Fifth Sun

FIFTH SUN

A New History of the Aztecs

CAMILLA TOWNSEND

UNIVERSITY PRESS

OXFORD
UNIVERSITY PRESS

Oxford University Press is a department of the University of Oxford.
It furthers the University's objective of excellence in research, scholarship,
and education by publishing worldwide. Oxford is a registered trade mark of
Oxford University Press in the UK and certain other countries.

Published in the United States of America by Oxford University Press
198 Madison Avenue, New York, NY 10016, United States of America.

Library of Congress Cataloging-in-Publication Data
Names: Townsend, Camilla, 1965– author.
Title: Fifth sun : a new history of the Aztecs / Camilla Townsend.
Description: New York, NY : Oxford University Press, [2019] | Includes
bibliographical references and index.
Identifiers: LCCN 2019003623 (print) | LCCN 2019004887 (ebook) |
ISBN 9780190673079 (updf) | ISBN 9780190673086 (epub) |
ISBN 9780190673062 (hardcover : alk. paper)
Subjects: LCSH: Aztecs—History. | Aztecs—First contact with Europeans. |
Aztecs—Historiography. | Mexico—History—Conquest, 1519–1540.
Classification: LCC F1219.73 (ebook) | LCC F1219.73 .T67 2019 (print) | DDC 972—dc23
LC record available at https://lccn.loc.gov/2019003623

Title Page Art: Mexica government officials in full battle gear. The Bodleian Libraries, the
University of Oxford, Codex Mendoza, MS. Arch. Selden. A.1, folio 67r.

7 9 8 6

Printed by Sheridan Books, Inc.
United States of America

Contents

Acknowledgments

As the Aztecs well knew, no one ever accomplishes anything alone. Certainly I owe my ability to write this book to the hundreds of people whose lives have touched mine along the way—those who raised me and loved me, educated me or studied with me, worked with me as colleagues, or shared their knowledge of early Latin America. The list is so long, and the influences so varied, that I sometimes find the thought overwhelming. Please know, every one of you, that I feel the gratitude I should, and like the Aztecs, hope to pay my debt to the universe through the way I live my life and my efforts on behalf of the people of the future.

There are two groups of people who have helped me so much on this project that I must call out their names individually. One group consists of the Nahuatl scholars whose work made this book possible. I dedicated the last book I published to two recently deceased intellectual giants, James Lockhart and Luis Reyes García, whose translations of Nahuatl texts formed the bedrock of much of my own work. In those pages I also referenced my gratitude to the late Inga Clendinnen and Sabine MacCormack. It has occurred to me since that I should not wait for people to pass away to the next world before speaking aloud of my debts. I deeply thank Michel Launey and Rafael Tena, two modest men who have made breath-taking contributions with their work in Nahuatl. You remind me of Nanahuatzin, though I certainly hope you have not felt your work to be a sacrifice.

The other group includes the Mexican intellectuals—teachers, professors, researchers, writers, publishers, and filmmakers—who in the past few years have personally welcomed my contributions and offered me their own, thereby enriching this book immeasurably. I humbly thank (in alphabetical order) Sergio Casas Candarabe, Alberto Cortés Calderón, Margarita Flores, René García Castro, Lidia Gómez García, Edith González Cruz, María Teresa Jarquín Ortega, Marco Antonio Landavazo, Manuel Lucero, Hector de Mauleón Rodríguez, Erika Pani, Ethelia Ruiz Medrano, Marcelo Uribe, and

Ernesto Velázquez Briseño. Your combination of pride in your heritage, openness to others, and intellectual acumen have inspired me more than I can say.

I must not wax poetic and omit to mention matters of daily sustenance; the Aztecs certainly would never have been been so naïve. Years ago, the American Philosophical Society awarded a grant that allowed me to travel to the Bibliothèque nationale de France and see the work of don Juan Buenaventura Zapata y Mendoza. I got the bug and have pursued the Nahuatl annals ever since. More recently, a fellowship from the John Simon Guggenheim Memorial Foundation and a sabbatical from Rutgers University allowed me to do the necessary research in the genre as a whole. A Public Scholar award from the National Endowment for the Humanities made it possible for me to take a year off from teaching and write, day in and day out.

The research would not have been possible without the years of painstaking work accomplished by the staffs of the institutions that safeguard the annals and other important texts. A number of them made me welcome over the years—the Library and Archive of the Instituto Nacional de Antropología e Historia in Mexico City, the Bibliothèque nationale de France, the British Library, the Library of Uppsala University in Sweden, the New York Public Library, and the Library of the American Museum of Natural History.

I thank my family for being who they are. My sister, Cynthia, and sister-in-law, Patricia, are the bravest of women. Your children and grandchildren will speak of you with love and admiration. My partner, John, and my two sons, Loren and Cian, have made me proud to know them as they have faced life's challenges. For years now, the three of you have shared me with many others—students, aging parents, former foster children, and the historical figures who live in my mind—but it is you who are my precious beloveds, always.

Glossary

Most of these terms are originally from Nahuatl (N) or Spanish (S).

Acolhua (N). A Nahuatl-speaking ethnic group inhabiting the territory to the east of the great lake in Mexico's central basin in the fourteenth and fifteenth centuries. The group contained several distinct altepetls, including such well-known ones as Texcoco and a town on the site of Teotihuacan.

Altepetl (N). Nahuatl term for any state, no matter how large, but most frequently used to refer to a local ethnic state. A close approximation would be our notion of "city-state."

Audiencia (S). The high court of New Spain, residing in Mexico City. In the absence of a sitting viceroy, the governing council of New Spain.

Cabildo (S). Any town council organized in the Spanish style. Used to refer to the local indigenous council governing their community's internal affairs.

Cacique. An Arawak or Caribbean indigenous word. A ruler, often used as the equivalent of tlatoani. Eventually, the word was used to describe any prominent indigenous person of a noble line.

Calli (N). Literally, a house or household. Often an important metaphor for larger political bodies. Also one of the four rotating names for years.

Calpolli (N). Literally, "great house." A key constituent part of an *altepetl*. We might think of a combined political ward and religious parish.

Chalchihuitl (N). A precious greenstone often translated into English as "jade." The Nahuas valued the gem exceedingly, and thus it served as a metaphor for that which was well loved.

Chichimec (N). Literally "dog people." Used in Nahuatl to refer to "wild" or nomadic, nonfarming peoples who lived primarily by hunting. The Mexica were proud of their Chichimec heritage.

Chinampa (N). Artificially raised plot for intensive agriculture built up in shallow water.

Cihua or cihuatl (N). Literally "woman" but with many embedded uses. A "cihuapilli" was a noblewoman or even queen. The "cihuacoatl" (literally Woman Snake) was the title of the Mexica king's highest-ranking aide.

Cofradía (S). A sodality, or lay religious brotherhood. Often established by indigenous and African people in colonial Latin America for mutual support in such things as paying for funerals.

Culhua (N). An ethnic group inhabiting the center of the central basin of Mexico in the fourteenth century.

Discalced friars. Mendicant orders whose members go entirely barefoot or wear only sandals, symbolic of their vow of poverty.

Doctrina (S). Spanish for Christian indoctrination but refers to an indigenous parish run by friars.

Don/doña (S). Spanish high title attached to a first name, like "Sir" or "Lady" in English. Applied by Nahuas in the early colonial period only to titled nobility from Spain and to their own highest-status local nobility.

Encomienda (S). Post-conquest grant of the right to receive labor and tribute from an indigenous altepetl through its existing mechanisms. In all but a handful of cases, these were given to Spaniards.

Flower Wars. A pre-conquest form of sport consisting of mock battles, which sometimes resulted in death.

Fray (S). The title given to a friar, or *fraile* in Spanish.

Gobernador (S). Governor and head of the indigenous cabildo. Early on, the position was filled by the tlatoani, but later, elections were held among all noblemen. Sometimes called a "judge" or "judge governor."

Guardián (S). The prior of a monastic establishment.

Macehualli (pl. macehualtin) (N). Indigenous commoner. Sometimes used by indigenous people to refer to themselves as a group in opposition to Spaniards.

Marqués (S). Marquis, lord of a border region. Several viceroys bore the title, but when the Nahuas used it without a specific name, they meant either Hernando Cortés or his legitimate son.

Mestizo (S). Person of mixed Spanish and indigenous descent.

Mexica (N). The ethnic group that dominated central Mexico at the time of the arrival of the Spaniards. Now most often referred to as the "Aztecs."

Nahua (N). One who speaks the Nahuatl language. The Mexica as well as dozens of other groups in Mexico were Nahuas.

Nahuatl (N). The politically dominant tongue that had become a lingua franca in central Mexico by the time of the arrival of the Spaniards.

New Spain. The large colonial jurisdiction centered on Mexico City and including much of present-day Mexico.

Otomí. An ethnic group whose people were scattered throughout various places in central Mexico. Perceived as "barbarians" by the Nahuas, they probably had a prior claim on the land.

Pilli (pl. pipiltin) (N). Indigenous nobleman.

Pinome. Speakers of the language Pinotl, or Popoluca, living east of the central valley. Perceived as "lesser" by the Nahuas, they had a prior claim on the land.

Pulque (S). An alcoholic beverage made from fermented sap of the maguey plant.

Quauhpilli (N). Literally an "eagle nobleman." A nobleman by virtue of deeds or merit rather than by virtue of birth. These were sometimes commoners promoted after success on the battlefield, or sometimes noblemen brought in from other altepetls.

Tacuba. The term used in Spanish to refer to the Tepanec altepetl of Tlacopan.

Tecpan (N). Literally, "place where the lord is." Originally, the palace of a local lord. After the conquest, used to refer to a community house where the indigenous cabildo met.

Tenochtitlan (N). Originally a small village established by the Mexica on an island in Lake Texcoco. Eventually the capital of a great state. After the conquest, the site of the founding of Mexico City. The people of the city were called the Tenochca.

Tepaneca (N). A Nahuatl-speaking ethnic group inhabiting the territory to the west of the great lake in Mexico's central basin. The group contained several distinct altepetls, including such well-known ones as Azcapotzalco and Tlacopan.

Teuctli (pl. teteuctin) (N). Lord, head of a dynastic household, with lands and followers.

Tlatoani (N). Literally, "one who speaks," and implicitly, one who speaks on behalf of a group. A dynastic ruler of an altepetl, in this book translated as "king." It was sometimes applied to a high Spanish authority, like the viceroy.

Tlaxcala (N). A large altepetl just outside the central valley that remained unconquered by the Mexica and their allies. The Tlaxcalans (or Tlaxcalteca) were among the very first to ally with the Spaniards.

Tochtli (N). Literally "rabbit." Often used as a metaphor to refer to ill fortune. Also one of the four rotating names of years.

Tollan (N). Literally "place of the reeds," often called "Tula" in English. A real town in central Mexico, but in ancient stories, often used to refer to a utopian community of the distant past.

Totonacs. An ethnic group living near today's Veracruz.

Triple Alliance. Used to refer to the fifteenth-century alliance between the ruling families of Tenochtitlan, Texcoco, and Tlacopan. There was in fact no formal alliance or political league, but the understanding was real.

-tzin (N). A Nahuatl suffix most often employed as an honorific, but sometimes merely conveying affection for a beloved person or object of humble status.

Viceroy or Virrey (S). The representative of the Spanish monarch in a region of the New World. At first, there were only two, that of New Spain and that of Peru.

Visitador (S). Inspector. These were sent regularly by the Spanish Crown to investigate local government in the Americas in a system of checks and balances.

Xiuhpohualli (N). Literally, "year count" or "yearly account." A traditional genre used by the Nahuas to recite their history verbally; often transcribed as written texts after the conquest.

A Note on Terminology, Translation, and Pronunciation

CONVEYING A PEOPLE'S history to outsiders in terms the people themselves would understand and approve of brings certain challenges. In this case, even their name presents a predicament, for technically speaking, there never were any "Aztecs." No people ever called themselves that. It was a word that scholars began to use in the eighteenth century to describe the people who dominated central Mexico at the time of the Spaniards' arrival. Its use is often confusing, as some people employ the term the way the eighteenth- and nineteenth-century intellectuals did; others use it to describe not only the dominant group but also all who were ruled by them, which included villages extending across most of central Mexico and a few others scattered more widely, extending as far south as El Salvador. In this book the term *Aztec* is used to refer to the people who controlled the region from their city-state of Tenochtitlan, as well as all those living in the central basin[1] who were closely allied with them. Despite the word *Aztec* appearing in the title and in the introduction—where it is desperately needed as a communication tool—I do not use it so unsparingly in the rest of the book. If I am speaking of the ethnic group that rose to power, I use the word they used, *Mexica* (Me-SHEE-ka), and if I am speaking of their close allies, I call them by name, too. If I am referring to the people spread across central Mexico who shared a language and a cultural outlook, many but not all of whom were conquered by the Mexica, I call them what they called themselves, the Nahuas (NA-was). After the introduction, I use the term *Aztec* only when I am discussing later perceptions of times past; then readers will hear about what "the Aztecs" are generally thought to have been or done.

There is a comparable issue regarding all the people who lived in North and South America long before anybody else. Over time, different words have been used to talk about them, some pejorative, some not. Today, people of descendant communities in various regions often have different preferences as to what they should be called. In Canada, they tend to prefer First Nations, and in Mexico, indigenous. In the United States, some choose Native American and others American Indian or just Indian. Each group has valid historical reasons for its preference. I do not choose between them, but instead use all these terms interchangeably.

There are also innumerable decisions to be made about the translation of words. When, for instance, the Mexica wished their hearers to understand that a woman in a noble family was understood to come from the line that would bear the heirs, they called her *inhueltiuh*, or "their Elder Sister." That phrase is cumbersome in English, so I have substituted the word "princess," although those who know the Mexica know very well there is no word meaning exactly that in their language. In another example, when people gathered of an evening for a celebration, performers told them their history and sang to them in varied combinations. When I write about these historians who were also artists, I sometimes refer to them as "the bards," but others might opt for "history tellers and singers." There simply is no perfect solution to translation questions of this kind. The footnotes will help those readers who seek greater specificity.

Presenting individual people's names in a foreign language can also be difficult. The word "Chimalxochitl" does not roll off the tongues of English-speaking people. A reader who is wrestling valiantly with the name can lose the point of the sentence. But if the girl is simply called "Shield Flower," does she become trapped in a world of charming and poetic names? Will we subtly condescend to her if she isn't named "Elizabeth," or "Maria"? This book attempts to resolve the issue by moving back and forth between the two possible names, but always using the English translation when the paragraph might otherwise become bewildering.

The first time each Aztec-language or Nahuatl (NA-wat) word is used, the approximate pronunciation is given in parentheses. Three rules will help readers speak most Nahuatl words relatively easily. First, the "tl" consonant is pronounced softly; in English, the closest equivalent is a simple "t" sound. Second, when "h" is followed by the letter "u," the intent is to produce a "w" sound. (Both of these rules are illustrated in the word "Nahuatl.") And finally, our "sh" sound is represented by the letter "x." Since the "sh" sound is common in Nahuatl, that guideline is worth remembering. The people we often call the "Aztecs," for example, called themselves the "Mexica," pronounced Me-SHEE-ka, and the word "xochitl," meaning flower, is thus SHO-cheet. For those who wish to expose themselves more thoroughly to this beautiful language, several excellent books are available.[2]

THE TENOCHCA ROYAL FAMILY

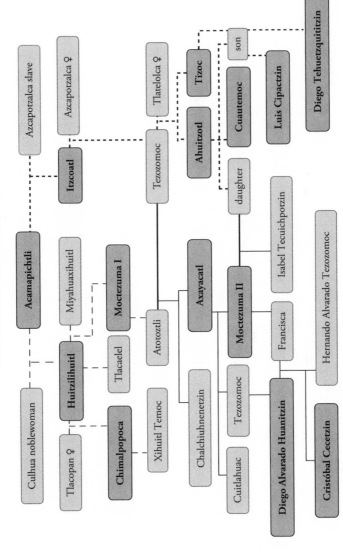

To
Tula

Huehuetoca

Citlaltepec

Xaltocan

LAKE
XALTOCAN

Tepotzotlan

Teotihuacan

Cuauhtitlan

Acolman

Tepexpan

Ecatepec

LAKE
TEXCOCO

Tlalnepantla

Texcoco

Huexotla

Tepeyac

Azcapotzalco

Coatlinchan

Tlatelolco

Tlacopan

Tepetzinco

TENOCHTITLAN

Chapultepec

Itztapalapan

Coyoacan

Colhuacan

Ixtapaluca

Tizapan

To Tlaxcala
Huexotzinco
& Cholula

LAKE
XOCHIMILCO

LAKE
CHALCO

Tlalpan

Cuitlahuac

Xochimilco

Chalco

Cuicuilco

Amaquemecan

VALLEY OF MEXICO, 1519

Introduction

The quill moving over the paper made a faint scratching sound, then almost a squeak as the pen was pulled backward suddenly at an odd angle to cross out a word. The ink blotted. The writer paused; he needed to think. That wasn't what he had meant to say. He stared down at the pale folio lying on the wooden table. The author was a Native American descended from migrants who had once made their way down from the desert lands of the north, but his own life was quite different from that of his ancestors. It was 1612, and outside the grated window, the streets of Mexico City were bathed in sunlight, glinting off the colored tiles, the metal doorknockers, the smooth adobe walls. People rushed by, laughing and talking, hawking their wares, urging their children to hurry, some in Spanish, some in "Mexican," as the Spaniards called the Indians' language. Inside his shadowy room, don Domingo—or Chimalpahin, as he sometimes called himself, after a great-grandfather—felt at peace. He was busy. It had been almost a hundred years since the arrival of the Spaniards, but the figures in his head had lived three hundred years earlier. He heard them in his imagination. "Please," a defeated chief begged of the man who had vanquished him, "take pity on my daughter." *"Xicmotlaocollili yn nochpochtzin."* The chief spoke in the language of the Aztecs, and don Domingo wrote down his words in that language. He believed in the defeated chief, knew that he had once lived and breathed, just as surely as Chimalpahin himself did now. His beloved grandmother, who had died only a few years earlier, had been a little girl in the years immediately after the Spanish conquest; her childhood had been peopled by elders who had lived their lives in other times, so don Domingo knew with every fiber of his being that those times had not been mythical. He turned to look at his source, a sheath of old, tattered papers, on

Mexica government officials in full battle gear. The Bodleian Libraries, the University of Oxford, Codex Mendoza, MS. Arch. Selden. A.1, folio 67r.

which someone else had described the events many years ago. He tried to find the right place in the midst of the dense writing. He was tired and considered stopping for the day, but then pushed on. His goal was nothing short of the preservation of his people's history as part of the world's heritage, and he had hundreds of pages yet to write.

***

CLIMBING DOWN from the dizzying heights of one of the pyramids of Mexico, a visitor almost expects to feel the presence of the spirit of an Aztec princess. A person less inclined to travel might hope to have an epiphany about the lives of ancient Native Americans while visiting a museum—gazing through the glass at a startling flint knife, seemingly brought to life by its embedded turquoise eyes, or admiring a tiny golden frog, caught by the artist preparing to leap. But no one would expect to hear an Aztec princess taunting her enemies in the stacks of a library. Yet that is exactly what happened to me one day about fifteen years ago.

Libraries are generally thought to be very quiet places, whether they shelter stacks of rare, leather-bound books or rows of computers. Another way to think of a library, however, is as a world of frozen voices, captured and rendered accessible forever by one of the most powerful human developments of all time—the act of writing. From that perspective, a library suddenly becomes a very noisy place. In theory, it contains fragments of all the conversations the world has ever known. In reality, some conversations are almost impossible to hear. Even someone who is desperately trying to distinguish what an Aztec princess is shouting, for instance, will generally have a hard time of it. She appears atop the pyramid, facing brutal sacrifice, but she usually remains silent. The voice overlaying the scene is that of a Spaniard, telling us what he is sure the girl must have thought and believed. Instead of her words, we hear those of the friars and conquistadors whose writings line the shelves of the library.

For generations, those who have wanted to know about the lives of ancient Native Americans have studied the objects uncovered in archaeological digs, and they have read the words of Europeans who began to write about Indians almost as soon as they met them. From these sources more than any others, scholars have drawn their conclusions and deemed them justified. But it was a dangerous endeavor that inevitably led to distortions. To make a comparison, it would never have been considered acceptable to claim to understand medieval France with access to only a few dozen archaeological digs and a hundred texts in English—with nothing written in French or Latin. Yet different standards have been applied to Indians.

The picture of the Aztecs that has emerged is bloodcurdling. The flint knives with their embedded eyes, the sacrificial stones, the skull racks, all leave indelible images in the imagination. We moderns look at them and then invent the accompanying scene—the spoken words, the music, and the context. We envision orgies of violence, like the one depicted in the film *Apocaylpto*. Textbooks present these same images and teach young people that the nobler native peoples were waiting to be released from a regime of such cruelty. The books written by sixteenth-century Spaniards likewise encourage readers to believe that the people whom the conquistadors defeated were barbaric in the extreme, that God willed the end of their civilization as it encapsulated all that was wrong with human nature. Even those written by more sympathetic observers—those Spaniards who lived in an indigenous community and learned the language—are filled with condescension toward the people they never quite came to understand, interpreting events through a European set of expectations, and thus seeing the choices the Indians made as bizarre at best.

The Aztecs would never recognize themselves in the picture of their world that exists in the books and movies we have made. They thought of themselves as humble people who had made the best of a bad situation and who had shown bravery and thus reaped its rewards. They believed that the universe had imploded four times previously, and they were living under the fifth sun, thanks to the extraordinary courage of an ordinary man. Elders told the story to their grandchildren: "When all was in darkness, when the sun had not yet shone and the dawn had not yet broken, the gods gathered and spoke among themselves." The divinities asked for a volunteer from the few humans and animals creeping about in the darkness. They needed someone to immolate himself and thus bring forth a new dawn. A man who was very full of himself stepped forward and said he would do it. "Who else?" the gods asked, but their question was met with silence. "None dared, no one else came forward." The gods called on a quiet man who sat listening. His name was Nanahuatzin (Na-na-WA-tzeen). He had not thought of himself as a hero, but he accepted the task readily on the grounds that the gods had been good to him in the past. The two men were made ready for sacrifice, the proud hero receiving beautiful, precious accoutrements, but Nanahuatzin only paper trinkets, reeds, and pine needles. At last it was time. The hero went forward. "The flames flared up high, and he became terrified. He stopped in fear, turned about, went back . . . he tried again . . . but he could in no way dare to do it." The gods turned to Nanahuatzin and stared at him. "He hardened his heart, shut his eyes firmly, and did not stop short." He jumped. "His flesh

crackled and sizzled." The gods sat waiting. "Then began the reddening of the
sky all around." And the sun rose in the east, its life-giving rays penetrating
everywhere. Without fanfare, Nanahuatzin had done what was needed to
save life on earth.[1]

The Aztecs were master storytellers, and they wrote down many of their
stories in the sixteenth century, in the decades after the conquest. Spanish
friars taught their young people to transcribe sound by means of the Roman
alphabet, and they used the new tool to write down many of the old oral performances. That had not been the Spaniards' original intention. The zealous
friars taught the boys the alphabet so they would be able to study the Bible
and help disseminate the tenets of Christianity. But the Aztec students did
not feel limited in its application. They were not startled by the principle of
writing, for their people already had a tradition of standardized pictographic
symbols, which they had long employed to create beautiful screenfold books,
some for the use of priests in their prognostications, and some for the use of
officials who maintained records of tribute payments and land boundaries.
None of these works survived the bonfires of conquest, but the fact that they
had once existed proved to be important: the Aztecs saw immediately how
valuable it would be to adopt this new, phonetic system. They could use it to
record anything they chose, writing not only in Spanish but also sounding out
words and sentences in their own language of Nahuatl (NA-wat).

In the privacy of their own homes, away from the eyes of the Spaniards,
what the Nahuatl speakers most often wrote was history. Before the conquest,
they had a tradition called the *xiuhpohualli* (shoo-po-WA-lee), which meant
"year count" or "yearly account," even though Western historians have nick-
named the sources "annals." In the old days, trained historians stood and gave
accounts of the people's history at public gatherings in the courtyards located
between palaces and temples. They proceeded carefully year by year; in
moments of high drama different speakers stepped forward to cover the same
time period again, until all perspectives taken together yielded an understanding of the whole series of events. The pattern mimicked the rotational, recip-
rocal format of all aspects of their lives: in their world, tasks were shared or
passed back and forth, so that no one group would have to handle something
unpleasant all the time or be accorded unlimited power all the time. Such
performances generally recounted stories that would be of interest to the
larger group—the rise of chiefs and later their deaths (timely or untimely),
the wars they fought and the reasons for them, remarkable natural phenomena, and major celebrations or horrifying executions. Although certain subjects were favored, the texts were hardly devoid of personality: different

communities and different individuals included different details. Political schisms were illustrated via colorful dialogue between leaders of different schools of thought. The speakers would sometimes even slip into the present tense as they delivered such leaders' lines, as if they were in a play. Occasionally they would shout questions that eager audience members were expected to answer.[2]

After the conquest, the young people trained in the Roman alphabet began to write down what various elders said, carefully transcribing their words onto paper and then storing the folios on a special shelf or in a locked box—another well-loved innovation the Spaniards had brought. As the colonial period went on, and fewer people remembered the old days, the genre became more terse, a simple annual record of major events. Still, the authors clung tenaciously to the traditional year-by-year format, usually including the calendar of the ancien régime, moving from the top of the page to the bottom, or sometimes left to right along a lengthy strip. The style belied the stereotype that Native Americans necessarily thought in a cyclical manner, for these were always linear accounts, offering theories of cause and effect, helping the readers or listeners to understand how they had arrived at the present moment, and teaching them what they needed to know about the past in order to make their way forward into the future. Some writers were descended from the Aztec conquerors themselves, some from their friends and associates, some from their enemies. Don Domingo Chimalpahin, from the conquered town of Chalco, was the most prolific of these indigenous historians, filling hundreds of pages in his clear penmanship, using materials other people had written down closer to the time of conquest as well as performances people gave for him to transcribe. By day, he worked for the Spaniards in one of their churches, but in the evenings, his time was his own.

For too long, little has been done with the xiuhpohualli, the annals. They are written in a language relatively few people can read, and their approach to history is quite different than Westerners' so they can be difficult to understand. Other sources have thus seemed preferable, and from them, some fine books have been written.[3] Nonetheless, the Aztec histories are worth considering carefully. They reward patience, just as the Aztecs themselves were wont to do.

In the annals, we can hear the Aztecs talking. They sing, laugh, and yell. It turns out that the world they lived in cannot be characterized as naturally morbid or vicious, even though certain moments were. They had complex systems in place regarding both politics and trade that were highly effective, but they were aware of having made mistakes. They were grateful to their

gods, but they sometimes lamented their divinities' unkindness. They raised
their children to do the right thing by their own people and to be ashamed of
selfishness, though individuals sometimes displayed this trait. They believed
deeply in appreciating life: they danced with joy; they sang their poems; they
loved a good joke. Yet they interspersed moments of lightness, humor, and
irony with other occasions laden with pathos or gravity. They could not abide
a dirty floor, which seemed to indicate a deeper disorder. Most of all, they
were flexible. As situations altered, they repeatedly proved themselves capable
of adapting. They were adept at surviving.

***

ONE DAY IN A LIBRARY, some Nahuatl words in one of Chimalpahin's
texts suddenly fell into place, and I heard an Aztec princess shouting at her
enemies. They had captured her, and she was demanding to be sacrificed. She
veered startlingly from the script I had been taught to expect. She was neither
threatening her enemies nor succumbing to them as a brutalized victim, nor
was she sanctimoniously or fatalistically promising to die in order to appease
the gods and keep the universe intact. She was raging about a specific political
situation that I had finally read enough to understand, and she was demonstrating courage. In that moment, I realized that these people whom I was
coming to know through their own words were far too complicated to fit
within the frameworks long imposed on them, based on the old sources—the
silent archaeological remains and the Spanish testimonies. Their beliefs and
practices changed as circumstances changed. Only by listening to them talk
about the events they experienced could I truly come to understand them.
I could not approach their world with a preconceived understanding of who
they were and what they believed, and then apply that vision as a key to interpreting everything they said and did. Only by moving through their own
accounts of their history, paying close attention to everything they themselves
articulated, could I come to understand their evolving beliefs and transforming sense of themselves.

This book, rooted in the Nahuatl-language annals, offers five revelations
about the Aztecs. First, although Aztec political life has been assumed to
revolve around their religiously motivated belief in the necessity of human
sacrifice to keep the gods happy, the annals indicate that this notion was never
paramount for them. It has traditionally been said that the Aztecs believed
they had to conquer others in order to obtain the requisite number of victims.
Or alternatively, some cynics have asserted, they merely claimed they had to
do so for this reason, in order to justify their inherent desire for control. The

Aztecs' own histories, however, indicate that they understood clearly that political life revolved not around the gods or claims about the gods but around the realities of shifting power imbalances. In a world in which chiefs had many wives, a leader could father literally dozens of sons, and factions developed among them based on who the boys' mothers were. A weaker faction in one city-state might eventually ally with a losing band of brothers in another city-state, and together, they might suddenly topple dominant family lines and change the political map of a region. The writers of annals explained almost all their wars in terms of this form of gendered realpolitik. The prisoners of war who ended up facing sacrifice were usually collateral damage in these genuine struggles. Only toward the end, when Aztec power had grown exponentially, did a situation arise in which dozens of victims were brutally murdered on a regular basis in order to make a terrifying public statement.

Second, there has been a problematic tendency to deem some people in the Aztec world evil and others good. What else could explain brutal warriors living side by side with gentle, Mexican corn farmers, or slaveholders existing in a land of beautiful poetry? But the same individuals could be farmers in one season and warriors in another; the man who at dusk blew the conch shell and chanted profound poems might call a terrified slave girl to him later that evening. Like other dominant cultures, they wielded most of their violence at the margins of their political world, and this choice made possible the wealth that allowed a gloriously beautiful city to grow and flourish—one filled with citizens who had the leisure time and energy to write poetry, create aromatic chocolate drinks, and sometimes debate morality.

Third, a great deal of ink has been spilled over the question of how the Europeans were able to bring down such a kingdom, but each generation of scholars has ignored certain aspects of the reality that the Aztecs themselves were explicitly cognizant of in their writings. Until the late twentieth century, historians condemned the Aztecs to fatalism and irrationality, regularly suppressing abundant evidence of their savvy strategizing. In more recent times, it has been assumed that a universal hatred of the Aztecs caused other people to ally with the Spaniards and thus defeat them. But the Aztec royal family was related to nearly every ruling family in the land. Some people hated them, but others aspired to be them. What is everywhere apparent in the historical annals is the recognition of a great technological power imbalance in relation to the newly arrived Spaniards, one that called for a rapid reckoning. It was possible, some thought, that this current crisis might be the war to end all wars, and many wanted to be on the side of the victors as they entered the new political era.

Fourth, those who lived through the war with the Spaniards and then survived the first great epidemic of European diseases found to their surprise that the sun continued to rise and set, and that they still had to face the rest of their lives. There was almost no time for self-pity. The surviving children were becoming adults with their own expectations, and the children born since the cataclysm had no memories of the events that had scarred their elders. Startlingly, the annals reveal that it was not just the young people who proved themselves disposed to experiment with the new foods and techniques and animals and gods brought by the people from across the sea. Some who were already adults when the strangers came helped lead the way in demonstrating the importance of a phonetic alphabet, for instance, or learning how to build a ship larger than any prior canoe, or constructing a rectangular rather than a pyramidal tower. Not everyone exhibited this remarkable curiosity and pragmatism, but many did. Moreover, the people proved adept at protecting their own worldview even as they adopted the more useful elements of Spanish life.

Finally, over the course of the next two generations, more and more people were forced to grapple with the enormity of the extractive economic policies the Spaniards introduced, and even more experienced racialized injustice. Yet even then, they were not destroyed but rather maintained their balance. Like so many people in other times and places, they had to learn to make peace with their new reality so they would not go mad. Certain figures in the generation of the grandchildren, like the historian Chimalpahin, became committed to writing everything they could remember of their people's history so that it would not be lost for all time. They became true scholars, even though the Spaniards did not recognize them as such. It is their efforts that now allow for the reconstruction of what their people once thought about. In short, the Aztecs were conquered, but they also saved themselves.

***

THE AZTEC HISTORY-TELLERS who once performed on starlit evenings would be the first to remind us that beyond any lessons we may derive from it, real history is exciting. The drama of humankind inherently constitutes a good yarn, and the Aztec past is no exception. Any history of theirs must explore the experience of a once-powerful people facing unspeakable disaster—and surviving as best they could. The Spanish conquest, for all its importance, was neither an origin story nor an absolute ending. The Aztec people lived for centuries beforehand, and they are among us still. Today about 1.5 million people speak their language; many more count themselves as the Aztecs' heirs. In the past, books about the Aztecs have either treated only the preconquest period, leading up to the crescendo of conquest in a final chapter, or have begun with an introductory chapter on pre-Columbian times and the arrival of the Europeans, and then presented a study of postconquest Mexico. This book is about the trauma of conquest, but it is also about survival and continuity—a paradox that reflects the nature of the actual lived experience of any devastating war. Here, the Spanish conquest is neither introductory nor climactic. Instead, it is pivotal.

The story begins in the deep past. In ancient times, the greater Mesoamerican world trade system stretched up into today's Utah. For example, the ornamental mineral—what we often refer to as jade—traveled on trade routes from the central basin of Mexico to the inner sanctum of Chaco Canyon in today's New Mexico; turquoise from the north made its way south. When the great corn-farming states of central Mexico fell, news passed by word of mouth to the mobile nomadic peoples of today's southwestern United States. In times of drought or duress, large groups listened to the rumors and moved south, looking to conquer fertile lands and make new lives. They had no horses: they learned to travel light, move with stunning speed, and employ deadly tactics. In wave after wave, they took the central basin, and the names of their leaders and the gods who advised them went down in legend. A series of great civilizations emerged, melding the practices of ancient corn farmers with the ideas of the innovative, daring newcomers. The last of the migrants from the north to arrive were a group called the Mexica (Me SHEE ka). Their late arrival might have been what rendered them among the scrappiest people of the central basin, for in the stories they told, they prided themselves on having once been underdogs, and they swore that they would rise.

As the peoples of the central basin jockeyed for power and access to resources, political alliances rose and fell. A woman who married with the enemy to protect an alliance might suddenly discover that alliances had shifted and thus might find herself demoted to a mere concubine. But her sons might not accept the change and instead choose to fight for power. Itzcoatl (Eetz-CO-wat), a Mexica ruler's son by a slave girl, brilliantly took advantage of the fissures that existed throughout the region and thus was able to help his family line rise to a position of prominence. This was no stable world of immutable beliefs but instead a shifting, constantly altering world, much like that of early Europe. The people's religion was both violent and beautiful. To thank the gods for what they had, they sometimes made an ultimate sacrifice: that of human life. Yet most of the time they were devoted not to death but to protecting their people's lives and working toward their future.

By the late 1400s, the Mexicas' village on an island in a lake had turned into a world-class city, tied to the land by three causeways. Great painted pyramids rose on all sides, surrounded by breathtaking gardens. The library of the ruler contained hundreds of books, and the music and the dancing performed at the palace brought renown to the city. Yet what made all this beauty and high culture possible was the Mexica rulers' increasingly draconian measures, their tightening bureaucratic organization and control in various arenas of life, the ritualized violence they regularly enacted before audiences, and the warfare they did not fear to wage at the edges of their realm. Life within the valley was stable, and some of the people were truly great artists. But the Mexica, like many others in comparable positions in world history, chose not to think much about the fate of those in the war-torn periphery of the world they had made.

Into this arena sailed the Spaniards, the first time in 1518 and with more serious intent in 1519. At this point the chronology of the book tightens: chapters One through Three treat multiple decades, and chapters Six through Eight do the same, but the two central chapters, Four and Five, are devoted to the arrival of the Spaniards, covering the years from 1518 to 1522 in great detail. Perhaps in some ways this gives too much power to the swaggering conquistadors, but it was indeed a critical time for the Mexica and merits careful consideration. Although the story of the arrival of Hernando Cortés has been told many times, it is done differently here, offering a tale of military rather than spiritual loss on the part of the Indians. The Mexica did not believe that the god Quetzalcoatl walked among them, nor were they impressed by a vision of Mary or one of the saints. Moctezuma, the king, simply found himself in possession of less military power than the newcomers, and he recognized this. Part of the story lay in the hands of the people whom the Mexica had rendered enemies—among them a young girl whom the Spaniards called Malinche, whose people had been under fierce pressure from Moctezuma prior to the arrival of the Spaniards, and she translated for the newcomers.

The war against the Spaniards was a horrific period in which all kinds of people—Malinche, for instance, as well as Moctezuma's captive daughter—simply did their best to stay alive. Aside from the destruction of the war, the death toll from the smallpox brought by the Spaniards led some native people to believe that they would all die . . . but they did not. Those individuals who had come to know the newcomers best began to counsel the people of the central basin—the Mexica, and those segments of the populace who had thus far remained loyal to them—to opt for peace and save their lives. As paramount rulers, the Spaniards would offer one advantage—they were even more powerful than the Mexica, which meant not only that they could defeat them but also that they could insist that all intervillage warfare cease in the regions they controlled. Many opted for that possibility and thus gave victory to the newcomers.

In the initial decades after the Spaniards' triumph, the people found that they faced overwhelming changes in many regards but that life continued much as usual in other ways. It varied considerably from place to place. In the great city of the Mexica, Moctezuma's daughter and Malinche, for instance, both did their best to ward off desperation and negotiate the pitfalls of life alongside the arrogant and powerful newcomers. Yet in a small town to the east, which thus far remained largely untouched, a young man who had learned the Roman alphabet from the friars tranquilly taught his father all that could be done with it. Working together, they wrote what was in effect the first permanently legible Nahuatl book. In this time of change, contradictions abounded.

In the Americas, within about a generation of the Europeans first establishing themselves in any one area, the indigenous nearly always mounted a sustained resistance. This was as true among the Aztecs as it was everywhere else. In the case of Mexico, the 1560s brought recurring crises. In the central basin, the Mexica were told for the first time that they would have to pay a tax or tribute as great as any other conquered people. The protests on the part of both men and women caused many to be imprisoned and sold into indentured servitude. The records they kept of their arguments with the Spaniards speak eloquently of both rage and pain. Their lives touched those of alienated Spaniards who were also considering rebellion. The son of Malinche by Hernando Cortés ended up being brutally tortured in what was in medieval courts a perfectly legal proceeding—the simulation of drowning, like today's waterboarding. By the end of the decade, the Indians had made clear to the Spaniards the limits of their suffering—but the Spaniards had also made clear to them the limits of their freedom.

By about 1600, the last of the people who remembered the days before the Europeans were dead or dying. Then, there was a great burst of effort among their grandchildren to write down what they knew of that past world. One of these historians was don Domingo Chimalpahin, the Indian from Chalco who worked for the church of San Antón at the southern gate of the city; another was don Hernando de Alvarado Tezozomoc, a grandson of Moctezuma. Some of what they wrote constitutes a fascinating and horrifying account of the colonial era they lived through. However, their manuscripts do more than record their own tumultuous times. They offer a glimpse of how at least some native people thought about what had happened to them and how they envisioned their futures. They would be the last for many years to write analytically as indigenous intellectuals. Thereafter, poverty and oppression largely held sway in their communities until the twentieth century, when a reservoir of remembered anger surfaced in revolution and rebellion, and ultimately new vistas on ancient traditions opened.

The story of the Aztecs is a grand and sweeping panorama, but it is also filled with real people, who experienced history as individuals. Admittedly, these individuals can sometimes be hard to construe from our vantage point. To make it easier to peer into their world, now so very foreign to us, each chapter begins by stitching various sources together to create a vignette about a single person who once lived. This is an imaginative act, and perhaps dangerous in a work of history. Yet conjuring the world of anyone long dead, even kings and presidents whom we purportedly know well, is also an imaginative act, but it is regularly undertaken. If we are very careful to have learned as much as we can before we try to leap the longer distances into more foreign territories, I believe it is the right thing to do. By carefully re-creating the world of Chimalpahin and that of his grandmother's generation, we may be able to hear more clearly what they have to say, not only its substance but also its tone. Chimalpahin and his peers wanted posterity to hear them—they said so clearly in their writings—and so we should listen for their sake. But we should also do it for our own. For who can say which is the more empowered, them or us, if we can speak to each other successfully across the chasm of time and difference? Do we ourselves not become both wiser and stronger every time we grasp the perspective of people whom we once dismissed?

I

The Trail from the Seven Caves

BEFORE 1299

The girl heard the voices of those who loved her in her head. They had petted her, sung to her, told her she was their precious, shining gem, their light, silken feather. She knew now she would never hear those voices again. They had warned her that it might come to this, that she might one day be taken in war and lose every-thing, that every flower was fragile. Now the worst had indeed come. For a time, terror left her mind blank. But after she slept for a few hours, she was able to remind herself what her mother and grandmother had taught her she must do.

***

SO IT WAS that in the year 1299, Shield Flower looked upon her own death and found the courage to pass from this earthly life with the dignity and style that befit a royal woman. At least so her people said in the stories they told of her for many generations after.[1] Sometimes they called her not Chimalxochitl (Chi-mal-SHO-cheet, Shield Flower), but the more valiant Chimalexochitl (Chi-mal-eh-SHO-cheet), meaning Shield-Bearer Flower. Her ancestors, going back six or more generations, had been among the last of the people to leave the desiccated, war-torn lands of the American Southwest and begin a trek across the expanse of desert in search of the rumored southern lands.

Two Nahua chiefs address each other. The Bodleian Libraries, the University of Oxford, Codex Mendoza, MS. Arch. Selden. A.1, folio 60r.

Some two hundred years had passed before their descendants made it to the central basin of Mexico, and the tales of the land's fertility had all proven to be true. Here the precious maize crop grew easily. Yet they found that the best lands had already been conquered by other bands of warriors from the north, people who were just as good with a bow and arrow as Shield Flower's grandfather and his warriors. In the absence of a better alternative, Shield Flower's kin hired themselves out as mercenaries, fighting other people's battles in exchange for the right to make their camp unmolested, hunt a few deer, and plant a little corn.

But the year 1299 had brought misfortune to her people. Indeed, their luck had been so poor that one storyteller would later insist that it had not all happened in a year Two Reed, as everybody else said, but rather in a year One Rabbit. One Rabbit was always associated with disaster; there was even an old saying, "We were really one rabbited," meaning "We were really up a creek."[2] In any case, Shield Flower's father judged that his people had grown strong enough to cease living in fear. He declared himself an independent king or chief, a *tlatoani* (tla-to-WAN-ee) meaning "speaker," implicitly the mouthpiece of the group. His declaration indicated that he would no longer pay tribute to others or work as a mercenary for them. He even taunted the area's most powerful chief, to be sure that he had made his point. Some said he went so far as to ask to marry the leading chief's daughter, but then sacrificed her when she arrived.[3] Since he was not a madman, it is more likely that his taunting took the form of attacking one of the strongman's allies or refusing to obey one of his direct orders. Whatever his uppity move was, it proved to be a significant error of judgment.

King Coxcox (COSH-cosh) of the Culhua (CUL-wa) people personally led the war party that came to destroy the upstarts. The party consisted of warriors from six communities working in unison. They killed without mercy, keeping only a few warriors alive to take as prisoners to the towns that had defeated them. The young women were divided up and led away to their new lives as concubines. Shield Flower and her father, Huitzilihuitl (Wee-tzil-EE-weet, Hummingbird Feather), were taken to Culhuacan, the most important Culhua town. Huitzilihuitl's heart wept for his daughter, whose torn clothes rendered her body visible to all, exposing her to shame. He begged Coxcox to have mercy on the girl and give her a little something to wear. Coxcox turned and looked at her, then laughed. "No," the people always remembered him as saying. "She will stay as she is."

Thus Shield Flower found herself bound hand and foot, waiting under guard to learn what her fate would be. Days went by, dragging out the torment. The Culhua people were searching the surrounding marshes for survivors who had escaped the battle. They counted on hunger bringing many of them forth eventually, and so it did. When they began to trickle into Culhuacan—some dragged by captors, some coming of their own volition to offer to act as slaves in exchange for their lives—Shield Flower was still a shamed captive. She had been able to bear it when none of her people were there to see, but she could not endure it now. She asked one of her people to get her some chalk and some charcoal. Her captors allowed it. Perhaps they were amused. The bound girl struggled to mark herself with the black and white substances in the ancient way. Then she stood and began to scream, "Why do you not sacrifice me?!" She was ready, the gods were ready; the Culhuas only dishonored themselves by delaying, as if they had no courage for the deed. Later, some of the bards would say that the Culhuas were shamed by her words and wanted to quiet her, so they lit the pyre. Others said that some among her own people valued her honor more than their lives, so they stepped forward and did the deed themselves, at her command. As the flames rose, Shield Flower stood tall: she now had nothing left to lose. Tears streamed down her face, and she screamed at her enemies, "People of Culhuacan, I go to where my god lives. My people's descendants will all become great warriors, you will see!" After she died, the Culhuas washed her blood and ashes away, but they could not wash away the dread that her words had awakened in them.

Many years later, when her people had achieved great power and then lost it again with the coming of the Christians, some would say that perhaps Shield Flower had never really lived. After all, in some of the stories her name was Azcalxochitl (a kind of flower; we might call her "Lily"). And in some of them she was not the chief's daughter but his elder sister, the one destined to mother the next chief in some communities. If the bards could not even agree on such basic plot elements, why believe any of it?

It isn't necessary to believe that we can hear the exact words of a conversation held in 1299 to know that the essentials are true. Archaeological and linguistic evidence, as well as the written historical annals of multiple Mexican towns, all indicate that the ancestors of the people now known as the Aztecs came down from the north over the course of several centuries, that those who came last found themselves without land, and that they then had to jockey for power in the fertile central valley.[4] We know how they waged war, and we recognize the symbolic significance of the chiefly daughters and sisters raised to mother the next generation's chiefs. We even know that the people of the valley educated their noble girls to be almost as stoical as their brothers in times of duress, and that Shield Flower and Lily were both common indigenous names for noble daughters. In short, the story of Shield Flower would have been the story of more than one young woman.

All of those young women, as well as their warrior brothers, learned their history while sitting around the fire in the evening and listening to the story-tellers. They all learned that their people had come from the far north and had crossed mountains and desert to build new lives for themselves, their leaders carrying the sacred bundles of their gods to their new home. The stories differed slightly, but there were certain commonalities, and we can add to the mixture the evidence of archaeology and of linguistic maps to form a coherent vision of what happened. The narrative has all the makings of an epic drama.

It stretches back to an era unknown to Shield Flower, except perhaps in myth and dream, to northeastern Asia in the time of the last Ice Age—to the time of the peopling of the Americas. By that time, humankind had emerged from Africa and had wandered far and wide, living almost everywhere in the Old World. Later, each group would learn to love the character of the land it called home, from Scandinavia's icy fjords to the arid promontories of India's Deccan. But twenty thousand years ago or more, the land was not so varied, still covered in many places by gradually receding glaciers, and "home" was not so clearly marked. Small groups of people followed big game from place to place, and valiant hunters brought it down with their relatively frail spears. Starting about thirteen thousand years ago, most scholars think, some who lived in northeastern Asia trekked across the Bering Strait into Alaska. At the time, the strait was covered in ice; the land bridge was miles wide. The strife of war or a shortage of resources drove waves of people across this strait at least three different times. They, or their children and grandchildren, contin-ued to pursue the mastodons, the caribou, and any other animal worth eating, and they gradually populated two continents. Here and there, they found a few groups who had preceded them in the new hemisphere, apparently travel-ing down the coast in canoes. By about fourteen thousand years ago, before the land bridge made sizable migrations possible, a few people had gotten as far as southern Chile. At a place now called Monte Verde, a child stepped in the mud next to a cooking fire and left a clear footprint for archaeologists to find countless generations later.[5]

Then, about eleven thousand years ago, the Ice Age ended. The ice melted; the sea level rose and covered the land bridge, separating the Old World and the New. Some of the more massive game species became extinct. Climates grew warmer; more plants flourished. Everywhere on earth, curious and hungry people experimented with eating more of the plants' blossoms and fruits and roots and seeds and stalks. It didn't matter if they lived where the weather was warm or cool, or if the land was woody and shaded or hot and dry. They did this everywhere. Yet despite the commonality of their actions, differences that began to emerge at this time would prove crucial to human history in later millennia. When the people of Eurasia later met those of the Americas, decisions that human beings had made about farming in those early times would determine their fates, in the sense that the past determined their degree of strength relative to each other. It is a tale worth telling if we wish to understand both the rise and the fall of the Aztecs.

In most places, it was men who hunted and women who gathered. In their lives, always on the very edge of survival, it behooved these women to notice everything in the natural world: they saw that the plants grew from the seeds; they sowed some of the seeds of their favorite plants in the damp earth and returned to gather the fruits of their labor the following year when the hunt drew them back to the same area. They learned, for example, that if they gathered seeds only from the bushes that grew the most berries, the next generation of plants would yield more berries. The women told the men what they had deduced, and those men who valued survival listened to them. Almost everywhere, humans became part-time farmers. However, hunting and fishing remained the main affairs—it was flesh that humans relied upon to obtain the protein they needed to live.[6]

People gradually became full-time farmers when and where it made sense to do so. That is, they dedicated themselves to cultivating the local flora instead of hunting only when the game grew thin on the ground, and they also had in their environment a constellation of protein-rich plants that could support human life.[7] It happened first—about ten thousand years ago—in the Fertile Crescent, a swath of land between the Tigris and Euphrates Rivers (in today's Iraq). There, the available wheat and peas rendered farming an obvious alternative when the overhunted deer began to disappear. In other places, such as New Guinea, where bananas and sugarcane were the tastiest plants available, people experimented eagerly with the sweet treats, but they continued to depend on wild boar and other game animals to feed themselves. They were not so foolish as to devote their lives to the full-time cultivation of desserts, and the wheat and peas native to the Middle East did not exist in their world. It might not have mattered in the long term except that full-time farming had such huge and momentous effects. Those who lived their lives as full-time farmers had to abandon the nomadic lifestyle. They could then construct big buildings and heavy items, experiment with metal forges, potters' wheels and looms. They could store food surpluses and thus increase their population. They had to devise ways to share water as they irrigated and developed new kinds of tools. It began to make sense to divide tasks and allow people to specialize in one area or another. Inventions proliferated. In short, the sedentary lifestyle of full-time agriculturalists eventually yielded more powerful civilizations.

Not that farmers are necessarily happier than hunter-gatherers, or smarter or more moral, nor do they always invent the same things in the same order, or even the things we would expect them to invent. The ancient Andean farmers, for example, never thought of straining plant fibers through screens to create paper on which to write, as those in the Old World did. Instead they "wrote" in knots and braids along colored cords and tied them together to record their prayers and their tax records. And the Europeans, later famous for their fighting, were not the ones to create the first explosives; the supposedly peaceful and self-contained Chinese did that. The point is that farming peoples always developed mightier civilizations in the sense of being able to defeat people who had not developed comparable weapons and goods, and whose populations had not grown equivalently.

The people of the Fertile Crescent made the shift first, but they were not alone for long in their new way of life. Wheat and peas spread quickly to nearby Egypt, southern Europe, and Asia, where people became far more dedicated to cultivation than they had been. In Egypt farming peoples included such local plants as figs. In Europe, they added oats and other crops to the mix. And in China, people were experimenting with growing more rice and millet. Large populations could now live in permanent towns—unthinkable to a population of hunter-gatherers—and trade routes between the towns soon fostered an exchange that gave peoples across the Eurasian continent regular access to each other's favorite domesticated plants and newest inventions.

Eventually the presence or absence of farming ceased to explain differences in power within Eurasia or people's ability to win a war there. With only a few centuries of difference between themselves and their neighbors, farmers soon found that their cleverest inventions and their best weapons could be bought, borrowed, or stolen by the more nomadic peoples who surrounded them. And once the nomads had such goods in their hands, they were just as powerful—or more powerful—than farmers. The Germanic tribes used Roman methods against their erstwhile conquerors. The Mongols of Asia's northern plains obtained horses and metal weapons from the Chinese. Then, when Genghis Khan and his men galloped down from the north, the farmers trembled—and with good reason.

Meanwhile, across the sea in the Americas, Shield Flower's ancestors continued as hunter-gatherers, with only a part-time interest in farming, for at least five millennia past the time when agriculture emerged with force in the Old World. Plants comparable to wheat and peas simply did not exist there. Later, the Native Americans would be known for their reliance on corn, along with beans and squash. But ancient corn, the plant called *teosinte*, was merely a wild grass with a tuft of tiny kernels, smaller than today's baby corn. Ancient wheat was almost exactly like today's wheat, but teosinte was not nearly so nutritious. It required thousands of years of effort on the part of Mexico's women to turn those little tufts into what we would recognize as ears of corn; they occasionally planted the larger kernels from the biggest tufts, just as they experimented with other plants. In the meantime, they and their menfolk followed the deer and other game. Even when the ears of corn began to grow to a substantial size, scraping off the kernels and eating them still left a person hungry. Eventually, the women began to notice that when they ate corn at the same time as they ate beans, they were better nourished.[8] Far more so than in Europe, the rise of agriculture was a long and protracted process that occurred in fits and starts. The shift did eventually occur: by 3500 BCE a few groups in Mexico were farming corn in earnest; by 1800 BCE, many more were doing the same.[9] But there had been several millennia of delay in comparison with the Old World, a fact that would matter a great deal in the future, as Shield Flower's descendants would discover.

In coastal and riverine areas of Mesoamerica, some people had established permanent villages even without access to significant, protein-rich plants because they could dedicate themselves throughout the seasons to the collection of different kinds of seafood. These people, who already had a tradition of sedentary living, may have been more interested than others in the benefits of farming. As early as 1500 BCE, near the southern shore of the Gulf of Mexico, on what is called Mexico's isthmus, the Olmecs began to collect in impressive towns, living primarily on the corn and beans they planted.[10] They built large, sturdy buildings where they stored surplus food, and their population grew rapidly relative to other groups. They divided up the necessary labor, and the distinctions allowed some segments of the population to become more powerful than others. They developed a calendar, and talented artists grew adept at sculpture. Their carvings honored gods or chiefs or godly chiefs—we cannot know exactly which—by creating mammoth statues of their heads. Later in the course of their descendants' history, other gifted individuals created a form of writing, scratching out symbols on tablets to represent words, such as the name of the Venus god, Ten Sky. Clearly these people took pride in all that they had accomplished and offered gratitude to their gods; their sculptures and inscriptions underscore the point.

Perhaps unsurprisingly, the corn-and-beans culture complex spread east and west from the isthmus, and Olmec influence expanded, its elements of grandeur firing the imagination of others.[11] To the east, great stone pyramids soon rose above the jungle canopy. The Maya artisans who built them added paint made from lime or plant pigments; others had learned to weave twisted strands of wild cotton into beautiful cloth, and soon colorful pennants fluttered in the breeze. They carved their writings on great slabs of stone that they set before the pyramids for all the world to see, commemorating the triumphs of their kings and staking their claim to greatness. Sometimes, they painted much tinier characters on ceremonial vessels and plates. These became veritable poems. One day in about the year 800, for example, a skilled artisan crafted a cup for drinking hot chocolate as a gift for a young prince. He connected the earthly world to the divine world, honoring at the same time both a powerful prince and a creator god: "He who gave the open space its place, who gave Jaguar Night his place, was the Black-Faced Lord, the Star-Faced Lord."[12]

The people were never utterly carried away by their philosophical musings, however. When the Maya population exceeded the number that their lands could provide for, or they needed a particular resource, they made brutal war upon their weaker neighbors. Thus, several kingdoms became powerful indeed, but time after time, they rose and fell. There was no single Maya state that dominated others permanently. In what scholars call the "classic" period, lasting until somewhere between 800 and 900, the decisive victory of a particular royal lineage often led to the construction of the monumental architecture that has stood the test of time; in the "postclassic" period most Maya kingdoms remained relatively small. Still many were indeed impressive, such as Chichen Itza in the middle of the Yucatán peninsula.

Meanwhile, to the west, other Olmec-influenced cultures took root and flourished. The civilization of Monte Alban, for example, near today's Oaxaca, ruled over a great valley; the central government drew representatives from many different village councils. And in the central basin in the heart of Mexico, a city state called Cuicuilco flourished from about 200 BCE. It far exceeded its neighbors in power until the day in the first century CE when nearby Mount Xitle erupted and lava covered the town completely (the volcano did its job so thoroughly that Mexican archaeologists were forced to use dynamite to uncover even part the city.) Cuicuilco's disappearance created a power vacuum, but this situation would not last. Nearly all the people of central Mexico had become corn planters by that time, and a number of them thus boasted impressive arts and crafts and a large population. One among them would surely rise to become a great state and take Cuicuilco's place.[13]

***

It was a place now called Teotihuacan (Tay-oh-tee-WA-kahn) that did so. The city rose out of the vacuum to such heights of power that even centuries after it fell, its ruins were known to Shield Flower and her people. When her ancestors came down from the north, they paused in their passage over the ring of mountains that encircled the central valley at the heart of the region and looked down at the panorama before them. All who came this way did this, and to a person of ordinary experience, it was a truly awe-inspiring vista. The valley was actually a basin without drainage. The damp earth of its frequently soaked plains was perfect for farming, and the encircling sweep of mountains formed a literal barricade against the outside world. It seemed to be the very center of the earth, created as a sort of enchanted place. In the pre-dawn darkness, the scattered villages were visible, for the women were already up, lighting their fires, and the points of light shone in the obscurity like clusters of stars in the midst of the blackness.

Perhaps that same month, or a bit later, the wanderers went to see the great ruins that lay in the northern half of the valley, ruins that were famous to everyone in their world and could be seen for miles. Shield Flower probably never saw them herself, for girls did not get out much in times of war, but her father or grandfather certainly would have in the days before the troubles started, when the group's menfolk spent their time as wandering bands of hired mercenaries. Those ruins were a holy place. The earliest arrivals from the north had given them a name in their own language, *Teotihuacan*, by which they were known ever after. It tied the place to the divine, for it meant either "the place of people who become gods" or "the place of those who had great gods," depending on what one heard.[14]

The descendants of the newcomers later envisioned Teotihuacan as the birthplace of their world. They said it was the scene of their storied hero Nanahuatzin's courageous self-immolation. Sometimes they told the tale in great detail, saying that when the first four imperfect worlds, each with its own sun and living creatures, had all been destroyed, and the earth was left in darkness, the gods met together at Teotihuacan. "The gods gathered and took counsel at Teotihuacan. They said to each other, 'Who will carry the burden? Who will take it upon himself to see that there will be a sun, that there will be a dawn?'"[15] They had great faith in one called Tecuciztecatl (tekw-seez-TEK-at) who volunteered, and they offered him the honor of a forked heron feather headdress for his sacrifice and other gifts; they chose Nanahuatzin for his very ordinariness. When midnight arrived and the moment had come, Tecuciztecatl found he could not do the deed. It was the ordinary Nanahuatzin who shut his eyes and threw himself into the flames "in order that the dawn might break." He suffered, and in his bravery he became the sun. All the gods honored him; his face had become so bright that none could look upon it. Suddenly Tecuciztecatl, inspired by another's bravery, found the courage he needed and threw himself in. And he became the moon. Then two ordinary animals, the jaguar and the eagle, modest but brave, threw themselves in likewise and thus proved themselves great warriors. Teotihuacan, the people believed, was the site of the beginning of everything.

The first newcomers from the north who stumbled upon the city's inspirational ruins must have been stunned at what they saw. The old city lay between two great pyramids, each of which was aligned with a towering mountain behind it; each offered homage to the power, the divinity, of the earth itself. Between them lay a great avenue, and along each side ran the houses and schools and temples of a people long vanished. Turning down the side streets, which were laid out in a grid pattern, and wandering among the remnants of an earlier world, the Nahuas found hundreds of apartments opening onto little courtyards. They found painted walls and aqueducts and holes used as latrines. In the temple precinct, carved snakes slithered down grand stairways, and the heads of giant feathered serpents jutted out of the wall at eye level. These creatures were the pale color of rock, but colorful patches here and there demonstrated that they once had been brightly painted.

In the past, the hum of the city's life had been audible from a goodly distance, and in the time of Shield Flower, the ruins still told that story. Between the 200s and the 600s, in the wake of Cuicuilco's destruction by the volcano, the population of the twenty-square-mile city rose to an astounding fifty thousand. The most sumptuous households were for the nobility, but each neighborhood was impressive in its own right and each had its own character and trade. The largest neighborhood was that of the obsidian craftsmen who worked with the volcanic material that resembled black glass, making spearheads, knives, statues, jewelry, and mirrors. Indeed, the city had been founded near an important obsidian mine, and when it was exhausted, the people found another mine seventy kilometers away and began to have the stone carried to them by slaves from conquered states. The potters were also known for their expertise. Like the obsidian products, their work was sent hundreds of miles away, where other goods were traded in exchange. In small enclaves in the city lived merchants from other regions, whose presence guaranteed the continuance of long-distance trade. In the remains of their cooking and their garbage pits, they left behind evidence of their foreign ways of doing things. All around the city, in a great circle, were the huts of the farming peoples and their irrigation ditches. The farmers did not feed the city all on their own, however; other food stuffs came in as payments of tribute from less powerful peoples. The city apparently even made war on or traded with some of the Maya kingdoms, far to the east, for the influence of Teotihuacan was later visible there.[16]

In about the year 500, the city's elites arranged for the founding of another city that Shield Flower's people later called Chalchihuitl (Chal-CHEE-weet), their word for the green stone that we call jade, at the site of a great gemstone mine far to the north. The site, in today's Zacatecas, in northern Mexico, is now called Alta Vista. A settlement had existed there for several hundred years, but it would be transformed into a place of grandeur. The ceremonial center was designed as a copy of that of Teotihuacan. The new city was charged not only with continuing to mine the precious jade but also with guarding the route to today's Arizona and New Mexico, from which turquoise and other goods came. The people who lived in Chalchihuitl did more than this, however. They had brought with them knowledge of the calendar in use at Teotihuacan, and there in the desert, they became expert astronomical observers. They aligned their built world with the celestial one, and people came from miles around to worship, just as they did at Teotihuacan.[17]

In around 650, a great crisis shook the world of all who lived under the sway of Teotihuacan. The working people—peasant farmers, or perhaps even slaves who had come as war captives—rose in revolt. They burned the palaces and the ceremonial precincts but left untouched the apartments of the ordinary folk. Archaeologists know that this was no foreign invasion: foreign enemies always try to destroy the common people's homes and livelihood, but they do not destroy the great monumental architecture they hope to acquire for themselves. It does not take much imagination to envision the kind of coercion that had to have taken place in Teotihuacan in order to maintain such a metropolis in a world without highways and railroad supply lines, or engines to aid construction projects. Add to this the fact that a major drought seems to have hit the area in this period, and the rebellion seems more like an event waiting to happen than a mystery in need of explanation.[18]

The fall of Teotihuacan created another great power vacuum. There was an almost inexhaustible supply of nomadic peoples living to the north who knew about the central valley due to the once-thriving long-distance trade networks. And those nomads were armed and dangerous. The people of the hemisphere had been killing their game—and each other—with spears for many millennia. They had grown expert in the design and production of what Shield Flower would have called the *atlatl*, or spear thrower, a device that considerably extended the trajectory that an individual man would otherwise have been able to achieve. Not long before the fall of Teotihuacan, however, a new invention had made its way down from the Arctic: the bow and arrow. These had not existed when the early migrants made their way across the Bering Strait, and although they had since become ubiquitous in the Old World, the same had not occurred in the New World. Bows and arrows did not give a decided advantage over the atlatl in the hunt; they only offered definite benefits in warfare with other humans, as they could kill from a greater distance, and they allowed for stealth. It was probably for that reason that this type of technology had not been vigorously pursued in the sparsely populated New World, where it was far easier to wander away to unclaimed territory than to attack one's neighbors. By around 500 CE, however, bows and arrows had definitely reached the American Southwest and northern Mexico and had rapidly become an important element of every warrior's gear.[19]

Waves of conquering nomads descended into central Mexico. Presumably drought or power struggles (or both) drove them out. The migrants would have been mostly young men, traveling without women and children when they started out, so they could move with greater speed. They learned to pride themselves on their ability to keep moving without complaint, even in grueling heat. Because nothing tied them to one place, they could strike sedentary people living in farming villages with lightning speed and then disappear again into the desert, where they were impossible to trace. They could take the farmers' stored food, their weapons, their precious stones, their women. If the interlopers did stay long enough in one area to engage in major battles, they generally won what fights there were, thanks to their bows and arrows, which at first the other side did not have. Then, if they chose, the newcomers could set the terms for their future residence in the area.

The migrants imbued their bows and arrows with magic and told stories about them. The stories were passed down through the generations until Shield Flower heard them in the form of entertaining tall tales about her ancestors: "They lived armed with the bow and arrow. It is said that they had bee sting arrows, fire arrows, arrows that followed people. It is even said that their arrows could seek things out. When the people went hunting, an arrow of theirs could go anywhere. If it was hunting something above, they would see it come back with an eagle. If the arrow saw nothing up above, why then it came downwards towards something else, maybe a puma or a jaguar or a snake or a deer or a quail or a rabbit. The people would follow along to see what their arrow had brought back to them!"[20]

There were no horses in the Americas at the time. Ancient equine species had become extinct much earlier, and the horses that would later arrive with the Spaniards had not yet made their appearance. So we must not envision the Apache of later centuries, who came galloping into farming villages on their painted ponies. Among the migrants' most famous war leaders was a man who went by the name of Xolotl (SHO-lot), according to the legends. He could never have appeared on horseback at the brow of a hill like Genghis Khan, the famed Mongolian. And yet, Xolotl was, in essence, a sort of Genghis Khan on foot. Wherever he went, he had the same bravado and aura of victory, though he maintained it on his own, in his own person, without the aid of a trusty steed. His nickname meant "Little servant boy," an ironic moniker intended to underscore his deadly power.[21]

In fact, the analogy to Genghis Khan goes much deeper. The Mongols certainly won their battles, but it was high Chinese culture that ultimately absorbed the nomads, not the other way around. It was the Mongols who changed their own lifestyles, to become farmers and merchants; some of their sons learned to write. Likewise, it was central Mexico's ancient culture that absorbed the incoming barbarians, as they were called (and as the latter proudly called themselves). The descendants of the newcomers eventually settled down and became corn planters; their children became adept in the complex ancient calendar of central Mexico.

In these same years, far to the north, in today's New Mexico, the Anasazi built extraordinary temples and apartments along a nine-mile stretch of the San Juan River's Chaco Canyon.[22] The intricate, three- and four-story brick buildings dazzle beholders even now; in their colorful heyday, when thousands of people came to attend the yearly religious ceremonies, they would have have been truly stunning. In the oldest part of the largest development (now called "Pueblo Bonito"), the builders guarded the precious jades and quetzal feathers that had come from distant Mexico. They aligned their buildings with the solar and lunar cycles, as did the people of Chalchihuitl, through whom the Chacoans traded with the Mexicans. After the collapse of Chaco, ever more migrants moved south, for in stories told around fires it was the south that was the stuff of legend to the people of the north.

Perhaps it was the south's calendar that carried the greatest mystique. Although elements of phonetic writing had moved from the central isthmus eastward toward Maya country, joining with and influencing writing traditions there, the tradition of writing had not moved westward with any great force. What writing did exist in the region was largely logographic, consisting of symbolic pictures, without phonetic representation of speech of the type the Maya were creating. The complex calendar system, on the other hand, had made its way to nearly every village in central Mexico, and a particular version had taken root there. Every child kept track of the basic elements of the system, although only learned priests ventured into the realm of more esoteric branches of the science. There were two ongoing cycles of time. One was a solar calendar, which consisted of eighteen months of twenty days each, plus five blank or unnamed, frightening days at the end, for a total of 365 days. The other was a purely ceremonial calendar containing thirteen months of twenty days each, for a total of 260 days. The two streams of time ran parallel, so on any day, one knew where one was both in relation to the sun and ceremonially. On a much simpler level, one could argue, we do something similar. We know what day of the year it is, which relates to our position in connection with the sun, and at the same time, we run a totally arbitrary, continuous seven-day series of Nordic gods' names, so we know it is Wednesday or Thursday as well.

The two cycles of time both returned to their starting point at the end of fifty-two solar years. Thus a "bundle" of fifty-two years, as they termed it, was as important to them as a century is today. To name each year, they tied it to the ceremonial calendar's most important number: thirteen. The fifty-two years were divided into four groupings of thirteen each, like this: One Reed, Two Flint-knife, Three House, Four Rabbit, Five Reed, Six Flint-knife, Seven House, Eight Rabbit, Nine Reed, Ten Flint-knife, Eleven House, Twelve Rabbit, Thirteen Reed, and then beginning again One Flint-knife, Two House, and so on. The priests and their people were proud of their knowledge of the calendar, revealed to them by the gods and aided by careful measurement and record-keeping.[23]

Or perhaps pleasure, not counting, lay at the crux of the southern realm's cultural prestige. The element of central Mexico's way of life that seems to have spread more easily than any other was the notion of a central town square surrounded by pyramidal structures, where people gathered and shared cultural events, and where there was almost always a ball court with slanted walls on two sides. There, athletes played before their people, using their hips to keep a rubber ball aloft, until finally they scored a point by causing it to hit the ground on the opposing team's side. Often there was a stone ring carved on each side of the court; only the most skillful could send the ball through such a hoop. The crowd yelled with excitement and frustration while watching the dramatic games. Later, when empires arose, there would be occasional games played to the death, with the losing team sacrificed. But it was not that rare practice that caused the ball courts to last for dozens of generations; rather it was the thrill of the game and the joy it brought. The town square with its pyramid temples and its associated ball court spread through Mexico and eventually northward as well.[24]

***

DESPITE THE GLORY of the southern realms, Shield Flower prided herself on her descent from northern *Chichimecs*, from barbarians, more than on her descent from the culture of corn planters and calendar-keepers they had married into. At her death, she cried out as a warrior maiden. The history she had been taught—and which she saw herself as a part of—focused on the wanderers, not on those who had occupied the valley before their arrival. Dozens of those stories survive, written down in her language by the first generations of her people to learn a phonetic transcription system. Each story is a little different from the others, depending on whether it came from her people or a neighboring people, whether it was written down in the first or the third generation after contact with Europeans, whether it was taken from a teller who valued humor or one who preferred high drama. Taken all together, although they may contradict each other in certain details, they reveal a great deal about her world.[25]

Almost all the wanderers believed they came from the northwest, from Chicomoztoc, "the place of the Seven Caves." Some groups said their specific origin was called "Aztlan," a word of uncertain meaning, but it was probably meant to be "Place of the White Heron." Where was Aztlan? We don't know, and we never will. It was likely a mythical name, used to mask the fact that the ancestors had migrated multiple times. The newcomers spoke Nahuatl, which belongs to the Uto-Aztecan family of indigenous languages. These languages stretch from that of the Utes (originally in today's Utah) down to Nahuatl. In between these areas, other peoples, such as the Hopi, also speak a Uto-Aztecan language. Thousands of years ago, along this linguistic route, people in neighboring villages would have been able to understand each other, yet a Ute would not have been able to understand a Nahua. It is very possible, even probable, that some of the migrating populations originated as far away as Utah and that others originated in northern Mexico. No single person ever traveled the entire path. No one in Shield Flower's day could or would have carried memories of a childhood in Aztlan; it was a communal memory of a home or homes abandoned long ago that they carried with them.[26]

Like all humans, the Chichimec barbarians seem to have spent most of their time forming alliances with others and deciding when and where to break them. This was the core of their political strategy as they made their way to power in central Mexico. They were proud of their alliances, and although they knew it was the stuff of life, their stories reveal that they were also guilt-ridden about the rages and the schisms. In their narratives, the worst of these crises nearly always occurred at a previously utopian place called "Tula." There was in fact a real city of Tula that rose to prominence about three centuries after Teotihuacan's fall, not far to the north of that once-great site. But it was never anywhere near as grand as Teotihuacan, and its period of ascendancy was relatively brief. Only a few groups of the arriving Nahuas actually spent time there, yet nearly all the old Nahuatl histories mention the glorious Toltec people, with their breathtaking arts and crafts, and allude to a political crisis at Tula as if it were a foundational moment for every group that had a story to tell. This was because the word "Toltec" was used to describe any of the artisan peoples of central Mexico who had inhabited the area for many generations, and a reference to a place called "Tula" (meaning "a reedy place" or "a swampy piece of ground," like most of the central valley) was a symbolic way of speaking of any nomadic group's first important moment of settling down with locals. The tensions, it seems, were always horrendous.[27]

One of the first—perhaps the very first—of the Nahua histories that was recorded using the Roman alphabet opens in "Tula." There the barbarians, who already had some ties to civilized folk (and are thus called the "Tolteca Chichimeca"), set up housekeeping with the decorous Nonohualca, who had closer ties to the more ancient people of central Mexico. The Chichimec barbarians bossed the others around, but it was not exactly the Chichimecs' fault that they exhibited such rough, uncouth behavior. One of the more malicious gods had tricked them: he left a foundling for them to find and take pity on and raise as their own. They adopted him, having no way of knowing that the creature's sole purpose was to make trouble for them. In a bawdy tale designed to catch the audience's attention, the 1540s storyteller described the ensuing crisis:

> When Huemac became a young man, he gave orders that the Nonohualca tend to his home. Then the Nonohualca said to him, "So be it, my lord. May we do what you desire." The Nonohualca came to tend to his home. And then he demanded women of them. He said to the Nonohualca, "You are to give me women. I order that the buttocks be four spans wide." The Nonohualca said to him, "So be it. Let us first

seek where we can get one whose buttocks are four spans wide." Then they brought four women who had not yet known sexual pleasure. But as to size, they were not enough. He said to the Nonohualca, "They are not of the size I want. Their buttocks are not four spans wide. I want them really big." The Nonohualca left in great anger.[28]

The audience had to laugh, but as the story continued, matters only grew worse. This Huemac proceeded to do the most terrible thing one could do to a conquered people's women: rather than keeping them as minor wives, he sacrificed them. He tied the four of them to an obsidian table and left them there to await their fate. At this, the Nonohualca had had enough. Naturally, they blamed the Chichimecs who had taken Huemac in, and they launched an attack against them. In their rage, they were about to attain victory, when the Chichimecs suddenly begged them to desist. Their leader cried aloud, "Was *I* the one who sent for the women over whom we are fighting and making war?! Let Huemac die! *He* made us fight!" Working together, the two groups managed to defeat their preposterously evil enemy, but in a sense it was too late. They had killed too many of each other's sons. "The Nonohualca gathered together and talked. They said, 'Come, what kind of people *are* we? It seems we have done wrong. Perhaps because of it something may happen to our children and grandchildren. Let us go. Let us leave our lands. . . . We should leave here.'" The Nonohualca thus departed that very night. The rest of the history is an account of their own and the abandoned Chichimecs' efforts to find peace and stability without the aid of their lost allies.

Alone and vulnerable, the Chichimecs became wanderers again. And now the ultimate message of the Nahua histories becomes clear: they did not simply tell exciting stories of the forging of alliances and the dramatic crises that would break them apart. What Shield Flower really learned as a girl as she listened to the elders around the fire was that her people were destined to survive. Their creator would see to it. "Here he has placed us, our inventor, our creator," one of the historians had a character say. "Will we have to hide our faces, our mouths [that is, will we have to die]? What does he say, how does he test us, our inventor, our creator, he who is everywhere? He knows if we will be defeated here. What will he dispose? O Tolteca, may you have confidence! Gird yourselves up, take heart!" Shield Flower learned that her people deserved to survive because they loved life and fought for it, using their smarts, their love, and their ferocity, each in turn, as might be necessary. And their young people were expected to carry on in the same tradition.

In the story, the Tolteca Chichimeca eventually found themselves living as the servants of another, more powerful ancient tribe. They were demeaned; they suffered hunger; they could not worship their own gods properly. They had no weapons, no way of fighting back. But they cleverly devised a plan. They offered to take responsibility for handling the festivities of an upcoming religious holiday. Dancing was involved, dancing that required weapons. Their leader went to speak to the overlord chiefs, asking permission for his people to collect broken-down, cast-off weapons for use in the performance. He returned with the needed permission and addressed the young people of his community with tears in his eyes. Their people's fate was now in their hands. "O my children, O Tolteca, go to it with a will!" he cried out. The story continued:

> Then they dispersed and went to do the borrowing, saying to the [powerful] town's residents, "Please lend us your old weapons, some of your old shields and war clubs—not your good equipment—if you gave us that we would break it."
>
> "What will you do with them? What do you want them for?"
>
> "Listen, we are going to perform for the rulers. It's for when we will dance in the homes, the households, of your town."
>
> "Maybe you want our good weapons?"
>
> "No, my lord, just your old weapons that lie fallen where you throw out the ash water. Let's fix them up, and with them we will entertain the rulers and lords."
>
> Then the town residents said, "Fine. Here and there our old weapons, our old shields, our old clubs, are lying around. Gather them up. Ha, we don't even need our new weapons." So then the people wandered everywhere, looking in the various houses and patios. Wherever they went, there was eating and drinking going on. The residents spoke to them. They just belittled them and laughed at them. But the Chichimeca, they prepared themselves.

They worked night after night, patiently, painstakingly gluing, sewing, and repairing, rendering the feathered, painted shields and spears truly beautiful. At last they were ready to launch their bid for their people's freedom—which of course they won.

Each group of Nahuas had their own traditions and stories that were variations on this theme of courage and survival. Shield Flower's people were called the Mexica (Me-SHEE-ka). They shared versions of the tales common to almost all the Nahuas, but they also told stories unique to their own group. They said, for example, that after Shield Flower died, the survivors among her people were given land by the king of Culhuacan, in exchange for which they had to act as his servants. He entertained himself by giving them impossible tasks and threatening them with dire punishment if they failed to perform them. They had to move a chinampa (a farmable field built in swampy ground by constructing a basketry-style fence and filling it with earth—nothing could be less movable); they had to capture a deer without piercing its hide or breaking its bones; they had to defeat an enemy unarmed. In each case, they managed the task, either through trickery or, in the latter example, the use of extraordinary violence. (After they ambushed the designated enemies, they cut off their left ears to prove that they had done so and placed them in a basket.) Each time they returned to the king of Culhuacan with the job done, he and his people marveled and asked themselves, "Who *are* these Mexica?!"[29]

At last Coxcox, the king of the Culhua, determined to be done with his unwelcome guests. He said that they might build a temple to their own god, but all the while he intended to retract permission and then have his people destroy them for their impudence. Hidden in the bushes, he watched as they prepared the dedication of their temple. Suddenly the people's god chose to intervene. "While the sacrifice was being made, the Mexica and Coxcox heard the sky howling. At that an eagle came down, alighting on the peak of the temple's thatch roof, just as if he had his nest there." Coxcox knew then that he could not destroy these people, who had the blessing of a powerful divinity. So he banished them. And they survived more wanderings.

Not so many years after 1299, in the mid-1300s, an eagle alighted before the Mexica where they were camping; they decided that the eagle wanted them to build a permanent town there. This was no longer the world of legend. The campsite was very real, and the people probably saw at least one veritable eagle land there, a bird they revered. They were motivated to find a good reason to stay. They were on an island in a great lake, a place no one else had claimed, probably because the land was so marshy. There grew in abundance the prickly pear cactus, with its edible fruit, the *nochtli*, being especially nutritious. And there were fish to catch, water fowl to shoot, and algae to gather. It was a lively, colorful world. The Mexica looked around and decided the site could definitely be made to work. The town they built would be called *Tenochtitlan*,[30] and it would soon have a tlatoani, or king, and be beholden to no one else. This was what Shield Flower's father had attempted to orchestrate years before, but he had acted prematurely. A generation or two later, in the mid-1300s, the Mexica were better prepared to defend themselves, and this time they began with no rash implicit declarations of war against their neighbors.

If only Shield Flower could have known! Her beleaguered, wandering, utterly exhausted people were to find some peace even before the close of the old age she should have had. On their island home, her people began to transform themselves into the great figures she had wanted them to be. Yet perhaps it is just as well that Shield Flower could not know with certainty what heights they were to attain. Had she known of the future good, she would have known of the future agony as well. She had to die as all do, knowing only that to posterity the fates would undoubtedly deal both blessings and trauma; she had to die as all do, hoping that those who came after her would demonstrate the same determination to be strong that she herself had shown.

2

People of the Valley

1350s–1450s

By 1430,[1] Itzcoatl (Eetz-CO-wat),or Obsidian Snake, felt confident that he had won the gamble of a lifetime. He felt sufficiently certain that he would be able to retain the position of tlatoani of the Mexica—and indeed, high king of all the central valley—that he took time off from the battlefield and ordered a ceremonial book burning. All the old painted histories that led their readers to expect a future different from the one he had in mind—those that led people to think his half brother's sons were the ones destined to rule, or that Tenochtitlan was bound to remain only a minor city-state—were to be tossed into a bonfire in a great sacrifice to the gods.[2] The paintings on rolls of deerskin and the accordion-fold books made of thick parchment crafted from maguey plant fibers—and all the stories they contained— crackled and popped in the red heat before they turned to ash.[3] There was an old riddle in Nahuatl: "What is the scarlet macaw leading, the raven following?" And the answer was *tlachinolli*, a conflagration.[4] It must have been satisfying for Itzcoatl to watch the black billows of rising smoke. He probably knew that many people were already saying he had only won his power thanks to the brilliant military performance of his more noble half brother's son.[5] But in the long run, it didn't matter what they said. It was he who had emerged as high king. His deeds would literally be carved in stone, and he would see to it that his descendants ruled. He would be known to have brought his people to their turning point; he was in the midst of pulling them out of obscurity and weakness to a position of extraordinary strength.

***

A young man goes to war. The Bodleian Libraries, the University of Oxford, Codex Mendoza, MS. Arch. Selden. A.1, folio 63r.

ITZCOATL'S WORLD HAD never intended him to govern. Although his father had been chief of the Mexica for decades, Itzcoatl himself was just the son of one of the *tecpan* (palace compound) women who was far from royal. His half brothers by more important mothers had names that harkened back to the thirteenth century—like his brother "Huitzilihuitl," Hummingbird Feather, named for the ancestor-king who had been father to the feisty Shield Flower. Itzcoatl's name was his alone—no one before him ever bore it, nor would it be passed on to descendants. His life story was uniquely illuminating.

Itzcoatl's chieftain father had been called Acamapichtli (A-cahm-a-PEECH-tli). Fittingly, the name meant "Fistful of Reeds," for it was he who had been set up as the Mexicas' first tlatoani after they built their town on the island in the reedy swamp. The Mexica had managed to turn themselves into an independent entity at last by making friends with their on-again, off-again enemies, the people of Culhuacan. Acamapichtli's father was a Mexica man who had married a Culhua woman of some rank, but he himself had been killed in one of the periods of rancor. The son had survived the violence. In the middle of the 1300s, the Mexica had requested that he be allowed to become their king; obviously, as a son of a Culhua woman, he would keep his people loyal to Culhuacan. And so it had been settled. The Mexica at last had a recognized tlatoani with his own, symbolic reed mat, or throne. In Nahuatl terms, they had finally arrived.[6]

Admittedly, their island was available only because no one else wanted it. People of the central basin had long lived by farming corn and beans, but the swampy conditions of the central lake area ruled out full dependence on agriculture. Not that the Mexica gave up the project entirely; they had observed that on the southern shore of the lake, their rivals the Xochimilca (whose warriors' ears the Mexica had, in the distant past, cut off) did very well by constructing *chinampas*. These were gardens arduously built in shallow waters by piling up mud and silt, and then trapping some earth above the water level by constructing a wooden or straw-basket ring wall. The chinampas, though difficult to build, were immensely fertile, and the Mexica were thus quick to follow their neighbors' example. They also developed their fishing skills, grew adept at collecting birds' eggs, and learned to gather certain kinds of insects as well as the highly nutritious blue-green algae. As a boy, Itzcoatl passed his days flitting about in a canoe (he called it a little *acalli*, meaning literally a "water house") and then contributing whatever he foraged to the family pot. He came to love the shimmering, aquatic world he knew so well. All his people did. The artists among them grew adept at painting on walls and deer hides, and their work often featured the tiny crayfish and spiral shells found in the blue-green waters.

Sometimes the themes of the evening music and song were also inspired by the vibrant waters of the lake. Someone blew a conch shell; another man played a drum decorated with blue-green gemstones; a third might dance, his legs covered in strips of tinkling bells. The mood was sometimes achingly sad: the kingdom of Tlaloc, the rain god, and of Chalchiuhtlicue (Chal-chew-TLI-kway) or Jade Skirt, his wife, could be a mournful world, representing as it often did, not only life but also death. "I cry. What in the world have we done to deserve this?!" The singer could take on the persona of a fish, perhaps a weaker one hiding in the reeds speaking to a stronger one, "I am a sand fish, you are a trout." In happier times, Itzcoatl's people often sang not of the dim watery world but of birds fluttering in the light. Sometimes, in especially haunting moments, they might bring together the two traditions, aquatic and aerial, and sing a special poem aloud, harkening back to their historical roots, and referencing their proud warrior tradition represented by the eagle and the jaguar: "Your home abounds in jade water whorls... You hid yourself [meaning, you died] among the mesquite plants of the Seven Caves. The eagle was calling, the jaguar cried. And you, a red flamingo, went flying onwards, from the midst of a field to a place unknown."[7] The "place unknown" was one manifestation of the land of the dead, a special one that received the spirits of those brave enough to die in war or by sacrifice. As they sang in the firelight, the Mexica felt that they had reason to be grateful to the gods who had brought them to this moment. It had not been so long ago that they were wanderers, dependent on the Culhua people, or anyone who would temporarily take them on as hired bowmen. Now they made war only when they wanted to. Now they had a town of their own. True, the water still threatened to take it back from them. Reeds grew everywhere, and their square adobe houses didn't last well in swampy conditions and had to be constantly rebuilt. The people, however, grew extremely practiced at building dikes, causeways and canals, and soon were able to build streets, like those of other towns. Neighborhoods contained an extended kin group or *calpolli* (literally, "great house"), with its own leading families who took responsibility for organizing labor and war parties in support of the chief, Acamapichtli, and in turn were offered greater deference. Such a family was termed *pilli*, or *pipiltin* in the plural; we would call them nobles. Others were called *macehualli*, or *macehualtin* in the plural. The word meant more than commoner; etymologically, it referred to those deserving of land, and hence of their own space in the polity.

At about this time the people made the collective decision to add a layer of gravel to their original adobe shrine—where the eagle had purportedly landed—so they would have a base platform strong enough to begin to build a large pyramid.[8] Certain priests dedicated themselves to caring for the temple and began to create painted books for posterity. With their history recorded on animal skins, the priests could announce that the people had reached the end of a fifty-two-year cycle, that it was time to ceremonially "bundle" the years, as they put it. They held a great feast day and marked it as a significant moment in their histories.

In taking their past seriously, they were implicitly taking their future seriously, too. The chief Acamapichtli, the half-Culhua nobleman who had attained authority through his tight connections to the powerful state of Culhuacan, also brought with him a noble Culhua bride. Some said her name was Ilancueitl (Ee-lahn-KWEY-eetl), Elder Woman Skirt, though others said that such a name must have belonged to his mother. Since it was a chosen, symbolic name, it could easily have belonged to both women. Certainly the Culhua wife, whatever her name, did not expect to remain Acamapichtli's only woman, but it was understood that she was the primary, or First Wife, not necessarily chronologically but in the sense that her sons would rule in the next generation. Later, the bards of other communities would make the claim that she was barren, and that it was a woman from their own hometown (whichever one that was, depending on who was telling the story) who had eventually mothered Acamapichtli's heirs, though the children were passed off as Ilancueitl's. Be that as it may, there was certainly no concept of primogeniture. It would have been utterly impractical in such a fluid world in which the people needed a highly competent leader, not merely one who happened to have been born first.

Older boys, however, certainly had an advantage over younger ones. As the sons of a chief's most powerful wife grew up, their personalities and relative athletic abilities caused one among them to be perceived as the most likely heir, while his full brothers grew to accept expectations that they would be high priests or powerful military figures who stood by his side. All would be equally well rewarded for their efforts with gifts of land and other forms of wealth, so it was to all of the full brothers' advantage to support the one who seemed most like an appropriate chief.[9] In this case, the child who was groomed as the heir was called Huitzilihuitl, Hummingbird Feather, in honor of the thirteenth-century chief of that name.

Besides his full siblings—the other children of Acamapichtli's noble Culhua wife—Huitzilihuitl had many half brothers, among them Itzcoatl.

Obsidian Snake's mother had been no one of any importance. She had been, in fact, a slave—a beautiful slave girl from the nearby town of Azcapotzalco (Ahz-ka-po-TZAL-ko). People said she had spent her days selling vegetables in the street before she was turned over to the king. Noblemen loved to gamble and often gambled away their slaves; or perhaps she had been used to settle some other type of debt or presented to the high chief as a gift to curry favor.[10]

It may seem unlikely that a future Mexica king could be the son of a slave. Traditionally, the subject of slavery in the Aztec world has been a vexed one. Because the Aztecs were disparaged for so long as cannibalistic savages, serious scholars have been loath to write anything that might be perceived as detracting from their moral worth; associating them in any way with famous slave societies was hardly going to help matters. Thus the idea was often promulgated that Aztec slaves by definition were prisoners of war taken for sacrifice to satisfy a religious compulsion, and that household servants were a different category altogether: they were a collection of people who had voluntarily sold themselves into temporary slavery to pay debts, or who had been condemned to enslavement as punishment for a crime. However, modern scholars now acknowledge that the reality was quite different. Some prisoners of war (usually men) were indeed sacrificed, and some household servants had in truth indentured themselves or been sold by their chief as a punishment. But there were also many other enslaved people. As in the ancient Mediterranean world, the households of wealthy and powerful men contained numerous female slaves taken in war. Some were princesses, and might be treated almost like wives, depending on the circumstances. Others were more ordinary, and Itzcoatl's mother was one of these.[11]

Yet it would be a mistake to assume that Itzcoatl's mother was brutalized. She may have been, but given what Itzcoatl later managed to accomplish, it isn't likely. Throughout Mesoamerica, it was understood that the children of enslaved women were never slaves themselves. Indeed, it was essential that the condition not be inherited; otherwise many towns would soon have had more slaves than free people, and their world would have been torn asunder. Thus even in her worst moments, Itzcoatl's mother would have known that her children by the king would be privileged. She may possibly have been proud and hopeful for her young son's future. But even if she harbored ambitions on behalf of her boy, she would never have thought it possible that he would one day rule. That privilege was reserved for the sons of noble women from the most powerful of towns.[12] Times of crisis, however, often bring unexpected results, and so it would eventually prove in this case.

In the meantime, the boy called Itzcoatl grew up expecting to serve his royal half brother as a loyal warrior, and he did so. Huitzilihuitl, the heir, became king, and he ruled successfully for twenty-four years, conquering numerous smaller and more vulnerable city-states and demanding tribute from all of them. The men of Tenochtitlan left their island with some frequency and set forth as a united group, armed and dangerous. They danced before they left and they danced when they returned, wearing gorgeous headdresses that transformed them into frightening beasts—eagles, jaguars, serpents and coyotes. Their shields, decorated with iridescent feathers, also bore the images of such creatures, but they could introduce an element of ironic distance from their animal alter-egos as well, showing not a coyote, for instance, but rather a man dancing as an upright coyote.[13] These eager warriors readily allied with others to bring down those who tried to lord it over them or who had resources they desperately needed. Xochimilco and even the once-dominant Culhuacan were reduced to subsidiary status. Huitzilihuitl began, in short, to put the new town of Tenochtitlan on the map, and from there it grew into a small city. Huitzilihuitl's list of conquests was long in the telling around the evening fires.

The most important war Huitzilihuitl waged was arguably the one against Cuernavaca, the region to the south where wild cotton grew so well that people had begun to cultivate it and use it to weave cloth. It was a valuable crop, for cotton did not grow in the mountainous region. Cuernavaca was thus a rich city-state and its chief a powerful man. He also had a "most admirable" daughter, the lovely Miyahuaxihuitl (Mee-ya-wa-SHEE-weet, Corn Flower Gem), whom many chiefs eyed with interest as a marriage partner. Rulers everywhere "asked for her," using the most respectful term for a marriage relationship. When Huitzilihuitl's emissaries approached the Cuernavacan chief, he laughed at them. The town of Tenochtitlan, although on the rise, was by no means the alliance he had in mind for his child. "What is Huitzilihuitl saying? What will he provide for my daughter there in the midst of the waters?" The king couldn't refrain from a bit of sarcasm. "Perhaps he will clothe her using the fibers of marsh plants, since he makes his own loincloths out of them?" Then he decided to move from the customary round-about speech to a more direct style. "Go," he said. "Tell your ruler Huitzilihuitl that you are definitely not to come here again."[14]

After that, the tellers of the tale opted to depart from a realistic account of events. They did not choose to dwell on the carnage of the ensuing war or the many years it lasted, since the two peoples later became allies:[15] such things are better forgotten. Instead, they used an old Nahua myth to interpret what happened. The disappointed Huitzilihuitl went off by himself and prayed to his people's god, Huitzilopochtli (Wee-tzeel-o-POCH-tli), meaning "Left-Footed like a Hummingbird." He thus had the special powers associated with both left-handedness and the magical, suspended (and fearsome) humming-bird, and he was especially tied to the king, Huitzilihuitl, whose name meant "Hummingbird Feather." As always, the god told the supplicant what to do, and naturally, Huitzilihuitl proceeded to do as the god directed. "He stood within the boundaries of the lord of Cuernavaca. Then he shot a dart, a pret-tily painted and marvelously crafted reed, in the center of which was inserted a precious jade—most valuable and shimmering brightly. And it fell in the middle of the courtyard where the maiden Corn Flower Gem was confined." The girl marveled at it and picked it up. Sensing the stone's power and feeling a strange desire for it, she suddenly popped it into her mouth. Then the mes-merized young woman swallowed the precious gem by accident and—like other girls in numerous other Native American ancient stories—conceived a child.[16]

The Nahua tellers of the tale and their rapt audience would have said in that moment that the joke was on the overly proud Cuernavacan king; his beloved daughter had been duped and would now bear a child by a father she would by no means have chosen herself. But they would have recognized that the situation was laced with irony. The lovely Corn Flower Gem may have shed tears that night, but the apparently powerless girl would eventually come into her own: her child, after all, was named Moctezuma[17] (later to be known as Huey Moctezuma, or Moctezuma the Elder), and he was destined to rule over the Mexica and many tens of thousands of others.[18]

For the moment, however, in the palace compound in Tenochtitlan, the Mexica high chief Huitzilihuitl probably was not paying a great deal of atten-tion to any children born to a Cuernavacan woman taken in war. He was lead-ing his people as effectively as possible in a series of military campaigns, enlarging the territory he governed. He was able to be so successful largely because under his leadership Tenochtitlan had become a client, so to speak, of what was currently the single most powerful city-state in the region. The head or "boss" state was Azcapotzalco, the leading town of the *Tepanec* people, a group of Nahuas who had arrived much earlier than the Mexica and domi-nated the western shores of the great lake in the center of the valley.[19] After each victory, the Tepanecs, of course, took the best lands for themselves, but a goodly share was set aside for their lieutenant-state, Tenochtitlan. Or, if the victors decided that the losers were not to forfeit their lands but to pay tribute instead, certain villages were told to pay the Tepanecs in future, and others

were instructed to deliver goods to the Mexica. It is not certain why the
Mexica were chosen as the favored lieutenant state. Probably the swampy
nature of their island territory rendered them more mobile than other peoples; because they did not have much farmable land, they were not as tightly
tied to cycles of planting and harvesting. No town in central Mexico had a
standing army; all the men were potential warriors, and they had to fit in their
fighting with their farming. The Mexica, however, lived as much off fish, bird
eggs, and algae as they did from maize. This meant they were relatively poor
and hungry compared to others to start with; working closely with the highly
agricultural Tepanecs, however, their mobility in any season gave them a kind
of power.

Unsurprisingly, given the patron-client political relationship, Huitzilihuitl
took a bride from a Tepanec town as his primary wife, meaning that her sons
were expected to rule after him.[20] (The town was called *Tlacopan* and was
later to be an important place; the Spanish, who couldn't pronounce it,
turned it into "Tacuba.") When Huitzilihuitl died, Chimalpopoca (Chee-
mal-po-PO-ka, Smoking Shield), a son by the Tepanec bride, inherited the
throne, exactly as expected.

By now, Tenochtitlan's ruler was fully recognized by everyone as tlatoani,
or "speaker" on behalf of an independent, self-governing community. In the
Nahua world, each community that boasted its own tlatoani was called an
altepetl. The word literally meant "water-mountain," for in the old days, the
Nahuas nearly always settled where they had not only a hill from which to
defend themselves but also a source of water. At Chimalpopoca's ascension,
there were days of prayer, followed by a great feast and a ceremony in which
Chimalpopoca seated himself on the symbolic reed mat and promised to protect his people as their tlatoani. At this point, the Mexica were powerful
enough to take themselves quite seriously: the public speeches and the com-
mitments made between Chimalpopoca and his people lasted for hours.
Eventually, a priest peppered the young ruler with rhetorical questions, to
which the new monarch and the people were ultimately meant to respond
"No" with all their energy:

> Will you see a time of fear? Will it fall to you to declare war? Will the
> altepetl be engulfed in war? Will it be your responsibility? Will the
> altepetl crumble in war? Will it be surrounded by enemies? Will there
> be agitation, tremors? Will the city lie abandoned, lie darkened? Will
> it become a place of desolation? Will our people be enslaved?[21]

"No!" they answered, and "No!" again. They would win the wars, not lose them. They would not be enslaved. Then, to demonstrate his prowess, Chimalpopoca set off on the initial military campaign required of every new king. He returned victorious; his people were optimistic. Chimalpopoca ruled for about ten years, bringing multiple new towns under Mexica control.

***

THEN IN THE MIDST of Chimalpopoca's reign a great political crisis rocked the Mexicas' political world. In 1426, the king of the powerful town called Azcapotzalco, Tezozomoc (Te-zo-ZO-moc), who had ruled since 1370, died in his bed. The Tepanec leader had personified power in the valley for so many years that when he died, people looked uncertainly at each other. Suddenly the old king's sons lunged forward into action—but they did not move to defend their family's turf, as one might expect. Instead, they turned on each other with murderous intent.

This seems puzzling at first. It seems less so when we think about the fact that polygyny had created a situation in which there were many potential claimants to any throne. The Nahuas were so accustomed to the phenomenon that they did not see it as a problem. They saw it as a net positive, and, in fact, they were not entirely wrong. Whatever our modern sensibilities may tell us, polygyny does have many benefits. It offers obvious pleasures to the senior male with multiple wives, and even the wives in such situations often say that it is a help to them as they age to bring younger women into the household, as many hands make light work. Nahua wives certainly never sought or expected romantic love from a husband; it did not surprise them when men were fickle, nor did anyone in their world blame the women. Furthermore, polygyny generally eliminates any possibility of a king dying without an heir, and it creates a veritable clan of young men who pride themselves on their relationships to each other and who will stand together in times of crisis.

Such, at least, is the theory. In reality, even a woman who has never expected a permanent partnership with a man can be hurt when she is supplanted by a rival. And the pain may possibly be not the woman's alone but also her children's. "Hey, mother," went one Nahuatl song, "I am dying of sadness here in my life with a man. I can't make the spindle dance. I can't throw my weaver's stick."[22] The singer was taking the role of a captive wife, and she meant that as an extraneous household woman, she could not look forward to a dignified old age as her children gradually took over the family wealth and family duties. Yet this, after all, speaks only of personal pain, likely to be utterly irrelevant in a political sense. What is far more important in a larger sense is that the system can work well only when the vast majority of people fully agree as to which wife is primary—that is, when they all think alike as to whose sons should inherit. If there is significant doubt about that, a civil war is imminent, for factions of royal half brothers born of different mothers, divided by visceral, childhood-based hatred are there at hand, ready and willing to lead the people as they defend their different visions of their people's future.

The annals tell us that warfare exploded at such moments in the towns across Mexico, time and again.[23] The extensive fighting at first seems confusing, but upon closer observation, it usually fits certain patterns. In the Nahua world, since the different wives of a chief were often from different city-states, these fratricidal conflicts often had an ethnic dimension as well. When Maxtla (MASH-tla), son of Tezozomoc of Azcapotzalco, rose against his half brother, the presumed heir, and killed him,[24] Maxtla was undoubtedly assuming that he would receive help from his mother's home village, and he did. At the same time, he turned against Azcapotzalco's former allies, whose royal houses were all intermarried with the maternal family of the half brother he had killed, specifically, the royal household of the town of Tlacopan. This meant that Maxtla also targeted Tenochtitlan's chief, Chimalpopoca, who had a Tlacopan mother. Nahua historians offered different versions of a terrible story of treachery and death. In one, Maxtla invited Chimalpopoca to his home, as if to welcome him to the celebration feast of his new reign, but then had him strangled to death.[25]

However the deed was done, there was pandemonium back in Tenochtitlan. The borders with Azcapotzalco were considered closed (they used the word that meant "closed off"), once it was understood that people who crossed into the other's territory were liable to be attacked. For years the Tenochca people's political choices had depended on the will of the boss state of Azcapotzalco. What were they to do now? For a brief spell of sixty days, Chimalpopoca's young son ruled, then suddenly he fell. His name was Xihuitl Temoc, or Fallen Comet.[26] The epithet seems too perfect to have been his real name; the boy did have ancestors of that name, but one wonders if the bards applied it to him after the events unfolded, as often happened. It is not known exactly how he died, but probably it was in some sort of battle or skirmish. It does not seem likely that he was also assassinated by Maxtla, for he would surely have known what had happened to his father, Chimalpopoca, and would have learned caution from that disaster.

Perhaps he had been betrayed in some way by Itzcoatl. It was, after all, Itzcoatl who came to power next. By now, Itzcoatl was at least forty years old.

No one tells us when his birthday was, but he had lived through the twenty-four years of his half brother Huitzilihuitl's reign, plus another ten years under his nephew, Chimalpopoca, and he would have been conceived at least a few years before his father's death. He may, indeed, have been much older than forty in 1426, as he would die of what was perceived to be old age fourteen years later. In any case, he was certainly a seasoned war leader, unlike Chimalpopoca's still-young children. That might explain why people followed him in this emergency. But Huitzilihuitl's son by the Cuernavacan princess was available, and other sons as well, among them one named Tlacaelel, who had been born in the 1390s and already held a high position.[27] There was no genuine need for the royal family to turn to Itzcoatl, Grandpa Acamapichtli's son by the slave girl. Itzcoatl, the "Obsidian Snake," must have been distinguished by more than a long year count or respected resume; others also had these qualities. He must have had charisma, and ambition, and a subtle mind.

Itzcoatl's plan was to take advantage of the very same type of fissures that had created this emergency in the first place: he clearly understood that polygyny lay at the very heart of politics. It was an issue to be taken extremely seriously. Itzcoatl planned to ally with the ousted noble family of Tlacopan, but it was going to take more than that to win the war that he had in mind. Maxtla wouldn't have killed his half brother by a Tlacopan mother if he hadn't believed that that he had sufficient allies to back him in his power grab. Itzcoatl would need additional allies—people who would join him because they had far more to gain than to lose by challenging the status quo in the polygynous system in which they were all enmeshed. He turned to another city-state suffering from a comparable polygyny-induced civil war, and he sided with those who were presently losing, who were hungry for allies and desperate with rage. He was taking a great risk, and some of the historians later said that many among his people begged him simply to implore Maxtla for mercy. Let Maxtla name a puppet king and be done with it. (Perhaps, indeed, that is who the ill-fated Fallen Comet had been.) They insisted that they would pay whatever tribute Maxtla set rather than face slaughter. But Itzcoatl did not listen to such counselors. Instead, he sent emissaries to a place called Texcoco (Tesh-CO-co).

On the eastern side of the lake, on the shore opposite that of the Tepanecs, the dominant ethnic group had for many years been the Nahuatl-speaking people known as the *Acolhua* (A-COL-wa). Their leading town was Texcoco, sometimes called the Paris of ancient Mexico, so beautiful were its buildings and so fine its artwork. Like Tenochtitlan, Texcoco had for years been somewhat dependent on Tezozomoc, the godfather-like king of Azcapotzalco who had died suddenly. Naturally, under these circumstances, Texcoco's king had as his primary wife one of Tezozomoc's daughters, and her sons were poised to inherit power.[28]

Among the Texcocan king's women, however, there was one whom he liked much better. She was Matlalcihuatl (Ma-tlal-SEE-wat, Blue-Green Woman), who was a Tenochca noblewoman, probably a daughter of Huitzilihuitl, and thus a sister of the murdered Chimalpopoca.[29] Texcoco, an old and well-established city-state, chafed more than Tenochtitlan did under the oppressive leadership of Azcapotzalco. (It is, after all, easier for a new kid on the block to accept the bossiness of a charismatic boy who offers to befriend him than it is for a longtime resident who once led the local gang to cede his place to such a figure.) Perhaps to make a political point, the Texcocan king sometimes favored Blue-Green Woman's children over his Azcapotzalcan primary wife's offspring more than was quite wise.

Meanwhile, as a result of Azcapotzalco's great power, a Texcocan princess had been given as a minor wife to the high chief Tezozomoc's son.[30] It was understood that her children were not to inherit. Indeed, her status in the household necessarily mirrored her hometown's status in relation to Azcapotzalco. Texcoco was the weaker state, and thus her children were necessarily weaker than their half siblings by Tepanec mothers. Tezozomoc may even have used the girl to underscore her hometown's dependency upon him by having her take lesser roles in public ceremonies or events. In any case, the young princess found her status humiliating and her life in general a misery. Still, she was by no means a prisoner, and eventually she fled home and took up with another man from her hometown. She simply acted as though she were free to marry. The history tellers loved it when they got to this part of the story on starlit evenings, for it allowed them to enact some of the dialogue they delighted in delivering: "Now, when Tezozomoc found out that his daughter-in-law had married, had taken a husband in Texcoco, it made him furious. He summoned his captain, and a few others who came along, too, and he said, 'I have heard, I have learned, that War Arrow of Huexotla (Way-SHO-tla) has bedded the former wife of [my son], your comrade. He has slept with her. My lords, hear me! I am angry, I am insulted.'"[31] Later, when war came, and the Tepanecs further discovered that the woman's son by their chief was also living in his maternal grandparent's lands of Texcoco and was fighting on his mother's side, not on their side, they were livid. "What a scoundrel! Would anyone want to make war on his own father?!?"[32]

In the tales that were told, women caused these wars: "It was said that there was war because of a concubine," one historian wrote in another case.[33] Yet in the 1420s war had not really come to Mesoamerica because of a runaway wife—she was only a metaphor for the uppity Texcocans—but because of a broader political situation. The Texcocan king had decided he was powerful enough to take a political risk to try to gain his ends. He began to insist that his sons by his Mexica wife would indeed inherit, thus indicating that he would no longer accept Texcoco's status as a client state of Azcapotzalco. Changing his relationship to his wives was tantamount to making an important public pronouncement. Tezozomoc and the Azcapotzalcans did not wait for more. Hundreds of them crossed the lake at dawn in dozens of canoes ringed by their bright-colored shields. The boats slid silently through the still waters. Then the warriors rushed ashore and began to kill without mercy.[34]

The Texcocans soon sent the young Azcapotzalcan-fathered nobleman who was living among them to try to make peace. It was a vain effort, and Tezozomoc's men killed him. Eventually, the old Texcocan king was also killed in a skirmish; he had paid a heavy price for attempting to throw off Azcapotzalco's yoke. Some said that his son by Blue-Green Woman, his Mexica wife, saw his father's death from high in a tree where he was hiding. Perhaps he did. Others said he was hiding deep in a cave at the time. That may have been more likely, but it could equally as easily have been a poetic device; in Mesoamerican storytelling tradition, crucial moments of transition often revolved around caves, whence a new form or force emerged from darkness. The boy's name was Nezahualcoyotl (Nez-ah-wal-CO-yot), or Hungry Coyote, and whether or not he was witness to the killing of his father, it was certainly emblazoned in his consciousness. He fled and hid in Tlaxcala (Tlash-CA-la), a town to the east that was not under Azcapotzalco's sway. It seems to have been there that Itzcoatl's emissaries came looking for him years later, during the great political crisis. The two lords—Nezahualcoyotl and Itzcoatl—were related, through Blue-Green Woman, Nezahualcoyotl's Mexica mother; now Itzcoatl had an offer to make to his young kinsman.[35]

He explained that he had a triple alliance in mind. If the Texcocan families who were loyal to Nezahualcoyotl would fight against Maxtla of Azcapotzalco, alongside the Mexica and the recently demoted people of Tlacopan, they could probably win. Victory over Azcapotzalco, the valley's most powerful city-state, would bring extraordinary rewards. Nezahualcoyotl's days as a scavenger would be over: he would become the recognized tlatoani of Texcoco, instead of the derided half brother of the ruling king.

Nezahualcoyotl responded that it would not be an easy task to collect loyal families to follow him into battle, as Tezozomoc, after attaining power, had made his own grandsons (his daughter's children by the old Texcocan king) the rulers of most of the region's villages. It was even said that Tezozomoc had his people ask local children who were no more than nine years old if their current ruler was the rightful one. At that age, the children did not have the circumspection necessary to edit their responses: they gave away their families' political position as it had been discussed it in the privacy of their own homes. Some of the prattling children's families had been brutally punished since.[36] But the fear that had been engendered by such acts had also bred anger. Nezahualcoyotl said that he was game, indeed eager, to join the alliance; he would gather what followers he could.

The ensuing battles were brutal, but village by village, the supporters of Maxtla the Azcapotzalcan were brought down. Within a year or so—the sources vary as to date—Itzcoatl was able to declare himself tlatoani of the Mexica. He was implicitly *huey tlatoani*, or high chief, of all the valley. He soon had Nezahualcoyotl ceremoniously declared tlatoani of Texcoco, and within another year or so after that, they had between them killed all of Nezahualcoyotl's remaining Azcapotzalcan half brothers and the husbands of his Azcapotzalcan half sisters. They recorded in their histories: "Nezahualcoyotl sought out the descendants of Tezozomoc in all the places where they were ruling; conquests were made in as many places as they were found." Maxtla himself fled and disappeared in 1431.[37]

The kings of Tenochtitlan (of the Mexica people), Texcoco (of the Acolhua people), and Tlacopan (of the Tepanec people) now ruled the valley as an unofficial triumvirate. There was no formal statement to that effect. Later generations would say that they initiated a Triple Alliance, even though in a literal sense there was no such institution. In a de facto sense, however, there most certainly was what we might call a lowercase triple alliance. No one moved in the central valley without at least one of these three kings being aware of it, and beyond the mountains that surrounded them, in the lands that they gradually conquered, they had many eyes. They worked together to bring down their enemies; they divided the resulting tribute payments judiciously between them. The Mexica, with the largest population and having played the most important role in the war, got the largest share, but they were careful not to engender resentment among their closest allies by taking too much.[38]

It was a complex web that they wove among them. In a certain sense, the political lay of the land remained almost unchanged. In general, each altepetl continued to rule itself, choosing its tlatoani as the people thought best, and rotating tasks and responsibilities among the various segments that composed it, in the same fair-minded way as they always had. And if several altepetls had a tradition of governing themselves as a unit, as a "greater altepetl" at least in their foreign affairs, then that tradition generally continued, too.[39] A sort of democracy continued on a local level, in the sense that people continued to discuss local matters among themselves and arrive at solutions that pleased most of them. The same arrangement was allowed even to the non-Nahuas who were conquered. The central valley's triumvirate was satisfied that it should be so, as long as these other communities fought alongside them when called upon to do so, participated in public works—like the building of roads or great pyramid temples—and paid their assigned tribute on time. "This was no Rome," one historian has commented succinctly, meaning that the Mexica had no interest in acculturating those they conquered, no desire to teach them their language, or to draw them into their capital or military hierarchy.[40]

Yet despite the maintenance of local tradition, in an economic sense the region was profoundly changed. Each altepetl that fell under the sway of the triumvirate had to pay tribute wherever it was assigned. Often the financial exigencies were head-spinningly complex. One part of a greater altepetl might be assigned to pay tribute, for example, to nearby Texcoco, their regional boss town. But by the terms of the peace agreement, the next segment of the same greater altepetl might pay their taxes to Tenochtitlan. They might pay part of the tribute (such as a certain number of bales of cotton) once a year, and another part (such as some bags of corn or beans) three times a year. By necessity, the calendar grew increasingly consistent across more and more territory, for Itzcoatl's collectors were timely, and the people had to be ready to receive them. Different villages had adopted the calendar at different times, so one altepetl's year One Reed might be another one's Two Rabbit. Now they were forced to try to synchronize their time counts. The calendars were never perfectly aligned, but they began to come closer.[41]

On one level, Itzcoatl enforced the same kind of tribute collection system that would have been in place under Tezozomoc of Azcapotzalco in the old days—and probably others before him in the deeper past. But now the central valley's net of power spread wider. With three altepetls working together, the armies they could send out were larger, the roads they had been able to build were longer. Altepetls that had been far from old Tezozomoc's grasp now came within the central valley's reach. Many resisted, but those who fought back against the new arrangements tended to lose. Then they were faced with tribute payments in perpetuity that sent shudders down every wise chief's spine: they were tasked not only with sending corn and beans, or chocolate and cotton, but also with supplying people to serve as sacrifices in the religious ceremonies of the central valley. A chief knew that this tax meant he would be forced to constantly make war against his neighbors if he were to avoid sending his own people's children to the cutting stone. It was enough to make anyone think twice before resisting. And chiefs had had it inculcated in them from an early age that a good chief was a responsible chief, one who avoided battles he was likely to lose and preserved his people's lives in order to protect the future of the altepetl. An impetuous chief could be referred to derogatively as a "child."[42]

If a town had fought strenuously against the Mexica with any significant degree of success, and yet ultimately lost, then its fate was even worse. The Huaxtecs (WASH-tecs) to the northeast, for example, fought back like wild animals; their reputation for it became fixed in local lore, together with their sad destiny. "The soldiers from all the allied provinces took many captives, both men and women, for they and the Mexica entered the city, burned the temple, sacked and robbed the place. They killed old and young, boys and girls, annihilating without mercy everyone they could, with great cruelty and with the determination to remove all traces of the Huaxtec people from the face of the earth."[43] Their story was to serve as a lesson to other potentially recalcitrant altepetls. And so it did.

After such a battle, the long lines of captives were tied together and taken to Tenochtitlan (or perhaps Acolhua or Tepanec country). The terrified prisoners first passed by other villages like theirs, with their flat-roofed adobe houses grouped in squares opening onto courtyards, where the women chatted as they worked, grinding corn and patting out tortillas, while their men labored in nearby fields.[44] As they approached the capital, the towns that were more closely entwined with the center of power were visibly wealthier, their buildings and religious pyramids grander, some even built of stone or wood.[45]

A great causeway was being constructed by the defeated people of Xochimilco. It stretched from the island to the southern shore of the lake, and along this the prisoners walked. Most prisoners were distributed among the nobility after a battle, but those who had been taken by a particular warrior were sent to their captor's neighborhood temple for sacrifice at local religious festivals, or, if they were young women whom he wanted, to his household. Some were earmarked to be sent to the city's two central pyramid temples, one dedicated to Huitzilopochtli (the Mexica protector god) and the other to Tlaloc (the rain god). The ones not needed in either temple were sold in a slave market—there was a huge one in Azcapotzalco—and might be bought by neighborhoods in need of ceremonial sacrifice victims, or occasionally by men seeking concubines. Women slaves bought for sacrifice could sometimes convince their new masters to keep them alive to work in their household.[46]

Horrendous misconceptions have grown around the Aztec practice of human sacrifice. In novels, movies, and even some of the older history books, hundreds of people at a time were made to climb the narrow steps of the pyramids to the top, where their hearts were cut out and their bodies hurled downward, while the people screamed in near ecstasy below. In reality, it seems to have been a gravely quiet, spellbinding experience for the onlookers, much as we suspect it was in other old worlds, like that of the ancient Celts.[47] The people who watched had fasted and stood holding sacred flowers. In the early decades of Tenochtitlan's life, when the altepetl was still gathering strength, only a few people would have been sacrificed on the monthly religious festival days, and they were always treated as a holy of holies before they died. After a sacrifice, the warrior who had captured and presented the victim kept the remains (the hair and ceremonial regalia) in a special reed chest in a place of honor in his home for as long as he lived.

Most of the victims were men, classic prisoners of war. Not all were, however. In one annual festival, for instance, a young girl taken in war was brought from a local temple to the home of her captor. She dipped her hand in blue paint and left her print on the lintel of his door, a holy mark that would last for years and remind people of the gift she gave of her life. Then she was taken back to the temple to face the cutting stone. It was an ancient tradition among native peoples not to give way before one's enemies: such stoicism brought great honor. Sometimes those who were to die could get through their part without letting their enemies see them sob; sometimes they could not. "Some, in truth, wept," one man remembered later.[48]

The Mexica, like all their Nahua neighbors, believed they owed everything to the gods. "They are the ones who taught us everything," their priests would later explain to the Spanish. "Before them, we kiss the ground, we bleed. We pay our debts to the gods, offer incense, make sacrifices.... We live by the grace of the gods."[49] Each group of Nahuas had carried sacred bundles devoted to its own deity in the long marches from Aztlan; in the case of the Mexica, it was the relics of Huitzilopochtli that they had protected year after year, until they were finally able to bury them beneath a permanent temple. Other altepetls had carried relics of the rain god Tlaloc or his water-world consort, Jade-Skirted Woman. Others honored Quetzalcoatl, Feathered Serpent, the god of wind, who was at home both on earth and in the sky, a crosser of boundaries, special protector of priests. Some were most dedicated to Tezcatlipoca, Smoking Mirror, a mischievous god who led humankind in a dance by assisting chiefs and warriors to bring change through conflict. Cihuacoatl, Woman-Snake, was known by many other names as well, but she was always sacred to midwives; she often bore a shield and spear, for she helped birthing mothers seize a new spirit from the cosmos. There were many gods and goddesses each of whom appeared with a range of possible traits; today, we do not always understand their characteristics as well as we would like to, for the Nahuas did not write freely of them in the colonial era. They could write openly of history, but it was dangerous to write of the gods. We do know, however, that just as in ancient Greece, all the altepetls honored and believed in a pantheistic range of gods, not just the deity who had especially protected them.[50]

The gods asked human beings to appreciate what had been given to them and to make sacrifices, mostly by bleeding themselves, but sometimes even by giving the ultimate gift, that of human life. If human beings refused to do this, the fragile world might come to an end. Other, prior worlds had ended in disaster; the Nahuas never forgot that they were living under Nanahuatzin's Fifth Sun. In more ancient days one of their own children was probably offered up. This seems to have happened around the world in the earliest eras, before writing existed to document the practice in any permanent way. In the Hebrew Bible, for instance, Hiel the Bethelite begins to rebuild the city of Jericho by burying his eldest son beneath the gate. Likewise, in English lore, Geoffrey of Monmouth, in speaking of Merlin, says that he had to talk his way out of becoming a foundation sacrifice for a king's tower.[51] The notion of a youth dying for his people was hardly unique to the Nahuas.

However, as the Mexica rose, they sacrificed not their own young people but rather, increasing numbers of prisoners of war. They and all the other Nahuas had sometimes sacrificed their enemies: the burning of Shield Flower in 1299 was proof of this. But now the Mexica were nearly always the winners; they were no longer the ones who sometimes died themselves, and the numbers of their victims gradually grew. They allowed politics and the outcomes of wars to affect the numbers who died in any one year. They did this even as they prayed devoutly, even as they wrote heartrendingly beautiful poems and painted their walls with images of shells that looked so real one might imagine oneself in an eternal sea, transcending the struggles of this earthly life.[52] Did they know that the world would not shatter like jade if they did not sacrifice living human beings? Did they laugh cynically at the terror they inspired and the political power they wielded as a result? Probably there were some brilliant strategists and far-seeing, experienced people who did—perhaps like

Itzocatl. They would not have been alone among world leaders; we know that there were some Greek and Roman leaders, for instance, who questioned the very existence of the gods yet did not let it shake their worldview.[53] Surely there were many more of the Mexica who simply never thought much about it—like people in so many times and places who choose not to see the pain inflicted on other people when it is more convenient not to. Can we blame them? Should we blame them?

Or perhaps they did think about it, as Itzcoatl himself must have done, and decided that whatever their philosophical views, there was no choice. After all, they did not live in a modern, liberal state, where certain protections are guaranteed to the majority. They simply could not afford too much generosity, for the real world that they inhabited was every bit as dangerous as the cosmos they envisioned. The Mexica themselves had been on the other side for more years than they cared to remember. For generations, it had been their own young warriors and maidens who faced the fire and the cutting stone. Even now, if they began to lose their wars at any point, it would be their turn again. They knew this, as they sent their sons to practice the arts of war and learned to construct maces with bits of jutting obsidian glass embedded in them. In the midst of words of love addressed to their "little doves," mothers taught their children that the world was a dangerous place. "On earth we live, we travel, along a mountain peak. Over here is an abyss, over there is an abyss. If you go this way, or that way, you will fall in. Only in the middle do we go, do we live."[54]

The image of mothers teaching their children to live with these realities is a compelling one. Everything we know about the Mexica tells us that mothers valued their children dearly, more than anything else in life—they said that they were precious, like polished gems, or iridescent feathers, treasures fit for high kings. They warned them of dangers and begged them to be responsible, to care for themselves and their communities so that the altepetl would go on forever.[55] And children heeded their mothers' words. This was far from a world in which maternal figures were disparaged or in which women appeared as interchangeable sex objects. In the first place, it was generally only the men of noble families—those of the *pilli* class, the *pipiltin*—who had the right to take numerous wives and bring home captive women from the battlefield, for one had to be rich to afford to do such a thing. Even in that situation, who one's mother was mattered to an enormous degree to each child; but one has to admit that from an elite man's point of view, the women may have been somewhat interchangeable. That, however, simply was not the experience of the majority. The majority of the people were of the *macehualli* class, the *macehualtin*, and in their families, one husband lived with one wife, whose cloak had been tied to his in a formal ceremony. Sometimes a household was multigenerational or contained several siblings, but even there, each woman had her own hearth in her own adobe apartment facing onto the common courtyard. A woman raised her own children, teaching them to help her in the labor that everyone recognized was essential. In a world without day care, restaurants, vacuum cleaners, or stores, who would have dared to think that childcare, cooking, sweeping, and making clothes were inessential activities? No one, it seems, for the indigenous sources leave no record of disrespect, or even of veiled misogyny. Women's roles were complementary to those of men, and everyone understood this to be so; the house, the four-walled *calli* was symbolic of the universe itself.[56]

So we should take seriously whatever the women said, for their own people did. Women comforted their children, yet in the same breath warned them in no uncertain terms that they must learn to be ruthless in maintaining order, to do their duty, to take lives or give lives in the eternal wars if necessary. They must be willing to be like the brave but modest Nanahuatzin, who had jumped into the fire to bring forth the Fifth Sun for his people. These mothers would probably have been confused if someone had tried to talk to them about "good and evil." They would have said that all people had the potential to do good or to do harm, that it wasn't possible to divide people into two camps on that basis. To do good, a person had to suppress egotism and do what was best calculated to keep his or her people alive and successful in the long term. Everyone was expected to give thought to the future. It wasn't always easy. Often one's fate involved doing just what one did not want to do. In some ways, it was not so much gratifying as exhausting, this playing "king-of-the-mountain" for life-or-death stakes.

For the system to work over the long term, Itzcoatl and, later, his heirs had to choose their military targets carefully. They had to be relatively sure of victory, based on rational calculations, not divine promises. Fortunately, the highest level priests were members of the leading noble families, and they seemed to understand this, too. At least, the gods whom they prayed to never demanded that they wage unwinnable wars. There were certain pockets of resistance that were more formidable than most and these had to be handled carefully. The best known was the greater altepetl of Tlaxcala, a large city-state composed of four independent sub-divisions, with four separate but united kings, located just to the east of the central basin. Tlaxcala was relatively wealthy—its name meant "place of the tortillas," or we might say "Bread Town." It was lodged securely in its own highly defensible valley and surrounded by pine woods that served as havens for deer and woodland birds and other game. These people were Nahuas, too, having arrived about the same time as the Mexica—they even shared some of the same myths and stories—and they weren't going to give the latter an inch if they could help it. Early on, the Mexica did launch several attacks against them, but it became clear that they were going to become mired in a stalemate. It was likely as a result of this that the Mexica initiated what they called the "Flower Wars," a kind of Olympic games played every few years, in which the winners, rather than earning a crown of laurels, saved themselves from death. It is unclear whether these games unfolded on a ball court or a battlefield, but probably the latter. The system worked well to keep young warriors on their toes even in times when there was no current war. And it made it unnecessary to explain to anyone why Tlaxcala was allowed to continue to exist without paying tribute. The world at large could assume that Tlaxcala was being left alone to serve as an enemy in the ceremonial Flower Wars. No one needed to discuss the fact that bringing down the large polity would have been far too destructive of Mexica resources, if it was even possible. Leaving Tlaxcala as a free enemy with a recognized role was a clever strategy. The leaders could not have foreseen that one day in the future it would cost them dear, when a new enemy, stronger than they, would land on their shores and find allies ready-made.[57]

Even a highly successful war-based polity of necessity faced certain problems. In this world that Iztcoatl negotiated so successfully, the ongoing wars could make it difficult for the Mexica to trade with far-off peoples. If the question of an attack was always imminent, few people would want to approach the Mexica or their allies even to discuss mutually beneficial business deals. Perhaps for this reason, not just the Mexica but all the Nahuas as if by common consent accepted the existence of certain neutral trading towns along the coasts and along the banks of rivers that led inland from the sea. Near to where the Olmecs had once lived, for example, there was a coastal town called Xicallanco (Shee-ca-LAN-co), and although it was nestled within Maya territory, numerous Nahua merchants lived there. They facilitated trade with the eastern realms, buying textiles and cocoa, beautiful shells, the plumages of rare birds—and eventually, the birds themselves—as well as other luxury goods. They sold these in exchange for the goods made by Tenochtitlan's craftsmen, as well as excess slaves from the wars launched by the Mexica and their allies, women and children who had not been sacrificed but rather turned over to long distance merchants. Further along the coast, the island of Cozumel was another such neutral zone, and several others existed.[58]

In most of the Mesoamerican world, however, permanent truces did not exist. Warfare and expansion were perennial, for the Mexica state needed to grow wealthier as its polygynous noble families grew larger. And people needed to be kept in a state of suspense in order for their old alliances to last, rather than breaking down over minor arguments. And the battle zones needed to be pushed outward if the inner sanctum of the valley was to know only peace. It would have been a familiar story to any great monarch. Gone were the days when the father of Shield Flower, the warrior maiden, could declare war or make decisions based on his own needs and desires and those of a few companions. Itzcoatl had won his gamble, attaining power, wealth, and glory beyond any of his childhood dreams. But as a result, he had forged a complex political organism, one that, for all his vaunted power, he could not control simply by making a declaration.

One of the greatest threats to Itzcoatl's control lay very close to home. Either because he really did love them or because it would have precipitated civil war, or both, Itzcoatl did not kill the surviving sons of his half-brother, the late tlatoani, Huitzilihuitl, Hummingbird Feather. They, presumably for a mixture of the same reasons, continued to support him. They were the ones who by the law of custom should have ruled, not Itzcoatl. But he was the one who had united the Mexica in a time of terrible crisis, found useful allies for them, and led them all to victory. So they worked together during the fourteen years of Itzcoatl's reign. One nephew, Tlacaelel, was an active and successful warrior who made a great name for himself as the *Cihuacoatl*: the name of a goddess had become a title reserved for the man who was the second-in-command after the tlatoani, the inside chief who governed domestic affairs. Supporters of Huitzilihuitl's old royal line—many of them Tlacaelel's own children and grandchildren—liked to say that Itzcoatl really owed everything to Tlacaelel, that he was the one who had defeated the Tepanec villain Maxtla, and that it was his savvy strategizing that helped Itzcoatl govern in the toughest of times. When all the annals, not just those authored or orchestrated by Tlacaelel's descendants, are considered, this version of events strains credulity. If the man were really so indomitable, he himself would have emerged as tlatoani, rather than the bastard son of a slave girl. Still, it is clear that he was a major force to be reckoned with. He must have been satisfied with the power and the income he was given by Itzcoatl, for he maintained his place and went on to become an adviser to four kings over the next several decades. A council of four men from the extended royal family always worked closely with the person serving as tlatoani, and Tlacaelel the Cihuacoatl was the chief of these.[59]

In order to guarantee the continuance of the compromise, it was essential to settle amicably the question of the succession. Years earlier, Itzcoatl had married a woman from the then-powerful boss state of Azcapotzalco; his son by her was named Tezozomoc, after the old godfather king whose death had unleashed pandemonium. Itzcoatl could not present a half-Azcapotzalcan son as the people's future tlatoani, not after the recent war to the death against Atzcapotzalco. Besides, Huitzilihuitl's noble sons would not have been kept in line if they thought they were going to be excluded from the succession forever. So probably even before Itzcoatl died, it was understood that Tlacaelel would keep his lands and titles in perpetuity, and that Moctezuma, Huitzilihuitl's son by the Cuernavacan princess, would be next in line to rule. This Moctezuma was an ancestor of the one who would become world famous in his meeting with Hernando Cortés. Moctezuma was a powerful warrior— his name meant Frowns-Like-a-Lord—whose maternal relatives lived in an important cotton-producing region. Better yet, he was reasonable. He agreed to do what much-less- important Nahua altepetls often did—that is, alternate power between different lineages in a politically expedient rotation. He agreed that though he himself would rule, his own sons would not rule after him. Rather, he would select a daughter or a beloved niece to marry one of Itzcoatl's grandsons (a son of the passed-over son, Tezozomoc), who would be elected as ruler in his turn. Like Itzcoatl, Moctezuma would forego the opportunity to have one of his own sons succeed, likewise on the understanding that a grandchild of his would eventually take over. In this way, they would allow the pendulum of power to swing back and forth between the two family lines, ultimately bringing the lines together through the birth of a child descended from all of them, and the heart of the kingdom would remain at peace.[60]

***

ITZCOATL WAS QUITE RIGHT that his successor would need to be able to count on peace and stability in the inner circle. Though he could not have foreseen exactly where the gravest problems would emerge, he knew that in this life, nothing ever stays the same, and thus no monarch is ever truly secure. It was fortunate that he and his kinsmen settled their differences as effectively as they did, for in their strategic handling of polygyny-induced factionalism, they cemented their hold on power. It was perhaps their greatest stroke of brilliance, what most set them apart in a political sense.

The young Moctezuma was destined to rule for twenty-nine years. In his time, he would expand Aztec territory dramatically and solidify control over rebellious city-states conquered in earlier years. But his successes would not come easily. Relatively early in his reign, a great drought afflicted his people. Locusts passed through the land in the 1450s, and in 1454, the corn did not yield nor did it yield for the next four years. The priests begged the gods to take mercy on the powerless people who suffered, the common folk and the little children. They chanted their prayers to Tlaloc aloud:

> Here are the common folk, the macehualtin, those who are the tail and the wings [of society]. They are perishing. Their eyelids are swelling, the mouths drying out. They become bony, bent, emaciated. Thin are the commoners' lips and blanched are their throats. With pallid eyes live the babies, the children [of all ages]—those who totter, those who crawl, those who spend their time turning dirt and potsherds, those who live sitting on the ground, those who lie on the boards, who fill the cradles. All the people face torment, affliction. They witness that which makes humans suffer. Already there are none who are passed over.[61]

In the countryside, the teenage children left home to look for food, hoping at least to spare their parents the need to feed them. Often they would die, alone on some hill or in some wood, and people would later find their bodies, half eaten by coyotes or vultures.[62] In the city, tribute payments no longer arrived regularly, and the urban dwellers thus could not feed themselves. Times were so bad that some families might sell a child to the merchants who were traveling to the east, to Totonac or Maya country. There the drought was not so grave, and people were interested in buying children cheaply. As slaves, their parents told themselves, their children would not starve. But the Mexica swore to themselves that they would never let themselves be this vulnerable again.

As soon as he could, Moctezuma mounted another military campaign, this time against a former ally that had earlier been subjugated by the Mexica but then had become restive during the drought. The place was called Chalco. It was a powerful Nahua city-state within the central valley, just to the southeast of the lake. Its name meant, in effect "by the shores of the jade waters."[63] There had been some earlier skirmishing, but the war began in earnest in 1455. It took ten years, but in the end the political entity of Chalco was no more. Most of the people still lived, but their royal lines had been ousted. Henceforth, announced Moctezuma, the Chalca people would not rule themselves but would be ruled according to his decrees. Power had been given him by the gods. His brother Tlacaelel, the Cihuacoatl, took as his primary wife a daughter of the Chalcan royal line, and then he took up the reins of power and gave out chieftainships to men of of the Mexicas' choosing. "And for [the next] twenty-one years," said one writer of annals, "there was rule by outsiders."[64]

In the courtyards of Tenochtitlan, the poets and the history-tellers once again told the tale of their altepetl's greatness. Under starlit skies, they held up their painted books. These were new books that they displayed, painted since the time of Itzcoatl's conflagration; the revised histories made it seem absolutely expected that Itzcoatl would rise to power in the place of Huitzilihuitl's sons, and that Tenochtitlan—and not Azcapotzalco—was destined to rule the known world. The bards pointed to the symbolic images of burning temples, representing the conquests the Mexica had achieved. Then they began to talk: they moved back and forth between the perspectives of the various components of the altepetl, telling their story as a conglomerate whole, twisting the strands together into one, to use their spinning metaphor. Their animated voices carried in the night.

The Mexica had come a long way, the speakers reminded their listeners, from the tragic last days of Shield Flower. They had been hunted wanderers—quite literally, at one point, after the war with Culhuacan—but under Huitzilihuitl, Chimalpopoca, Itzcoatl, and Moctezuma they had strategized and fought and jockeyed for position with such success that the surrounding people who once abused them now feared them, and hunger stalked them only intermittently. Sometimes, it was true, it felt as though they were still just barely hanging on, that there was still a threat at every turn.

But not most of the time. Most of the time, they were feeling quite successful; their stories were laden with their sense of themselves as underdogs-made-good. No one had ever handed them anything. They had been realists and strategists, and they were determined that they would continue to be. Each year, they knew, there would be more to add to their tale. All Nahua peoples were proud of the enduring life of their altepetl, the water-mountain, the community that outlived all individuals. Like Shield Flower, though, the Mexica exhibited an added panache in their pride. They weren't merely poised between the days that were gone and the days yet to come: they beckoned to the future.

3

The City on the Lake

1470–1518

Outside, the bright sun seared the stones of the patio; inside the thick adobe walls, all was coolness and shadow. One afternoon in 1479, Quecholcohuatl (Ke-chol-CO-wat), a young Chalcan nobleman, paused on the threshold of the Mexican tlatoani's palace, letting his eyes adjust. "He was considering what judgment would come forth from the king," a man from his altepetl explained many years later.[1] Never had Quecholcohuatl felt such fear in his very gut, for he could tell from the looks passing between his compatriots that they thought he had been summoned inside to face a brutal punishment. They thought he would be escorted to one of the dreaded wooden cages the capital city was famous for; from there he would be taken to be burned to death. "Will we all be burned to death?" his friends wondered. Quecholcohuatl found it almost impossible to move forward, following the signals of the servants. But he did so. His name meant "Flamingo Snake"; it was a chosen name, in keeping with the gorgeously colored, finely embroidered clothing he wore when giving a musical performance before the king, as he had just dared to do.[2] The tassels swayed as he walked. Here in Tenochtitlan, he represented the greater altepetl of Chalco. He did not want these Mexica people to see his fear, only his pride. He steeled his nerves and put one foot in front of the other.

***

A musician plays his drum. The Bodleian Libraries, the University of Oxford, Codex Mendoza, MS. Arch. Selden. A.1, folio 70r.

AT A DISTANCE of more than five hundred years, it is impossible to know exactly what happened on that day in the palace of Axayacatl (Ah-sha-YAHK-at). The existing account was written at least one hundred years after the fact, by someone who obviously could not have been there. Nevertheless there is much to be gleaned from it. The author was Chimalpahin, the Nahua historian who lived in Mexico City in the early 1600s. He was Chalcan, and his beloved grandmother had known Quecholcohuatl in her girlhood—though by then, he was an old man and had taken the Christian name of don Jerónimo.[3] So the Chalcan historian got his information from aging relatives who had known people of the ancien régime. The story that he recorded fits perfectly with numerous other sources that illuminate a variety of subjects—including political relations between Tenochtitlan and Chalco, the architectural patterns in Tenochtitlan, and even the cultural mores of the city. For instance, at about the same time as Chimalpahin was discussing this event with his grandmother, some Mexica men were telling the Spanish friar Bernardino de Sahagún how terrifying it used to be to present musical pieces before the ruler, as he might punish an inept performer.[4] There is thus no reason to doubt the gist of Chimalpahin's account, and in fact, much can by learned by analyzing it in the context of other extant sources, for the author vividly describes life in Tenochtitlan's imperial court.

By 1479 almost fifteen years had passed since Chalco had been destroyed by the Mexica, its royal houses disbanded. Enough time had gone by that there was a new generation of young adults who did not clearly remember the horrors of the war; yet not enough time had passed for the Chalcan people to forget their ancient royal lines and the self-governance they had enjoyed for centuries. So Quecholcohuatl's generation had grown restive: they had begun to talk among themselves and insist that Tenochtitlan give them a place at the council table and treat them as relative equals, as they did the other major powers of the central valley.[5]

Flamingo Snake and his fellow singers and drummers had come to perform before the high king Axayacatl at his palace. They were there only to entertain him, or so they said. In reality, they had carefully chosen their song with a political agenda in mind. The piece was called "the Chalca Woman's Song," and when they sang its words, they were lodging a protest of sorts.[6] The singer adopted the persona of a female prisoner of war, of a concubine. Everyone in their world understood the parallels between a captive woman and a conquered altepetl. In ordinary times, in ordinary marriages, women were understood to be complementary to men and in no way inferior. But in times of war, the female sex truly suffered. A captive woman lamented her fate, not necessarily because she was subject to any daily violence but because she had lost her sense of self as an honored being; she could no longer take pride in the idea that her children would inherit her place and carry her family line forward. She had become a nonentity in a social sense, a sexual object without lasting power, a bearer of relatively unimportant children; she had lost, in short, her future. The singer of the song varied in her reactions from stanza to stanza. Sometimes she flirted, as any young girl in such a situation would do, trying desperately to regain a sense of agency in her own life. "What if I were to pleasure him?" she wondered. She cried out, "Go stoke the pot and light a big fire!" And finally, in case the point still was not clear, she began to make direct allusions to sex and even to the king's penis:

> Will you ruin my body painting?
> You will lie watching what comes to be a green flamingo bird flower ...
> It is a quetzal popcorn flower, a flamingo raven flower.
> You lie on your flower-mantled mat.
> It lies inside.
> You lie on your golden reed mat.
> It lies in the feathered cavern house.[7]

Then suddenly, in the very next lines of the song, the young woman found her heart breaking. She remembered what her life used to be, how her family had thought she would bear the children of her people's future. "As a noble girl child, I was spoken of in connection with my marriage." Her hopes had all come to nothing, and she did not think she could bear it. "It is infuriating, it is heartrending, here on earth. I worry and fret. I consume myself in rage. In my desperation, I suddenly say, 'hey, child, I would as soon die.'" *Manoce nimiqui*, I would as soon die. It was a strong statement.[8]

In the performance that afternoon, another nobleman from Chalco had originally been the lead musician, but either the heat or his fear of what the group's punishment might be—or both—had caused him to faint. Quecholcohuatl knew that his own fate and his altepetl's hung in the balance: if they were going to convince Axayacatl to consider Chalco's feelings about the current situation, the entertainment would have to be superb. He stepped around his unconscious compatriot and took the lead himself. He gave the performance everything he had: he made the gilt-edged drum throb and call aloud.[9] He sang the lyrics with feeling. The song ended with an offer on the part of the concubine to live with the king, her new master, without rancor, if only she were treated with respect. "Don't let your heart take a needless tumble....Here is your hand. Come along, holding me by my hand. Be content. On your reed mat, on your throne, sleep peacefully. Relax, you who are king Axayacatl."

In the midst of the performance, the ruler Axayacatl suddenly began to pay attention. "He came out from inside where he was with his women, and went to dance. When he got to the dance floor, Axayacatl lifted up one foot, completely happy in hearing the music, and began to dance and move in circles." He wore a gold headpiece trimmed with symbolic clusters of feathers: each element represented not only his own rank but also his city's relationship to others. The carefully crafted diadem was itself an object of awe. It was considered a great honor, a momentous occasion, when the tlatoani joined the dance. So the signs were good; the Chalcans were hopeful. When the song ended, however, the king suddenly went inside and sent a messenger to summon the lead performer. The Chalcans did not know what to think, but they feared the worst.[10]

When Quecholcohuatl came before Axayacatl, he found him surrounded by his women, all wearing lovely embroidered skirts and blouses, edged with dyed rabbit fur or yellow parakeet feathers or other colorful features.[11] He made the traditional Nahua sign of obeisance, kneeling and making the gesture of scooping up earth and touching it to his lips.[12] He said something along the lines of "Oh, lord king, may you burn me, I who am your vassal, for we have done wrong in your presence." Self-denigration was a polite style of greeting, and Quecholcohuatl apparently thought it might be useful here.[13] He was overly cautious, as it turned out. "Axyacatl did not want to hear these words." The tlatoani liked the song, and he liked the singer. He took Quecholcohuatl to bed forthwith and asked him to promise to sing only for him. Chimalpahin claimed he even said joyfully to his wives, "Women, stand up and meet him, seat him among you. Here has come your rival."[14]

Understanding the nature of homosexual sex among the Aztecs has long been a troubled issue, for scholars have largely relied on sources produced under the auspices of the friars, in response to direct and highly judgmental questions about the matter.[15] The people answering those questions were well aware that they were not supposed to approve of the practice, and they made some negative comments, but it is hard to know what they really thought. In later years, indigenous writers of the seventeenth century would describe brutal punishments meted out by the church to homosexual men, but they apparently did not relish such scenes. If anything, they seemed to disapprove slightly. "One [of the men] was named Diego Enamorado [Diego In-Love]...The [authorities] did not specify the reasons why they hanged them."[16] It is clear from the few available sources that before the conquest there was no category of people who lived their lives full-time as gay individuals in today's sense. However, Nahuatl-language sources produced beyond the purview of the Spaniards suggest that many men sometimes chose to have sex with other men. There was a range of sexual possibilities during one's time on earth, understood to be part of the joy of living, and it certainly was not unheard of for men to go to bed together in the celebrations connected with religious ceremonies, and presumably at other times as well.[17] In any case, king Axayacatl was a famous warrior and a man who fathered many children, and he could be drawn to a man as well as to a woman. "The king really loved Flamingo Snake because he got him to dance," Chimalpahin, the Chalcan historian, later commented. Chimalpahin made no judgment at all, unless perhaps he evinced a bit of pride, for Flamingo Snake's song became a multigenerational hit, with repeat performances over the next several decades, and it brought fame to his hometown. "Because of it Amaquemecan (Ah-mah-kay-MAY-kahn) was [once] famous, an altepetl which now appears small and unimportant," he said.

At the time, the singer's relationship with the tlatoani was definitely a source of great pride. To reassure the Chalcans waiting tensely on the patio, Axayacatl sent Quecholcohuatl back outside, bearing aloft symbolic gifts: a full outfit—cloak, loincloth, and sandals—embroidered with jade, all of which items had been the king's own. Flamingo Snake's companions were aware of what such gifts meant, for public gift-giving was a political language, a code that everyone knew. In the *Annals of Cuauhtitlan*, for instance, all the narrator had to do to establish that the Azcpotzalcan ruler, Maxtla, was abusive and planned to undo Nezahualcoyotl was to state laconically, "He gave him only one *tilma* (or cloak)."[18] When the Chalcans saw the richness of Axayacatl's proffered goods, they let out a great whoop of joy, and those who had been more confident turned to tease those who had predicted only doom and gloom. Their laughter rang out.[19]

That night, the visiting musicians celebrated in the greatest city in the known world. They were lodged in the very middle of the island, in a house maintained for entertainers.[20] Tenochtitlan was divided into four subdivisions (Moyotlan, Atzacualco, Cuepopan, and Zoquiapan), and each one occupied about a quarter of the city. As with most conglomerate altepetls, the people of each segment placed their finest buildings in the "four corners" area where the quadrants came together, thus creating a truly urban area in the center of a partly agricultural world. Around the edges of the swampy island, they still had their chinampas (the gardens hanging in the muddy water), and they reserved certain areas for fishing and aquatic foraging for birds' eggs and other delicacies. In the center of the island, where the visitors were, rose the temple precinct, including the huge, gleaming pyramid dedicated to their own Huitzilopochtli, and next to it, the edifice dedicated to Tlaloc, the rain god. Directly behind these was Axayacatl's palace. It received fresh running water, the supply fed by a clay aqueduct that originated on a hill on the lake's western shore and then crossed over a causeway to the island, part of an extraordinary waterworks system containing dikes and sluices as well as causeways and aqueducts.[21]

The palace of the former king Moctezuma (the Elder), on the far side of the temple precinct, was dedicated to other purposes than the housing of royalty now that Moctezuma was dead. The most powerful monarchs each left impressive architectural remnants of their reigns, visible to all the world for all time (or so they hoped), and the state found plenty of practical uses for them. In this central area, for example, the war captives who faced sacrifice in the near future were closely guarded; some of them were housed sumptuously, others much less so, depending on the ceremonial role they were to fill.[22] Not so many years earlier, Chalcans would have been among the prisoners, but they were not now. Nearby, the Mexica king maintained a sort of zoo filled with animals brought as tribute from subject states far and wide. Some of these, too, would face the cutting stone on holy days, but many were displayed indefinitely as a testament to Mexica power. The visitors could have seen fascinating reptiles, or jaguars, wolves, and mountain lions, among dozens of other creatures.[23] Unlike in the wild, the visitors didn't need to fear the yowling of an animal. In the forest lands, if one suddenly heard the mewling or scream of a flesh-eating animal, some people feared it meant that one would soon be taken prisoner and enslaved or killed, or that one's children would become prisoners.[24] On Quecholcohuatl's evening in the city, however, he had nothing to fear, but rather much to hope. He and his peers were focused on the possibility that their beloved Chalco might yet be restored some measure of independence.

Their hosts offered them food, and they feasted. The tamales boasted decorative designs on top, such as a seashell outlined with red beans. Guests could choose between turkey, venison, rabbit, lobster, or frog stewed with chilis of various kinds. On the side, there were winged ants with savory herbs, spicy tomato sauces, fried onions and squash, fish eggs, and toasted corn. There were all kinds of fruits, tortillas with honey, and little cakes made of amaranth seed. Indeed, a former servant once counted two thousand different dishes made for the Mexica king and then passed on to be sampled by his councilors, servants, and entertainers. At the very end of the meal always came chocolate—crushed cacao beans steeped in hot water and flavored with honey and various kinds of dried flowers, such as vanilla pods or roses. To render it even more special, the drink was served in carved or painted gourds, often from faraway lands.[25]

Yet perhaps it was neither the zoo nor the food that the visitors especially recalled in later years. People who saw the city always remembered first its beauty. It was because of the gardens—the gardens overflowing from ordinary people's flat rooftops, as well as the gardens of the tlatoani. There, Mexico's most gorgeous flowers—many with names never perfectly translated into European tongues—blossomed amid trees whose fascinating shapes could make them appear enchanted. In large, finely wrought wooden cages, the brightest birds from the jungles in the east and south fluttered and sang—quetzal birds and parrots, flamingos and tufted ducks, parakeets and pheasants—too many kinds to count. As the birds flew quickly in and out of the foliage, the colors of their wings glinted in the evening light, like flashes of magic, the result of some spell, just like in the stories people told back in Chalco. As the darkness grew, the stars appeared. Priests observed and charted them, but ordinary people just admired them. The stars looked, the Mexica sometimes joked, like popcorn scattered in the night sky.[26]

***

WHERE HAD THIS CITY COME FROM? Tenochtitlan in the 1470s and 80s was a far cry from the somewhat scruffy, marshy town inhabited by Itzcoatl when he made his initial bid for power. But under him and Moctezuma the Elder, victories had multiplied until the Mexicas' relative wealth and power were truly significant. The central valley of Mexico now contained about 1.5 million people, most of them farmers. In the very center of the fertile basin, on this little island of 5.5 square miles, there lived as many as 50,000 people.[27] Counting the people of other altepetls who clustered on the far shore of the lake, facing the island, there were perhaps a total of 100,000 in the wider urban area. Tenochtitlan's population growth had outpaced that of other regions. This was partly because the city's wealth and political dominance encouraged in-migration, but victory in war also brought more captive women to the city, and as any demographer would predict, more wombs had birthed more babies. Clearly, the relatively few chinampas on the outskirts of the city could not support so large a population. Instead, the city folk obtained much of their food from the rural hinterland. Mexica success in warfare made it possible to demand greater amounts of food as tribute, and in addition, their growing population made it economically attractive for the people of the basin to voluntarily bring food to sell, in exchange for the artisan craftwork the urbanites were becoming so adept at producing. In this context, the city's location on an island in the center of a great lake rendered it almost easy for its market to become a great hub of trade, tying together all the peoples who lived near the surrounding lake shores.

Because the city had grown so quickly from scratch, rather than evolving gradually, like ancient Paris or London, its construction was planned and organized. The buildings ranged along orderly, straight streets. Ordinary households consisted of adobe buildings on three or four sides of a central courtyard. The flat roofs held gardens and sometimes additional small rooms, often used for storage. Generally each woman had her own hearth—whether the women of the house were co-wives or mother-in-law and daughters-in-law—and each one had her own supply of *cihuatlatqui*, woman's gear arranged in orderly baskets and boxes—spindles and looms, grinding stones and pots, brooms and dustbins, as well as clothes and jewelry for adults and children. In a prominent location in the home, men kept their own gear hanging on the wall—their carefully accumulated handmade weapons, battle headdresses, and mementos of war. There was no furniture; people sat and slept on thick, comfortable mats and pillows.[28]

Over the simple structures loomed large neighborhood temples in the form of pyramids, with highly decorated compounds near each of these for the nobility. Towering above were the great twin temples of the central plaza, bordered by the royal tecpan (or palace) where the Chalcan visitors performed. Itzcoatl had long ago begun the process of turning the simple shrine that had once stood at the center of the island into an ornate structure on a broad stone platform. Since then, there had been several more building stages, each enhancing the splendor of the two temples, for the city's architects and builders—in the pay of the tlatoani—never rested. An early aqueduct, built to bring fresh water to the island, had collapsed in a flood in 1449, just before the great famine had started, and under Axayacatl a new one had recently been built, significantly higher, and with two water troughs, so that even if one needed to be cleaned or repaired, there would be no interruption of water flow.[29]

The Mexica were able to bring all this about so successfully largely because the transition to the next generation of leadership had twice gone relatively smoothly. Itzcoatl's son, Tezozomoc, had kept his word and willingly foregone the possibility of ruling, as agreed long ago (accepting lands and tribute payers in Ecatepec near Azcapotzalco instead). Itzcoatl was succeeded by

Moctezuma, from Hummingbird Feather's line; after Moctezuma's death, the selection of a ruler was made from among Tezozomoc's sons, also as agreed. Tezozomoc's elder sons had been born to wives whose marriages predated the rise of Itzcoatl and his family, but the youngest one, Axayacatl, or Water Beetle, was his son by one of Moctezuma's daughters, Atotoztli. Perhaps the young woman was actually Moctezuma's granddaughter (child of a daughter of Moctezuma's who had married Tlacaelel); the bards did not agree on this point. In either case, she was a close connection to Moctezuma, someone whose sons he was directly related to, and whom he wanted to envision as occupying the reed mat someday. Axayacatl was thus the son of Tezozomoc whom Moctezuma desired as a successor.

Before Moctezuma died, he did everything to ensure that the royal clan would elect to follow the boy when he himself was gone. He bribed and threatened and, whenever possible, displayed young Axayacatl to advantage. It worked. After he died, at the customary council of royal family members, two of Axayacatl's older half brothers, Tizoc (TEE-zoc) and Ahuitzotl (Ah-WEETZ-otl), complained loudly. They insulted the young prince in crude terms: "Is he really a manly warrior? Does he really take captives? Are they not really…slaves whom he buys and brings here, so that he appears to be a manly warrior?"[30] However, although the two older brothers insisted that they be considered themselves if there were to be another transition in their lifetimes, they let the matter drop when they were given high military titles and lucrative sources of income. Axayacatl became king in 1469, immediately after Moctezuma died. This seemed to bode well for the consolidation of Mexica power.[31]

Unfortunately for the athletic young Axayacatl—who did indeed zip around in a war canoe like a water beetle on the surface of the lake—one specific issue related to the succession had never been resolved, and it exploded into a crisis. Many years earlier, not long after the Mexica settled their island and began to make a home for themselves, some sort of internal disagreement broke out, and a dissident group established a separate village on the north shore of the island, where they became known for hosting the island's largest market trading with villages on the perimeter of the lake. Their separate altepetl was called Tlatelolco (Tla-tel-OL-co), and it had its own tlatoani, as the smaller, breakaway group had no wish to live and work under the power of the larger group's king.[32] Still, despite the split, the Tlatelolcans were nevertheless Mexica, with Mexica history and pride, and they continued to face the outside world alongside the people of Tenochtitlan. When Maxtla of Azcapotzalco murdered Chimalpopoca back in 1426, he sent some of his relatives to kill

Tlatelolco's king as well. So it was without hesitation that the Tlatelolcans threw in their lot with Itzcoatl when he roused the Mexica of Tenochtitlan to follow him in bringing down Azcapotzalco. For the next half century, Tlatelolco acted as Tenochtitlan's junior partner, helping the larger town to secure victories and collecting a share of the winnings. The people of Cuauhtinchan (in the east) and of Toluca (in the west), for instance, later remembered the high-handedness of the Tlatelolcans who collected tribute from them.[33]

By 1470, however, the people of Tlatelolco had grown resentful. They believed that Tenochtitlan's meteoric rise was due to the military support that the Tenochca had always received from their kin on the north shore of their island, and they therefore felt that they had a right to a larger share of the available wealth and power. Moreover, they were the ones who operated the great market patronized by all the people of the valley. They were undoubtedly irritated that it was Axayacatl who had become king, rather than one of his older half brothers, some of whom had a Tlatelolcan mother. Had one of the half-Tlatelolcans become king, Tlatelolco might have expected richer payoffs in future. Now they wanted to make it clear that they would no longer unquestioningly support Tenochtitlan unless changes were made. Their tlatoani, Moquihuixtli (Mo-kee-WEESH-tli), began to do what Nahua kings were wont to do in such situations: he rearranged his marital relations in order to make a statement about the succession. Moquihuixtli started to insist that his Tenochca wife would no longer be his primary consort and that her children would not inherit power. Indeed, he said, she would have no children, for he certainly would not sleep with her. Such a thin, fragile-looking little thing could appeal to no man, and he preferred his other women, he added snidely. Whether Moquihuixtli really believed he would elicit better terms from Tenochtitlan, or whether he actually wanted to provoke a war and try to topple Axayacatl is not clear; the latter seems plausible, as he was known for bellicose statements that verged on the irrational—or even crossed the line.[34]

In either case, the young Tenochca wife whom he turned against was called Chalchiuhnenetzin (Chal-chew-ne-NE-tzeen, Jade Doll), and she was Axayacatl's full sister. When the young tlatoani heard what Moquihuixtli was saying, he publicly sent his sister rich gifts as a gesture of political support. Moquihuixtli took them from her; he also took the fine clothing she had brought with her to the marriage and left her to borrow coarse skirts and blouses from the household's working women. Eventually, so the gossips and storytellers said, he even beat her and made her stand naked with the other women while he looked them all over. Chalchiuhnenetzin now slept among the grinding stones used to make the corn meal. But perhaps the borrowed clothing and the adoption of the role of servant helped her. One day, she was able to slip away, presumably traversing the streets incognito, and she made her way back to her brother's palace. She told Axayacaatl everything. "He has given [his allies] shields and obsidian-bladed war clubs. I have heard what he says. There are consultations by night.... He says he will destroy us Mexica Tenochca, that the only rulership will be in Tlatelolco."[35]

In 1473, the war came swiftly. Moquihuixtli had prepared by establishing numerous alliances, mostly with altepetls that were his tribute states and whose royal lines were intermarried with his family. Numerous others rejected his overtures—or at least told Tenochtitlan that they had. Axayacatl did not wish to appear to be committing many resources to a shameful, internecine squabble. So at first, the Tlatelolcans held their own. They swarmed into the center of the island suddenly, via dozens of canoes. They were beaten back, but by no means destroyed. The results of the battle were inconclusive. Each group retreated and hunkered down in its own part of the island. People long remembered the grim silence.

Such a situation could not last though: Tenochtitlan was too powerful. Eventually—it is not clear if it was days or months later—the men of the city and the allies who had come to them were fully prepared for what they had to do. They went forth in a great body. Some said that the people of Tlatelolco were by now so enraged that the women bared their bodies in an insulting gesture, and that those who could squeezed milk at the oncoming enemy. It might be true: the author of the *Annals of Tlatelolco* claimed almost proudly that their women fought in the last stages of the war against the Spaniards, too, as if it had been something they considered culturally appropriate for their women to do in moments of extremity.[36] If the women of Tlatelolco fought on this occasion, though, their actions did not deter the men from Tenochtitlan, who were led by Axayacatl himself. There were far more of the Tenochca. They drove the remaining Tlatelolcan warriors off the northern tip of the island into the marshy lake. And still they chased them, beating the reeds and killing them wherever they found them. It was said that the Tenochca "made them quack like ducks," and thereafter, if anyone wanted to taunt a Tlatelolcan, they had only to call him a "duck."[37]

More importantly, perhaps, the Tenochca ended Tlatelolco's royal line, forbidding anyone to sit on their reed mat ever again. Moquihuixtli was either thrown from the heights of his people's temple pyramid or he chose to hurl himself downward and end his own life. The history tellers could not agree about this; probably few men ever knew the truth, only those who battled their way to the top of the temple. The story of his fall lived on in popular memory. A drawing of his great descent from the pyramid made a dramatic image in a history later prepared for curious Spaniards.[38] From now on, said Axayacatl, the Tlateolcans would pay tribute like everyone else, including a quota of slaves for sacrifice. The latter was a heavy charge, for it committed the losing party to waging wars against others that they were presently ill-prepared for. In the end, however, he does not seem to have enforced the demand. An old man who was a relative of both his and Moquihuixtli's prostrated himself before the king and begged for mercy for the Tlatelolcans in this regard.[39]

During this period of the 1470s and 80s, Mexica power grew significantly. Axayacatl intervened routinely in the governance of other city states. In 1472, for instance, old Nezahualcoyotl of Texcoco, who had joined with Itzcoatl to bring down Maxtla and the Tepaneca in the 1420s, had died, marking the end of an era. He left behind him, according to one count, sixty sons and fifty-seven daughters, with a significant number of the boys wanting to rule. Axayacatl naturally wanted a son by a close female relative of his own to be the heir. One had already been picked out: Nezahualpilli, his name meaning "Hungry Prince" and encompassing a reference to his father, "Hungry Coyote." The problem was that he was only nine years old—some said he was actually only seven—and it was going to be difficult for him to best fifty-nine older brothers, several of whom had noble mothers of their own. Later, the Spaniards would nod sagely and say the tiny child must have inherited because he was the only *legitimate* heir. One friar imagined tragic scenes in which an aging Nezahualpilli had almost given up hope of his wife producing an heir. At the time, however, the idea that only one woman's son could conceivably inherit was not a notion that existed in the polygynous Nahua world; the people would have been highly amused at the idea that there were no other possible choices when there were 117 siblings in existence. The problem was not that Nezahualcoyotl had no heirs, but that he had too many.[40]

Axayacatl was proactive in protecting Nezahualpilli's claim. Some of the older sons had actually been gotten rid of even before their father's death. One called Tetzauhpiltzintli (Te-tzow-pil-TZEEN-tli, literally, Prince Terrifying) by the history tellers was accused of stockpiling weapons and failing to obey his father; he was put to death. The Tenochca king insisted on this, even though the aging Nezahualcoyotl was said to have wept. Whether or not that was true, after the old king's death, Axayacatl sent both warriors and bribes to Texcoco posthaste. Most of the half brothers accepted a buyout, but a few, fathered in Nezahualcoyotl's early years as a fugitive in the Tlaxcala region, came to make war. Their arrival helped some of the other brothers—who had been raised in Texcoco—to make common cause and side with their baby brother, Nezahualpilli, in order to keep power out of the hands of the easterners, their father's children by a long-ago wife.[41]

It also helped that the child was the favorite candidate of Tenochtitlan. Naturally, there were some resentments about the Mexica always dictating to them, but Axayacatl paid the rejected candidates generously in lands and titles. And because there were so many potential heirs, his emissaries' arrival on the scene averted an internal Texcocan bloodbath that might otherwise have ensued. Axayacatl implicitly promised to continue to support Texcoco faithfully in its dealings with other altepetls, as long as his chosen candidate was king. Mexica rule, in short, was not all terror tactics, at least not among their friends. On some occasions, Axayacatl even knew enough to step back and let the local people have a bit more of their own way. Such was eventually the case in Chalco. After the 1479 performance of Quecholcohuatl's political song, parleys were initiated, and eventually, the royal lines of the four altepetls of Chalco were reinstated. They in effect became part of the inner circle of theTenochca state. Within the central valley, Axayacatl sought to maintain perfect stability.

Then in 1481, after only twelve years of rule, Axayacatl died. Since he was young when he took the throne and was an active warrior, it seems likely that he died in battle, but his people's historians do not say, though they do mention moments when he was wounded or nearly captured or made marvelous captures himself.[42] His death apparently occurred before his people were quite ready for a transition, as a fraternal struggle ensued after his death. His oldest half brother, Tizoc, was elected to the reed mat by the royal clan. He must not have mustered the needed margin of support to maintain power, however, for he went down in the histories as a coward despite waging nearly constant warfare. He died after only about five years of rule—some said four, some said six—and people talked openly about the probability that he had been poisoned by an enemy faction. His brother Ahuitzotl now followed. He ruled successfully enough, but by the time he died in 1502, it was certainly expected that the pendulum of power would swing back to the other branch of the family—the one descended from Huitzilihuitl, not Itzcoatl. Under Ahuitzotl, Tlacaelel, the old Cihuacoatl, had died and been replaced by one of his sons; the institution of the council had solidified and its meeting continued uninterrupted despite the loss of a key individual. In their selection of the tlatoani, the royal clan overwhelmingly backed a son of Axayacatl, Moctezuma Xocoyotl, or Moctezuma the Younger.[43]

In 1502, Moctezuma was a young and charismatic figure. Posterity would later characterize him as fearful and pusillanimous, but early Nahuatl sources portray him quite differently. He was a hard man, with a hard agenda. Although he himself wouldn't have used such terms, not having studied twentieth-century political science textbooks, his goal was nothing less than the creation of a true state apparatus, capable of exerting control far beyond face-to-face situations. By now, there were no more upheavals coming from within the central valley—no more rebellions on the part of such altepetls as Chalco or Tlatelolco. The Mexica were thus ready to establish a more complete dominance over the several hundred altepetls outside of the inner basin, from whom they (and their partners in empire) already extracted tribute, but who generally had been left to their own devices as long as they did not rebel.

Moctezuma wanted to increase the level of direct control. He started by setting up thirty-eight administrative provinces (there were later fifty-five provinces), each with its own tightly organized bureaucracy. Representatives of his government were sent to live in each. In a town far away in the Toluca valley, they created such neighborhoods as (in Nahuatl) "Place of the Temple Lords," "Place of the Merchants," "Place of the Rulers," and "Place of the Mexica people."[44] Permanent military garrisons were built at key locations in order to support the Mexica who were scattered far and wide. The chain of command between the tlatoani's highest officials in Tenochtitlan and those lesser figures who lived locally was carefully delineated, and then recorded in documents that illustrated these political relationships.[45] Archaeological studies have revealed that people in the countryside outside the central basin largely continued to prosper. The prior "Triple Alliance" rulers had encouraged interregional trade: local markets sold such useful items as copper needles, jars of salt, and small bronze bells (for dancing and ceremonies). There was no reason for life to change much. Only rarely did a recalcitrant local noble find his compound attacked and his lineage destroyed. That was generally not what Moctezuma had in mind.[46]

The local Mexica officials' most important task was to collect all required tribute on time. They continued to work on synchronizing various altepetls' calendars, so it would be clear when tribute was due, and they held public ceremonies, recorded in paintings, delineating what and when each altepetl owed.[47] But tribute collection was no longer the officials' only task. They supported Nahua merchants engaged in long-distance trade, who were at the mercy of locals if not backed by Mexica royal authority; with such support, they could orchestrate luxury trades over impressively long distances.[48] The officials also oversaw local diplomatic negotiations concerning, for the most part, chiefly marriages and inheritance, and they acted as judges upholding certain notions of law and justice, especially regarding landholding, which Moctezuma wished to see standardized, since in each area some lands were dedicated to helping to support Tenochtitlan. The tlatoani of each local alte- petl would continue, as he always had, to distribute farmlands among his own people, but in the case of any unresolved disputes, and certainly of any dis- putes with other altepetls, it was the prerogative of Tenochca judges to decide upon the proper distribution. They intervened with some frequency; years later, long after the Spaniards were in power, some local families were still sim- mering about Tenochtitlan's decisions, which were generally still in force, by then having the weight of custom behind them.[49]

The vision Moctezuma and his councilors held of a well-regulated body politic was in some ways a product of generations of Nahua tradition. Their political organization had long revolved around what a leading historian has called a sort of "cellular principle."[50] That is, no individual human being was considered to stand alone in life but existed only in relation to others; nor did any group exist alone but rather thrived by virtue of their connections with those who surrounded them. Families were grouped into kin-based clans (usually called *calpolli* but sometimes by some other name), and these in turn were grouped together to form an altepetl, and altepetls in turn were often collected into a greater altepetl. It was understood that harmony among the whole depended upon each cellular segment doing its part: from time imme- morial, unpleasant tasks (like maintaining a local temple, or clearing weeds away from a lakeshore to form a port, or collecting tribute to turn over to a conqueror) had been rotated between the different component parts of a polity. So, too, was there the tradition of passing the chieftainship back and forth between lineages, so as to avoid breeding resentment. In a sense, the Tenochtitlan state had become powerful enough to formalize some of these traditions on a vast scale, but with a twist—they, and no others, would always be the head of this carefully balanced body politic, a position they had worked hard to achieve.

The social organization began at home: Tenochtitlan offered a shining example of the world Moctezuma had in mind. There, the city's four quarters or sub-altepetls were further divided along the lines of the calpolli, in units akin to parishes or wards, each with its own noble (*pilli*) families, in the midst of the commoner (*macehualli*) families. The macehualli families supported the noble families by paying them tribute; they worked hard in the chinamp- sas or a craftsman's workshop, while the noble families organized their endeavors. In general, over the years, there had been relatively little tension

within each calpolli: certain families had been more special than other families for so many generations that their lineage was unquestioned. And, as in all
aspects of life, it was understood that every category of person had an important role to play. Often the Mexica conceived of society as one of their beloved
birds; the pipiltin might be the head, but the macehualtin were "the tail, the
wings." And what bird could fly without its tail and wings? It was a beautiful
idea and one deeply familiar to the Mexica.

There are signs, however, that in later years the relative peace was threatened more often than it had been before. As the nobility brought home
increasing numbers of captive women, they had more children. The families
of the pipiltin threatened to become unmanageably large relative to those of
the macehualtin. As far back as the reign of Moctezuma the Elder, it had been
concluded that the king had too many children to expect the macehualtin to
support them all with their tribute. He was remembered as saying, "Not all of
my children will rule." And he concluded that they should be trained to support themselves as elite artisans, such as lapidaries, sculptors, and scribes.[51]
The problem only grew. It was the same in Texcoco. One old woman in the
sixteenth century remembered how it had been in her girlhood in the late
1400s: "Back when I was growing up there was an infinite number of nobles.
How many noble houses there were, the palaces of those who were nobles and
rulers! It was like one big palace. There were countless minor lords and lesser
relatives, and one could not count the commoners who were their dependents, or the slaves; they were like ants."[52] All of this created more than a few
logistical problems. The nobility worked out complex understandings as to
which family members would count as nobles in the sense of depending on
tribute from commoners, and who could and could not be considered a possible heir; they even created an accompanying terminology. One absolutely
had to inherit one's official status through the male line, they decided, thus
reducing claimants by half.[53]

At this point, the organization of each calpolli was tightened. Each had its
own officials charged with storing tribute and organizing public works (like
the repair of the temples), and with hearing and settling disputes. There were
separate officials to handle commoners' grievances and those of the nobility,
as well as a sort of high court that supervised both: the latter was called the
tlacxitlan, meaning "the place at the foot [of something]"—implicitly, in this
case, the foot of the ruler. No laws were written down, but certain principles
of legal tradition were understood by all, and the judges issued penalties for
breaking them. Adultery, for example, was a crime for everyone, punishable
by stoning or strangling. The exact nature of the crime differed according to

sex. A married woman could not have any sexual relations outside of her marriage; a married man could, but if he slept with a woman who was married, then he, too, was guilty. An indebted person could sell his or her child into slavery, but a young person who became a slave in this way was entitled to certain protections and to buying his or her way out of slavery if it were ever possible. In theory, those rights persisted everywhere. When questioned by Spaniards, some people later insisted that the Mexica kings sometimes tried to help families buy their loved ones back from distant places; in reality, it would have been impossible to find them once they were taken to the east. Still, the concept of a fixed law existed in the minds of many thousands of people, even without a written code.[54]

The many markets—the small ones in each calpolli neighborhood, as well as the massive one that had grown up at the north end of the island, in Tlatelolco—were also carefully administered by officials who ultimately answered to Moctezuma and his council. Women were an important part of market life, as both buyers and sellers, and for this reason, some of the officials who governed commerce were themselves women. They carried their staffs of office proudly, and were not afraid to report on and punish any delinquents. Anyone who stole from vendors or cheated customers or even got into a fight at the market would regret it.[55] Later, a Spaniard who saw the market at Tlatelolco four days after the Europeans first arrived remembered it with a sort of awe, as it was both so huge and yet so well controlled: "We were astounded at the great number of people and the quantities of merchandise, and at the orderliness and good arrangements that prevailed, for we had never seen such a thing before. The chieftains who accompanied us pointed everything out. Every kind of merchandise was kept separate and had a fixed place marked for it."[56]

One part of the market featured luxury goods—gold and silver, turquoise, jade and other gems, the feathers of exotic birds. Merchants sold these to artisans as raw materials, and to wealthy customers as finely crafted textiles and beautiful jewelry. Likewise, they sold plain cotton thread or cloth and also beautifully made embroidered cloaks and other clothing. In another area, they offered firewood and lumber, as well as wood carved into tool handles, paddles, and columns for buildings. They sold copper axe-heads and needles, white bark paper, pitch pine for torches, rubber balls, herbal medicines, tobacco, pipes, and row upon row of ceramic pots and dishes. They hawked goods made of sisal: twine, rope, nets, and sandals, as well as all manner of animal furs, tanned or untanned, dyed or undyed. They sold rough grinding stones and fine obsidian knives or mirrors, in which one could see every detail of one's face.. In one corner, men could pay to have their hair cut. In another, they could buy a slave or find a prostitute.[57]

It was the section selling food stuffs, though, that most impressed people who had never been to the marketplace before. The stalls offered everything—every type of corn and bean, all varieties of salts and herbs. Birds and animals rustled in their cages. There were fruits and vegetables, cacao and honey, bird eggs and the delicious bars of dried algae from the lake. But what was remarkable about Tlatelolco, what made it different from neighborhood food markets, was that food could be bought partially prepared, for urban customers too busy to make everything from scratch. One could buy pre-made tortillas and little cakes, squash already cut into pieces, smoked chilis, and ground cacao. Hungry shoppers could go to what was effectively a restaurant—a stand where prepared meals were available for sale.[58]

Doctors and healers, both men and women, also operated out of the market. They sold a variety of herbs that experience had taught would help with different ailments—blisters, constipation, diarrhea, itchy skin, eye sores, headache, or fever. They could also cast stones, a like throwing dice, to try to determine the best treatment for a mysterious ailment, or make a house call to perform a ceremony designed to oust a malicious force from the body. Later, well-meaning Spanish friars would try to insist that there had been some doctors who dealt only in efficacious herbs, while other evil ones preyed on people's superstitions. It was the friars' way of trying to save the reputation of some of the indigenous doctors in European eyes. But the extant descriptions make it clear that those who often worked with medicines and those who conducted ceremonies were one and the same.[59]

Startlingly—at least to newcomers—the market also served as a repository for the urine collected in clay pots in households across the city. Whether people were paid for what they brought or fined for what they didn't bring is not clear. In either case, the practice served two purposes. The collection of the waste in one place rendered most of the city very clean. Ammonia was also needed for tanning hides and making salt crystals, and there was no better source than the urine from the island's tens of thousands of people. Canoes full of basins of it were lined up near the market, and there the tanners and salt-makers brought their requisite supplies.[60]

It was not just the courts and the markets that were governed by an increasingly well-defined apparatus: the temples and schools were likewise becoming the bastions of a highly organized set of officials. By the time of Moctezuma, almost all of the city's children, boys and well as girls, nobles as well as commoners, were educated in temple-run schools. They entered these boarding schools around the age of thirteen and stayed a few years. Thus they passed the most trying adolescent years away from home—much like European youths who entered apprenticeships. Every girl learned the proper prayers for her marriage ceremony and for daily life. She learned to spin and weave and embroider if she had not already become adept, and she also learned her duties as a future wife and mother. She discovered, for instance, that she would have very little sleep for much of her adult life, and that she must not resent it. "Here is the task you are to do: be devout night and day. Sigh many times to the night, the passing wind. Call to, speak to, cry out to it, especially in your resting place, your sleeping place. Do not practice the pleasure of sleep." Nursing mothers and the mothers of young children could expect to be up part of every night, and they must still rise early to haul the water, rekindle the fire, and start the breakfast without complaint. When that time came, a young woman should not be surprised. The adults in her life were preparing her to handle the harshness of reality.[61]

Every boy studied warfare, unless he had been selected as a likely priest or had been born into a merchant family. Merchants formed their own tight-knit group and educated their children for the harrowing treks across unknown country; priests were educated in a separate school, where they would learn far more than other boys about religious matters, the calendar, and the pictographic writing system. Those two groups aside, every young male had to learn to be a warrior. That had always been true in almost every village in Mexico, but now the Mexicas' predominant position absolutely depended on their success; there was no room for failure or for doubt if they did not want all the surrounding altepetls that hated theirs to rise up against them. The boys learned a craft from their parents at home—perhaps sculpting ceramic vessels, or making tiny golden animals with charcoal and wax molds, or gluing the velvety fibers of exotic feathers in intricate designs on shields—but when they were about thirteen, they all left home to train as warriors. In the early weeks after starting school, they swept and collected firewood; they sang in the evenings and enjoyed themselves. The violent exercises began gradually. The boys learned to withstand pain and to fight. As older teenagers, they might accompany warriors to battle, on the understanding that whole groups of them should try to bring in a captive by separating a man on the battlefield from his cohort and then working together as a well-practiced unit to bring him down.[62]

By about the age of twenty, the period of apprenticeship was finished. If a man did not then make kills or take captives on his own, he had to fear a life of shame. If in the years of training, it became clear that a particular boy simply could not fight successfully in any capacity, he could be designated as a burden bearer. For the rest of his life, he might, for instance, ply the aquatic edges of the town in a canoe loaded with vats of fresh water, leaving them in appointed places, and everyone would know why. How often such a fate became real we do not know, but the threat of such a destiny must certainly have weighed heavily as a boy grew into manhood.[63] If, on the other hand, a young man was especially adept at fighting, he won honors for himself and his whole family. A commoner could rise to become a *quauhpilli* (kwow-PIL-li), an eagle lord, or honorary nobleman. The slaves and other loot he brought back from battle made him rich. If he liked, he could take more than one wife, just like a born nobleman, for he could support them and the resulting children. Often such men were honored with an official position, and no one quarreled with their right to hold it.[64]

In the meantime, other boys were educated to become priests. The priests who trained them, who held such power in their lives, seem to have encompassed a wide range of personalities. Some were remembered as wise and thoughtful; others, unsurprisingly, were brutal. They were there, after all, to teach a new generation to take over their duties in the bloody sacrificial rituals. When a student at a *calmecac*, as the schools were called, committed a particularly serious infraction, such as drinking, he was doomed to participate in a ceremony in which the priests attempted to drown him—or seemed to attempt to do so. "They plunged him under the water and dragged him. They went pulling him along by the hair. They kicked him. As he swam under the water, churning, beating, and swirling it up as he went, he escaped the hands of the priests.... When he finally reached the shore, he lay half dead, breathing his last, gasping in his last agonies." At that point the boy's parents were allowed to take him home. The system was not without a certain moral impurity. If a mother and father were convinced that their child was not a good swimmer and thus might actually die, they could bribe the school officials. "They would give the priests a turkey or some other kind of food, so that they would let [their boy] be."[65]

The priests in general wielded increasing power as they became professionalized and closely entwined with the state. Traditionally, every month in the Nahua ceremonial calendar had seen sacrificial victims die, but by the end of Moctezuma's reign, so many were killed in Tenochtitlan every month that a significant number of priests had to have worked full time preparing for, orchestrating, and then cleaning up after the deaths. They cleaned the skulls and plastered them into great *tzompantlis* (skull racks). They no longer killed only specially arrayed impersonators of the god but also a variable number of ordinary captives, whose dead bodies, sprawled on the lower steps, were understood to receive the god figure into their arms as he or she fell down the pyramid. The priests who drugged the victims, tied them down, cut out their hearts, and burned what was left of them must have become inured to their activities over time. Spiritually infused potions were made with the remains of the dead; undoubtedly priests had touched these to their lips from time immemorial. But now parts of the sacred stew were sent to elite households for them to partake of as well, figuratively if not literally. As the polygynous noble families grew rapidly, this practice touched the lives of an increasing proportion of the people. Moctezuma himself spent an exorbitant amount of time playing a sacrificial role: he was constantly called on for participation at key junctures in many of the monthly ceremonies. For him, going to the battlefield was no longer feasible as he would have been too busy participating in the public ceremonies that ran with blood.[66]

Only a few decades earlier, Mexica society could not possibly have dedicated so much time, manpower, and psychic energy to the rituals of death. But their strength enabled them to do so by the later decades. And their leaders were convinced that if they could do so, they should, as they believed the practice reduced distant altepetls to abject terror. By this time, a number of elite figures and their priests clearly took a cynical view of the question of human sacrifice. When they were making war on peoples at the edge of their empire whom they wished to incorporate into the realm, they would seize some of the men and bring them to Tenochtitlan, not in a public procession so that they might serve as sacrifices, but secretly, so they could be made to watch. Then they were released to bring word home to their people of what awaited them if they did not accept Mexica terms peacefully. "Thus they were undone, and disunited," a man who had seen these spectacles later commented.[67] Moctezuma especially liked to bring such visitors to see the gladiatorial sacrifice ceremony in the month of Tlacaxipeualtli, when captured warriors were forced to fight for their lives—only to be slain anyway. There was definitely an underside to the controlled, well-oiled workings of the beautiful city.

The levers of control sometimes even threatened the central valley's most elite citizens. In 1498, just before Moctezuma took office, daughters of many of the city's leading families were taken to nearby Texcoco to see a horrifying spectacle as a lesson on the importance of obedience and self-control. Years ago, before he died, Axayacatl had married off his daughter, also named Chalchiuhnenetzin, or Jade Doll, like her tragic aunt, to the young Nezahualpilli, the boy whom he himself had set on the throne of Texcoco.

When the two young people grew up, they found they were not suited. Perhaps Jade Doll was arrogant, given who her father was. Then Axayacatl died, and his daughter was left vulnerable. Her uncle Ahuitzotl—who had never accepted that Axayacatl was chosen before him—now ruled in Tenochtitlan. He undoubtedly wanted a different primary wife for Nezahualpilli. Gossips claimed that the Mexica princess had committed adultery with at least two men. Nezahualpilli either believed that she had done so, or was convinced by the hostile Ahuitztotl that he must pretend to believe it. He ordered that his wife and her lovers and all the many people who had covered for them be put to death by stoning and strangling, just as the law demanded for all adulterers. Many years later, an old woman would recall the day's events. "People came from the towns all around to see. Ladies brought along their daughters, even though they might still be in the cradle, to have them see.... Even some Tlaxcalans, and people from Huexotzinco and Atlixco, although they were our enemies, came to see."[68] She remembered that Nezahualpilli had regained his honor by hosting an unforgettable feast; she said it put to shame any that the Mexica had ever held. She had been a child, and the food had made a great impression on her, more so than the public executions.

We will never know if Axayacatl's daughter really showed such poor judgment as to take lovers. Even if she did, she might have gotten away with it had there not been those in Nezahualpilli's court who wished to see another woman become the primary wife. The enemies of her lineage had clearly moved quickly, thinking they could improve their own position in regards to the succession.[69] Her death, however, did not settle matters in favor of anyone in particular. It merely left the playing field open. A noblewoman from the Atzacualco quarter of Tenochtitlan was a favored wife who bore Nezahualpilli eleven children, and many assumed that one of her sons would inherit.[70] The eldest, Huexotzincatzin (Way-sho-tzeen-CAH-tzeen), was a popular man. In Moctezuma's reign, he became known for his participation in the evening entertainments of singing, dancing, and the telling of histories. Unfortunately, in the politically competitive environment in which he lived, his love of these arts was to cost him dearly.

What happened to Huexotzincatzin is a long story that illuminates both politics and gender at the peak of Mexica power. There was among his father Nezahualpilli's women one who was particularly valued. She was not from a noble lineage but was the daughter of a merchant from Tula; thus the bards did not even give her name, as they nearly always did for princesses, but merely called her "a lady from Tula." What made her famous was not her beauty—for there were many beautiful women in the household of any tlatoani—but rather her ability to spin poems and turn them into songs like any man. She was not the only woman with this skill—the art of speaking was always valued in the Nahua world, and other women are on record as having been painters, speakers, and singers—but among young women, who were ideally supposed to be demure, she was nevertheless a rarity.[71] Still, when the Lady of Tula later got into trouble, it was not because she was a woman, or even because she was an assertive woman in public. Rather, it was because she, too, like everyone else, was enmeshed in the dangerous politics born of polygyny.

In the courtyard performances of Tenochtitlan, Texcoco, and other alte-petls, there was always give-and-take among those who held the floor. It was expected that representatives of more than one sub-altepetl would offer their version of a crisis moment in history, or that more than one noble would offer a song lauding a leader or remembering a battle. Different performers would take their turn in succession. The expression of different points of view, they knew, worked to bind people together. What Huexotzincatzin and the Lady of Tula became known for, however, seems to have been a bit different. They earned a reputation for composing works addressed directly to each other, and for teasing and being witty in front of an audience. In breaking with tradition, they created art.[72]

What poems did they sing aloud? We have the lyrics of dozens of Nahua song-poems from the era, which overlap in theme and metaphor, but we cannot know exactly which lines were their favorites or how they spun them into new works, as all performers did.[73] We can, on the other hand, get a good sense of the possibilities. At some point one of them must surely have sung one of the perennial favorites about the fragility of flowers, the fleeting nature of earthly joys. Such a song would have flowed easily from the heart of a woman taken from the land of her birth to serve others until her death:

My heart is angry.
We are not born twice, not engendered twice. Instead we leave this earth forever.
We are in the presence of this company but a moment! It can never be—I will never be happy, never be content.
Where does my heart live? Where is my home? Where does my house lie? I suffer on this earth.

The singer's next lines were addressed to the creator god, who had such power to dispense joy in the midst of earth's sufferings: "You are a giver of jade stones, you unfold them spun like feathers, you give flower crowns to princes."[74]

Huexotzincatzin could have responded to such a salvo with a typical poem of joy and laughter, trying to get the woman to smile, rather than continuing the lament. If so, the change of genre would have been a startling move to the audience. Or perhaps the man did continue with the same type of song laced with sadness, but looked meaningfully and directly at the originator of the dialogue, reminding her that, like all who have lived on earth, she would not be forgotten. He could easily have referenced their common Nahua ancestors—for the songs were full of such images—and complimented her beauty at the same time. The old song, known in Itzcoatl's time, ran thus: "You died among the mesquite plants of the Seven Caves. The eagle was calling, the jaguar cried. And you, a red flamingo, were flying onwards, from the midst of a field to a place unknown."[75] In reading the surviving songs, hearing their cadences, and noting their powerful imagery, it becomes clear that the possibilities for a charged literary encounter were virtually infinite.

Whatever the two young poets did, Huexotzincatzin was the king's son and the lady his woman, and the aging Nezahualpilli did not like it. Under normal circumstances, he surely would have handled the matter in private, since the culprit was his son. But in Tenochtitlan, Moctezuma the Younger had been looking for an excuse to replace Huexotzincatzin as the presumed heir, and now he had one. He wanted the Texcocan's king's heir to be a close relative of his own, someone who would always do exactly as he said. His nephew Cacama, a son of Nezahualpilli by a granddaughter of Tlacaelel, seemed a likely candidate. But first he had to get rid of Huexotzincatzin and his numerous brothers without causing a civil war in the central valley.

In the mid-1500s the elderly woman who remembered seeing the executions of 1498 also remembered Huexotzincatzin's strangulation a number of years later. She didn't like it. "He was punished just for composing songs to the Lady of Tula," she said briefly. Rumor had it, she added, that Nezahualpilli shut himself up in his palace to suffer his grief. But Moctezuma had been implacable. He claimed there would be no order if the nobility were allowed to flout the laws and even make cuckholds of their own fathers. He insisted that the cord be tightened around Huexotzincatzin's handsome neck. (No source says explicitly what happened to the Lady of Tula, but undoubtedly she died, too, since other sources show culprits being punished in pairs.)[76] Moctezuma must have hoped that this tactic would frighten Huexotzincatzin's younger brothers into allowing his nephew to become the heir. Two of the older ones did come to bargain immediately: they accepted lands and titles, which their sons and grandsons still held in the 1560s. The younger boys were not considered a threat, and so Moctezuma left them alone, and this was a tactical error. Not so many years later, one of them would be among the first to ally with the newcomers from across the sea.[77]

But for now, in Nezahualpilli's and Moctezuma's courts, voices rose in song, and then dropped to relate the passionate tales of history. Conch-shell trumpets called hauntingly. In the early 1500s, Flamingo Snake, the drummer and singer who had so pleased Axayacatl, was still alive, and he loved to hear the performances. As a Chalcan, he knew all about the darker side of Mexica power. But he also knew and loved the beauty of the world the Mexica had helped to build, for he saw artists of the different altepetls responding to each other's work and inspirations. They were not caught in traditional patterns but were eager to experiment. He listened to it all, and then bent to his drum and made it speak (as he would have put it), just as he had when he was young. If he were of a philosophical turn of mind, he might have said that in order for the central valley to have such peace and space for their art, then the chaos of warfare and the predicament of hunger had to be expelled to the distant villages of strangers whom he himself would never see. Thus it had always been, and thus it would always be: the residents of great cities almost never saw the vulnerable, shattered peoples in distant lands who supported them—except briefly, in an almost unreal sense, as honored sacrifice victims in magisterial ceremonies. The people who lived in Tenochtitlan were convinced that they had built something worth protecting for whatever time on earth they could.

***

NOT FAR FROM THE PALACE courtyards where the voices rose, there stood many storage chambers. Some of these were for *in tlilli in tlapalli*, the black and the red, meaning the painted texts of the scribes. They were carefully rolled or folded up accordion style and placed in the proper wooden bins and reed chests. A few were timelines illustrating histories, and the history tellers used these to remember what to say during performances or to help determine when a song might be appropriate. Most of the painted texts, however, had nothing to do with art or beauty. Whether Flamingo Snake knew it or not, most were business records—records of boundary decisions and chains of authority, of noble lineages, and tribute due. Moctezuma even sent people—often frightened merchants—to record their observations of the type of business conducted in as yet unconquered areas and the kinds of resources available there. About 1515, Nezahualpilli died and tensions broke out in Texcoco, as some of Huexotzincatzin's younger brothers had proven unwilling to keep quiet about their right to inherit; they again had to be bribed with a large share of the realm, at least for a while. Moctezuma was very busy with that matter, and with a brief war involving the ornery altepetl of Huexotzinco: When they lost a war with Tlaxcala that he himself had incited them to begin, he had to receive many refugees from their land. He nevertheless kept track of what was going on in more distant regions as well. In 1518 he sent observers to investigate some strangers who had apparently made several appearances in Maya country along the sea coast. Governing the precarious lands he ruled required eternal vigilance, for the collectivity was a finely tuned organism—like life itself, where ferocity and peace lay side by side—and such an organism could not be expected to maintain itself. As king of the Mexica, he certainly believed that it was worth protecting. And his people trusted him to guard it; it was their very definition of the duty of a tlatoani. "The ruler used to keep vigil through the night," they remembered.[78]

***

FROM WHERE THEY WERE HIDDEN, Moctezuma's messengers could see a long stretch of the beach. The newcomers galloped their beasts—like huge deer, they thought, but much more stalwart—up and down the hard-packed sand, wheeling around suddenly and giving great shouts of laughter. Their arrow-shattering metal raiment glinted in the sun. The strangers glanced self-consciously at the bluffs, knowing they were being watched. The observers knew they knew…but didn't care. It was not their mission to maintain secrecy but to gather intelligence. They took notes, carefully recording in glyphs all that they saw before them. Beyond the beach, the strangers' great boats were anchored in the waves. The watchers had seen many canoes in their time, but none as big as these. In a stroke of pure genius, the boats' makers had thought to hang cloth blankets from poles, so as to catch the wind and speed their travel. Men could live for many days on boats that size; they could have come from far away indeed.[79]

When the messengers were ready, they turned to begin the trip back to the city. They knew the shortest routes leading from the humid lowlands up into the pine forests. They knew where to find passage through the ring of mountains that surrounded the great valley. They knew when to rest and when to push forward relentlessly. In a matter of days, they knelt before their king.

4

Strangers to Us People Here

1519

The frightened girl and her companions followed the winding path from the Maya town of Potonchan, on the shore of the Gulf, down to the beach where the strangers were encamped. They moved through the shadows, surrounded by gnarled and twisted trees—ceiba, mahogany, rubber—the exposed dirt path glinting silvery-gray wherever the sunlight managed to strike it. Warriors armed with spears walked with them, in case anyone should suddenly try to run. The young women were to be peace offerings to the fearsome newcomers; they could not outrun their fate. As the group came out into the bright sunlight, they saw the giant boats they had heard so much about, with their cloths hung to catch the wind. The bearded ones turned from their smoking camp fires—they were desperately trying to keep the mosquitoes away—to stare brazenly at the offered women.[1]

***

WHEN SHE WAS young, the girl would have been called something like Daughter Child. Some girls in her world earned funny, affectionate names—like She's-Not-a-Fish or Little Old Woman—or poetic ones—like Deer Flower—but most were simply called "Elder Daughter," "Middle Child," or "Youngest," at least until their personalities became better known.[2] Living at the fringes of empire, this Daughter Child had no illusions about the agonies

---

A girl learns to weave. The Bodleian Libraries, the University of Oxford, Codex Mendoza, MS. Arch. Selden. A.1, folio 60r.

of war; she harbored no belief that it was for a greater good. It was simply the way things were. If she allowed herself to have any feelings about the Mexica at all, her sentiment was hatred.

When she was born to a Nahua nobleman of Coatzacoalcos, farther west along the coast—close to today's Veracruz—her mother had undoubtedly buried her umbilical cord near the hearth, as almost all Nahuatl-speaking mothers did. She would have uttered a prayer something like this: "You will be the heart of the home. You will go nowhere. You will not become a wanderer anywhere. You become the banked fire, the hearthstones."[3] It was what anyone would have wanted for a beloved daughter. The mother's prayers, however, had been in vain. Although the child's father was a highly ranked nobleman, her mother was no one important, probably a slave. It was such women's children who were most vulnerable in moments of crisis.

And the crisis came. The Coatzacoalcos region was the next target in the Mexicas' perennial expansion. When the Mexica and their allies approached other altepetls to demand their allegiance, it was the children of less powerful mothers who generally found themselves in harm's way. Unless the aggressors happened to be in need of child sacrifices for the annual festival of Tlaloc, no one thought of killing the young. They were far too valuable. They could be raised as loyal household dependents, or sold as slaves. That is what had happened to Daughter Child. Whether her father's people had managed to prevent war with the Mexica by offering a sort of preemptive tribute, or whether they had actually lost a battle and been forced to sue for peace by offering a gift, is unknown. Regardless, the child was ripped from her kin and placed in a canoe with other captives. As the boat pulled away from the shore and sliced rapidly through the water, bearing her in the direction of the rising sun, she had no reason to believe she would ever see her home again.[4]

Daughter Child would have guessed that she was being taken to one of the neutral trading ports that rendered long-distant trade possible in war-ridden Mesoamerica. At the coastal town of Xicallanco, lying not far to the east, where many Nahuatl merchants lived, she was sold to some Maya, either for a certain weight of cacao beans or for bolts of cotton cloth. These were the two kinds of currency in the busy, polyglot town that nestled in a giant blue lagoon. Here, there were no pyramids or stone monuments, just buildings made of mud and sticks of wood. No one had time to construct anything more, for they were there to trade, not to pray. People came from far and wide, and no one attacked the place, for it was too important to all of them. Every kingdom's merchants depended on the existence of such towns.[5]

From Xicallanco the girl was brought back westward to the town of Potonchan, near the mouth of the Tabasco River. It was a leading settlement of the Chontal Maya, the "Phoenicians of Mesoamerica," as they have since been dubbed. These were a powerful people, for their nobles, nearly all of whom were merchants, were extremely wealthy. They used their riches to buy food and favors from the surrounding farmers and to purchase slaves from the long-distance Nahua traders. Those slaves made it possible for them to produce large quantities of beautiful cotton cloth that others were willing to pay a great deal for.[6]

It was the honored wives and daughters of Chontal men who did most of the weaving, not the enslaved women. The creation of cloth, of tapestry, was a holy task, beloved by the gods. But while the honored wives devoted their time to weaving, other women were needed to grind corn, make tortillas, fetch water, and care for young children. A host of other textile-related activities could be assigned to slaves as well. Someone had to sow and harvest the cotton plants. Then the fibers needed to be beaten and carded for many hours to rid them of the dirt and flecks. The fibers then had to be spun into yarn; dyes had to be made out of plants or shellfish and then the yarns repeatedly boiled in them until they reached the desired color. Finally the looms needed to be warped in preparation for the actual weaving. Then at last the great lady of the house could begin the sacred task of weaving. As a Nahua girl child, the newly purchased child would have adapted to her assigned chores relatively easily: back home, she would have begun by the age of five to learn to use a little spindle to make yarn, and she would have been taught to cook and clean as well.[7]

Years passed, and Daughter Child had a new name, a slave's name. In her new life, no one claimed her as kin. She was no one's Elder Sister, or Youngest Child. We do not know what the Maya who had purchased her called her. Whether she was coerced into having sexual relations, we will also never know, although that would have been a typical part of an enslaved woman's experience. As the girl grew to early womanhood, not much differentiated one year from another. Then in 1517, the townsfolk heard that some strangers with remarkably hairy faces had landed a very large boat at Champoton, another Chontal town lying to the east. After a skirmish, the outsiders were driven off, with many of their men badly wounded, but they left many Chontal warriors wounded and dying. The strangers were clearly dangerous to the political order—a political order that required the Chontal to appear invulnerable to the surrounding peoples.

The strangers returned the next year. This time, they bypassed the feisty town of Champoton. Messengers on speeding canoes came to say that they had stopped near Xicallanco, but didn't find it, hidden as it was in its lagoon. They kidnapped four young boys who had boarded the boat to trade and then proceeded west. All of Potonchan waited. Within days, the strangers found the mouth of the Rio Tabasco. From where they floated, they could see the town clearly. Hundreds of Chontal warriors gathered along the shore; they made their way out toward the larger boat in dozens of canoes, arrows notched, ready to fly. A huge dog aboard the strangers' boat spotted land, jumped overboard, and began to swim toward the shore. The young Chontal men gave a great shout and showered the creature with arrows. Within moments, something aboard the massive boat seemed to explode, and bits of metal flew everywhere, wounding many. Some slumped over, apparently dead. The Chontal retreated.[8]

All the households buzzed with gossip. The next day, the town's leaders sent a few canoes of men out to try to parley, and the strangers brought forward a young prisoner who spoke their language. He told the Chontal he had been kidnapped years ago near Cozumel. Yes, the warriors said, they had heard rumors that strangers were occasionally appearing along the eastern coast of the Yucatan peninsula, and some even asserted that they governed a huge island six days' sail to the east of Cozumel, but the previous year was the first time they had heard a full and coherent story, from Champoton. The interpreter told them the strangers were indeed dangerous and that they sought gold and food in regular supplies. To the indigenous, this signified that they were demanding tribute; it was not good news. The Chontal asked the interpreter to explain that the Mexica, far to the west, were really the people to seek if they wanted gold and other precious goods, but that they would barter what they had, if only the strangers would return the four boys they had kidnapped near Xicallanco. Some goods were brought out and traded, but the boys were not returned. Later that day the winds were right, and the strangers rapidly put up a sail and departed.[9]

No one could tell if they were gone for good. The Chontal leaders built a few stockades and arranged for neighboring peoples to fight at their side if it came to that. The people harvested their corn and cacao and wove their cloth. Many undoubtedly forgot about the incident or put it out of their minds. But if the women had ceased to gossip and speculate about the strangers, the subject nevertheless resurfaced dramatically less than a year later. In 1519 a messenger arrived, saying that no fewer than ten of the big boats were sailing westward from Cozumel.[10]

The ships came straight to Potonchan. In the talks that unfolded between Spaniard and Indian on the very first day—undoubtedly while the women and children were being led out of the city—the Chontal leaders said bluntly that they would kill anyone who entered their land. They offered food and advised the strangers to leave before anything unpleasant happened. The foreigners' leader, a man in his early thirties who called himself "Hernando Cortés," refused to listen. Instead, he made plans to come ashore. He divided his men into two groups. One landed at the mouth of the river on the coast and then moved overland toward the town, and the other sailed upriver, then drew near the settlement in smaller boats and began to wade ashore in a tight formation. Their glinting swords were bared, creating a circle of space around them, and their outer clothing was likewise made of metal, so they could move with relative impunity, as the Indians' stone arrowheads and spear tips shattered against it. Still, it was tough going for them. One of the strangers later described the scene:

> With great bravery the [locals] surrounded us in their canoes, pouring such a shower of arrows on us that they kept us in the water up to our waists. There was so much mud and swamp that we had difficulty getting clear of it; and so many Indians attacked us, hurling their lances and shooting arrows, that it took us a long time to struggle ashore. While Cortés was fighting, he lost a sandal in the mud and could not recover it. So he landed with one bare foot.[11]

As soon as they were ashore, the invaders began to use their crossbows and lances against the indigenous, who were armored only in padded cotton, forcing them to retreat. With their metal weapons, the strangers broke through the wooden stockades that had been constructed, and then the other group of outsiders, who had been making their way overland, arrived. The Indians rapidly withdrew, and the newcomers were left in command of the abandoned center of Potonchan, a square surrounded by empty temples and halls. There they slept, with sentries standing guard. Armed and armored and in a large group, they were relatively invulnerable. But they soon grew hungry. When they sent out foraging parties, the Chontal attacked them guerrilla-style and killed several men.[12]

Two days later, the strangers, determined to make something happen, moved out in a body onto an open plain. Wave after wave of warriors attacked the group of metal-clad foreigners, perishing before the lethal steel weapons, but wearing them down nevertheless. The battle continued for more than an hour. The Chontal lords thought the strangers would surely tire soon, and then their own greater numbers would carry the day. Then, from behind, there suddenly came thundering over the plain more enemies mounted on huge quadrupeds, twenty times as strong as deer. Under cover of night, the Spaniards had unloaded ten horses from the ships that were still in the mouth of the river. It was a time-consuming and difficult task, requiring pulleys and canvas slings, but the men were protected by darkness and their armor, and whichever Chontal were watching could not possibly have known how significant these actions would turn out to be. The horsemen, who had been struggling through the coastal swamps all morning, came charging over the flat grasslands, cutting down Chontal foot soldiers with wild exhilaration. The warriors had no alternative but to withdraw.

The leaders of Potonchan counted their missing men, whose bodies lay strewn over the field of battle. They had lost over 220 warriors in only a few hours. Nothing comparable had ever occurred in all the histories recorded in stone or legend. They simply could not afford to keep up a fight like that. Even if in the end they could drive these men away, the battle would do them no good, for everyone in their world would learn of it. They would be left weak and defenseless, vulnerable to their enemies, having lost many hundreds of their own.[13] Moreover, it seemed likely that more of these strangers would arrive the following year. So it was that the Chontal sued for peace. One of the enemy, strangely enough, spoke some Yucatec Mayan, a language well known to the Chontal. He had been a prisoner on the peninsula for years. He said that his leader, Cortés, would forgive them if they made amends.

Among many other gifts, the Chontal leaders sent twenty slave girls down to the shore. The young woman from Coatzacoalcos was among them.[14] She watched as a man who was evidently a religious figure approached them in a costume different from that of all the others. He made gestures and murmured prayers of some kind, finally sprinkling water on each new arrival. Daughter Child's new name, she learned, was Marina. Her captors did not ask what her former name had been, nor did she tell them.[15] Almost immediately, she was presented to a confident, even arrogant man whom the others deferred to. She could not yet pronounce his name, but she heard that it was "Alonso Hernández de Puertocarrero."[16] Later she would learn what gave the man his authority among these people: he was first cousin to a nobleman, the Count of Medellín, across the ocean in the place called Spain. Cortés had been so excited to have someone of his stature along that he had given him a sorrel mare as a gift and would now present him with the most beautiful girl in the

group. Marina's spiritual baptism, it turned out, had simply been a preliminary to rape.[17]

Marina learned a great deal in the next few days. This wasn't only because
she was an astute observer who could hold her feelings in check. She found
she could speak easily to the foreigner named Jerónimo de Aguilar, who had
been relaying messages to the Chontal.[18] Over eight years earlier, when he was
about twenty years old, he had been aboard a ship that capsized near Cancun.
A good swimmer, he made it to shore. But then he was taken prisoner by the
Yucatec Maya and had labored as a slave among them ever since, learning
enough of their language to function. When Cortés arrived in the area where
he was living and learned of his existence, he ransomed him so that he might
serve as an interpreter, one who would be more loyal than any the strangers
had ever had. Aguilar did not speak Chontal, but Marina and some of the
other women spoke enough Yucatec Mayan that they could communicate
with him easily. Fortunately, Marina had a razor-sharp mind, and she soon
realized that there was a staggering amount of information that she needed to
absorb and process rapidly if any of it was going to be of use to her.

It seemed that the sea that surrounded their world was not boundless after
all. It was larger than she could imagine, but within about ten weeks' sailing
toward the rising sun, there lay a land full of people who worshipped a powerful god of their own. They called themselves *cristianos*, among many other
names. In any case, explained Jerónimo de Aguilar, his people were one group
among many who worshipped this same god. He himself was, he said, a
Spaniard, and it was the Spaniards who had first discovered this part of the
earth, this New World, and conquered and settled the great islands that lay a
few days to the east in the Caribbean Sea. At first the Spaniards thought that
they had reached the islands off the coast of a place called Asia, such as the
famed Cipangu (Japan), or perhaps India. The explorer called Columbus was
so convinced of this that he had named the people he met "Indians," and the
name stuck. After more than ten years, the newcomers had acknowledged
that what they had found was not Asia, but a landmass hitherto unimagined
by anyone. They sent out many exploratory expeditions from the Caribbean
and kidnapped a number of interpreters. They thought they had learned that
on this mainland there was a rich nation somewhere to the west. It was important that they find it, Aguilar added, for there were now about five thousand
Spaniards living in the Caribbean, and there simply was not enough wealth
for all of them. Over four hundred men and another hundred or so servants
and retainers had come away with Cortés on his expedition, convinced as
they were that better things awaited them over the western horizon. They

would be grievously disappointed and therefore dangerous, at least to their own leaders, if they did not find what they sought. But Hernando Cortés had no intention of letting them taste such bitterness.[19]

In the days after peace was made with the Chontal, the two sides did a brisk business together, the Spaniards presenting goods they had brought for the purpose in exchange for food. The priest they had with them said mass. Jerónimo de Aguilar may have tried to explain some of what he was talking about, but it would have been difficult. Later, a linguistically talented missionary would try to translate Hail Mary into an indigenous language. He heard the murmured words in his head: *Hail Mary, full of grace. The Lord is with you. Blessed are you among women and blessed is the fruit of your womb, Jesus. Holy Mary, Virgin, mother of God, pray for us sinners. Amen.* He tried to convey these words in an utterly foreign tongue to people who were completely unfamiliar with any of the ideas. He struggled. "May you be joyful, oh sainted Mary, you who are full of *gracia.*" He left just that one word in Spanish; it was too difficult to translate. He went on, "God the king is with you. You are the most praiseworthy of all women. And very praiseworthy is your womb of precious fruit, is Jesus. Oh Saint Mary, oh perfect maiden, you are the mother of God. May you speak for us wrong-doers. May it so be done."[20] The much less articulate Jerónimo de Aguilar could not even have gotten this far. As they listened, the Chontal looked non-committal, but politely kept their impatience to themselves. When they were given a chance to speak, they said nothing about God or his mother. Instead, they worked to convince the Spaniards that the type of tribute they sought could best be delivered by the Mexica, to the west.

On the day that the Spaniards called Palm Sunday, they took to their ships with the twenty enslaved women and headed west. About three days later, they passed near the land of Marina's birth, drawing into the entrance to the Coatzacoalcos River at the foot of the Tuxtla mountains. This place, however, seemed to be of no interest to her new masters. They sailed on, and she watched the coast of her homeland recede once again in the distance. A day later, they anchored at a point that had been charted by the previous year's expedition, on the site of today's Veracruz.

Within half an hour, two canoes approached the flagship of the fleet, which bore Cortés and Puertocarrero and their Indian servants. Moctezuma, they would later learn, had ordered that this spot be watched since the strangers had visited it the year before.[21] Cortés called for Jerónimo de Aguilar and asked him to translate. The man tried. In his desperation, he may even have considered feigning comprehension, but that could only go so far. Aguilar spoke Yucatec Mayan well enough, but unbeknownst to him, the expedition had now left Maya territory. He was hearing Nahuatl and could make nothing of it. Cortés grew angry. He had gone to a great deal of trouble and expense to ransom the castaway, and the man had assured him he could speak to Indians. Now it seemed he couldn't, after all.

The young woman now named Marina did have alternatives. She could have remained silent. No one expected a young slave girl to step forward in that moment and become an international conduit. But she chose to explain what the Nahuatl speakers were saying. By the end of that hour, she had made her full value felt. Afterward, Cortés claimed that he took her aside along with Aguilar, and promised her "more than her liberty" if she would help him find and speak to this Moctezuma of whom he now had heard so much. He meant that he would make her rich; it was what he promised everyone who agreed to help him.[22] But it is doubtful that Marina acted out of any interest in the riches promised by an interloper whom she had no real reason to trust. Her motivations would have been quite different. As it was, she was the concubine of Puertocarrero—a man with so few morals that he had once even abandoned a Spanish girl whom he had persuaded to run away with him. When he tired of his Indian slave girl, or when he was killed, Marina would be passed on and might even become the common property of all the men. Alternatively, she could speak aloud, earning the respect and gratitude of every Spaniard there, especially their leader. If she did that, the group might survive longer, and she along with them, for if she rendered it possible for them to communicate with the local people, she could help stave off battles, gain important information, and aid them in trading more efficiently for food. She does not seem to have hesitated. Within days, the Spaniards were calling her "doña" Marina, a title reserved for highborn ladies in Europe. Over the months to come, she proved herself to be both courageous and charming; she even managed to laugh at times.

Mexicans today generally consider Marina to have been a traitor to Native American people. But at the time, if anyone had asked her if she should perhaps show more loyalty to her fellow Indians, she would have been genuinely confused. In her language, there was no word that was the equivalent of "Indians." Mesoamerica was the entire known world; the only term for "people native to the Americas" would have been "human beings." And in her experience, human beings most definitely were not all on the same side. The Mexica were her people's enemies. It was they who had seen to it that she was torn from her family, and their merchants who had sold her in Xicallanco. Now this relatively small group of newcomers wanted to make war on the

Mexica. No one in her world could have imagined that she owed loyalty to the Moctezuma's people. While she lived, and for many years afterwards, no one expressed surprise at the course she chose. Only modern people who lacked knowledge of her situation would later say that she was some sort of traitor.

Gradually, Marina and others of her generation did begin to understand that the people on the American side of the ocean were profoundly different in some regards from the people on the other side of the sea, and that the former were eventually going to lose to the latter. None of them, however, could see that at first contact. The indigenous people struggled with categories and eventually began to refer to themselves as *nican titlaca* (NEE-kan tee-TLA-kah, "we people here"), whenever they needed to distinguish themselves as a whole from the outsiders who were arriving. Moctezuma's messengers, for example, told him that the interpreter the strangers had with them was not one of the ones from across the sea, but rather "one of us people here." They explained that she was from the eastern lands; they never meant that she was "one of us" in the sense of being one of the Mexicas' own. It would not have occurred to them to expect any loyalty from her, any more than they would have from anyone else whom they had made war against.[23]

In the first few days after Cortés discovered that he had such a marvelous translation chain at his disposal, he worked hard to convince Moctezuma's messengers that he needed to be taken to meet their lord in person. Meanwhile, the emissaries worked hard gathering information and preparing their report. Sometimes they questioned Cortés though Marina and Aguilar; sometimes they spied on the Spanish encampment, watching them race their horses up and down the hard-packed sand of low tide. Soon they decided they had as much information as they could glean easily, and they departed.[24]

The Spaniards covered themselves with stinking grease to try to ward off the mosquitoes that swarmed them, driving them nearly mad. And then they waited.

***

MANY YEARS LATER, it would become an accepted fact that the indigenous people of Mexico believed Hernando Cortés to be a god, arriving in their land in the year 1519 to satisfy an ancient prophecy. It was understood that Moctezuma, at heart a coward, trembled in his sandals and quickly despaired of victory. He immediately asked to turn his kingdom over to the divine newcomers, and naturally, the Spaniards happily acquiesced. Eventually, this story was repeated so many times, in so many reputable sources, that the whole world came to believe it. Moctezuma was not known for his cheerful disposition. Even he, however, had he known what people would one day say, would certainly have laughed, albeit with some bitterness, for the story was, in fact, preposterous.[25]

What really happened when the messengers returned with their report was that he sent scouts out to every important town between Tenochtitlan and the coast, and then set up a veritable war room. This is exactly what one would expect him to have done, given his history as a ferociously successful tlatoani who believed whole-heartedly in order, discipline, and information. Years later, a man who had been young at the time remembered: "A report of everything that was happening was given and relayed to Moctezuma. Some of the messengers would be arriving as others were leaving. There was no time when they weren't listening, when reports weren't being given."[26] The scouts even repeated a summary of the religious instruction that was being regularly offered by the Spanish priest and translated by Aguilar and Marina. When the Spaniards later got to Tenochtitlan and tried to deliver a sermon to Moctezuma, he cut them off, explaining that he was already familiar with their little speech, his messengers having presented it to him in full.[27]

Only one European recorded the events in writing as they were unfolding— or at least, only one account from that time has survived. Hernando Cortés himself penned a series of letters that he sent back to the king of Spain between 1519 and 1525. These are our only existing direct source, all other commentaries having been written years later when their authors were older men and the events deep in the past. And in his letters, written on the spot, Cortés never claimed that he was perceived as a god.

The idea first appeared, albeit in somewhat incoherent form, in some writings by Europeans in the 1540s. Fray Toribio de Benavente wrote of the indigenous observers' purported understanding: "Their god was coming, and because of the white sails, they said he was bringing by sea his own temples." Then, remembering that he had earlier claimed that all the Spaniards were supposed to have been gods, the priest quickly added, "When they disembarked, they said that it was not their god, but rather many gods."[28] It was a deeply satisfying concept to this European author and his readers. In such a scenario, the white men had nothing to feel remorse about, no matter how much the Indians had suffered since their arrival. The Europeans had not only been welcomed, they had been worshipped. Indeed, could there be a European man living who *didn't* like the idea, who didn't feel flattered and pleased by the notion? In years to come, other invaders would try out comparable assertions. John Smith, for example, would claim that in Virginia, the local chief's daughter had been wildly in love with him and had been willing to sacrifice her very life for his. He didn't mention that when he had known her, she had been only ten years old. And interestingly, he only told the story of her adulation when she and her English husband had both been dead for years and couldn't possibly refute what he said; in the report he sent back to London during the period in question, he said nothing remotely similar. There are, in fact, numerous such tales in the annals of colonialism.[29]

In retrospect, the story of Cortés being mistaken for a god seems so obviously self-serving and even predictable that one has to wonder why it was believed for so long. In a fascinating turn of events, by the 1560s and '70s, some of the Indians themselves were beginning to offer up the story as fact. The first ones to do so were the students of the very Franciscan friars who had originally touted the idea. The young indigenous writers were from elite families, the same ones who, forty or fifty years earlier had lost everything with the arrival of the Spaniards. And they were longing for an explanation. How had their once all-powerful fathers and grandfathers sunk so low? They were intimately acquainted with both sets of people—their Mexica families and their European teachers. They knew them both too well to believe that their own people were simply inferior, necessarily weaker or less intelligent than Europeans. Their own personal experience taught them that this was definitely not the case.

Here, however, was an explanation. God had been on the side of the Christians, of course; their own immediate ancestors had been trapped by their own loyalty to a blinding faith, tragically imprisoned in their own religiosity. The students of the Franciscan friar Bernardino de Sahagún, author of the Florentine Codex, beginning in the 1560s and '70s, wrote down what no indigenous person had ever said before—namely, that their forefathers had been paralyzed even before 1519 by the appearance of a variety of terrifying omens. Interestingly, the stories they told bore a distinct resemblance to the narrations in certain Greek and Latin texts that were in the Franciscan school library.[30] They waxed eloquent in their tales of pillars of fire and a trembling king. A few pages later, the students turned to a new phase of the project and began to write down what certain old men who had actually participated in the events had to say, and then both the substance and the tone of their writings changed dramatically. They became much more specific and the indigenous people they described much more pragmatic. "At the first shot the wall did not give way, but the second time it began to crumble," someone remembered, for instance. Gone were the pillars of fire.[31]

The students weren't done with the subject of influential prophecies, however. They liked an idea that one of their teachers had offered, which was that the great schism that had occurred in ancient Tula, present in so many of their early histories, had really been a battle between a brutal leader who believed in human sacrifice and a peaceful one who did not—one who was in effect an early Christian, unbeknownst even to himself. The group that had wandered away to the east had been following the peaceful leader. If they decided the man's name was not Huemac, as a leading culture hero of numerous ancient stories was called, but rather Quetzalcoatl, as the former teacher fray Toribio was the first one to suggest, the story would work perfectly, as one of the many year signs associated with the god Quetzalcoatl corresponded to 1519. The mortal man could have become a god and been expected to return then. Unfortunately, the students got the matter a bit confused. From their people's own records, they knew of the arrivals along the coast in the two preceding years, and they said it was the second captain who was thought to be Quetzalcoatl returning from the east.[32] That one was actually Juan de Grijalva, sailing in 1518, not Cortés arriving in 1519. But no matter. The gist of the story was there, and it could be taken up in generations to come and embellished as much as future authors saw fit to do.

None of the original Nahua histories written down by the earliest generation of students in the privacy of their own homes had said anything like this. In fact, none of the elements ring true, given what we know about Mexica culture. The Mexica did not believe in people becoming gods, or in gods coming to earth only in one particular year, or in anybody having a preordained right to conquer them. They didn't consider Quetzalcoatl to be their major deity (like the Cholulans did) or originally associate him with an abhorrence of human sacrifice. When we add the fact that we can actually watch the story's birth and evolution in European-authored and European-influenced works, the case for its being a later fabrication seems closed.[33]

However, even if the notion that the Mexica mistook Cortés for the god Quetzalcoatl is discounted, the fact remains that they did refer to the Spaniards for a number of years as *teules*. Beginning a generation later, Spanish writers delighted in this, as it was a bastardization of the Nahuatl word *teotl*, meaning "god." But the word carried other connotations as well. In religious ceremonies, a *teotl* was a representative of the god, destined for sacrifice. In certain other contexts, the word implied strange and unearthly power, such as some sorcerers or priests might wield. At the time, the Europeans seemed to understand this: in an early letter back to Cortés, the Spanish king instructed him to take special care to convert the Indians' political leaders (their "señores," he said) as well as their priests (their "teules," he called them).[34] Later generations, however, forgot what the Spaniards had initially understood about the word's use, probably because they hadn't seen the chaos and confusion of the earliest interactions. In general, the Nahuas struggled to come up with terms that would apply to the Spaniards. In their world, everybody was named for the place from which they came (the Tenochca from Tenochtitlan, the Tlaxcalteca from Tlaxcala, the Culhuaque from Culhuacan, etc.). If a person's geographical origins were unknown, then it wasn't clear what to call him. The newcomers presented a problem in this regard. The only element that rapidly became clear was that the strangers considered themselves to be representatives of their god. That made sense to the Nahuas. Until they were certain what the name of the newcomers' god was—and the strangers used a confusing array of terms—it apparently seemed most logical to refer to them by a word that conveyed they were the representatives of a revered divinity.[35]

Their choice of labels apparently left even some of their own grandchildren believing that the white men really had been considered gods. The fact remained that those grandchildren desperately needed to come to terms with the conquest. That their ancestors had been benighted savages, as the Spaniards sometimes said, they knew to be false. But their ancestors could perhaps have made a mistake of this nature, and if they had, it might explain a great deal.[36]

Indigenous youths of the late 1500s had no way of knowing the deep history of either the Old World or the New. They had no way of knowing that in the Old World, people had been full time farmers for ten thousand years. Europeans had by no means been the first farmers, but they were nevertheless the cultural heirs of many millennia of sedentary living. They therefore had the resultant substantially greater population and a panoply of technologies—not just metal arms and armor, but also ships, navigation equipment, flour mills, barrel-making establishments, wheeled carts, printing presses, and many other inventions that rendered them more powerful than those who did not have such things. In the New World, people had been full-time farmers for perhaps three thousand years. It was almost as if Renaissance Europe had come face to face with the ancient Sumerians. The Mesopotamians were stunningly impressive—but they could not have defeated Charles the Fifth of the Holy Roman Empire working in combination with the Pope. Had the young indigenous writers of the late sixteenth century known all of this, it would have been a relief to their minds. But that relief was denied them. And so they participated in constructing a version of events that Moctezuma would have derided—but that he had no power to change from the land of the dead.

***

IN THE RAINY SEASON OF 1519, neither the Spaniards nor the Mexica knew what stories would someday be told about them. At the time, both sets of people had pressing realities to contend with. Neither could spare time or energy for philosophical musings about the future, historical memory, or the nature of truth.

First of all, the Spaniards were hungry. Marina bargained as effectively as she could. From the people living nearby, she bought cages full of turkeys, and some of the other women plucked and stewed them. She bought tortillas and salt, fruits and vegetables. The people grew used to dealing with her and sought her out. They did not have an "r" in their language, so they heard her name as "Malina." They added the honorific "-tzin" to the end, and it became "Malintzin," which sometimes came out as "Malintze." As the Spanish speakers did not have the "tz" sound in their language, they heard the "Malinchi" or sometimes "Malinche." Thus when they did not call her "doña Marina," they called her "Malinche," and so she has remained to historians ever since. What the Spaniards found disorienting was that to the various groups they dealt with, this woman seemed to be the most important member of their party. They did not even seem to see Jerónimo de Aguilar, and they called Hernando Cortés himself "Malinche," as if her name must be his name, too, though the Spaniards felt it should have been the other way around.[37]

Cortés knew he was dependent on Malintzin, and he did not like it. In his letters home to the king, he referred to her as little as possible. He might not have referred to her at all, but then his whole story would have been suspect, as there were moments where an interpreter simply had to have been present in order for events to have transpired as they did. What Cortés did not want others to realize was that if Malintzin hadn't been there, they could not have succeeded. Of course, it was possible that if she had not appeared when she did, someone else might have filled this role later. After all, women who had been ripped from their homes and had no love for the Mexica were now scattered all across Mesoamerica. But Cortés had been especially lucky, and on some level he knew this. Not all women who hated the Mexica spoke both Nahuatl and Yucatec Mayan. And of those who did, not all of them were the daughters of noblemen and spoke with such finesse, with the ability to understand and use the high register of the nobility, which even had its own grammar. Nor did all of them have such a subtle understanding of complex situations. It soon became clear that Malintzin actually had a special gift for languages. She began to learn Spanish from Jerónimo de Aguilar, without a blackboard or a grammar book. Within a few months, she no longer needed her teacher at all.[38]

In the meantime, she helped Cortés to lay his plans. Messengers came back from Moctezuma twice, each time bearing gifts and promising more in the future, but also categorically refusing to escort Cortés and his party to Tenochtitlan. There was a drought, said Moctezuma's emissaries, and the king could not entertain them in the style to which they were undoubtedly accustomed. Cortés, however, was absolutely determined to get there. He had decided that he would either conquer this city, or if that was impossible, then he would trade for marvelous goods and bring back specific intelligence of the place to Spain; in either case, he would be hailed as a great discoverer. Undaunted, he considered what he had learned from some nearby Totonac villagers and from Malintzin herself—namely, that Moctezuma had many enemies who would help him in his travels. He could proceed by making his way first to a rebellious Totonac town, and then go on to Tlaxcala, where the people hated the Mexica. There, his forces would have access to food and water and other support.

There was a serious obstacle, however—namely, that he had left the Caribbean without the governor's permission, so he was, technically speaking, an outlaw.[39] The governor had at first assigned him to go on an exploratory expedition, which was the reason that more than four hundred landless men had flocked to join him. At the last moment, however, the governor began to fear that Cortés planned to exceed his authority and attempt to establish some sort of fiefdom on the mainland, one that would cut the governor out of all the profits. He sent a messenger to convey that he was revoking his permission. What could Cortés do but leave immediately and pretend he had never received the word? (The messenger himself he dealt with by bribing him to come along to find the rumored land of riches.) Yet even if his venture into the heart of the mainland succeeded, he was still liable to be arrested when he returned. Even the permit he pretended to believe was still in effect only gave him the right to explore, nothing more.

Cortés knew Spanish law well—some historians even believe he had attended law school for a while—and he clearly had been trained by a notary. He knew that the Spanish legal apparatus was based on the idea that an organic unity of purpose bound together a leader and his subjects. Any leader, even a king, could be set aside by "all good men of the land" if he was behaving outrageously. In that case, the good men of the land were not traitors when they refused to obey, but were acting instead for the common good. Cortés therefore needed a citizenry to demand that he lead them in settling the land. He arranged for all the Spaniards present to band together and sign a document insisting that they found a Spanish town (it was to be called the Villa Rica de la Vera Cruz, or the "Rich City of the True Cross"), and that he lead them where they wanted to go—which was to Tenochtitlan.

There was more to do, however, before they set out. Cortés asked Puertocarrero, the most influential man on the expedition because of his high social status, to return to Spain and speak directly to the king, in order to ensure that the Caribbean governor not prejudice him against their case too much. This was not just a maneuver on Cortés's part to get rid of the man who kept him from having Malintzin all to himself. Crucially, Puertocarrero's high status meant that he could take responsibility for sending more men, supplies, horses, and arms. Five hundred Europeans could not bring down the Mexica, but Renaissance Europe could, so Cortés needed to make sure that more of mainland Europe was on its way to support him. At this point Puertocarrero and his party left. Finally, Cortés ordered that the remaining ships be beached. They weren't permanently destroyed, but leaving would now be a major undertaking requiring many weeks of repair work. It was a way of preventing discontented men from easily going home.[40]

With this done, Cortés led the ascent from the hot coastal lands up into the mountains. Two Totonacs guided them toward Tlaxcala. They entered a pine wood, where it was unexpectedly cold at night. Many of the men weren't dressed for it, and a few of the enslaved Indians the Spaniards had brought from the Caribbean died after a drenching rain with hail. At length the path began to lead downhill, into a valley. There they came upon a nine-foot-high wall built of stone, stretching to the right and left as far as they could see. It was shaped like an extended pyramid: at its base, it was twenty feet across, and at the top it culminated in a flat walkway only a foot and a half wide. This, it seemed, was the Tlaxcalan border. Despite the forbidding boundary, the Totonacs continued to insist that all would be well. The Tlaxcalans, they explained, truly hated the Mexica, for although they had remained independent, they had done this by participating in the dreaded Flower Wars against them for years.[41]

The travelers soon found an opening in the wall, and Cortés along with half a dozen men rode forward to explore. They soon caught sight of about fifteen warriors up ahead and called out to them. Cortés sent one of the riders galloping back in case reinforcements were needed, and then he and the others approached the Indians. Suddenly, hundreds of warriors seemed to rise out of nowhere and surrounded them completely. Cortés actually claimed it was thousands in his letter home, but he always exaggerated numbers for dramatic effect whenever anything went wrong; it wouldn't have been possible for the Tlaxcalans to have placed a guard of thousands at the entrance, given their total population. In any event, two of the horses were killed and their riders gravely injured before more of the Spanish cavalry approached and the

Tlaxcalans retreated. Cortés had learned a crucial lesson: a handful of armored men was not enough to withstand an onslaught, not even if they were mounted on horseback. His men simply had to move in larger groups in order to remain relatively invulnerable.

Late in the day, some Tlaxcalan messengers arrived. They apologized for the incident and blamed it on foolish and rambunctious Otomí who lived in their territory. They claimed to desire friendship and asked to tour the impressive camp. Malintzin had misgivings; she wasn't sure what to expect.

A huge Tlaxcalan force attacked at daybreak. The Spaniards were ready for them, and with their armor on, they could inflict more casualties than they received, but they were weakened from their travels and distraught at this reception. They had to fight without food or respite all day long, surrounded by a sea of enemies who only withdrew when darkness made it impossible for them to tell friend from foe. That night, Cortés took the thirteen remaining horsemen galloping over the plain to the nearby hills, where lighted fires signaled the presence of villages. "I burnt five or six small places of about a hundred inhabitants," he later wrote to the king.[42]

The next morning, the Tlaxcalan warriors attacked once more, in such numbers that they were able to enter the camp and engage in hand-to-hand combat. It took four hours for Spanish armor and weaponry to drive them back. This time, the Spanish even used their guns, which were really tiny cannons that couldn't be aimed well but could scatter grapeshot with deadly effect. "The enemy was so massed and numerous," commented one of the Spaniards later, "that every shot wrought havoc among them."[43] Many dozens of Tlaxcalan men died that day, each one swept up into the arms of his comrades and carried from the battlefield. Yet only one Spaniard died.

Before dawn the next day, Cortés once again led the horsemen rapidly out of the camp, this time in the opposite direction. "I burnt more than ten villages," he reported. For the next two days, the Tlaxcalan chiefs sporadically sent emissaries suing for peace, but they somehow sounded unconvincing, perhaps because no gifts were forthcoming. Cortés tortured one of them, demanding the truth through the interpreter, Malintzin—who was quickly ascertaining that the Christian god was not truly one of peace. The emissaries learned nothing, and Cortés cut the fingers from the hands of a number of them, so that "they would see who we were," as he said, and then sent them home.[44]

The Indians attacked again, and again were driven back. After a few days of silence, Cortés took his now-rested horsemen out again during the hours of darkness. "As I took them by surprise, the people rushed out unarmed, and the women and children ran naked through the streets, and I began to do them some harm."[45] He had Malintzin on horseback with him and had her shout aloud that the strangers offered peace and friendship, if they chose to accept it. Something she said convinced them, for the war ended that night. Peace talks began in earnest in the morning.

Tlaxcala was in effect four countries in one. The altepetl consisted of four well-populated sub-altepetls. Each had its own king, but they were so tightly bound by intermarriage and tradition that they remained an unbreakable unit in their relations with outsiders. So it was that they alone had been able to resist Mexica aggression. For many years, they had been allies with nearby Cholula and Huexotzinco, but recently these two, facing the possibility of destruction by Moctezuma, had gone over to his side and fought against the Tlaxcalans. The Tlaxcalans remembered proudly that they had gotten word of the defection while they were playing a ball game and then had roundly defeated the Huexotzincan traitors. "We pursued them right to their own homes," they bragged in their annals.[46] Their courage notwithstanding, they were still surrounded by enemies, their trade routes cut off. The Mexica could not bring them down without losing more men than they could spare, but they did not really need to, because they could use the traditional enmity to fuel the ritual Flower Wars that often ended in death.

Over the years, the Tlaxcalans' survival had depended on their ability to prove that their warriors were the match of anybody's. Although they would have been aware of the approach of an expedition of over four hundred strangers, they would not have had a ring of spies and messengers bringing them detailed reports or anyone to explain to them ahead of time the newcomers' hope that they would help bring down the Mexica. It fell to Malintzin to convey the situation to them. Fortunately, until the recent wars had cut them off, Malintzin's people in Coatzacoalcos had been among Tlaxcala's trade partners. She apparently presented herself as a gracious and authoritative noblewoman, for they decided that they could trust her.

The Tlaxcalans brought the Spaniards to the imposing palace of the tlatoani Xicotencatl (Shee-ko-TEN-kat) of Tizatlan, one of the two largest sub-altepetls. There, they offered the newcomers women, ranging from princesses whom it was intended the lords should marry, to slave girls meant as a form of tribute. Cortés gave the most important princess—a daughter of Xicotencatl himself—to Pedro de Alvarado, a charismatic man with a bright blond beard who was one of his lieutenants. One of the minor lords' daughters was given to Jerónimo de Aguilar, and the rest were distributed to other men in the company who were proving their worth in the eyes of Cortés. Not many years later, Tlaxcalan artists painted a record of the politically important event on

Tizatlan's palace walls and made another copy on bark paper. They wished the early alliance to be recalled in perpetuity. Strings of young women being given to the Spaniards, together with the names of the most important ones, looked out from the painting; they personified the treaty of alliance that the Tlaxcalans believed had been made.[47]

Meanwhile, Cortés was bargaining for more through the women. He wanted several thousand warriors to go with him to Tenochtitlan. The Tlaxcalans agreed. It was the kind of alliance they had had in mind when they offered Xicotencatl's daughter as a bride to one of the strangers' leaders. When the company set out, it was at least three times larger than it had been before. It gave the appearance of an army of victory.[48]

***

AT THIS POINT, Moctezuma decided he could not delay any longer what he had so dreaded having to do. He sent messengers offering annual tribute—including gold, silver, slaves, and textiles—to be delivered as the strangers desired. The only provision was that they not enter his lands, as he could not host so large a company. Moctezuma and his council assumed that this arrangement was what the foreigners' sought. It was certainly what the tlatoani himself would have sought in like circumstances. He had hesitated to make the offer before because it would constitute such a drain on his resources, and he had hoped there might be another way of turning the newcomers aside. What he absolutely could not afford, politically speaking, was a confrontation with such a force anywhere close to home. He knew from his sources that the strangers won their battles. Even if he collected a mighty army and did manage to bring them and their allies down, his kingdom would still be lost, for the casualties would be immense, beyond anything calculable from past experience. And if he could not deliver an easy victory at the heart of his kingdom, his allies would not continue to stand with him. Under no circumstances could the Mexica be made to appear weak in the central basin; it would be political death to them. Moctezuma could not afford a battle; he did not even want the strangers to come close enough for comparisons to be drawn. In later years, scholars would delight in arguing that Moctezuma did nothing at this point because he was paralyzed by some aspect of his culture which the scholars could perceive and specify (he was relying on man–god communication rather than man–man, or perhaps unable to fathom warfare to the death) but there is no genuine evidence that overwhelming fatalism had anything to do with it. Moctezuma had, as he had always had throughout his adult life, a pragmatic agenda.[49]

However, his plan failed. The strangers and their newfound friends, the Tlaxcalans, turned down his offer of tribute and continued to approach. They stopped in Cholula, now a subject town of Moctezuma's. He gave orders to the Cholulans that they not feed the strangers well. It seems that he also commanded them to attack the party as they left the city, when they would be forced to pass through certain narrow ravines as they entered the ring of mountains surrounding the central valley. At least, Cortés claimed that Malintzin gathered this news from an old woman who lived in the city. It is eminently logical that Moctezuma would have done this: Cholula was the last stop outside of the central valley, and the town was a new ally. He had little regard for the lives of the people who lived there, and if their attack failed, he could easily dissociate himself from it, both in his own people's eyes and those of the Spaniards. But perhaps he was too cautious to order a confrontation even this close to home; we cannot be sure. Whether he wanted a battle or not, the Tlaxcalans were spoiling for a fight. They had not forgiven the recent turncoats in Cholula. If they could bring down the present chiefly line and install one more sympathetic to Tlaxcala, the result would be of lasting benefit to them. It may, indeed, have been the Tlaxcalans who planted the story of the planned attack, and the Spaniards were merely their dupes. However it came about, the Spaniards and the Tlaxcalans combined forces in a terrible rampage. The temple to Quetzalcoatl was burned—Quetzalcoatl was the primary protector god of the Cholulans—as were most of the houses. "The destruction took two days," commented one Spaniard laconically.[50]

That business done, the combined Spanish and indigenous force moved on. They safely traversed the mountain pass between the volcano Popocatepetl (Smoking Mountain) and the snow-capped Iztaccihuatl (White Woman) and entered the valley. As they approached the lakeside towns at the center, the Spaniards—as well as many of the accompanying Indians—began to feel a sensation of awe. A Spaniard named Bernal Díaz wrote of his impressions many years later: "These great towns and cues [pyramids] and buildings rising from the water, all made of stone, seemed like an enchanted vision from the tale of Amadís." (Amadís was a legendary knight, and a book about him had recently become a best seller in Spain.) "Indeed," the Spaniard remembered, "Some of our soldiers asked if it were not all a dream." When the men stopped to rest at the town of Iztapalapan, they were literally stunned. The lord's palace there rivaled buildings in Spain. Behind it a flower garden cascaded down to a lovely pond: "Large canoes could come into the garden [pond] from the lake, through a channel they had cut....Everything was shining with lime and decorated with different kinds of stonework and paintings which were a marvel to gaze on.... I stood looking at it, and thought that no land like it would ever be discovered in the whole world."[51]

Bernal Díaz was writing these words as an old man. He had reason to feel a bit maudlin as he thought of his lost youth, and then also recalled all that had happened since. At the end of the paragraph, he almost visibly flinched with shame. "Today all that I then saw is overthrown and destroyed; nothing is left standing."

***

ON THE MORNING of November 8, 1519, the Spaniards and the Tlaxcalans crossed the wide, clean-swept causeway that led straight to the city. Cortés rode on horseback towards the front of the cavalcade; Malintzin, her small shoulders squared, walked at his side. Moctezuma had wisely decided to handle the situation by putting on a grand show of two brother monarchs meeting. At the gate at the edge of the island, hundreds of dignitaries had gathered, including multiple representatives of each of the central altepetls. Each person in turn stepped forward and made the gesture of touching the ground and then kissing the earth upon it. The joint performance was a classic Nahua method of expressing the strength of a united body politic. The chiefs were nothing if not patient as they carried it through. But Cortés was different. "I stood there waiting for nearly an hour until everyone had performed his ceremony," he said huffily.[52]

Then Cortés and his company were led across a bridge and found themselves looking at a broad, straight avenue leading to the heart of the metropolis. It put the tiny, mazelike streets of European cities to shame, and the small downtown area of Tlaxcala also paled in comparison. For the newcomers, there was a moment of doubt as they tried to make sense of the scene, and then the various elements resolved themselves before their eyes. Not far down that wide sun-lit road, there stood a royal company, which now moved toward them. Every man there was dressed in bejeweled cloaks, and at the center came Moctezuma, the tlatoani, speaker for his people. Anyone could see that he was the high king. Over him his retainers held a magnificent canopy, a great arc pointing toward the sky, its bits of gold and precious stones glinting in the light.[53] It was as if he carried with him a reflection of the sun itself.

5

A War to End All Wars

1520–1521

The smell of the burning bodies was rank in the air. But worse was the smell of the *miccatzintli*, the poor dead woman who had not been moved for days. She lay where she was, because there was no one left in the palace strong enough to cope with the problem. The sickness, like nothing ever seen before, had struck not long after the unwelcome strangers had been forced to leave Tenochtitlan. Now Moctezuma's young daughter looked at her sisters lying with her on the soiled sleeping mats. They were still alive. When they looked back at her, their dark eyes reflected her own terror. Their faces, their arms, all their parts were covered with the vile sores. But they were beginning to heal; they did not seem to be at the point of death. Not like before, in the fevered haze, when she thought she knew they were all perishing, all disappearing—it was the same word.[1]

***

NONE OF THE royal children had ever known a day's hunger until now. Even through this scourge, they had had good care as long as there were any servants left to tend to them: their good fortune had helped them survive. It helped that they were grown girls, too. Later, Moctezuma's daughter would find that her younger siblings—children recently born to the newest wives— had died.[2] Nor were they the only ones gone. Others had been "erased"—as she would have described it—weeks before the pox struck. Two of her brothers had been accidentally killed when she herself was rescued from the

---

Temples burn in war. The Bodleian Libraries, the University of Oxford, Codex Mendoza, MS. Arch. Selden. A.1, folio 6r.

strangers,[3] the night the Spaniards were ejected. People said that her father, the Lord Moctezuma himself, had been found strangled by the Spaniards like a common criminal.[4] It was probably true. However it had happened, he was gone, as were the others. Like the heroes in the songs, they would never come back. Time on earth was fleeting, the singers always said. "Are we born twice on this earth?" the singers called out when people died. And the chorus knew the tragic, angry, tear-laden response, "No!" The child understood what they meant now.

Tecuichpotzin (Tek-weech-PO-tzin, Lordly Daughter) was about eleven years old.[5] She had experienced so much horror in the past year that her mind had almost certainly chosen to forget some of it, as she needed to use the wits she had left to make it from day to day. It had been a joyous moment when the Spaniards left, when they were pushed out of the seething, resentful city and forced to flee for their lives. If she had known then that the ordeal was far from over, that the worst was yet to come, she might not have found the fortitude to forge ahead and join her people in putting their world back together. But she was eleven, with a child's zest for living, and she had her beloved sisters at her side. And of course she had not known that the sickness stalked them. So when the Spaniards left, she—like all the other women—reached for a broom and began the holy act of sweeping.[6] She swept the cobwebs, both literal and figurative, out the door.

***

HAD ANYONE ASKED Tecuichpotzin, she undoubtedly would have said that the problems had started even before the strangers and their Tlaxcalan allies had crossed the causeway into her world. Her father's temper had been frayed for months before that moment, as he had struggled to determine the best course of action. He could not afford the casualties of a battle with the newcomers so close to home, in front of all their allies. His offers of tribute, no matter how great or dedicated to what god, had proven ineffective in turning the marching army from its course. Eventually he determined that there was nothing to be done but to welcome them, even act as though he expected them—and gather as much information as he could. There had been tensions from the earliest moments of their arrival when Hernando Cortés dismounted from his horse, took a few steps forward, and made as if to embrace Moctezuma. The tlatoani's shocked retainers had stepped forward quickly to prevent such marked disrespect. They waited nervously as gifts were exchanged. Cortés presented a necklace of pearls and cut glass. Moctezuma signaled that a servant bring forth a necklace of red snail shells, hung with beautifully crafted shrimp made of gold. Then he gave orders that the new-comers follow him, as he would speak with the leaders indoors.[7]

To this day we do not know exactly what the great men said to each other. Tecuichpotzin did not hear what passed between them; few did. A year later, Cortés made the remarkable claim that Moctezuma had immediately and contentedly surrendered his kingdom to the newcomers, on the grounds that an ancestor of his had gone away generations before, and that he and his people had long expected that his descendants would return and claim the kingdom. Cortés added that a few days later (because he doubted that he really had full control) he had placed Moctezuma under house arrest and never let him walk free again. Cortés's statements would be utterly mystifying—except that they were absolutely necessary for him to make at the time. When he wrote of these events a year later, the Mexica people had ousted him and all his forces from the city. At that point, he was desperately trying to orchestrate a conquest from near the coast, in conjunction with indigenous allies and newly arrived Spaniards. He did not want to look like a loser, but instead like a loyal servant to the Spanish monarch who had already accomplished great things and would soon do more. According to Spanish law, he was only in the right in launching this war in the name of the king . . . if in fact he was attempting to retake a part of the kingdom that was in rebellion. He had no authority to stir up trouble by making war against a foreign state that had just ejected him. Thus it was essential that the Mexica people were understood to have accepted Spanish rule in the first place, so that their present choices could be interpreted as acts of rebellion.[8]

When Cortés's men wrote about these events in later years, they often forgot what they were supposed to say. Cortés, for example, claimed that his control had been complete from the beginning, and he asserted that he had ended human sacrifice. "While I stayed . . . I did not see a living creature killed or sacrificed." But Bernal Díaz admitted, "The great Moctezuma continued to show his accustomed good will towards us, but never ceased his daily sacrifices of human beings. Cortés tried to dissuade him but met with no success."[9] Another man seemed to remember mid-paragraph that Moctezuma was supposed to have been their prisoner. "[His people] brought him river and sea fish of all kinds, besides all kinds of fruit from the sea coast as well as the highlands. The kinds of bread they brought were greatly varied. . . . He was not served on gold or silver because he was in captivity, but it is likely that he had a great table service of gold and silver."[10]

It is more than likely that Cortés had heard about the Mexica history of schisms and migrations through Malintzin or perhaps others. Moctezuma knew well that his own ancestors were invaders and that there had been other waves of invaders, some of whom had moved on or turned back. It would make sense for him to believe—or at least seem to believe, in front of his people—that the strangers were other descendants of his own fearsome ancestors, in short, that these visitors were long-lost relatives, whose existence did not surprise him at all. Such a scenario makes perfect sense. But we can't know with any certainty what really passed in that first conference between the Mexica tlatoani and the men from Europe. All that the children of the indigenous elites ever mentioned was that Moctezuma recounted his own ancestral lineage in great detail, before calling himself the newcomers' "poor vassal." If he really said that, then he was only underscoring his great power in the speech of reversal that constituted the epitome of politeness in the Nahua world. It certainly would not have been an indication that he actually intended to relinquish his throne without further ado.[11]

What is clear is that Moctezuma continued to govern in the weeks and months that followed, and that he treated the strangers, even the Tlaxcalan leaders, like honored guests, despite the drain on his resources that feeding so large a company entailed. He persistently questioned them through Malintzin. The Spaniards toured the city, rudely demanding gifts everywhere they went. Their hosts remembered them chortling and slapping each other on the back when they saw Moctezuma's personal storehouse and were told they could take what they liked. The Spaniards took beautiful gold jewelry and melted it down to make bricks; the Tlaxcalan warlords preferred polished jade. Moctezuma showed the strangers maps and tribute lists in an effort to get them to name their price and go away. He clearly hoped to convince them to leave and to have established the most favorable possible relationship with them by the time they did.[12]

Tellingly, Moctezuma sent for Tecuichpotzin and two of her sisters to be turned over to the newcomers as potential brides. It was a test. If the strangers treated them only as concubines and not as brides, it would be bad news, but he would at least know where he stood. The royal sisters, presented in all their finery, kept their eyes down and maintained a respectful silence as their elders made the requisite rhetorical speeches and Malintzin listened.[13] The translator learned that Moctezuma had a number of older daughters who were already married into the royal houses of Chalco, Culhuacan, Tlacopan, and other important altepetls. These three daughters were the girls presently of marriageable age. The mother of two of them was the daughter of the Cihuacoatl, the leading military commander.[14] The mother of Tecuichpotzin, or Lordly Daughter, was a daughter of the former king Ahuitzotl, so this child's marriage was of great political significance, as her heritage brought together both the rival branches of the royal family, the one descended from Huitzilihuitl and the one descended from Itzcoatl.[15] Moctezuma kept the existence of a younger sister of hers a secret from the Spaniards, so that they did not even know of her until years later. Perhaps he thought she might be useful as a political pawn some day in the future, or her Tepanec mother had insisted on hiding the girl, or both. Another young boy, the child of a woman from Teotihuacan, was also purposely hidden from the Spaniards.[16]

Malintzin managed to convey to the strangers—utterly ignorant of the complex politics of marriage in this part of the world—that Tecuichpotzin was the daughter of a high-ranking mother and thus a princess of significance. This they understood. When they baptized her, they named her Isabel, in honor of Queen Isabella, who had launched the first ships to the New World. They called the other girls "María" and "Mariana."[17] Then they were taken away to live with the Spaniards in their quarters in Axayacatl's former palace. What happened to them there is undocumented, but some of the Spaniards later said that Cortés violated multiple princesses during those early years; and other, less public figures than Cortés would never have been brought to account for anything they might have done.[18]

The weeks of tension dragged on. Then in April of 1520, the situation changed dramatically. Moctezuma received news from his network of messengers that at least eight hundred more Spaniards in thirteen ships had arrived on the coast.[19] The Spaniards did not yet know. The tlatoani eventually decided to tell them, in order to gauge their reaction. He gave the news to Malintzin, who turned to tell Jerónimo de Aguilar, who said the words aloud in Spanish. Cortés could not hide the panic he experienced in that moment.

***

WHEN ALONSO DE PUERTOCARRERO had sailed from Veracruz, the plan had been to make straight for Spain. But one of the Spaniards on board had lands and loved ones on the north coast of Cuba. Stopping briefly at his plantation had proven irresistible. They left within just a few days, but word soon spread. The angry governor, Diego de Velázquez, made a futile effort to overtake the scofflaws on the high seas, and he brought in for questioning all those who had learned anything during the ship's brief stopover. Velázquez, who had once led the brutal conquest of the island of Cuba, now decided that he was extremely concerned about the violence Cortés had inflicted on the Indians along the Maya coast. He wrote of his concerns to the king, and assured him he would immediately send Captain Pánfilo de Narváez in pursuit of the renegade. Narváez had been his second-in-command in the taking of Cuba and now held a legal permit to explore the mainland. Unlike Cortés, he said, he would establish a suitable relationship with the people there.

Puertocarrero docked in Spain on November 5th, and the letter from the enraged Cuban governor arrived shortly after. Puertocarrero and other speakers on behalf of Cortés's expedition—such as his father, Martín Cortés—did their best to defend the operation in the king's eyes. They delivered all the gold and other exotic treasures the expedition had been able to collect along the coast. Some of the material was sent on tour for exhibition throughout the realms of the Holy Roman Emperor. In July, in the town hall in Brussels, the artist Albrecht Dürer saw some of the tiny, lifelike animals the indigenous people had made out of gold. "All the days of my life," he wrote, "I have seen nothing that rejoiced my heart so much as these things, for I have seen among them wonderful works of art, and I have marveled at the subtle intellects of men in foreign parts." The stories, of course, traveled even faster than the exhibit—many of them full of wild exaggeration. Unbeknown to him, Cortés became a famous man in Europe. His father immediately began to outfit a shipload of supplies. Ships and printing presses ensured that the news passed from port to port in weeks rather than years, a speed that was to make a huge difference. Within months, there were people in every part of western Europe considering the possibility of investing in the newly discovered lands or even going there themselves.[20]

***

IN THE MEANTIME, across the sea, both Cortés and Moctezuma were busy assessing future possibilities. Cortés knew that his messengers had not been gone long enough to have sent the many well-outfitted ships so rapidly. The recently arrived fleet had to have come from his would-be nemesis, governor Velázquez. Somehow, either through Malintzin or some other Nahua who was learning Spanish—perhaps even Tecuichpotzin—Moctezuma learned of Cortés's tension and the reason for it. He detected an opportunity to divide the Spaniards and, hopefully, defeat them. For the first time, he ordered his people to begin preparations for war—though he could not have been entirely certain which group of the outsiders he would initially side with.[21]

In desperation, Cortés risked all by doing what he only claimed he had done before: he took Moctezuma hostage—literally put him irons, where he would remain for about eighty days.[22] Only with a knife at Moctezuma's throat could Cortés assure the newly arriving Spaniards that he was in control of the kingdom and thus hopefully win their allegiance. And only in doing that could he stave off a violent rejection on the part of the Indians: this was a tried-and-true practice of medieval Spanish warfare.[23] The Spaniards took Moctezuma by surprise, dragged him back to their quarters, and guarded him around the clock, threatening to kill him if he ordered his people to resist. Then Cortés took Malintzin and a substantial portion of his men and traveled with haste down to the coast.[24]

Once there, they sent messages and bribes to key men in Narváez's camp, assuring them that they were welcome to join them in dividing up the riches of Mexico if they chose. At the end of May, they attacked the camp suddenly in the middle of the night. The fighting was brief—only about ten men died—for once the obstreperous Narváez was captured, few others seemed to have the heart to go on with the battle. They reached an accord almost immediately. Cortés now had approximately eight hundred more men armed with steel, eighty additional horses, and several ships full of supplies at his disposal. Now he could truly bring down Moctezuma, he thought. They even had wine from home with which to celebrate.

On the twelfth day, however, as Cortés was in the midst of making plans and arrangements, some Tlaxcalans brought Malintzin a devastating piece of news. The people of Tenochtitlan were in open rebellion. The Spanish forces had turned Axayacatl's palace into a fortress, but they could not hold out much longer. They had every reason to believe it was the beginning of the end. The next day, two more Tlaxcalans arrived, this time carrying a smuggled-out letter from the Spaniards. Cortés remembered reading it. "I must," they begged, "for the love of God come to their aid as swiftly as possible."[25]

They set out at once. The trek up into the mountains was more than a little disconcerting. "Not once in my journey did any of Moctezuma's people come to welcome me as they had before," Cortés wrote. "All the land was in revolt and almost uninhabited, which aroused in me a terrible suspicion that the Spaniards in the city were dead and that all the natives had gathered waiting to surprise me in some pass or other place where they might have the advantage of me."[26] Later he would learn that a much smaller group that had traveled separately, whom he had dispatched before receiving the bad news, had in fact been attacked in a mountain pass, imprisoned, and eventually killed down to the last person—and animal. This group had included Spanish women and children, enslaved Africans, and other servants carrying burdens and leading livestock. Despite what Cortés had learned about the need for numbers and cavalry, they had been sent ahead because they would travel more slowly and would need more time to cover the same ground. As it turned out, they paid for their commander's arrogant decision with their lives.[27] Cortés's own force was large enough to be relatively invulnerable while on the move. No one tried to stop them, not even when they reached the city. They passed easily through the silent streets to Axayacatl's palace, where they were greeted by their compatriots with great joy. It was to be the last laughter the Spaniards shared for quite some time, for the next morning, the Mexica attacked.

The signs of trouble had begun three weeks earlier. The resentment of the city's people had become evident when they stopped delivering food to the strangers. A young woman who had been paid to do their laundry was found dead near their quarters, a clear sign to others not to do business with them. The Spaniards sent clusters of armed men to the market to obtain food, and they stored what they brought back. Meanwhile, the city people were preparing for an important holy day, the celebration of Toxcatl, at which the altepetl's warriors danced before a huge figure of the god Huitzilopochtli. Pedro de Alvarado, who had been left in charge, said that he began to fear they planned to use the dance to launch a war. This seems highly unlikely; there were far more efficient ways for the Mexica to overcome the Spaniards, as events would later prove. But Alvarado was not known for his acumen. Perhaps he simply believed that a struggle was coming and that whoever attacked first would secure victory. In that case, he sought only an excuse, and the days of warlike dancing provided one.[28]

What followed was etched in the altepetl's memory for many years to come. Thirty years later, a survivor told a young listener what had happened:

> The festivity was being observed and there was dancing and singing, with voices raised in song. The singing was like the noise of waves breaking against the rocks. When . . . the moment had come for the Spaniards to do their killing, they came out equipped for battle. They came and closed off each of the places where people went in and out [of the courtyard]. . . . And when they had closed these exits, they stationed themselves in each, and no one could come out anymore.
>
> When this had been done, they went into the temple courtyard to kill the people. Those whose assignment it was to do the killing just went on foot, each with his metal sword and leather shield. . . . Then they surrounded those who were dancing, going among the cylindrical drums. They struck a drummer's arms; both of his hands were severed. Then they struck his neck; his head landed far away. Then they stabbed everyone with iron lances and struck them with iron swords. They struck some in the belly, and then their entrails

came spilling out. . . . Those who tried to escape could go nowhere. When anyone tried to go out, at the entryways they struck and stabbed him.[29]

Yet a few did escape, for it was they who told posterity what had happened. They hid where they could. "Some climbed up the wall and were able to escape. Some went into the various [surrounding] calpolli temples and took refuge there. Some took refuge among those who had really died, feigning death. . . . The blood of the warriors ran like water."

That evening, Mexica warriors raised their cry promising vengeance. The Spaniards and those Tlaxcalans who were still in the city walled themselves into their "fortress" and waited. The Mexica attacked en masse, but they couldn't penetrate the wall of crossbows and steel lances. Then suddenly, they ceased their attack. For more than twenty days, they left the Spanish alone in silence and uncertainty. Thirty years later, an old man recalled what they had been doing. "The canals were excavated, widened, deepened, the sides made steeper. Everywhere the canals were made more difficult to pass. And on the roads, walls were built, and the passageways between houses made more diffi-cult."[30] They were preparing, in short, for a cataclysmic urban battle. During that period, Cortés and his army reentered the city and made their way back to their quarters.

When the warriors were ready and felt the strangers had grown hungry enough, they attacked. For seven days, Tecuichpotzin and her sisters listened to the sounds of battle—to the rising murmurs and then shouts of their own warriors, and then the noise of the harquebuses (a heavy matchlock weapon) firing grapeshot among them, and the hissing crossbows slinging forth iron bolts or whatever came to hand. The fighting began anew every day at dawn as soon as it was light enough to see. The Spaniards could not escape, but the Mexica could not penetrate their defenses, either. At length Moctezuma tried to speak to the people from a rooftop, conveying his words through the booming voice of a younger man who served as his mouthpiece. His message went something like this:

Let the Mexica hear! We are not their match. May the people be dis-suaded [from further fighting]. May the arrows and shields of war be laid down. The poor old men and women, the common people, the infants who toddle and crawl, who lie in the cradle or on the cradle board and know nothing yet, all are suffering. This is why your ruler says, "We are not their match. Let everyone be dissuaded."[31]

In later years, these words were taken out of context and used to try to prove that Moctezuma was a coward, interested only in saving himself. But all the old histories and prayers make it clear that the Nahuas understood a ruler to have one paramount duty—and that was to save the lives of his people, down to the youngest babies, so that the altepetl could continue into the future. A ruler who lost his head, or who was arrogant and stubborn and committed his people to unwinnable wars, was the lowest of the low. He did not have a chief's wisdom, the perspective of a true leader.[32] Moctezuma had eighteen years of experience as a ruler of tens of thousands of his people and was well aware of how many of the people around them hated the Mexica. Furthermore, he had spent the last half year conversing in depth with Malintzin and the Spaniards, and he knew that many more of the strangers were coming. He understood that in this case, no victory would be permanent. He was simply telling his people the truth as he saw it.

The young warriors, however, did not see the situation this way. It was not their duty to be circumspect but rather to fight to the death, if necessary, to defend their honor. A younger half brother of Moctezuma, the militant Cuitlahuac of Iztapalapan, emerged as the de facto leader of the city's enraged young men. The long-term consequences of their actions were not uppermost in their mind. What they knew was that they could endure no more. Speaking through Malintzin, Cuitlahuac's messengers informed Cortés in no uncertain terms of how things stood:

> They were all determined to perish or have done with us, and . . . I should look and see how full of people were all those streets and squares and rooftops. Furthermore, they had calculated that [even] if 25,000 of them died for every one of us, they would finish with us first, for they were many and we were but few. They told me that all the causeways into the city were dismantled—which in fact was true, for all had been dismantled save one—and that we had no way of escape except over the water. They well knew that we had few provisions and little fresh water, and, therefore, could not last long because we would die of hunger if they did not kill us first.[33]

Cortés understood that escape from the island city offered the Spaniards their only hope of survival. There was one causeway left still connecting the isle and the mainland, but the segments connecting its separate segments had been destroyed, so that it was impassable. They would not let this stop them: some of the men worked all through one night constructing a portable bridge out of whatever wood they had available. Others packed the most important tools and valuables, including the gold they had collected for King Charles. Cortés organized a guard of thirty men who would surround and escort Malintzin and the Tlaxcalan princess "Luisa" (the nobleman Xicotencatl's daughter, now the common-law wife of Pedro de Alvarado), the two women being at this point the Spaniards' most valuable assets. He also ordered that "Isabel" and her siblings, Moctezuma's children, were to be taken along as hostages. According to the Indians, this was the moment when he commanded that Moctezuma be killed, lest the tlatoani serve as a rallying point for his people, though Cortés himself never admitted he had done so. He insisted that the angry young warriors had killed their own king.

Before midnight on the seventh day, the Spaniards suddenly broke through the gates of the palace in what was at first an organized body; they then traveled as quietly as possible down the avenue that became the causeway over the lake. The portable bridge served them well at the first place they found themselves facing open water, but they were unable to pick the bridge up and move it to the next location where it was needed. They went forward with only some wooden beams they had taken from the palace to help them with the next crossings. Some later said it was a woman who first saw them and shouted aloud, sounding the alarm. Warriors in canoes descended on their fleeing enemies from all sides: they were intent on destroying the makeshift bridges and stabbing upward at the armored horses on the causeway, as they were vulnerable from below. They killed fifty-six of the eighty or so horses that night. At the second place where the causeway was broken—and where there was no bridge, just a few boards—the escaping forces drowned in droves. The Mexica later recalled what the Spanish never spoke of: "It was as though they had fallen off a precipice; they all fell and dropped in, the Tlaxcalans . . . and the Spaniards, along with the horses and some women [they had with them]. The canal was completely full of them, full to the very top. And those who came last just passed and crossed over on people . . ."— they hesitated over the words—". . . on top of the bodies."[34]

Approximately two-thirds of the Spaniards died that night, and probably an even greater proportion of the many Tlaxcalans still in the city, about six hundred Europeans and many more Indians. Cortés estimated the dead at two thousand, including the indigenous.[35] Almost all of the men who had come with Narváez were killed, for most of them were in the rear. The only ones who stood a good chance of surviving the ordeal were those who departed first. They had surprise on their side, and the makeshift bridges were still in good condition. Those who came later faced a disaster zone. Bernal

Díaz, who had a horse at that time, had been ordered to act as a rear guard. When he was old, he still struggled with his conscience whenever he thought of the "Noche Triste," as it was called, for he had certainly not remained behind until the bitter end. "I declare that if the horsemen had waited for the soldiers at each bridge, it would have been the end of us all: not one of us would have survived. The lake was full of canoes. . . . What more could we have attempted than we did, which was to charge and deal sword thrusts at those who tried to seize us [from below], and push ahead till we were off the causeway?"[36] They had lost everything—the gold, their guns, most of the horses. But the few hundred who were left still wore their armor, still had their swords—and could not be easily attacked if they stayed together. And they still had Malintzin and the Tlaxcalan princess. It was toward Tlaxcala that they now turned.

Cortés was told that all the Mexica hostages, including Isabel and her siblings, had been killed in the mêlée, but that was not the truth. The girls had been recognized, and their people surged forward to help them. Isabel's brothers had, in fact, accidentally been killed. Later, as the people collected the masses of bodies, "they came upon Moctezuma's son Chimalpopoca lying hit by a barbed dart."[37] But Isabel was pulled into the arms of her people, along with her sisters, and taken to Cuitlahuac.

Then, in a matter of weeks, the smallpox struck.

***

LA VIRUELA HAD COME ABOARD one of Narváez's ships as an invisible passenger, perhaps in a scab in a blanket. Or perhaps it was carried by a man who did not know he was sick until they landed, since the ten-day incubation period was longer than the voyage from the Caribbean. In essence, the microbe was part of the panoply of military advantages that had accrued to the Old World. The people had always lived with their farm animals, exposing themselves to myriad viruses, but then the highly developed trade and transportation routes had spread the germs with deadly efficiency. The only silver lining was that those who did not die of a particular pest were immune from it for the rest of their lives. And in this regard, their vulnerability suddenly became a source of strength when they met the people of the New World. Most of the Europeans had been exposed to the smallpox before, and they were, in effect, inoculated. But the indigenous were a previously unexposed population, utterly without defenses.[38]

When the pox reached a new altepetl, the wave of death rose for about sixty days, in some places taking as many as a third of the people. Then the epidemic receded, for by that time there was no unexposed person left to contract the disease. It had been carried to surrounding towns, and so the wave arose somewhere else. It had already reached Tlaxcala by the time the Spaniards and their surviving allies had dragged themselves back there. Maxixcatzin (Ma-sheesh-KAH-tzeen), one of the four kings, was dying of it, along with many thousands of his people. Those leaders who were able came together for a series of great council meetings; there they debated for twenty days. Many saw the Spaniards as a plague of hungry grasshoppers who had come in a time of sickness; they pointed out that the strangers' war-mongering had already cost the lives of hundreds of young Tlaxcalan warriors. These leaders were for killing the Spaniards, finishing the job that the Mexica had started. But others reminded the more militant that they knew from their own experience that twenty-odd horses and a few hundred Spaniards could inflict extraordinary damage. And the woman who the strangers called doña Luisa—the Tlaxcalan princess who was in a relationship with Pedro de Alvarado—informed the men in council that the Spaniards who were here were but the forerunners; thousands more were coming. Malintzin likewise agreed that it would be wisest to stay the course, cement the alliance, and use the victory they would ultimately attain to gain the upper hand over Tenochtitlan. Eventually, this side carried the day.[39]

The Spaniards were in bad shape. The Mexica had harried them at several points, so that they had to travel in a tight cluster, with the horsemen surrounding those on foot. Whenever they stopped to rest, they established lookouts in every direction. They had found that most of the villagers fled before them, afraid not only of Spaniards but also of what the Mexica would do to them if they were thought to have helped them. The beleaguered travelers ate the supplies they found in the abandoned altepetls; they even ate a wounded horse when he died. By the time they found succor in Tlaxcala, many of their wounds had festered, and more men died. Cortés himself needed to have two fingers on his left hand amputated.

While they rested, Cortés and his closest companions discussed their options. Some were for making for the coast and either leaving or regathering their strength there. But Cortés was convinced that they should do the opposite, that they should stay where they were and make a show of strength. The Mexica had many enemies, but they had some friends, too; perhaps more importantly, they had the entire the countryside living in fear of them. If the Spaniards were going to gain and keep enough indigenous allies to secure a permanent victory, they had to be perceived as the strongest force in Mexico, the one group most feared on a long-term basis, not a group who would soon leave. They could not be just another playing piece on the chessboard of local politics; they had to be by far the most frightening figures in the game.

Through Malintzin, Cortés gathered intelligence from the Tlaxcalans. Whenever a nearby altepetl was found to have entertained emissaries from Tenochtitlan, he gathered his horsemen and made another one of his famous early morning raids. The Mexica let it be known that they were offering a year's tribute relief to all who refrained from going over to the strangers— implicitly reminding everyone that they were the leaders who were there to stay and that they wouldn't forget who their friends and enemies were after these interlopers were forced to withdraw. But that was a distant reward compared to the immediate threat of having mounted lancers ride through town, burning and killing with impunity. Meanwhile, the Spaniards also offered to reward those who came over to them. "They see," wrote Cortés in the midst of these events, "how those who do so are well received and favored by me, whereas those who do not are destroyed daily."[40] Malintzin, who had always counseled that responsible leadership entailed caution, circumspection, and peaceful overtures toward the powerful strangers, would have reminded all those to whom she spoke that if they swore loyalty to Cortés's king, the Mexica would be destroyed, and the endless wars between the altepetls would cease forever. The Mexica had been strong enough to guarantee peace among their subjects in the central basin, but these newcomers were far stronger. It was a foregone conclusion that the Spaniards would ultimately be victorious, went the argument for laying down arms, for they had the edge, and they weren't leaving. Their victory would prevent future chaos and retaliatory wars throughout a much larger swath of land than just the central valley.

More of the indigenous were gradually learning what Malintzin and Moctezuma had understood months before—that far more Spaniards were coming, and would bring more of their arsenal with them. While resting in Tlaxcala, Cortés had forced every man to turn over whatever gold he possessed so it could be collected and used to buy horses and weapons in the Caribbean. He then sent a number of mounted men to the coast, charged with repairing one of the boats and setting forth to make the purchases. They found to their delight that seven more ships had already arrived. One came from Cortés's father, who had been working to collect goods for his son since his message first arrived with Puertocarrero. Early the next year, three more fully stocked ships appeared. Cortés grew increasingly jubilant. "When on the 28th of April [1521], I called all my men out on parade and reckoned eight-six horsemen, 118 crossbowmen and harquebusiers, some 700 foot soldiers with swords and bucklers, three large iron guns, fifteen small bronze field guns and ten hundred weight of powder, . . . [we] knew well . . . that God had helped us more than we had hoped."[41]

Word spread quickly among the local communities about the present strength of the Spanish forces. We know that they were always assessing whether or not to believe Malintzin's argument from various incidents. At one point after the war had actually started, the Spaniards lost a battle: several dozen men were cut off from their company and then captured and killed. Some of the indigenous allies withdrew at once, but they soon returned. Spaniards later said that they returned because their priests had augured a great Mexica victory within the next eight days, which did not occur, and thus the people lost faith in their priests. That may have been part of the reason for their return to the Spaniards' side. After all, in one of their own histories— indeed, one of the earliest written, probably in the 1540s—the indigenous writer recalls the people's profound disappointment on another occasion when some priests promised them a victory on the eightieth day, which never occurred, and in fact the promise only cost them more lives. But in this case, something else had occurred: messengers had come from the coast carrying word of the arrival of yet another ship, and they brought powder and cross-bows as proof, which would have been visible to any indigenous who were spying on them. Almost immediately, in the words of Cortés, "all the lands round about" made the decision to return to their erstwhile allies.[42]

Many altepetls—or rather, certain lineages within altepetls—needed little convincing to throw in their lot with the strangers. Due to old internal tensions, these family lines and their followers were ready and willing to fight with the powerful newcomes. In Texcoco, for instance, Moctezuma had only recently worked to dispose of undesirable heirs to the throne to make way for his nephew, Cacama, and Huexotzincatzin had been executed for singing with the Lady of Tula. Some of Huexotzincatzin's full brothers had accepted bribes in the form of land. Yet since the death only a few years before of the old king, Nezahualpilli, the altepetl had literally been split in two, as the youngest brothers of Huexotzincatzin, the executed poet-heir, had emerged as a potent force and had been given—or had taken—the northern half of the realm. One of these younger brothers, Ixtlilxochitl (Eesh-tlil-SHO-cheet), an extremely successful warrior, decided to seize the day and ally with the strangers in order to oust Moctezuma's favorite, Cacama, and unite Texcoco under his own and his full brothers' control. Cortés was delighted with him, calling him "a very valiant youth of twenty-three or twenty-four years" who worked hard to bring along "many chiefs and brothers of his." He admitted that the brothers were not at first "so firm in their friendship as they afterwards became." But thanks to the efforts of Ixtlilxochitl, thousands of Texcocans were soon fighting on the side of the Spaniards.[43]

In the meantime, as the Spanish forces waited for reinforcements and worked on creating alliances with the local people. Martín López, a ship-builder in their company, taught the Tlaxcalans how to build brigantines to sail on the great lake. Canoe makers, carpenters, ropemakers, weavers . . . all were needed. They built twelve different boats in pieces, and then, when the time was right, carried them to the shores of the great lake and assembled them there. The Tlaxcalans quickly learned to work the sails and maneuver the large, fast-moving boats. In later years, when they told their children about the conquest, this was what some of them mentioned first and recorded in their earliest annals.[44] It was an empowering, even thrilling experience, and it became an important long-term memory. In the short term, though, it meant that Cortés and his forces would never be dependent on the cause-ways again.

***

IN TENOCHTITLAN, TECUICHPOTZIN lived each day in fear. Her joy at being rescued from the strangers and seeing them in flight had been short-lived, for the terrible disease had come soon after her rescue, and her relief at seeing the epidemic abate had been even briefer. Cuitlahuac, her father's younger brother and the new tlatoani, had died of the smallpox after only some eighty days of rule.[45] With every family in the city devastated, they could not even mourn their ruler properly, as their religion demanded. The people did their best to regather their strength and rebuild, managing just day-to-day efforts. In the meantime, the man who emerged from the council as the new tlatoani was Cuauhtemoc (Kwow-TAY-moc). He was from the other branch of the family—the one descended of Itzcoatl—a son of the former king Ahuitzotl. He had a Tlatelolcan mother,[46] so he had Tlatelolco's support. And as the Tlatelolcans were the possessors of the big market on the north side of the island to which many local people were still bringing their produce, they had significant strength in these tumultuous times. Cuauhtemoc's election would have seemed appropriate to Tecuichpotzin at first, but within weeks, the full force of a new horror struck her.

Cuauhtemoc and his advisers understood all too well what was happening in the Mexican countryside—that despite their resounding victory in July, people far and wide were still considering allying with the strangers. The Mexica had not been too afraid that they would be attacked while they were laid low with the pestilence, for all the people in the country were affected by it at about the same time, including all the Spaniards' allies and potential allies. But the Mexica became afraid as the survivors recuperated and regained their full strength, for the season of warfare would start again soon. If they could not prevent the defection of the majority of the surrounding altepetls, then they would almost certainly be destroyed. Cuauhtemoc believed the only response was to make a show of brutal force.

Moctezuma's living sons were a threat to Cuauhtemoc and his policies. Two had died in the fighting on the night of the Spanish retreat, but a number were still alive. Cuauhtemoc had the support of most Tlatelolcans, but the sons of Moctezuma had the support of many, possibly most, of the Tenochca. Perhaps more importantly, these sons would have been taught by their father, Moctezuma, that overt warfare against these strangers was futile and counter-productive. They thus represented an opposing school of thought; they offered an alternative to the war that the city was undertaking. Fortunately for Cuauhtemoc, they were also vulnerable: these sons of Moctezuma could be presented as weak, as emblematic of the mistakes that had been made. That is how Cuauhtemoc went about describing them. Then, in short order, he had six of them killed; some said he even killed one with his bare hands. The Tlatelolcan noblemen—who held Cuauhtemoc entirely blameless—explained, "The reason these nobles were killed is that they were favoring the common people [in desiring peace] and trying to see to it that shelled white maize, turkey hens, and eggs should be collected so that they could have them submit to the Spaniards." Among those who were killed was Tecuichpotzin's only full brother, named Axayacatzin, after the past king. Now, Tecuichpotzin was left with only two living half brothers, little boys who had managed to survive the pox and were too young to be considered a threat.[47]

In the midst of the carnage, Cuauhtemoc came for Lordly Daughter Tecuichpotzin herself. He did not want to kill her, though. Instead, he wanted to marry her and make her bear his children. Doing this rendered his rule legitimate in many more people's eyes, for his heirs would thus be tied to both branches of the royal family. The union was in keeping with the custom of having a new tlatoani from a different branch of the family marry a daughter or another close relative of the man he had replaced. In this case, it was even more important that Cuauhtemoc have the girl by his side. Ever since she had been gifted to the strangers, her name was sometimes paired with that of their enemy, Cortés, by the people in the countryside, whenever they weren't pairing him with Malintzin (with whom they sometimes confused Tecuichpotzin, probably to the royal family's shame). It had to be shown that this symbolically important girl who carried both royal lines within her belonged to him, and to no one else. This he told her, in deeds if not in words.[48]

In the wider world, however, Cuauhtemoc's power remained far from absolute. Despite his ferocity—and he did bring many allies to the city, among them some of the loyal Texcocans, even some of the brothers of Ixtlilxochitl— he was unable to keep enough of the altepetls on his side. Gradually, as the Europeans' technological advantages won over the surrounding peoples, the city folk found themselves increasingly cut off from food supplies. Their isolation was not yet complete, but it was growing. They were grateful for their chinampas, for the birds and the fish and the algae in the lake, and for those who still flocked to their banners. Around the fire at night, they sang songs in celebration of loyalty.[49] And as weeks turned into months, they prayed.

Then one day, the enemy came. Though the Mexica had anticipated this, it was still somehow a shock. The strangers had been moving around in the local area for a number of months and had been seen assembling their boats across the water in Texcoco, on the eastern side of the lake. Still, everybody had assumed that their approach to the island would be a gradual affair. The people had not realized how fast the ships could move when in full sail with the wind behind them or how many people they could carry. One morning, the brigs made straight for the neighborhood of Zoquipan (or "Mudflats") on the island's shore. The residents ran about frantically, calling to their children. They tossed the little ones into canoes and paddled for their lives. The lake grew full of their craft, and the Spaniards and Tlaxcalans entered an uninhabited quarter. They looted it, then returned to their ships.[50]

Over the ensuing weeks, a pattern emerged. The foreigners used their cannon to knock down the walls that the Mexica had built as obstructions and even demolished whole buildings. Then they sent in their indigenous allies to fill in the canals with rubble or sand, while the long-range crossbows and guns guarded them. Once the Spaniards had access to a flat, open space, they could easily maintain control of it with their horses and lances. Every day, the Spaniards killed dozens of the Mexica at a minimum; once they killed several hundred in a single day. One of the warriors, when he was an old man, remembered: "Bit by bit they came pressing us back against the wall [at Tlatelolco], herding us together."[51]

The old one remembered other elements as well, especially how hard he and his companions had made the Spaniards' task. They contested every single foot of ground; at night, they sometimes managed to re-excavate canals that had been filled in. Famous warriors performed death-defying deeds and occasionally managed to topple a horse and bring down the rider. Twice they were able to isolate and bring down large groups of the Spaniards (once fifteen of them, once perhaps fifty-three). They sacrificed the prisoners atop the tallest pyramid in full view of their ashen compatriots, then strung their heads in a grisly necklace and left it hanging in the air. The courage of individual warriors sometimes stunned the younger boys who watched. On one occasion the Spaniards reached a neighborhood no one had thought they would reach until the next day. They began to seize the women and children who had not yet evacuated. A warrior named Axoquentzin (Ah-sho-KEN-tzeen) came running. His rage seemed to lend him superhuman strength. He ran out into the open and picked up a Spaniard and whirled him around until he dropped a girl whom he had seized. Then Axoquentzin picked up another man and flung him about. But this sort of action couldn't go on forever, and the Spaniards brought him down: "They shot an iron bolt into his heart. He died as if he were stretching out when going to sleep." Thirty years later, such stories lived on in the people's collective memory and in the songs they sang. The fearlessness of their greatest warriors made them deeply proud.[52]

At no point do the warriors seem to have been awestruck or paralyzed with fear by the strangers' weapons. Instead they analyzed them in a straightforward way:

> The crossbowman aimed the bolt well. He pointed it right at the person he was going to shoot, and when it went off, it went whining, hissing, and humming. And their arrows missed nothing. They all hit someone, went all the way through someone. The guns were pointed and aimed right at people. . . . The shot came upon people unawares, giving them no warning when it killed them. Whoever was fired at died if some dangerous part was hit: the forehead, the nape of the neck, the heart, the chest, the stomach or the abdomen.[53]

Unfortunately, when the Mexica secured some of the powerful weapons and tried to use them themselves, they were unable to do so. At one point, they forced captured crossbowmen to try to teach them to shoot metal bows, but the lessons were ineffective, and the arrows went astray. The guns, they soon learned, would not work without the powder the Spanish had. Once, when they captured a cannon, they concluded that they had neither the experience nor the ammunition needed to make it useful. The best they could do was to prevent it from falling back into enemy hands, so they sank it in the lake. They learned not only to make extra-long spears to rival Spanish lances but also to zigzag their canoes so quickly in unexpected patterns that the Spaniards could not easily take aim from their brigantines. Yet such tactics could not bring them victory; they could only hinder their enemies. The old men remembering their people's efforts found it too painful to say this directly, but one came close. "In this way, the war took somewhat longer."[54]

On one occasion the Spaniards decided to build a catapult, thinking that it would petrify the Indians. Cortés wrote: "Even if it were to have had no other effect, which indeed it had not, the terror it caused would be so great that we thought the enemy might surrender. But neither of our hopes was fulfilled, for the carpenters failed to operate their machine, and the enemy, though much afraid, made no move to surrender, and we were obliged to conceal the failure of the catapult by saying that we had been moved by compassion to spare them."[55] Here, Cortés was merely assuaging his feelings. The Mexica by no means believed his claim that only compassion stayed his hand, and in fact, for them, the incident bordered on the humorous:

> And then those Spaniards installed a wooden sling on top of an altar
> platform with which to hurl stones at the people. . . . They wound it up,
> then the arm of the wooden sling rose up. But the stone did not land
> on the people, but fell [almost straight down] behind the marketplace
> at Xomolco. Because of that the Spaniards argued among themselves.
> They looked as if they were jabbing their fingers in one another's faces,
> chattering a great deal. And [meanwhile] the catapult kept bobbing
> back and forth, going one way and then the other.[56]

But the moments the warriors could joke about were few and far between. The Mexica knew that they were losing. They had no way to explain the discrepancy between their power and that of their enemies; they had no way of knowing that the Europeans were heirs to a ten-thousand-year-old tradition of sedentary living, and they themselves the heirs of barely three thousand. Remarkably, through it all, they seem to have maintained a practical sense of the situation: they knew what needed to be explained. They did not assume greater merit or superior intelligence on the part of their enemies. Rather, in the descriptions they left, they focused on two elements: the Spaniards' use of metal, and their extraordinary communication apparatus. The old men talking about their experiences used the word *tepoztli* (metal, iron) more than any other in reference to the Spaniards: "Their war gear was all iron. They clothed their bodies in iron. They put iron on their heads, their swords were iron, their bows were iron, and their shields and lances were iron." They grew ever more specific: "Their iron lances and halberds seemed to sparkle, and their iron swords were curved like a stream of water. Their cuirasses and iron helmets seemed to make a clattering sound."[57] When the elderly speakers paused in wonder at the events, it was to ask how the word had gone out so efficiently to so many people across the sea about their marvelous kingdom.[58] The warriors had seen the ships—but not the compasses, the navigation equipment, the technical maps, and the printing presses that made the conquest possible. What is striking is how quickly they realized that these issues were at the heart of the matter.

***

THE FIGHTING LASTED for three months, far longer than the Spaniards would have thought possible, given the effects of the smallpox and the starvation to which the Mexica were ultimately reduced. Once, after more than four weeks of war, the warriors shouted to the Tlaxcalans that they wished to speak to the woman, she who was one of the people from here. When Malintzin came, they offered full and immediate peace—on condition that the Spaniards would return to their home across the sea. "While we stood there arguing through the interpreter," Cortés remembered, "with nothing more than a fallen bridge between us and the enemy, an old man, in full view of everyone, very slowly extracted from his knapsack certain provisions and ate them, so as to make us believe that they were in no need of supplies." The Mexica went on to outline terms—undoubtedly giving the specifics of the tribute they would offer—for they stood in conversation for some time without having Malintzin pause to translate. It was agreed that she would summarize afterwards. "We fought no more that day, for the lords had told the interpreter to convey their proposals to me," said Cortés. He rejected those proposals in the morning.[59]

The Mexicas' efforts to demonstrate that they were not short of courageous warriors or of food supplies could not mask the truth for long. By August 13, their remaining corner of the city had come almost to a standstill. "On the roads lay shattered bones and scattered hair. The houses were unroofed, red [with blood]. Worms crawled on the roads, and the walls of the houses were slippery with brains."[60] The survivors had eaten everything they had, down to deer hides and tiny insects and lizards, and even softened adobe bricks. Dysentery was now widespread among them. Cuauhtemoc went to the Spaniards in a canoe and gave himself up, together with some close advisers and his wife, Tecuichpotzin.[61] He asked only that his people be allowed to go to the countryside to seek food. The fighting stopped, and word spread among the populace that they could walk out, go to family in other altepetls if they had any, or bring precious possessions to trade for food, or simply beg.

Those who were children at the time remembered the feeling of release, the surge of hope and joy as they sped along the broken causeways or waded and swam across the lake with surviving adults. The young ones heard cries of lamentation in the distance, as some of the adults gave vent to their grief, and some saw young women being seized by individual Spaniards despite the agreement.[62] But the children couldn't help feeling happy at this change in their fortunes. They did not understand as yet that their world as they knew it was ending. A hollow-eyed Tecuichpotzin watched them go.

6

Early Days

1520s–1550s

The walls of the adobe houses burned slowly, as the tongues of flame sought wooden beams. But the resistance of the humid mud did not effectively slow the disaster, for the thatched roofs went up in a great blaze, and then came crashing downwards, destroying everything in the homes below. The inhabitants had emerged screaming as the mounted Spaniards set their village alight. They stood and watched as all their worldly goods crackled and disappeared. Some cried; some were too stunned to react. The riders, whom everyone knew had been sent by the prior of the nearby Franciscan mission, thundered off into the distance.[1]

***

THIS WAS A moment in 1559, in a town to the east of Mexico City. The Spaniards had been in the region for more than thirty years, but until now their presence hadn't been very meaningful to most of the villagers. One of the old men nearby had grown too blind to see much, but the sounds and smells told him everything. He was an aging chief, still known to his people as Chimalpopoca ("Smoking Shield," like one of the Mexica kings of old), but years earlier he had taken the official name of don Alonso de Castañeda, after one of the first Spanish conquistadors to come to the area. He and a number of other community leaders had spent much of the last two years attempting

A boy paddles his acalli, or canoe. The Bodleian Libraries, the University of Oxford, Codex Mendoza, MS. Arch. Selden. A.1, folio 63r.

to convince the local villagers that the Spaniards really meant it when they said the people must now leave their rural hamlets and move to the larger town of Cuauhtinchan (Kwow-TIN-chan), where they could be more efficiently turned into Christians, taxed, and generally kept in line. Those who resisted were to be burned out. Now it had happened in the little village of Amozoc. On this dreadful day, Chimalpopoca would have reflected on all the years of his life, both before and after the arrival of the Spaniards. Many in his generation faced comparable moments of crisis, of course, but Chimalpopoca is unique in that he left us records of his experiences and even, to some extent, his thoughts. A few others who came of age before the arrival of the Spaniards are quoted in the works of younger men, but Chimalpopoca orchestrated the writing of a book that survives to this day.[2]

The man's anguish must have been intense, for over the years, Chimalpopoca—or don Alonso de Castañeda—had worked ever more closely with the Spaniards, on the firm understanding that if he did so, the perennial local warfare would end, and his people would cease to suffer. The burning of Amozoc was not exactly what he had had in mind. He did not lose control of himself, however. He had lived many years and had a long memory; he knew that the morning would bring a new day. He would try to help his people get through these times. Their children and their children's children still constituted the future of the altepetl, whatever they had lost in their village.

Political crises and war had predated the arrival of the Spaniards, and this was not the first time that don Alonso had been a witness to pain. One of his formative memories was of the murder of his father and uncle, long before the arrival of the "strangers to us people here." It was a long story, and he was not averse to telling it on starlit evenings.[3] His ancestors had come from a place far to the north at the invitation of other Nahuas who were already intermarried with the long-settled people of Cholula. His people helped the Cholulans defeat their enemies, and, as a reward, had been allowed to settle on the still wild lands to the east, where eagles soared but few people lived. They even named their new home Cuauhtinchan, meaning "Home of the Eagles." Most of the clans continued to intermarry with the Cholulans, but a few, living on the far reaches of their new settlements, forged closer bonds with the peoples farther east who did not speak Nahuatl but a language called Pinotl (its speakers Pinome). Those eastern sub-altepetls were the minority voices in Cuauhtinchan, and they grew tired of their subordinate status. Eventually, in the second half of the 1400s, one of their chiefs made a strategic alliance with the Mexica of Tlatelolco, asking them to come and intervene. Then the Pinome chief quickly gained the upper hand, and his group began to take over the lands of all the others and demand payments of tribute (part of which they in turn had to pay to their new godfathers, the Tlatelolcans).[4]

Chimalpopoca's father, Cotatzin, was born into one of the Nahuatl-speaking chiefly families still closely allied with Cholula; they were among those who were weakened when the eastern upstart made his alliance with the Mexica. In 1510, when Cotatzin had only recently inherited the chieftainship of his family's set of villages, he was invited to the home of Tozcocolli, the Pinome chief who was now the paramount chief of all of Cuauhtinchan, by a messenger who spoke with extreme courtesy. The optimistic Cotatzin went to Tozcocolli's village. It turned out to be a mistake. "The murderers were already there," his son later remembered, and they strangled him. Another brother—who apparently responded to the sight with belligerence—fared even worse. He was placed on the cutting stone but not treated with the honor of a true sacrifice to the gods. Chimalpopoca—a child then—always remembered, "When they cut his breast, they did not quickly take his heart out. They stopped in the middle. So he went into convulsions before he died." Yet another brother of the murdered chief, Tecuanitzin ("Man Eater"), Chimalpopoca's uncle, took over the rulership of the sub-altepetl and wisely said nothing about the lands of his people that Tozcocolli had usurped or about the murders. Most likely he had a different mother than Cotatzin, making it easier for him to accept the situation. Indeed, he might even have been in league with Tozcocolli.[5]

Ten years later, the ruler Tecuanitzin, too, was dead, but not from treachery. He died of the foul disease that spread not long after the mysterious strangers arrived in the land.[6] When he died, no one in Chimalpopoca's world had actually seen the newcomers, for the sickness moved faster than the foreigners. However, gossip about them was already rife. The first concrete news that the people would have heard was that strangers had allied with the people of Tlaxcala to destroy their beloved Cholula, home of Chimalpopoca's grandmothers. Then the new enemy moved on to Tenochtitlan, whence they were eventually ejected. Word of that event spread far and wide. Cholulans celebrated and with them, Cuauhtinchan. Not long after that, however, the great smallpox epidemic broke out, carrying off thousands from Cuauhtinchan, including the chief, Tecuanitzin. Chimalpopoca was a strong young man by then, and he survived the disease. In this time of trouble, he took his uncle's place and became chief of his family's set of villages, one of the major sub-altepetls of Cuauhtinchan.

Less than a year later, in 1521, word came that Tenochtitlan had fallen to the Spaniards. Like much of central Mexico, the people of Cuauhtinchan waited tensely, wondering what this would mean for them. It was not many months before the Spaniards arrived—alongside their battle-hardened Tlaxcalan allies, who were showing the newcomers the way to all the key alte-petls that needed to be defeated if their victory were to be considered secure.[7] Some of the local chiefs might have celebrated the fall of the Mexica, but they could not celebrate the arrival of the Tlaxcalans, who had waged such brutal war against Cholula. The men of a number of altepetls in the region gathered together to make a stand. This was a subject upon which Chimalpopoca did not like to dwell in later years. "We were defeated," he said tersely, using a form of the verb that implied absolute destruction. "We all withdrew to the marshlands."[8] As Nahuas had so often done in the past after great losses—as when Shield Flower's father had been defeated in 1299—the people went to hide in the swamps. There, they elected emissaries to approach the Tlaxcalans and the strangers and thus sue for peace. They had already heard that their enemies were accompanied by a woman from the eastern lands who not only spoke their own language perfectly but could also communicate with the strangers. Yet they were not reassured by this, for in their experience commu-nication was not always effective in bringing peace. Sometimes, emissaries were simply killed.

Hiding with his surviving people among the reeds, Chimalpopoca waited. The messengers reappeared. They could all return to their homes, they announced, if they agreed to deliver annual tribute to an overlord, who would be one of the newcomers, people from a place called Castile. "What was the tribute?" they asked. A certain number of woven blankets, gold pieces, and turkeys, as well as a goodly supply of corn. Smoking Shield considered his options. He sent the emissaries back to get more specific numbers and to work out an exact measuring unit for the corn, a basket size that both parties recognized as the right amount.[9] When he received clarification on the terms, he agreed. This was a tribute payment his people could realistically make. The survivors went home to their villages. They were hopeful that, after mourning their dead, they would be able to pick up their lives and carry on. And for a few years—like most of Mexico—they did just that.

***

AT THAT POINT in the early 1520s, the eye of the storm was not the rural hinterland but Tenochtitlan, the City of Mexico as the Spaniards called it, and its immediate surroundings. The Spaniards still made their camp across the water from Tenochtitlan in the lakeshore town of Coyoacan, since Tenochtitlan itself was in shambles. "Our lords the Christians had not yet come to settle here," a man who lived near the island's marketplace remembered later. "They gave us consolation by staying for the time being in Coyoacan."[10] The level of chaos in the early months of foreign governance was horrifying. The Spaniards were only able to maintain some semblance of order by ruling through the indigenous elites; in Mexico City, this meant ruling through Cuauhtemoc. He was kept in a locked room and heated rods were applied to the soles of his feet when he claimed not to know where his forebears' stores of gold were held. If Tecuichpotzin, or Isabel—still a girl but rapidly growing into a woman—had ever feared her husband, she could only pity him now. The two of them heard that in the beautiful towns of Texcoco and Xochimilco, the Spaniards loosed their giant dogs and even let the mastiffs kill some of the men when the people there likewise denied knowing where the treasure hoards were. In altepetl after altepetl, the translator Malintzin was made to stand on a parapet and shout orders to bring the treasure; then she had to watch the punishments meted out if the Spaniards judged that the orders were not obeyed.[11]

The conquerors seemed to be in a veritable frenzy to amass riches and generally please themselves. When not enough gold and jewels were forthcoming, they began to brand prisoners of war they had collected—undoubtedly including some of Smoking Shield's compatriots from the battle in Cuauhtinchan—and marched them to the coast for shipment to the Caribbean as slaves. In 1522, one-fifth of the profits of this venture (5,397 pesos, as the meticulous records specified) were set aside as tribute for King Charles. The Spaniards kept the prettiest of the captive young women for themselves; other starving girls whose families had been destroyed came to them voluntarily. In at least one case, a group of these girls was kept locked in a building in forced prostitution. Conscience-stricken observers of the treatment meted out to the girls told tales back in Spain, and in June of 1523, the king issued a plea to his people that they rein themselves in and cease their abuse of the native women.[12]

By then, the situation had calmed down somewhat; Cortés had begun to make progress in imposing order and constructing a new political apparatus. The market at Tlatelolco reopened and a relatively normal urban life resumed. Spanish artisans were training crews of indigenous men in Tenochtitlan—it was Cuauhtemoc and the translators who had to use their moral authority to make sure that the crews showed up—and the workers learned astonishingly quickly to construct fine examples of European Renaissance buildings. The great central square of Tenochtitlan became the Plaza Mayor, flanked by a newly rising cathedral, as well as a massive government building with battlemented towers at either end. The sound of hammering could be heard morning to evening. By 1524, the Spaniards would be ready to relocate their center of operations from Coyoacan to the City of Mexico.[13]

At the same time as the urban Mexica were dragooned into building a great European-style downtown, Cortés was distributing the surrounding rural altepetls as gifts to his followers. He did not receive official permission to do so until the end of 1523, but he began the process long before that.[14] Each conquistador was awarded the villages of a particular altepetl or sub-altepetl as an *encomienda*, or "package." This did not mean that the people living there became that conquistador's chattel slaves. In theory, it meant that the conquistador was to guard their spiritual and political well-being, and in exchange, the people were to pay him tribute in goods and also labor on his behalf for part of each year.[15] Cuauhtinchan, for example, was assigned to Juan Pérez de Arteaga, a conquistador who had spent long hours studying Nahuatl with Malintzin as an assistant interpreter.[16] Malintzin often needed help in this period, for she was frequently called upon to help with more sophisticated negotiations than the war itself had necessitated. Rather than merely demanding submission and food supplies, she now had to convey the exact nature of the Spaniards' political and economic demands, and then try to communicate the nature of indigenous political and economic realities to the Spaniards. It often had to be decided which chiefly line was to rule and which ones were to take a step back. Naturally, only those lines apparently sympathetic to the Spanish cause were to be supported. In Texcoco, for example, the power of Ixtlilxochitl was upheld and that of other family lines reduced.[17]

The Spaniards had the upper hand in all these arrangements, yet at no point did Cortés and his peers lose sight of the fragility of the peace. There were, after all, still millions more Indians than Europeans in this vast land. In early 1524, Cortés issued a new edict insisting that all Spanish men maintain a full set of arms. Each one was required to own a dagger, sword, and lance as well as a shield, helmet, and breastplate. Any man who did not acquire these goods within six months and then appear on command at military parades was subject to stiff fines. Those who had received encomiendas of up to five hundred Indians also had to arrange to purchase either a crossbow and bolts, or, failing that, a firelock musket and enough ammunition to fire two hundred times. If an encomienda contained between five hundred and one thousand Indians, the recipient additionally had to obtain a horse. Those who received even larger encomiendas had to purchase more such goods. If an encomendero did not comply, he stood to lose his grant in its entirety.[18]

In 1524, not long after this new ordinance was issued to the Spanish population, local indigenous leaders were summoned to meet in Tenochtitlan with the newly arrived "Twelve Apostles"—twelve Franciscan missionaries charged with launching the proselytization of Mexico. What the Indians were thinking when they first had Christian doctrines preached to them has long been a matter of great interest. Generally, Europeans have made their own assumptions without much evidence. At first the earliest friars enthusiastically reported that the indigenous were deeply moved and that they, the friars, had been able to baptize many thousands right away. Later, they walked back their assertions that all the Indians had truly been devout converts from the moment they were sprinkled with holy water, but the friars also remained generally confident in their overall success. They convinced the whole world that they had successfully converted Mexico to Catholicism in relatively short order. Only in the 1990s did it become commonplace for scholars to argue that this premise was indeed false—that in fact the indigenous had not simply rejected generations of belief and accepted Christian teachings without question.[19]

In these more recent discussions, scholars have had to rely upon indirect evidence—for instance, if the Nahuas didn't have a word for "the Devil," how could they possibly have come to believe in him so immediately? In their proselytizing efforts, the friars were reduced to using the word *tlacatecolotl* (tla-ka-te-KOL-ot) for a more generic type of "devil." This term had been used before the conquest to refer to a type of malicious shaman who could take the shape of a horned owl and fly about casting spells and generally wreaking havoc in unsuspecting people's lives. A tlacatecolotl generally came forth at night and was at all costs to be avoided. These creatures were hardly on par with Lucifer, but the friars decided that the word would have to do, as there was none better for their purposes. There are innumerable examples of such incommensurate cultural beliefs.[20] One historian has argued that both sides were much too quick to assume they understood each other, leading to a kind of "double mistaken identity" that made it very difficult for true Christianity to spread with the rapidity the friars had once hoped for.[21] This is indirect evidence for indigenous psychological resistance to the imposition of a European worldview, but it is nevertheless very real.

Yet there is in fact a surviving source that quotes the words of deeply religious Mexica men at the 1524 meeting, apparently giving direct insight into what they thought at first. Bernardino de Sahagún, the famous Franciscan friar who spoke Nahuatl and orchestrated the production of the Florentine Codex, left a record of the exchange, which he called "the

Colloquies." It is, however, a somewhat problematic source. First of all, Sahagún himself was not there; he had to have been working with someone else's notes. Second, the Indians were actually summoned on numerous occasions; the text that has come down to us today is a set of notes purportedly taken on one day, but the document likely represents a crystallization of what observers heard at several different meetings. Furthermore, the notes must have been taken in Spanish and the translation back to Nahuatl done years later, for no one alive in 1524 could possibly have written in Nahuatl with the fluency that the document exhibits. There were, in short, numerous opportunities for European editors to adjust the record. Yet despite these problems, the source remains credible in essence, for what it quotes both sides as saying is in keeping with assertions they made elsewhere. And what it claims the Indians said is in no way what the Spaniards would have wished them to say.[22]

The interpreter—almost certainly Malintzin, though it could conceivably have been one of her apprentices—did her best to translate as the friars expatiated for hours on the basic tenets of the Christian faith. When they finished, one of the indigenous leaders present stepped forward and in the most courtly Nahuatl speech offered a welcome to the strangers who had come from afar, thanking them for their precious words, like precious jades, precious feathers, he said, using the Mexicas' favorite cultural similes. Then he transitioned to express his anguish that most of the wise men who had once ruled in this city had died and that those who survived were their predecessors' inferiors in knowledge and experience. He said that it would be best if they called together the wisest of the surviving priests and let them determine how best to respond.[23]

That evening, the governing noblemen spoke to the priests and made the necessary arrangements. They must have insisted that they needed help: they were attempting to maintain order among their people in virtually impossible circumstances, and they could not risk making any politically inflammatory, dangerous religious statements themselves. If the Mexica were to defend their faith, someone who was not in a political hot seat would have to do it. So it was that in the morning, a collection of priests from the ancien régime came to hear the Christians speak of their beliefs. They asked to hear from the beginning all that had been uttered the previous day, and the Franciscans were only too happy to comply. "One of the twelve, using the interpreter, repeated everything that they had said to the lords the day before." If the interpreter was growing tired, no one made any mention of it. Finally, the leading Nahua priest rose and began to speak. He began, as was customary, in the most polite of tones, saying that he was overwhelmed by the honor of meeting the new-comers. But then at length he changed direction:

> You have told us that we do not know the One who gives us life and being, who is Lord of the heavens and of the earth. You also say that those we worship are not gods. This way of speaking is entirely new to us, and very scandalous. We are frightened by this way of speaking, because our forebears who engendered and governed us never said any-thing like this. On the contrary . . . they taught us how to honor the gods. . . . And they told us that through our gods we live and exist, and that we are beholden to them. . . . They said that these gods that we worship give us everything we need for our physical existence. We appeal to them for the rain to make the things of the earth grow.[24]

The priest spelled out the myriad reasons they had to be grateful to their gods and concluded, "It would be a fickle, foolish thing for us to destroy the most ancient laws and customs left by the first inhabitants of this land." He added that if the Spaniards were so daring as to insist on the destruction of the old gods, they would be courting political disaster. He spoke as if he were giving friendly advice, but he conveyed a threat. "Beware," he said, "lest the common people rise up against us if we were to tell them that the gods they have always understood to be such are not gods at all." Eventually he came to his climax: "All of us together feel that it is enough to have lost, enough that the reed mats, the thrones [political power, the royal jurisdiction] have been taken from us. As for our gods, we will die before giving up serving and worshipping them. This is our determination; do with us what you will. This will serve in reply and contradiction to what you have said. We have no more to say, lords." A more literal translation of his last words was, "That is all with which we return, with which we answer, your breath, your words, O our lords." It was a typical way to end a political speech that had wended its way from a courte-ous opening to the stark and angry statement the speaker really wanted to make. In another context some years later, an angry Mexica prisoner would end a speech to his Spanish judges on behalf of himself and a friend with the same sentiment, albeit in less flowery terms, in the style of a commoner: "That is all we have to say!"[25]

One of the twelve friars muttered under his breath something to the effect that they would just have to wait for these old men to die; the young people would be better listeners.[26] And that is more or less what the Spaniards pro-ceeded to do. They decided they had no interest in causing a huge upheaval by tormenting these recalcitrant pagans. Indeed, they reminded themselves, the Indians were not actually rejecting Jesus. Some seemed quite willing to add him to their pantheon. They were simply adamant about not replacing their old gods. It made most sense to wait, the friars concluded, and continue with their teachings and explanations. The so-called twelve apostles went to establish missions in the four places where the Spaniards had greatest control: Tenochtitlan and nearby Texcoco, as well as Tlaxcala and its neighbor, Huexotzinco. There they would begin the work of more effectively proselytizing the people of Mexico, largely by working with young people.

***

IN MID-1524, the exhausted Malintzin was also preparing to travel, but not in order to accompany the friars to any of their missions. Instead, she was to accompany Cortés overland to Honduras. Cortés had heard that one of his captains, Cristóbal de Olid, who had been sent on an exploratory mission, had set up a rival government in Central America, and he was determined to root him out. Cuauhtemoc and several other indigenous lords were forced to come along as hostages, so that their people would not rebel in Cortés's absence. Tecuichpotzin, however, was to stay home and guard the interests of the Mexica royal household. If Tecuichpotzin saw Malintzin during the weeks of preparation for the expedition, she must have pitied the older girl—though that was something she was not in the habit of doing. Both young women knew the trip would be futile and likely to be deadly.

Tecuichpotzin had not been in the habit of pitying Malintzin, because in the past three years, while Tecuichpotzin herself languished in virtual imprisonment alongside her beleaguered husband, the former concubine Malintzin, from a once tribute-paying land in the east, had grown startlingly powerful. It wasn't merely that as translator, she was at the heart of all negotiations as they unfolded. As soon as the acute strain of the war of conquest had ended, Malintzin had conceived a child by Cortés. It was a boy, Cortés's first son, and they named him Martín, after Cortés's father. In letters to others, Cortés revealed how much he loved the child, and for a while he even considered him his heir. He did not, however, live with the boy and his mother. Malintzin had been removed to her own household, for Cortés had a Spanish wife in Cuba, and as soon as the peace was made, she traveled to Mexico to join her husband. Theirs was not, it seemed, a happy marriage. Cortés and doña Catalina fought in public and in private. Later, when Catalina died suddenly, people whispered that Cortés had strangled her, but he was never indicted for the crime, and it was never proven.

Probably even Malintzin herself did not know the truth of the matter. She was so preoccupied with other matters that she may not have thought about it much, especially since she no longer had to live with the hot-tempered Cortés. She was translating in multiple venues, high and low, and was committed to training other translators. She ran her own household, earning money to maintain herself, her son, and her staff through small business ventures that her language skills and connections rendered it possible for her to operate. She wore an elaborately embroidered *huipilli*, or blouse, over a fine skirt, as well as sandals— unlike other women, who mostly went barefoot. All of this signaled her status, but she never grew overbearing or boastful. Nor did she ever choose to switch to Spanish dress. Everyone who had dealings with her liked her—except perhaps for Jerónimo de Aguilar, who was no longer needed in a translation chain, since the young woman had become so adept in Spanish. He later bitterly accused Malintzin of promiscuity, after she herself was dead, but no one supported this idea. Others remembered her as a cheerful, honorable, and extraordinarily competent person who had done her best to help establish order in the nearly lawless early months. They did recall that Cortés at one point went into a rage when he imagined that Jerónimo de Aguilar himself had been eyeing Malintzin.[27]

When Cortés came to Malintzin and demanded that she leave her son behind and accompany him as translator on a massive overland expedition through the jungles and mountains of Maya country, the land where she had been enslaved, she would have been far from overjoyed. She had a great deal to lose and nothing to gain. Cortés, likewise, had far more to lose than gain, but he either couldn't or wouldn't see it. Some have assumed that Malintzin was wildly in love with the conqueror and made his desires her desires. However, concubines in the world she came from knew better than to expect lasting romantic love from their masters. And Cortés in recent months had bedded so many women—and enraged so many mothers and husbands—that it would have been impossible for Malintzin to believe that there was a special bond between them. If, reminding him of their son, Malintzin ever spoke of marriage, Cortés would have made it clear that he was determined to marry a fine lady from Spain, not an indigenous slave girl; it was the only way he could be certain of maintaining his present power and influence. And the boy, Martín, could be legitimized by petitioning the pope.[28]

One might assume that Cortés simply forced Malintzin to accompany him, but this cannot reflect reality. All the records of the expedition indicate that Malintzin did more than go through the motions. For the next two years, she actively, energetically, and good humoredly pursued the entourage's best interests at every turn, and Cortés, remarkably for him, even expressed in writing some veiled gratitude for the dedication she demonstrated. Why did she behave so? What could a Nahua woman hope to gain from fulfilling the whims of the apparently addled conqueror?

Malintzin, like other indigenous people at the time of conquest, left behind no diaries, no letters, no explicit record either of her motivations or of the concessions she demanded. But the events that unfolded tell us that she bargained hard and astutely to secure protection for herself, her children, and her people in the best way she could. The expedition was first to travel through Coatzacoalcos, the land of her birth. Significantly, just before they crossed the river that bordered that territory, the enormous cavalcade came to a grinding halt for a full week. There Malintzin was suddenly married to a high-ranking lieutenant of Cortés's named Juan Jaramillo. Of the few single men in Cortés's circle at that time, there were only two others equally or more highly ranked, and one of them preferred to live with a young man he called his "nephew." Malintzin, married to Jaramillo, henceforth would have the legal protections of a Spanish lady. In addition, Cortés gave a significant wedding present, the kind of gesture he would never have made of his own accord; she had to have made the demand herself. Malintzin was assigned her natal village of Olutla as an encomienda. She would rule there, rather than a Spaniard. Legal documents were signed, though they were later lost in the disastrous expedition.[29]

As soon as these arrangements were made, the cavalcade moved forward. The river was higher than they had hoped, and much of the baggage was lost in the current, though no lives were. In a few days, Malintzin came face-to-face with her kin. It was an emotional greeting, Bernal Díaz later said.[30] The words she uttered are lost to us, as is so much of the indigenous experience of the immediate upheaval of conquest. We see this phenomenon everywhere in the history of the Americas. Sacajawea, for instance, another war captive who was traded away to white newcomers, would later meet her birth family as well, on the overland trek with Lewis and Clark. No one recorded her feelings, either, before she was pressed back into service as a translator for the travelers making their way to the Pacific. Letters and diaries sometimes bring us close to grand moments or touching scenes in the history of Euro-Americans, but harkening back to the thoughts and feelings of the less powerful, we meet only silence.

In any case, after all the years apart, Malintzin's time with her family and friends was brief, for she had a promise to Cortés to keep; for the sake of herself, her children, and her people, she would not break that promise. In a matter of days, they moved on toward their goal of Honduras. It was to be a long slog; weeks in the dark forest turned into months.

In a town called Acalan ("Land of Boats"), about fifty miles inland from the Gulf Coast, at the head waters of the River Candelaria, Cortés made a decision that has traumatized Mexicans to this day: he executed Cuauhtemoc. Accounts of what happened differ. Cortés later claimed that an indigenous informer revealed a plot hatched by the Mexica ruler: he had purportedly suggested that the Indians rise against the Spaniards in the midst of the jungle and free themselves, then return to the central valley in secret to inspire a rebellion there as well. Others, including a number of Spaniards, believed it was all a misunderstanding. Cuauhtemoc and his companions had merely been celebrating a rumor they had heard that Cortés had at last come to his senses and was ready to turn back. They joked and said things they perhaps should not have said—that they would prefer to die at once, for instance, rather than perish slowly of starvation, leaving their bodies scattered along this accursed route. Cortés had each of the men involved tortured separately. Malintzin had to translate the words they uttered in their agony. When Cortés had the evidence he sought, he had Cuauhtemoc hanged from a ceiba tree, along with at least one of his cousins, the ruler of Tlatelolco, and probably one other nobleman. Was Cortés truly in a panic, and was it only the efforts of Malintzin and others to translate what they understood to have been sarcastic comments and jokes that saved at least a dozen others? Or had Cortés always planned to rid himself of these two Mexica preconquest rulers when he was far from Tenochtitlan, where their deaths could not cause rioting and unrest among the people? In either case, Malintzin and numerous indigenous men were forced to watch and even to participate. It comes as no surprise that the event is referenced both directly and obliquely in several indigenous texts produced later. Cortés left nothing in writing that might illuminate the situation. Indeed, no writings survived the trek; almost no baggage of any kind did. A good proportion of the people were left dead along the route, just as Cuauhtemoc had apparently sarcastically predicted.[31]

When what was left of the cavalcade emerged from the forest on the shores of the Atlantic coast, they found that Cristóbal de Olid had been killed by Spaniards loyal to Cortés months earlier. As it turned out, the expedition had been entirely unnecessary. What was worse, the Spaniards living there on the coast were almost as hungry as those who had survived the overland trek from Mexico City. Once again, Cortés began coercing the local Indians to promise to offer tribute in the form of food and other valuable goods. He used the settlement's lone ship to send messages to the Caribbean seeking support. Soon enough, he received word in response that the power vacuum in the Mexican capital had given rise to a period of chaotic in-fighting among the

Spaniards, which the Indians were watching with interest. Rumors of Cortés's own death had been rampant in the city.

In desperate need of cash to solve his many problems, Cortés instructed his underlings to sell some local indigenous people into slavery in the Caribbean. In order to avoid being accused of wrongdoing, he insisted that they sell only those who had been enslaved by other indigenous peoples prior to the conquest. To do this they asked the indigenous people to identify them in Spanish: no arrangements were made for a translator.[32] Malintzin would have learned of these plans around the time she gave birth to Jaramillo's child, roughly nine months after their arrival on the Atlantic shores. This time, she had a girl, named María, after the Virgin. Shortly afterwards, they embarked for Veracruz; from there they would head for the capital. Other departing boats were loaded with human cargo that had been branded for sale in the Caribbean. Such, Malintzin knew, could so easily have been her fate or her daughter's. If she had ever harbored any doubts about her course of action, this would have convinced her that she had made the right decisions in her life, given her limited options. Her baby daughter, if she lived, was one girl who would never be sold as a slave, either by the Mexica or the Europeans.

***

MEANWHILE, THE POSTCONQUEST political storms in Tenochtitlan continued to rage. Once returned to the city, Cortés found himself embroiled in a struggle to regain his former power. Even his lands and encomienda Indians had been taken over by others, the interim government having believed the rumors that he was dead. One of his first acts was to officially inform Tecuichpotzin, now the lady Isabel, of the death of her husband, Cuauhtemoc. Then he brokered a marriage between her and Alonso de Grado, another conquistador. He gave de Grado the office "Protector of Indians"—which was rather ironic, given that de Grado had been known for brutalities toward Indians during the conquest—and he gave Isabel the large encomienda of Tlacopan, one of the three cities of the so-called Aztec Triple Alliance, where she had maternal relatives. The couple would thus be both rich and powerful. Cortés thought to please both the indigenous nobility and the Spanish Crown, as well as gain a loyal and wealthy sup-porter in de Grado. But a year and a half later, in early 1528, the elderly de Grado was dead.[33]

Cortés was feeling ever more besieged by his enemies and detractors. It was uncertain whether the king would ultimately side with him or punish him for having caused the tumult in the first place by decamping to Honduras to continue his adventures. "I am in purgatory," Cortés agonized to his father. "And the only reason it's not hell is that I still have hope of redress."[34] In his desperation, Cortés grew ever more rebellious and even reckless. When de Grado died, Cortés told the pretty eighteen-year-old daughter of Moctezuma that because she was a wealthy, highly desirable widow, he was going to move her into his own household "for her own protection." He was already in the habit of telling the Spanish world that Moctezuma, on his deathbed (struck down by rocks thrown by his own people, according to Cortés), had tearfully asked Cortés to protect his daughters.[35] It was only a bit more fantastical to pose before Isabel herself as her protector.

Isabel really had no choice. Her friends and family in the indigenous world could not afford to confront Cortés. Perhaps she believed his promises that she would be safe with him. She allowed herself and her few worldly goods to be taken to Cortés's home. Once there, she had no defenses. A close friend of Cortés's once commented laconically that "he had no more conscience than a dog."[36] Isabel became pregnant almost immediately.[37]

Cortés decided that he would travel to Spain himself to speak directly with the king about his affairs. He would take along young Martín, his son by Malintzin, and have the child legitimized by the pope in case he never produced other male children. Then he would leave Martín in Spain as a page to the young Prince Philip. Before he left, it was essential that he solve the awkward problem of Isabel's pregnancy. He would not have seriously considered marrying her himself. He dreamed of a Spanish noblewoman as a spouse, but there was an additional reason as well. If there were ever an indigenous woman whose social position might have made him consider a match, Isabel was that woman, but her high position meant that marriage to her would fuel rumors that Cortés was trying to establish a fiefdom in Mexico. He could easily alienate the king. Pedro Gallego de Andrade, a follower of Cortés, stated that he had no objections to marrying Isabel in her present condition, provided she still kept the extensive encomienda of Tlacopan, which Cortés assured him she would. Indeed, it was important to the Spanish government that she keep it, as her possession of it encapsulated the idea that the Mexica royal family was recognized as such by the Spaniards, and that they in turn accepted Spanish legal jurisdiction over themselves and their people. Cortés saw Isabel married to Gallego, and then he and his young son sailed away.[38]

Four months later, Isabel faced childbirth, what she thought of as *nomiquizpan*, "my moment of death." Among her servants, there were Nahua women, which was fortunate at this time of pain and uncertainty. "Beloved daughter," they would have comforted her in her own language, "exert yourself! What are we to do with you? Here are your old mothers. This is your responsibility. Grab hold of the shield. My daughter, young one, be a brave woman. Face it . . . bear down. Imitate the brave goddess Cihuacoatl."[39] All her life, Isabel-Tecuichpotzin, had thought of a woman giving birth as a warrior who had the opportunity to win honor, not as someone who begged for mercy in the face of a great punishment inflicted by the deity on all her sex, as the Spaniards did. But in her case, pride did not accompany whatever courage she showed. She was not capturing a spirit and bringing it home to her family to carry on their traditions. When the child was born—a girl—it was taken from her and carried to the home of one of Cortés's cousins, who had promised to raise the child for him.[40]

In her misery, Isabel found to her surprise that her husband, Pedro Gallego, was kind to her and sympathized, and she came to value him. The next year, she bore him a son, named Juan. They held a great baptismal party in honor of Moctezuma's first grandson born in Christian matrimony, a child who would enter the Spanish world. Church bells rang, and the people lit bonfires to celebrate. Two months after the baby's birth, Pedro Gallego died suddenly, and Isabel seemed devastated. She turned even more fully to the child. All her life, she loved Juan best among her children; her next marriage to a Spaniard named Juan Cano lasted more than twenty years and seemed a happy one, but her other children never displaced Juan.[41]

Isabel—always known as Tecuichpotzin by the indigenous city folk[42]— was known for her quiet demeanor. She was never entirely comfortable with the symbolic role the Spaniards had carved out for her. She gave as many of the profits from her encomienda as she could to a favored Augustinian friary. She breathed the suggestion to both of her daughters that they could become nuns if they wanted to, rather than the wives of Spanish men, and this is what they later did. In her will, she freed all the Indian slaves who served in her husband's household.[43] We cannot know if she envied her sister, christened "Francisca"—the one who had not been presented to the Spaniards as an emissary wife but was instead sent to her mother's birthplace, in the countryside of Ecatepec, near Azcapotzalco. The Spaniards never even knew about this royal daughter in the early years. Her fate more closely resembled that of the majority of indigenous people, who lived their lives beyond the direct observation of the Spaniards. Most, after all, were not initially caught up in the maelstrom, like Malintzin and Tecuichpotzin.

As the Spaniards fanned out in the countryside, however, every community eventually faced its moment of crisis. In 1529, about the time Malintzin at last succumbed to one of the European microbes and died,[44] and in 1530, as Isabel sang Nahuatl lullabies to her newborn, it was Cuauhtinchan's turn to face such a crisis.

***

SMOKING SHIELD GUIDED HIS PEOPLE through most of the 1520s without major incident. The Spaniards built a little church in the neighboring town of Tepeaca, and a priest visited as often as he could. He told the people of Cuauhtinchan that they should attend mass in Tepeaca, but few did and no one came to make any trouble about it. The requisite tribute gradually became more of a problem as it increased over time, and Smoking Shield was convinced there would be trouble if they ignored that mandate as well. By the end of the decade, Cuauhtinchan was committed to providing 24,000 woven blankets every four years, as well as twenty turkeys, six thousand bushels of corn, sixteen baskets of beans, eighty of chile, sixteen of chia, and sixteen of salt.[45]

In addition, thirty Indians had to provide domestic services to the encomendero and various Spanish officials: they could rotate that duty among themselves in any way they liked, as long as able-bodied workers presented themselves to the right people at the right time. The tasks were growing more onerous than the town could handle, especially in the wake of so many deaths from the new diseases. It was becoming more and more difficult to plant and harvest their own crops—without which their children starved and became more vulnerable to disease.[46]

Just as Smoking Shield must have been considering the possibility of protesting in some way, a large force of armed Spaniards arrived in the region and made camp; he was forced to relinquish any ambitions he harbored of becoming a renegade. It was 1529, and Nuño Beltrán de Guzmán, who would soon launch a war of conquest in the west of Mexico, had just been named to preside over the governing high court in Tenochtitlan.[47] Cortés was absent in Spain, and it was not yet clear who would be named viceroy, the representative of the king. In the meantime, Guzmán was in charge. He made the decision to arrest Ixtlilxochitl, the Texcocan nobleman whose family line had benefited from the arrival of the Spaniards. Throughout the 1520s, he had made the most of his alliance with Cortés and waged war against his neighbors when he deemed it necessary. Now Ixtlilxochitl was deposited in a dungeon cell in a Franciscan monastery, where he languished and died.[48] Next, Guzmán sent his henchmen out into the countryside east of the city with instructions to conscript several thousand indigenous warriors for the military campaign he was planning.

In Cuauhtinchan, the Spaniards demanded that the local nobles attend a meeting, and through an interpreter they made it clear that only those who immediately converted to Christianity and promised to cooperate would be able to retain their seats. Although Smoking Shield did not mention the matter in the book of history he later wrote, other sources reveal that the local chiefs did indeed decide to accept baptism at that time.[49] He accepted as his patron and godfather a man in the Spaniards' company named Alonso de Castañeda. Chimalpopoca (now Alonso) bowed his head; a priest splashed water on him and his fellows, praying as he did so and turning them all into namesakes of Spaniards. Smoking Shield was presumably a good performer and a talented negotiator: when the Spanish force moved on, he had managed to prevent most of his men from being conscripted. Their population was not devastated. He led his people to church and tried to look interested, as he understood that this was of central importance if he wished the Spaniards to treat his people with any respect. "But no one knew yet what was happening, if it was 'Sunday' or some other day [in the new calendar]," one of his connections later recalled. "We were really new at it. . . . We didn't know what was going on."[50]

With the arrival of Christianity, noblemen began to feel some pressure to choose only one among their several wives—as if they would somehow be willing to expel the ones not chosen. At first they could ignore the hints and requests, but it wasn't clear how long that situation would last. The writers of the annals in the next generation touched on the subject of conjugal discord only gingerly, never giving any details. The whole subject was extraordinarily painful, not only for the potentially rejected women but also for their children. In the long run, only generational change brought the noblemen around to monogamy. In the meantime, there were more public issues to contend with.[51]

In 1531, two bedraggled and exhausted chiefs appeared in Cuauhtinchan, begging for succor. They were the leaders of nineteen families who had fled desperate situations; their former chiefs had apparently been less effective than Smoking Shield at staving off the effects of conquest by the Spaniards. Perhaps they had simply been unlucky. The people came from different backgrounds—some were not even Nahuas but Otomí and Pinome—but in their mutual need they had come together under the leadership of two charismatic men named Elohuehue (Eh-lo-WAY-way) and Apiancatl (ah-pee-AHN-kat), who had promised to try to care for them all. The name of the first meant "Old Man Like a Fresh Ear of Corn"; the second was a stylized traditional title, the meaning of which is now lost, but it conveyed authority. "They were suffering people who came from distant lands," Smoking Shield remembered.[52] According to custom, all the Cuauhtinchan leaders came together to decide what to do. They agreed to offer the newcomers some unoccupied lands at the start of the road to Tepeaca. As in the old days, these arrangements were rendered permanent through formal public statements repeated by multiple parties; then a designated person painted a representation of the agreement, with known symbols for water, hills, and roads indicating the boundaries of the land. To this the people now added another ingredient: they brought with them to the meeting a young man who had learned the Roman letters from one of the Christians, and he wrote out the statements they made using symbols that he manipulated adeptly. Smoking Shield used his Nahuatl name, but to it he added "Alonso de Castañeda," and also included a title that the Spaniards had told him indicated he was a nobleman. So he became "don Alonso de Castañeda Chimalpopoca."[53]

Don Alonso and the other chiefs explained to the newcomers that in order to render the agreement binding in the eyes of the Christian authorities, the people needed to build a thatch-roofed temple where they could honor the Christian god; a priest would soon come from Tepeaca to bless their endeavor. The grateful settlers called their new village *Amozoc* and promised themselves they would never abandon it. Their resolve was to cost them dearly when the Franciscans later ordered everybody to leave the countryside and move to the town of Cuauhtinchan. It was the people of Amozoc, stubbornly devoted to their new home, who were burned out of their houses in 1558.

But all that was still in the future. At the moment, don Alonso was facing another crisis. In early 1532, a fellow Cuauhtinchan chief named Huilacapitzin (Wee-la-ka-PEE-tzeen), or Heart of a Snail Shell, was accused by the Spaniards of practicing human sacrifice and executed. Don Alonso had appeared alongside him only recently, at the meeting where land was gifted to the settlers of Amozoc. There, Huilacapitzin had used both his Nahuatl name and his new Spanish name "don Tomás." On the surface, at least, he seemed to be adjusting to the new ways just as Smoking Shield was, but apparently this was less true behind the scenes. He was the heir of the leading Pinome dynasty, a member of the family that had arranged to have Smoking Shield's father killed some twenty years earlier. But Smoking Shield did not seem to hold this fact against him, at least not since having fought together in their failed attempt to defend Cuauhtinchan from the outsiders. When Smoking Shield spoke of Heart of a Snail Shell, he used the Nahuatl honorific "-tzin" at the end of his name, which he withheld from the man who had actually ordered his father killed. He tried to avoid mentioning the events of 1532 altogether: in later years, when he was dictating a history of his people, a questioner apparently forced him to return to that moment and mention the matter, as it appears as an insert. He spoke very succinctly, saying only that don Tomás was hanged that year.[54] If his children wanted to know more, they had no choice but to ask someone else who had been involved. It turned out it was a young Tlaxcalan aide to the Spanish friars who had informed the representatives of the new religion of what was going on. The Franciscans arrested Heart of a Snail Shell, whom they persisted in calling Tomás, and tried him and sentenced him to death.

The Franciscans ordered the nobility of all the sub-altepetls of Cuauhtinchan and other neighboring towns to attend the hanging, and the images of what they saw that day remained burned into their memories. The man's legs kicked until all life was driven from his body. Even then, one who mourned him did not give up hope: "His dog, white with black spots, stayed lying there beside his hanged master."[55] Then two other men who had been accused of assisting Tomás—presumably native priests—were hanged, after which their bodies were drawn and quartered. Finally, the men and women said to have been present at the sacrificial ceremony were tied up to be shamed in the hot sun.

Probably even Smoking Shield and other near neighbors of don Tomás and his people did not know exactly what had really transpired. Each village— or close-knit set of villages—struggled on its own to make sense of the new religion and to decide how to comply with the authorities' expectations without being disrespectful of the ancient gods. Rumors swirled through the countryside of varying activities and varying Spanish responses. Don Tomás Huilacapitzin was not the only indigenous lord in Mexico to face a death sentence because he had been accused of spiritual crimes. There were many who still held rituals honoring the old gods.[56]

In this environment, Smoking Shield don Alonso received instructions that he and his people were to participate in building a stone church in Cuauhtinchan. They threw themselves into the project with enthusiasm, determined that if they were going to do it, they would certainly show some pride in their altepetl. Their church would rival that of Tepeaca, a neighboring town and longtime rival. A friar by the name of Juan de Rivas explained that the building was not to be shaped like a pyramid mountain like the temples of old, but instead like a great cube, with a tower rising from it. The people painted the insides with swirling flowers, placing a jaguar and an eagle in prominent positions. These were the characters of the ancient Nahua story— the ordinary animals who bravely jumped into the fire at the creation of the Fifth Sun and who had symbolized the qualities of warriors ever since.[57]

One Sunday in 1536, when the people of Cuauhtinchan were still in the midst of the building project, a Franciscan who had come to preach told them he had an important announcement to make.[58] His order was going to establish a school for the sons of the indigenous nobility. It would be in the country of the Mexica, in Tlatelolco, where the Franciscans had their great *convento*. They wanted boys who were ten to twelve years old—old enough not to require constant supervision like small children but still young enough to mold and educate in the Christian tradition. At the school, they would study religious precepts, as well as reading and writing, Spanish, Latin, music, and the illumination of manuscripts.

So it was that Cristóbal,[59] a son (or perhaps a young cousin) of don Alonso's named for an Old World saint—a Canaanite who converted to Christianity and helped travelers cross a river—found himself with a passel of other boys being conducted by one of the friars to the Franciscan establishment at Tlatelolco. He had his most precious possessions packed in a wooden chest with a lock and key, and a rolled-up mat for sleeping. When the boys arrived, they were told to place their belongings in the long dormitory chamber, and then were given something to eat in the refectory.[60]

In the coming weeks and months, Cristóbal apparently found the lessons to his liking. The friars showed them a "Cartilla" or letter primer, which the religious men had copied out themselves—later they would have copies of the little textbook printed up—and the boys rapidly learned the sounds associated with the symbols (ba be bi bo bu, bam bem bim bom bun, fa fe fi fo fu, fam fem fim fom fum). In a matter of weeks, several of them were reading the new phonetic code. The teacher, fray Bernardino de Sahagún, promised the stellar students that if they kept it up, they could soon begin their study of Latin. Then they would be able to access all the knowledge of the ancient world. He showed them the venerable books kept in the school library and promised them the keys to that kingdom. The drawing master hurt the group by speaking scathingly of the paintings their forebears had done, but in the eyes of some of the boys, he made it up to them when he taught them how to introduce perspective; they were soon entertaining themselves drawing true-to-life animals: dogs, birds, and horses. The study of Christian theology proved much easier for Cristóbal than his elders had thought it would. The depth of commitment to the doctrines that shone in the eyes of his teachers convinced him the material was as much worth learning as the religious lessons he had learned at home, and when the boys were brought together to offer thanks to God in the form of song, he felt that for long moments, he was lifted into another world; he heard the music of the divine.[61]

Of course, school wasn't always so uplifting. Sometimes the students argued with each other or told raunchy jokes in Nahuatl, and to their amazement, some of the friars actually understood and punished them.[62] And sometimes their teachers entertained themselves by gossiping about European politics. Henry VIII, the king of England, had lost control of his passions only a few years earlier and set aside his Christian wife, Catherine, daughter of the Spanish monarchs Ferdinand and Isabel, in favor of a young English woman, Anne Boleyn—shameless, the friars called her. Now came the news that, having grown tired of Anne Boleyn, Henry had had her imprisoned and then beheaded. All of this he had done to prove that he could break away from the Roman Catholic authority of the pope; as a king, Henry had set a very bad example, something the teachers hoped their own students would never do when they grew up to become chiefs. They should never behave as English monarchs did—or as their forebears had done, the teachers sometimes added. Whether the students were shamed, or rather were heartened by the idea that European politics sometimes resembled their own, their later writings do not make clear.[63]

When Cristóbal returned home a few years later, he had become a fluent writer, a master of a beautiful handwriting, and an expert in grammar and punctuation.[64] He prayed to the Christian god and dressed in Spanish clothing. Not surprisingly, he found himself dragged into the tensions between those families who had chosen to have their sons educated in Spanish ways and those who had not. A relative of his wrote a sly comment in Spanish in the margins of a book: "Well-born noblemen who do not know their letters have no understanding. They are noble beasts."[65] Useful tamed animals were often called "noble beasts" and were worthy of mankind's sympathy and kindness; but calling indigenous noblemen "noble beasts" was in effect a vicious insult. It was even worse than calling them animals. It was a pun, as "bestia" (beast) also meant "stupid"—thus the phrase could mean "noble beasts," but it could also mean "stupid noblemen." Sometimes these tensions made themselves felt not just between families but even within families, between generations. Young don Felipe de Mendoza from one of the Pinome lineages, a connection of the hanged don Tomás, was invited without his respected father to another nobleman's house specifically because he was, like his host, "raised afterwards, educated in the church."[66] That only he was welcome, not the elders in his family, apparently gave young Felipe pain, since he remembered the words and repeated them later.

Before long, a much larger crisis trumped whatever agonies were caused by these social rifts. It had been more than twenty years since the terrible epidemic of 1520, and now a whole new generation had arisen that lacked immunities. Then, in 1544, worms ate the corn crop and people starved; and in 1545, the most terrible epidemic since the time of the conquest devastated the land. Cristóbal and his father must have lost family members—everyone did—but no record of the names of their dead has survived.[67]

Many lands on the outskirts of Cuauhtinchan lay fallow, as the villagers assigned to work them were dying or dead, and the people of Tepeaca, a populous town, decided to move in and live in those areas. They were old enemies, and rage smote Smoking Shield. Part of him wanted to go by night and attack the intruders and drive them away as he once would have done, but that era was past: now he was don Alonso de Castañeda. In March 1546, instead of launching a war, he and his fellow chiefs decided to make the most of their sons' new style of literacy. They would sue the people of Tepeaca in a Spanish court of law. At root, this was a concept easily understood, as the Mexica overlords had been arbiters in their local affairs for many years.[68]

Don Alonso and his entourage made their way to Mexico City. Old pre-conquest roads led to the city they themselves still called Tenochtitlan. These paths were familiar to chiefs, but the terrain seemed strange in other ways. Travelers no longer had to worry about being attacked by those who perceived them as enemies. There would always be robbers, but no one would imagine the travelers as bringing war. They made their way to the center of the valley and crossed the lake to the island city. Although the outskirts of the town still belonged to indigenous fisherfolk and chinampa farmers, new Spanish-style buildings rose everywhere in the bustling downtown area. Don Alonso's little group made their way to Tlatelolco, where they had acquaintances from the days of their sons' being at school there. They found acceptable lodgings, but soon discovered that they had to spend frightening amounts of money to maintain themselves in the metropole. They were not, however, going to be beaten back now. They pursued their case, determined not to leave until they had conducted enough of the business to feel that it could be safely left in the hands of a representative.[69]

From May to August 1546, they made their way regularly to and from the court. When they entered the first time, the great stone walls and the darkness within intimidated them, but they soon grew accustomed to it. That first day, the leader of Cuauhtinchan's indigenous governing cabildo, or council, spoke for the group, but don Alonso's personality was so much more forceful that he soon took over. In their records, the Spaniards took to referring simply to "don Alonso and the other nobles." It was he who demanded that certain witnesses from Tepeaca be made to appear, and he also organized the presentation of witnesses from his side. After the words of each witness were transcribed, he would ask to have the statement read back to him by the court interpreter and then nod his assent.[70]

Don Alonso was eagerly absorbing lessons about the European world. This City of Mexico, whatever else it was, was a place of grandeur and a center of visible power. Here, in the chambers of the High Court, he saw for himself how power was enacted in the world the Europeans were making. Just as in his world, power was wielded through statements made publicly, gravely, and with ritualistic language, then commemorated on paper. But he also noted a significant difference. Here, decisions were rendered permanent through the medium of a certain kind of writing. This was not the pictographic writing that he knew so well but which younger men in his world could no longer read easily. He was observing the process of alphabetic writing, of phonetic transcription of spoken language. These marks on paper encoded the human voice. In court, his exact words were read back to him smoothly. Young men like Cristóbal assured him that anyone could learn to interpret the sounds of the letters; they were not the special province of priests who spent decades memorizing hundreds of pictographic symbols and creating others, and then took much of their knowledge with them to the grave. Even if a terrible epidemic were to strike dead all the specially trained men of the High Court tomorrow, others would be able to read these documents fully. It would be possible for men to hear his exact words generations later. That was certainly worth thinking about.[71]

In August, don Alonso was ready to leave the lawsuit in the hands of a lawyer and return home with his entourage. He then turned his attention to a new project: he had decided to orchestrate the writing of a great work of his people's history, one using the new letters. In some ways, the book he had in mind would look like a collection of the old-style painted documents, representing important historic moments and the establishment of the boundaries to various altepetls' lands with glyphs and drawings. But in other ways, it would be quite different, for year by year, it would present a full verbal performance of his people's history. All that would once have been said out loud around the communal fire would be written down, transcribed using the new letters. His son and other young people could help him. He and others of his generation would provide the information, and the young ones would do the writing. The pictorial elements they could work on together. It would be a history of all the Tolteca Chichimeca, focusing most specifically on those who had eventually settled in Cuauhtinchan.[72]

Don Alonso envisioned concrete uses for the volume over the years—it could provide evidence in Spanish courtrooms regarding traditional landholding arrangements, for example, or it could be carried to indigenous ceremonies as a sacred object lending authenticity to the procedures. But don Alonso dedicated untold hours of his family's time to this project for deeper reasons than these. He foresaw that once his people's memory of the meaning of the glyphs had faded, and their communities had sunk into the poverty that Spanish demands were pushing them toward, narrowing their horizons and forcing them to focus on survival, a great social amnesia would ensue. And if they could not remember their past, how could they articulate demands for their future?

Cristóbal picked up the quill, ready to write. And don Alonso de Castañeda Chimalpopoca began to speak. He told an ancient tale, about the breakup of a happy community centuries earlier. It was a story his people had been telling for many, many years, since they were wanderers. "When Huemac became a young man, he gave orders that the Nonohualca tend to his home. Then the Nonohualca said to him, 'So be it, my lord. May we do what you desire.' The Nonohualca came to tend to his home. And then he demanded women of them. He said to the Nonohualca, 'You are to give me women. I order that the buttocks be four spans wide.'" Surely don Alonso stopped here to have a good laugh at the preposterous arrogance of the man. But then he would have faced the cultural divide that was beginning to form between him and his descendants. Was young Cristóbal's Nahuatl still good enough for him to get the joke? Did don Alonso have to explain everything to the younger man, brought up in a different time? Did he tell him that the story was particularly rich because "Huemac" meant "Big Gift"? He had been a foundling and was supposedly a gift from the gods. Some "Big Gift" he turned out to be! It was because of him that all the discord between the ancestors originally arose. "Huemac" indeed! He had been no gift, but he certainly had brought the unexpected—like so much of life, don Alonso must have thought, as one who had seen one world give way to another and who had survived with his humor intact. He was living proof that the New World in which he and his people found themselves would not obliterate the old one.

Later, when the houses of Amozoc burned, don Alonso de Castañeda Chimalpopoca would be ready to comfort the afflicted. It had long been a Nahua leader's role to shoulder responsibilities on behalf of the people: he would not shirk his duty. His people would survive these times of trouble, he was determined.

7

Crisis: The Indians Talk Back

1560s

Late in the evening of January 7, 1568, the guards came to collect don Martín, the son of la Malinche by Hernando Cortés. The huge metal key turned in the lock; the heavy door creaked as it opened. The cell was in the basement beneath the High Court of Mexico, and don Martín knew what they had come for. The judge's decision that he was to be tortured had been read aloud to him several hours before, according to law, and he had been required to answer at that time that he understood the pronouncement and accepted it. Yes, he said, he understood that he had been accused of treason against the king, but he had not committed any treason and still refused to make a confession. He understood what would follow.[1]

***

DON MARTÍN—HE was called "don" because his father had been made a marquis by the king—was escorted to the chamber where the rack was kept. Judges all over Europe had found that merely showing an accused man the apparatus generally had the desired effect. A representative of the court asked don Martín again if he would like to confess that he had plotted against the Crown, but he responded, "I have already spoken the truth and have no more to say." A scribe recorded the prisoner's statement and prepared to transcribe any other words he might utter. He was only to omit the screams, groans, or

---

A tlacuiloc, or scribe, writes a history. The Bodleian Libraries, the University of Oxford, Codex Mendoza, MS. Arch. Selden. A.1, folio 70r.

any other testament to pain. The guards removed don Martín's clothing and tied his naked body to the two ends of the rack. They turned the levers and dislocated the bones of both arms and both legs.

The High Court judge, who was present, asked don Martín for the names of any conspirators against His Majesty the King. The scribe reported that the prisoner once again said that he had already told the truth and had no more to say. The judge signaled that the guards should turn the rack again. They did. The man said once again that he had nothing to say. But the judge was not yet discouraged. Every single prisoner that they had brought in regarding the purported plot of rebellion had ended by confessing and mentioning names. It was already time, he decided, for the water torture. The guards lowered don Martín's head below his body. One held his nose closed and inserted a horn deep into his mouth and even into the throat. Then the other poured buckets of water in slowly, then faster, never ceasing, so that eventually the man would drown if it went on. There had been occasions when the procedure went too far and a prisoner died, but in general the judges involved knew enough to signal that the guard should stop just before it was too late.

Now the judge made the signal; he questioned don Martín again. The man gasped and could not speak. They waited. At length he spoke. "I have already spoken the truth and have no more to say." Two more times they applied the water, and two more times he repeated his statement. Then the guards poured the water down his throat and into his lungs a fourth time. It went on and on and on. The judge waited. It went on. At last it stopped. And now don Martín faced his crisis.

He could talk. He had been part of no plot, but he could make up anything they might believe. Every other man they had brought here had done so. They had been the sons of Spanish noblemen, highborn and proud, committed to maintaining their honor, yet they had caved quite quickly. They had been accustomed to sunlight and to public contests. Those other men had never imagined even the possibility of a world in which they would be utterly powerless, alone in the darkness in the presence of men who were not afraid to kill them.

Don Martín was different. His early childhood memories were of his mother, Malintzin, or doña Marina as the Spaniards called her, twice a prisoner, ever a survivor, the bravest of women, as all men said. When he was eight years old, his father took him to Spain and left him there to become a page to Prince Philip, and he then learned the meaning of the word alone. He grew up a "half-breed Indian" in the eyes of those who surrounded him in the Spanish court. Silent, distant, he survived, but he was not stunned when humanity turned its face away from him. If anyone had ever looked past him, belittled him, or made him feel insignificant, they would learn who he was. In his world, honor came to a man by birth, but it also came from courage. His honor was all he had left, and he would keep it, in the eyes of all. He was the son of Hernando Cortés and doña Marina. And he believed deeply in the god of his father's people: the story of Jesus had touched the inner recesses of his heart. He whispered, "I have told the truth, and in the holy name of God who suffered for me, I will say nothing more from this moment until I die." He would die, then; he was ready. Two more times they poured the water, before the judge at last decided that it was truly useless. He made the signal to desist.[2]

When dawn came, word spread throughout the city of what had happened. People spoke in hushed tones of the son of Cortés. To some of the Spaniards, he embodied the myth of the silent, stoic Indian, who suffered at the hands of others. In others' eyes, he was simply a brave man, a man of honor, in the same way that any man might aspire to be. In whispered Nahuatl, the Indians told each other that the tecpan, the royal office, had been closed down again by armed men, this time in order to torture don Martín.[3]

***

MALINTZIN HAD DONE HER BEST for her children and launched them as citizens of the Spanish world so they would not be utterly powerless in the future they faced, but don Martín, like many first-generation mestizos, had nevertheless had a difficult life. The ship bearing the child and his father away from the port of Veracruz towards Spain had departed in March of 1528, when he was just seven years old. As a youth, he lived at the Spanish court, along with several other sons of noble fathers, providing companionship and entertainment for young Prince Philip, the heir apparent, who was five years his junior. Don Martín's father, as the most famous of conquistadors, had not only received the title of "marquis" for himself, but had also petitioned for and received a papal bull giving Martín the status of a legitimate child.[4] The paperwork was all in order, whatever people may have whispered about the boy. Early on, after Martín's father had returned to Mexico, and about the time the boy received word that his mother, Malintzin, had died, he became deathly ill with an infection in the lymph nodes. It was believed that he would die. Yet he survived. As Martín grew up, he received occasional messages from his father, living in Mexico, who assured him of his love for him. His father wrote to a cousin who was supervising his education: "Indeed I tell you that I don't love him any less than the other [boy] whom God has given me with the Marquesa, and thus I always want to know about him."[5] Cortés had married a

duke's daughter during his sojourn in Spain, and she had proceeded to bear
her husband a legitimate son, whom they also named Martín. This boy would
supplant Malintzin's son in the inheritance—he would become the marquis,
the recognized son of Hernando Cortés—as the half-indigenous child well
knew. He learned to live with that knowledge.

In 1539, the boy turned eighteen. That same year his father returned to
Spain. He brought with him the second Martín, the one destined to inherit
the title and the lands. This boy, too, was to join Prince Philip's household.
The adolescent don Martín took the eight-year-old brother under his wing
and tried to love him. The two of them traveled with their father while the
famed conquistador conducted his business throughout Spain. In early 1540,
for reasons we can never be certain of—but understandable youthful yearn-
ing must surely head the list—don Martin decided to part from his father and
brother, not to return to his life in the palace, but to visit Mexico, his childhood home. Across the ocean, he seems to have visited María, his sister on his
mother's side, Malintzin's daughter by Juan Jaramillo , and to have stayed at
his father's estate in Cuernavaca. Then, about a year later, he acknowledged
that he had become someone different and did not belong there. He returned
to Spain and took up his duties in the palace. As a knight, he went wherever
the royal household needed their retainers to fight. He went at different times
to wars in the Piedmont in Italy, to the Barbary Coast, to Germany, and
to France.[6]

In subsequent years, don Martín remained connected with his brother,
the heir, and they both attended their father's deathbed. They had a somewhat stormy relationship. They lent each other sums of money, paid it back or
failed to, quarreled and made up more than once. Eventually they had a spec-
tacular fight, and the older Martín sued his brother to obtain his inheritance
in a lump sum rather than an annuity, saying he wanted nothing more to do
with his brother. The younger Martín must truly have been a handful: his own
mother sued him at about the same time, in an effort to force him to provide
dowries for his sisters. Philip—who had become king in 1556—was called in
to negotiate between the brothers, who had been his childhood companions.
Perhaps the older don Martín felt chastened, or perhaps both did, for they
were reconciled, and then made plans to travel to Mexico, together with
another half-brother of theirs named Luis. They would take up their abode in
the fabled land conquered by their father and live as rich men.[7]

Don Martín had recently married a girl named Bernardina, whom he
apparently met, most romantically, while on a pilgrimage to the shrine of
Santiago de Compostela. An illegitimate son (named Hernando, for his

famous grandfather) whom he had with a poor woman a few years earlier came to live with the couple, and soon Bernardina bore a daughter. In 1562, Martín and his wife decided that he would travel to Mexico, while she would return to her parents' household with the two children. Later, if all went well, he would send for them. It was a fortunate decision, as it turned out, for the ship bearing the three Cortés brothers was damaged off the coast of Yucatan. Although they all survived the wreck, they made their way overland to Mexico City in a bedraggled and exhausted state.

The city welcomed the legitimate son of Hernando Cortés and his two half-brothers with great fanfare. The young marquis, however, quickly wore out his welcome. His wild and reckless behavior, combined with his arrogance, alienated potential allies. He had a rather sordid and very public affair with doña Marina Vázquez de Coronado, the daughter of the man who had led the conquest of New Mexico and the wife of a good friend of his. A witty lampoon began to circulate: "A good man won this land by Marina, and now another man of the same name will lose it by another woman of the same name."[8] In the meantime, don Martín had once again sought out his sister María, the daughter of Malintzin. The young woman he had seen in 1540 had turned into an exhausted middle aged woman, weakened and demoralized by countless pregnancies that had yielded only two living children. Sadly, she died within months of her reunion with her brother. And with her disappeared Martín's last human connection to his early childhood—to Nahuatl nursery rhymes or common memories of a mother. His wife and children still had not arrived. He grew extremely depressed and spoke to others about the possibility of returning to Spain. He went to confession often, imagining he might be near death.[9]

Bernardina had been delayed in Spain as she sought travel permits for a number of young women from her home town—a barber's daughter, for example, and a young woman who had been born illegitimate—so that they might accompany her to Mexico and find husbands far outranking those that would be available to them in Spain. It helped her application that her husband was the king's old playmate, and eventually, in 1565, she and her entourage arrived in Mexico City. Don Martín was overjoyed to see her and the children—but by then, he was in the midst of other, overwhelming difficulties.[10]

The City of Mexico had become a political tinder box. First, the Mexica residents had exploded with anger when, in 1564, they were told that they were going to have to pay tribute just like all the other indigenous peoples of central Mexico. Ever since 1521, it had been their role to give their labor free of

charge to the construction of city buildings and other projects, but they had
not been given out in encomienda to individual Spaniards, nor had they been
given cash tribute to pay, as had the people of the countryside. Because don
Martín had been given the post of chief constable, it had fallen to him to calm
the roiling indigenous populace.[11] At the very same time, the encomenderos
were becoming increasingly fearful that King Philip was planning to use his
monarchical powers to limit their own ability as individuals to extract wealth
from indigenous people, or even to hand down their encomienda grants to
their heirs in perpetuity. It was certainly true that the Spanish king wished to
prevent the growth of an all-powerful noble class in Mexico. Unfortunately,
the legitimate don Martín went about making tactless comments, as was his
wont. He loudly insisted on the right of the gentry of New Spain to make
their own decisions and direct their own lives. Of course he valued his childhood friend, the king, but he nevertheless loved to play the leader of disgrun-
tled young men. Then in July of 1564, the longtime viceroy, don Luis de
Velasco, died suddenly. In the power vacuum, the commotion and complaints
increased exponentially. By the time Bernardina arrived the following year,
her husband was forced to spend a good deal of his time explaining away some
of his younger brother's wilder statements and trying to convince him to tell
his fellows that he was certain King Philip would address their grievances soon.

Despite all his efforts, Malintzin's tactful son was unable to stave off disaster. One day in July, 1566, in the midst of some jousting celebrating the birth
of a set of twins to the wife of the young marquis, the guards of the Audiencia,
or High Court of Mexico, came to arrest don Martín. That same day, they also
arrested the marquis himself, and well as Luis. These three Cortés brothers
were accused of conspiring with others to take over the Audiencia chambers
by force, publicly renounce allegiance to the King of Spain, and set the marquis in place as ruler of Mexico. Over the ensuing weeks, each of the three was
interrogated. Don Martín confessed to having heard a great deal of angry talk,
but said he did not believe it amounted to anything more than the swaggering
of boys. He was then formally accused not of having participated, but of having known about the conspiracy for months without having done anything
about it.

Within a few short weeks, two other brothers of noble lineage, Gil
González and Alonso de Avila, emerged as the center of the somewhat incho-
ate "conspiracy." They were tried, convicted, and immediately hanged. The
residents of Mexico City were stunned. They had not thought it would come
to this for highborn Spaniards.[12] The judges of the Audiencia then turned
their attention fully toward the Cortés brothers. They equivocated in the

case of the two Martíns, but they sentenced Luis to death. He had behaved as arrogantly as the young marquis and had likewise made enemies everywhere he went, but he did not have the necessary wealth and connections to protect him.

Then suddenly there came a reprieve. A new viceroy at last arrived, don Gastón de Peralta, Marquis of Falces. He was a congenial man and a practical one, to boot. He ordered all trials and executions to stop until he had familiarized himself with the matter. He soon determined that the judges had exaggerated the danger and sent the marquis and Luis home to Spain to be judged by the king himself. Malintzin's son was released on house arrest while the viceroy considered his case further. He clearly hoped that in his case the whole matter would soon be forgotten, as it was perfectly evident that he was entirely loyal. And he wanted to stay in Mexico, the land of his birth.

In November 1567, however, a tribunal of special prosecutors arrived from Spain with instructions to reopen the matter. Men had been whispering in the king's ear that perhaps the new viceroy had reasons to cover up a plot against royal authority. Falces was to be sent back to Spain. And Bernardina had to watch when her husband was arrested again on November 15. A number of men were tortured and tried. Two were executed. So it was that in January of 1568, don Martín was put on the rack and given the water treatment. When he would not confess even under torture, his lawyers were able to intervene successfully. For the first time, they made official mention of his mother, pleading for mercy for her sake. Martín was sentenced to perpetual banishment from Mexico. He died not long after, when the king sent him to fight the rebellious Muslims in the south of Spain. At about the same time as he and Bernardina and the children sailed for Europe, two more special judges arrived in the land. The king had learned that the City of Mexico was once again dripping with blood, and he sent representatives to check the carnage once and for all.

It had taken the Spaniards long enough to come to their senses. Why had they been so taut with fear as to lose the ability to reason? If don Martín ever spoke to his dead mother as he lay in his prison cell, they must have laughed bitterly together. They would have known the answer to the question. What the Spaniards were afraid of was, ironically, the Indians.

***

WHAT HAPPENED IN MEXICO CITY in the 1560s was much more complex than what first meets the eye. There was much more afoot than a conflict between different groups of powerful Spaniards. In traditional accounts of the era, Aztec history has been missing; including it renders the chaotic period much more comprehensible. What seems to be a story of random violence and inexplicable mutual hatred is actually a predictable political crisis. By now, forty years had passed since the initial conquest. The Mexica who were young children at the time or born in the tumultuous decade that followed—if they had survived the epidemics—were now at the peak of their adult lives. They were fully cognizant of the world of their fathers and mothers, but they themselves had been raised in a different moment. As a result, they were sometimes torn in their reactions to pressing issues and were prepared to respond to Spaniards in terms the Spaniards could understand.

Tenochtitlan's royal family still survived as a politically viable entity. The war, the epidemics, and the imposition of monogamy had cut it down to size, but the descendants of Acamapichtli still carried the banner of their ancient history forward. In the late 1520s, after the murder of Cuauhtemoc, the Spaniards had named Indians they knew and liked to lead the people. The Nahuas used an old term for them, *quauhpilli*, or "eagle lord," the term they had always used for commoners or outsiders who rose to positions of power through merit rather than birth. Members of the Mexica royal family still had much of the respect traditionally accorded to them as well as access to some of their former material resources, but both sources of prestige were dwindling. The prospect of penury pressed at them, and they also sometimes faced opprobrium on the part of the people for having lost the war.[13] Then in the mid-1530s, a new viceroy arrived from Spain with full authority from the Crown to take over the governance of New Spain. To Hernando Cortés's chagrin, he himself was forced to take a backseat as a wealthy private citizen. The new viceroy, don Antonio de Mendoza, decided to select a member of the Tenochca ruling family to act as *gobernador*, or head of an indigenous cabildo, a collective that would be charged with maintaining order and assembling needed labor drafts. His goal was to establish such a body in every altepetl, and thus it was especially important that a proper model be established in Tenochtitlan, or the City of Mexico, as it was now called. The Indians, he thought, would govern themselves more effectively than any outsider could; offering self-rule was also a gesture of good will, for this was what the Indians said they wanted.[14]

The only question was whom to choose as a royal gobernador in the capital. Moctezuma's sons had mostly been killed by Cuauhtemoc. Only the two youngest had survived his rampage. One, Nezahualtecolotl (Ne-za-wahl-te-KOL-ot, or Hungry Owl), whose name recalled Nezahualcoyotl and Nezahualpilli, was almost certainly the son of a Texcocan mother. He was probably with the Spaniards during their original occupation of the city and thus became known to them, for immediately after the conquest, he was taken up as a protégé by Cortés. The conquistador had the boy baptized with the same name he gave his own sons, "Martín Cortés," and then sent him off to Spain for a Christian education, as befit the son of Mexico's late king. Nezahualtecolotl or "Martín" traveled back and forth across the Atlantic over the next decade and a half, and became so acculturated in Spain that he was soon known only by his Christian name, and eventually married a highborn Spanish woman. He died young, just as a different member of the royal family was about to be instated as gobernador, and some whispered in Nahuatl that he had been poisoned by Mexica noblemen who did not want to see this young man, who was effectively a Spaniard, live to claim power over them— though this story was undoubtedly apocryphal, as the man the gossips said was responsible had actually died before him.[15] Moctezuma's youngest son, don Pedro Tlacahuepantli (Tla-ka-way-PAN-tli), whose mother was from Tula, had been seven or eight years old at the time of the conquest. He would have been a friend of don Martín, Malintzin's son, since the two youths traveled to Spain on the same ship in 1528; the young prince was to serve as a royal prop in the roadshow Cortés intended to put on in Spain. When don Pedro later returned to Mexico, he had almost no cultural capital, as the marriage that had produced him had not been a welcome event in Tula, but rather forced upon them by the Mexica, nor was his mother anybody important. Indeed, the pipiltin of Tula seemed to hate him. "Go back to Mexico City," they are recorded as saying. "That is your land. Leave Tula [to us]; there is nothing for you here." Don Pedro would spend his life fighting for an inheritance in Tula, and though he eventually won in Spanish courts, he was far from being in a position to claim authority over the Mexica.[16]

Fortunately, don Pedro was not the only possible royal gobernador, for Moctezuma had surviving nephews who were more warmly embraced by the Mexica nobility. The one generally accorded the most respect was Huanitzin (Wa-NEE-tzeen), who had before the Spaniards arrived already been established by Moctezuma as the very young tlatoani of Ecatepec. He ruled over an important Tepanec town, the Tepanecs forming a key element of the Aztec Triple Alliance. Predictably, he was among the close allies who went to fight by the side of Cuauhtemoc during the war, and he was taken up and imprisoned with the latter in Coyoacan when the peace was made. In addition, he was later among those forced by Cortés to travel to Honduras and back.[17] He had since married his cousin, doña Francisca, the daughter of Moctezuma who had not been turned over to the Spaniards along with the long suffering

Isabel, but who had instead been sent to her mother's people in Ecatepec. (Huanitzin had had children with at least one other woman in the past, but they were not counted as his legitimate offspring in the new Christian world.)[18]

The Spanish viceroy decided that Huanitzin was the perfect candidate to serve as ruler of the indigenous cabildo. His people ranked him highly indeed.[19] He spoke some Spanish and had worked with the Franciscan Pedro de Gante, probably at some point during his imprisonment. Christened Diego de Alvarado, he used his Spanish and indigenous names together and styled himself, "don Diego de Alvarado Huanitzin." After the reinstatement of the royal line in 1538,[20] the new tlatoani wanted to make a sort of declaration on behalf of his people. Working together with Pedro de Gante, Huanitzin arranged to have the city's most talented feather workers, who had once made gorgeous shields, craft a shimmering picture of the mass of Saint Gregory—at which an early pope had proved transubstantiation (the miracle by which the bread and wine of the mass become the flesh and blood of Christ) before a doubting audience. It was meant to be a perfect parable for what the Christian fathers had managed to achieve in Mexico. Then in a grand public gesture Huanitzin sent it off to the pope in Rome as a gift with a message in Latin embedded in the work itself: "For Paul III, pope. In the great city of the Indies, Mexico, this was composed under don Diego, governor, under the care of fray Pedro de Gante, Franciscan, in the year of our Lord, 1539."[21]

Huanitzin lived only a few more years. After his death in 1541 the indigenous council arranged to have power alternate to the opposite branch of the family, just as had been the custom in the days of old. Don Diego de San Francisco Tehuetzquititzin (Tay-wetz-kee-TEE-tzeen), a grandson of Tizoc, whose reign in the 1480s had been so short, came to power and governed his people for almost fourteen years, until 1554. Tehuetzquititzin seems to have been generally well liked –his Nahuatl name meant "He-Makes-People-Laugh"—but his reign, like that of every Mexica tlatoani, was fraught with tension. He began by accompanying the Spaniards to the west, to participate in the Mixton War. In their histories, his people cast him as a warrior, going to fight as all new kings did. When he returned, the terrible epidemic of the mid-1540s had begun. It devastated both city and countryside. Tehuetzquititzin spent the subsequent years trying to defend his community's resources from rapacious Spaniards as well as attempting to prevent the erosion of his own family's wealth, without which they could not function as leaders. Throwing himself into the center of events, he earned some criticism. But he also met with significant success. He worked hard to unite the noble families in and around Tenochtitlan and was partly successful. Two years after his death in

1554 the heads of family gathered together to sign a petition, asking that the Spanish Crown appoint a protector to safeguard the Indians' interest; the highly literate group suggested Bartolomé de las Casas, whose writings were drawing attention to the situation in the New World.[22] From 1554 to 1557 there was a hiatus, during which time the Spaniards postponed approving a new royal gobernador. Perhaps they were rendered nervous by such strong indigenous voices. Instead, a respected nobleman from Xochimilco (another quauhpilli or "eagle lord") was brought in to rule. Eventually the eldest son of Huanitzin, don Cristóbal Cecetzin, agreed to serve and was elected. When he died unexpectedly in 1562, the pendulum once more swung back to Itzcoatl's side of the family, and in 1563, don Luis de Santa María Cipactzin, a grandson of Ahuitzotl, was chosen.

It proved an unfortunate moment to become leader of the Mexica people. Beginning in the 1550s, the Spaniards had started to discuss the prospect of having the indigenous people of the island city pay tribute, just like all the other native peoples of Mexico, except that their payment would be made to the Crown, rather than an individual encomendero. In the 1520s, when the Spanish state apparatus was first put in place, the fact that the Mexica did not pay tribute had in theory been explained by their history: they had not been tribute payers when the Spaniards came. But it was also a consequence of the reality that the urbanites were already being asked to do as much as any strug-gling population could do. Although they did not pay any kind of tax in cash, they were nevertheless coerced into building downtown Mexico City, and they also provided food, fodder, and service to the households of important Crown officials as well as to the friars. The city's people had grown used to these requirements, and they handled them as they had always handled public chores: they rotated them amongst the different wards of the city, which still matched the old calpolli units. Now the Spaniards spoke of adding tribute payments in cash and in kind, and the people grew restive, explaining that since they were artisans and merchants and did not have farmlands, they could not cope with such demands. The people had some staunch defenders in the Spanish population, among them the Franciscan friars as well as the viceroy, don Luis de Velasco, who believed that the Indians could not realisti-cally be expected to do more.[23]

Spain, however, had more power over the Indians now than they had had when the conquest was new. King Philip was in no mood to humor the Indians of the New World. He was strapped for cash—and would in fact later declare bankruptcy.[24] In a time-honored Spanish tradition, he sent a *visitador*, or inspector, with full powers to investigate the situation and all prior actions of the viceroy. Jerónimo de Valderrama arrived in the City of Mexico in September of 1563. He ostentatiously established his quarters in the mansion of the young marquis, Martín Cortés, rather than in the offices of the government complex, thus distancing himself from the viceroy. He immediately sent a report back to Spain blaming the Indians and their friends, the friars, for the king's cash flow problems. Specifically, he argued that the reason the people perceived themselves as poor was that they were currently pressured to give a ridiculously large quantity of money to their own indigenous nobility and to their religious caretakers. "All that has been taken from the Indians and has accrued to Your Majesty used to be consumed by the indigenous governors and noblemen, and the friars. The governors and noblemen drink their share up. The friars do, I am sure , use it for good in buying silver and ornaments for their churches and monasteries, but they do wrong to take the property against the will of its owners."[25] Valderrama insisted that he had it on good authority that the ordinary people would be delighted to pay a head tax to the king, if in exchange for that they were freed of their responsibility to labor on public projects and no longer had to support their own nobility.

The inspector was so biting in his attacks on the present policies of Velasco the viceroy—all in the name of the king—that by January of 1564, the viceroy had no choice but to cave. Though he predicted a crisis, he nevertheless signed into law the edict that the king so obviously desired: a requirement that the city's indigenous people pay 14,000 pesos annually into the coffers of the Crown and that they make an additional substantial payment in corn. The law was effective immediately; the first of three annual payments was to be made in July.[26] Three days after Velasco signed, a copy of the document was taken to the cabildo, the indigenous council, and formally presented to the leaders there. The gobernador, don Luis Cipactzin, appealed immediately, but to no avail. He was threatened with prison if he did not comply with the demands of the royal government. In February he signed the paper.[27]

Valderrama and his colleagues were determined to try to direct popular resentment away from themselves and towards the Mexica nobility. In March, they encouraged the filing of a lawsuit against don Luis Cipactzin and his fellow councilmen. The case was brought by a group of craftsmen from the neighborhood or sub-altepetl of Atzacualco. The leaders were Juan Daniel, a bread baker, and Pedro Macías, a tailor. The royal family lived mostly in the sub-altepetl of Moyotlan, and so at first glance, one might suppose that the resentments of Juan Daniel and Pedro Macías were based in a competitive spirit between neighborhoods, or possibly in anger at the expectations that the nobility had of the common people. Today, however, we can see the heavy-handed guidance of the Spanish lawyers who claimed to be taking Juan's and Pedro's statements. They gave some odd reasons for insisting that their current indigenous governors should not be empowered to rule—saying that they were not literate in the Spanish letters, that they loved to celebrate feast days with old-style dancing and even the wearing of feathers, and that they did not care who was a polygamist or how many taverns there were in the city. These were not complaints likely to emanate from an ordinary indigenous baker and tailor. Only at the very end was a statement added that the nobility robbed the people through exorbitant tribute demands that they placed upon the commoners. The two might indeed have voiced resentments of this kind, possibly going back many decades.[28]

Don Luis Cipactzin fought back. In court, his lawyers denied some of the charges and creatively defended their client against others. They gently pointed out, for example, that it was their understanding that even in Spain municipal office holders were not always fully literate. More importantly, perhaps, don Luis defended himself in the eyes of his people. In June, he married doña Magdalena Chichimecacihuatl (Chee-chee-me-ka-SEE-watl, Chichimec Woman), who was apparently the ward (the grandniece) of the former gobernador, don Diego Tehuetzquititzin. The girl was thus the youngest in the lineage of Tizoc. In making this marriage, don Luis reminded everyone of their joint proud ancestry in the lineage of Itzcoatl, son of Acamapichtli, the first seated king of the Mexica. Don Luis himself ostentatiously danced before the crowd, wearing the traditional feathers and playing a gold-painted drum, recalling the celebrations and ceremonies of untold generations as well as the significance of a king dancing.[29]

Within days of the wedding, don Luis sent emissaries to speak to key groups. The indigenous church painters and scribes who worked for the Franciscans received them with interest. Two elders came who presently were serving on the cabildo. The speakers used ancient metaphors to remind their listeners that they should remain devoted to the cause of keeping the Mexica polity alive and viable, speaking poetically and formally, just as their fathers had done in trying political times. "Does it not stem from here, the breath, the words of the altepetl, its years of blood sacrifices?"[30] If the church artisans and scribes—who themselves had studied with the wise friars and were descended from the artisans of the ancien régime—were going to behave inharmoniously and rebelliously, there would be no altepetl left to fight for. It would implode, and then the Spaniards would crush whatever pockets of political organization remained. The emissaries reminded them that don Luis and his colleagues among the nobility did not take any of this lightly. They regarded their responsibilities seriously, as good chiefs always had. "They suffer anxiety in the night. They don't eat with tranquility, worrying about how they will care for the wings, the tail [the commoners]."

In the waning days of June 1564 and the first few days of July, the Mexica talked of little else. They spoke to the friars and even recorded arguments with them, disputes which the Spaniards themselves never mentioned. They also debated each other and grew even more vociferous. They all felt they simply could not afford to pay the required new head tax every four months. Most did not blame don Luis for the change in the law, as Valderrama wanted them to (they did not accept the idea that it was his or his predecessors' corruption that had caused all this), but many were nonetheless convinced that their governor could have done more to stave off the disaster. His Nahuatl name "Cipac" meant "Alligator," but now they began calling him "Nanacacipac" or "Mushroom Alligator." He was as insubstantial as a mushroom that sprouted overnight, like a "paper tiger."[31] Often they called him simply "Cipac" without the "-tzin" suffix acting as an honorific, which they still applied to all the other royal figures of the recent past. Relatively few people seemed to understand the enormous pressures on him from both sides.

On Monday, July 3, seven members of the indigenous council were arrested. They were to be held hostage while the Crown's office demanded popular participation in some public works projects in addition to the collection of the tribute. On Friday it was announced that three hundred people would be arrested at random and sold into indentured servitude if the community did not cooperate. On Monday, July 10, armed Spaniards went house to house collecting "volunteers." To stop this, don Luis Cipac called a great public meeting for Thursday.[32]

At two o'clock in the afternoon people surged into the tecpan, the indigenous government building, and climbed to the second floor. Don Luis Cipac and the other cabildo members were seated in the center; those who had been jailed had been released to participate in the meeting. Juan Cano, Isabel Moctezuma's Spanish husband, was there to lend his authority. Almost all community leaders and master craftsmen were present, as well as many ordinary people, including dozens of women. If the tax were not repealed, it was in effect mostly women who would have to pay it by increasing their spinning and weaving for Spanish markets; their husbands' income really could not be stretched any further. Don Luis asked the clerk of the cabildo to read aloud a statement he had prepared about the futile efforts he had made to protest the new law; the speaker finished with a summary of the new tribute, the first installment of which had to be collected without any further delay.

At the end of the speech, people cried out, "Where will we get it from?!" One old woman made an impassioned statement and began to cry. Public tears were symbolic for the Mexica; they were laden with political weight and shed only at significant moments.[33] It was as if the woman had touched the core of years of anger. The situation devolved into pandemonium. A man who was present later recorded what happened:

> There was more raging and shouting. And they insulted the governor himself. . . . Pedro Maceuhqui [a member of the indigenous council] jumped in, separating people and restraining them. He had his staff of office on his shoulder. Suddenly they grabbed it from him and were going to kill him. They ganged together to kill him. They pulled his shirt off. Just naked was how they left him. They got Juan Cano out of there. He took out his sword so they would [back off and] let him go. Otherwise he would have died at the people's hands. And while people were crying out, everybody gathered on the rooftops, and the Spaniards on their roofs. Some ran to hear what was happening at the tecpan, and others ran away. The ones doing business at the market all came. And all the people in the houses came out, the old women and the old men, the children, the people of the altepetl. People threw stones at the upper floor of the building. They destroyed a floral carving that ran around the wall. Then a Spanish officer came and took out his sword and chased people. The Spaniards and some of the mestizos who were there all took out their swords and dispersed people. The women broke through the patio wall on the left side, where people were flung. Men and women just climbed over each other so that they fell back and screamed and shouted. Many really got hurt, and they hammered one old woman's face. The Spanish officers gathered really fast and pursued people and dispersed them. Right away they took people prisoner. The ones whom they collected they took upstairs and put into the hands of the governor, who beat them. When they were beaten, their hands were tied. The Spaniards went to close all the roads everywhere. Everywhere people were seized along the roads. They armed them-selves with lances, shields, and other weapons.[34]

Evening approached. The writer remembered, "The Ave María was ringing." The Spaniards' chief constable arrived. The people gave a great shout. Perhaps they knew who he was—the son of Hernando Cortés by his indigenous woman, the lady Malintzin. It was indeed don Martín himself who had come

on this day in 1564, not long after his arrival in the city. As a preliminary step
in his investigation, Valderrama had temporarily removed the viceroy's officers from their positions of power and replaced them with interim figures. To
the post of chief constable, he had named don Martín. Now Malintzin's mestizo son faced the sea of angry indigenous faces. He had not spoken much
Nahuatl—if any at all—since he had bid farewell to his mother as a boy, and
so he spoke through an interpreter. Like his mother once had done, he counseled peace, asking the people to save their lives and fortunes. He said if they
did not go home, orders would be issued to arrest them and sell them into
slavery. "Everyone must go home. Go home, Mexica." Whatever he felt inside,
and however much he had lost the ability to express himself in Nahuatl, don
Martín certainly understood those closing words from the interpreter's
mouth, mirroring his own words in Spanish. *Xicallaquican, mexicaye*. (Shee-
kal-ah-kee-kan, Mesh-ee-ka-ye.) "Go home, Mexica, go inside." They could
not turn the tide of power, he reminded them; they should salvage what they
could of their lives.[35]

Forty-six men ended up being arrested—thirty-one Tenochca and fifteen
Tlatelolca. They were quickly tried over the next few days; all were found
guilty. On July 21, their heads shaven to mark their shame, they were marched
through the streets and given two hundred lashes as they went. Then they
were sold into servitude for terms of two or five years. The town crier
announced the punishment at every corner, so that everyone in the city
should know of their crimes. The indigenous man who had been writing
about the events carefully recorded a list of their names, so that posterity
should not forget what they suffered.[36]

That Sunday, July 23, the writer mentioned, there was a public performance of the Chalca Woman's Song, the same vehicle for subtle protest that
had been sung years before by the musician known as Flamingo Snake, when
he wanted to call the Mexicas' attention to the unnecessarily draconian measures they were using to repress the Chalca people. "It is infuriating. It is
heartrending, here on earth. Sometimes I worry and fret. I consume myself in
rage. In my desperation, I suddenly say, 'Hey child, I would as soon die.'" The
familiar notes echoed through the streets. It made the authorities nervous.
On Monday morning, the Spaniards set up eight poles by the indigenous
market; they announced they would tie anyone who criticized the authorities
to these poles.[37]

Inspector Valderrama, meanwhile, was in a state of shock. He had genuinely convinced himself that the indigenous people wanted to enter into a cash
economy with payments made directly to the king rather than continuing

with the status quo. He wrote to Philip II, blaming the friars. "One can't believe that this riot by a few Indians could have happened if they hadn't been incited to it, because besides the fact that they are naturally so obedient, the [new] tax has been of great benefit to them. An animal without reason understands and recognizes the good that is done for him, more than a man, even though he has a bit of reason. I have made a great effort to understand them [meaning the Mexica], and the situation has not become clear."[38] It had, apparently, never occurred to him that the children and grandchildren of the Aztecs who had ruled the Mesoamerican world only forty years earlier might protest becoming impoverished, tribute-paying plebeians in such short order.

The viceroy, don Luis de Velasco, was not surprised at all. He knew the situation on the ground and had expected something like this to happen. But he was in no position to use the recent events to regain his prior authority, for he was dying. After a long illness, his kidneys were failing. He had spent the last fourteen years working tirelessly to cement relations between the various sectors of the new colony, and he now watched as his creation devolved into chaos. He lost the will to struggle; on July 28, he died.[39] The senior Audiencia judge, Francisco Ceynos, became the interim authority in the colony. He was a deeply cold man, who once said scathingly to a group of indigenous petitioners who were complaining of Spanish policy, "When it was still the time of Moctezuma, didn't the people used to give their own children to have their breasts cut open for their devil-gods?"[40] He was also a good friend and supporter of Inspector Valderrama. Malintzin's son don Martín insisted on resigning as chief constable the moment he learned that don Luis de Velasco had breathed his last. Apparently he could not bear the thought of enforcing the orders of Ceynos and Valderrama.[41]

In this don Martín made a wise decision, for Ceynos and his colleagues immediately embarked on a major effort to sow dissension among the Indians by attempting to pit the enraged populace against their own nobility. In August, Juan Ahuach, a church painter who worked for the Dominicans, was arrested for demanding an investigation of the gobernador's actions in accepting the imposition of the new taxes. Ceynos sentenced him and a companion to hang. The gobernador, don Luis Cipac, put his personal anger aside—though Ahuach was still shouting that he would take the gobernador down with him if he died—and together with the entire cabildo and numerous friars he went to plead for the lives of the two dissenters. By the end of the day the advocates had succeeded, and the two men were released. However, the troubles were not over: the Audiencia chief took Ahuach aside as he left and encouraged him to continue to complain about the indigenous authorities, even inviting him to create a painting that showed their abuses.[42]

In September, the attorneys for the plaintiffs who had originally brought suit against don Luis Cipac and the cabildo were forced to appear before the Audiencia judges and confess that their clients—Juan the baker and Pedro the tailor—had disappeared. They had run off to the countryside during the tumult in July and had not returned. Messages given to their connections had not led to their reappearance; they seemed to want nothing more to do with the case. Ceynos and Valderrama were displeased, and soon a new suit was filed against Cipac and his cohort. This time the leader of the petitioners was Toribio Lucas Totococ, a rebel who had been among the forty-six rioters sentenced to servitude. He was now suddenly released, most likely in exchange for participating in the case against don Luis Cipac—terms he would have been only too happy to accept. Don Luis loathed him, calling him "a seditious, offensive outsider." Toribio Lucas Totococ produced many years' worth of complaints he had previously filed against the cabildo for excessive demands, complaints that only now were going to get a serious hearing, thanks to the efforts of the current Audiencia judges to focus popular anger against Cipac rather than themselves.[43]

Meanwhile, some of the people continued to protest the tax itself, rather than directing their energies against their gobernador and his supposed collusion or irresponsibility. Among these was one of the leaders of the church painters who worked for the Franciscans, a man named Marcos Tlacuiloc. He was probably the same person who had become famous for painting a wildly popular image of the Virgin of Guadalupe at a chapel near an ancient fountain shrine in Tepeyac, just north of the city. It attracted so many visitors that it made the Franciscans nervous and generated a great deal of agitation amongst them.[44] (Later, in the seventeenth century, the story would be born that the site had become famous because an Indian named "Juan Diego" had seen an apparition of the Virgin of Guadalupe there, just a few years after the conquest.[45]) Marcos, like a number of others, refused to pay the four pesos required of him and was carted off to prison. The friars apparently paid, or at least petitioned, on his behalf, for they asked his brethren with concern what had become of him, and he was subsequently released.[46] While Marcos was jailed, he witnessed a set of exchanges that he would never forget. Ceynos himself came to the prison and tried to reason with (and possibly threaten) the jailed protestors. One in particular, Pedro Acaçayol, talked back to the colonial authority:

Ceynos said, "There's nothing more for you to wait for. You can't keep the pulque you've already drunk. Look around! Things are becoming clear. You've been here for three Sundays. Doesn't it hurt you, all that has already happened to you? Are you here to make a point?" Then he said to Pedro Acaçayol, "Listen, you. Four pesos are what you have [assigned to you]. In order to accomplish a little something, put down one peso and three tomines, and a basket of corn. Three tomines can be instead of a basket of corn, because you don't have lands and fields. That is all [the corn] you will have to give in one year." At that Pedro answered. He said, "It will not be possible, O king. Where will I get it from? I have only saved one half-peso and ten cacao grains. Please listen, O king. Even though I might be paid four pesos [for my craftwork] it doesn't stretch [to cover everything]. It is needed for my children."

"And do you serve only your children?"

"Whom if not my children? Our Lord gave them to me. . . . And if I had the money, [you ask]? Yes, if I had it, I would put it down. But all this is to what end? Where am I to get it?"

Ceynos said, "Fine, you will be sold to the metal works."

"Fine, you know what to do, for you are the king."[47]

Pedro Acaçayol's last words were clearly laced with irony. To the Nahuas, a king by definition knew what was best for his people and considered their future. Yet Ceynos understood nothing about the community he temporarily governed and persisted in making reckless demands, causing social unrest and producing poverty. Although Acaçayol's words were remembered and repeated, and probably gave both him and others some satisfaction, they did little for him in a practical sense. He was sentenced to labor in the metal works manufactory, just as the Spaniard had threatened.[48]

One ardent protestor who had not yet been jailed asked to meet with don Luis Cipac and the other cabildo members. He had what he considered a brilliant idea, designed to unite the nobles and the commoners behind one cause. Commoners raged that the nobles had not protected them and that the tax would not hit the wealthy noble families as hard as it hit the ordinary people. Nobles railed against the commoners for not understanding the extraordinary agony entailed in being an intermediary between the masses and an uncaring and powerful government. Now this man suggested that two Mexica individuals, one pilli and one macehualli (one nobleman and one commoner), come forth and agree to sacrifice themselves for their community. They would stand together, each loudly refusing to pay the tax. They would probably be executed—but they would have made the point to the Spanish authorities that they could not push the Mexica beyond a certain point. That would give the Spaniards pause; it would pressure them to readjust their demands. The gobernador and his colleagues heard the idea out. Then they looked at each other, amazed at the man's innocence, for they knew the Europeans well. They laughed harshly. "You propose that [only] two will die? When they have died, then you will die."[49]

At the end of September, don Luis Cipac himself was arrested and jailed for failing to cause his people to conform. He remained in prison for three days, and then was released on September 30, with instructions to begin the public collection immediately. The pressure was clearly affecting his mental state. The day he was released, he heard an old woman shouting outside about the injustice of the tax. He leaned out the window and shouted, "Bring her in! Tie her up!" Then he had her and at least one other woman beaten. One observer described the blood that came from their torn flesh with disgust.[50] Word spread throughout the city both of the gobernador's arrest and of his whipping of the women. In the first week of October, indigenous officials began to move through the neighborhoods of the city, house by house, collecting the tax, or as much of it as they could. The city's women now worked into the night, spinning yarn and thread. This work that had been their badge of honor during the time of their city's power, when they did not have to do it and could buy the cloth if they chose, or demand it as tribute, now became a dire necessity.

On Sunday, October 14, the cabildo members held a public counting of all that had been collected: 3,360 pesos. It was not the required one-third of 14,000 pesos, but it was a good start, enough to buy the community some time. The officials looked so exhausted as they stacked the coins and sorted and double counted and recorded the results in front of everyone that it was difficult to blame them. "How can we be confused?" the people asked. "Aren't we a conquered people?"[51] Then the cabildo members went in procession to deliver the funds to the Royal Treasury. When they returned to the tecpan, they held an open meeting. A representative from each of the city's four quarters spoke. Two of them wept, marking the political significance of the moment. Don Martín Ezmallin of Moyotlan, a grandson of Ahuitzotl (through one of the tlatoani's daughters), who was old enough to remember the days before the conquest, actually sobbed. He spoke of the injustice of asking men without land to produce more income as if by magic, along with the tragedy of having to ask the women to make the money by spinning. But then he spoke angrily of those who had been rebellious. "You elders, you men of experience, you have hurt the altepetl by confronting it and rising up. Did anyone here order this? It came from Spain."[52] Older people, he thought, should not behave with the naiveté of young hotheads who knew no better. He reminded them that with the might of Spain behind the tax, there was nothing anyone in Mexico could do to stop the collection. He concluded by forecasting political doom if they didn't somehow find a way to raise the rest of the required 14,000 pesos, this year and every year, for the Spanish state had not yet exhausted its strength.

***

DURING ALL THESE MONTHS, one young indigenous man had been listening to all that was said with particular fascination and horror. His name was Paquiquineo, though he was more often called by his Spanish name "don Luis de Velasco"—after his godfather, who had been the viceroy himself. He was an Indian from the Chesapeake Bay, in the far north (a kinsman of Powhatan, father of Pocahontas). He now lived with the church artisans who worked for the Dominicans, among them Juan Ahuach, the angry painter. In 1560, he had been kidnapped from his homeland when he and another companion boarded a Spanish ship, one that was exploring the coast of North America. Since he was the son of a chief, the ship's captain eagerly took him to be presented at court as soon as he returned to Spain. He thought the boy might possibly serve as an intermediary in the forbidding wildlands of the north, where no fully settled peoples like the Mexica had yet been found. Perhaps he might turn out to be an effective go-between, like Malinche. Back in Spain, King Philip spoke to the young man with interest, for the latter had already learned enough Spanish to make conversation possible. It turned out that he was still an entirely unrepentant pagan, not an eager middleman, and he asked only that he be returned to his homeland. Hoping to make an ally of him, and believing that something was due to a fellow prince, however savage he might be, Philip agreed. He ordered that Paquiquineo be taken on board the next fleet to Mexico, and then returned to the shores of North America on the fleet's return trip, following the winds.[53]

Paquiquineo traveled in the same fleet that carried the Cortés brothers and, like them, arrived bedraggled after a rough crossing in 1562. Until the outbound convoy was ready to sail, he was deposited in the Dominican monastery in Mexico City. Whatever he may have felt, he did not live in complete isolation, for not only had he learned some Spanish, but he had also acquired some Nahuatl from a Mexica Indian named Alonso who had been aboard the ship that had originally picked him up. The companion from home who had been kidnapped along with him was also still with him. The two of them almost immediately became deathly ill in the teeming metropolis. "They got so sick," wrote the head of the Dominican order, "and arrived at such a state, that it was not thought they would escape."[54] In this condition, Paquiquineo finally accepted baptism and took the Christian name of his noble patron, the viceroy, don Luis de Velasco. He was given attentive care, and he recovered.

Only then did Paquiquineo learn how poorly it had served him that he had impressed the Dominican provincial, fray Pedro de Feria, with his courage and his intelligence. Suddenly the friar decided that he saw in him the key to his order's future. The Nahuas had by and large become good friends with the Franciscans and thus, thanks to that order's influence over the Nahuas, the Franciscans had become the leading order in Mexico. Now the Dominicans would work with this young man to gain a similar influence over the hitherto untamed lands of North America. He spoke to the archbishop—who was himself a Dominican—and obtained a document forbidding Paquiquineo from returning home. Surely, the Dominicans reasoned, the king would not want him to return alone to his homeland now that he was a Christian, for if he were to backslide, his soul would be consigned to hell. Paquiquineo, they decided, would have to wait until the Dominicans were ready to launch a great undertaking in the north, in which he could serve as translator and guide. Paquiquineo argued, but to no avail. The provincial told him suavely that if he was so distressed about the situation, he could travel back to Spain and speak to the king again. But the young man demurred; if that were his only choice, he would rather stay in Mexico. At least he was on the right continent.[55]

So it was that the young Algonkian-speaking Indian from the Chesapeake was privy to all the protests that the Nahuas of Mexico City launched in 1564, as well as to all the agonies they suffered. He saw the violence and heard all the plans to try to get the Spanish overlords to change their minds, but it all came to nothing. In early 1566, a direct order arrived from the king to send Paquiquineo to Cuba where he was needed to help launch an expedition to his homeland, and he finally left Mexico. It would end up taking four more years before he at last made landfall in the Chesapeake region near his home village, in the company of a Jesuit mission.[56] There, above the James River in Virginia, he was welcomed by his people. Not long after the ships that had brought the settlers left, he arranged to have all the Spaniards present killed, except for one young boy, who later told the story. The Spaniards concluded that if even a beloved protégé could do such a thing, then the northern Indians must be inherently barbaric; they steered clear of the northern lands for a long time afterward and allowed the English to gain a foothold at the place they called Jamestown. But perhaps Paquiquineo had simply learned something very important from his years among the Mexica: namely, the futility of rebellion once Europeans had gained a secure foothold.

***

DESPITE THEIR POWER, or perhaps because of it, the Spanish authorities of the Mexican Audiencia certainly feared all kinds of social unrest as the tense year of 1564 turned into 1565. Reports of the full extent of the rioting had reached the king—undoubtedly through the sympathetic Franciscans—and now Valderrama found himself on the defensive. He whined in his letters to the king, "I have told the truth in everything that I have written. Your Majesty has been badly served here before I came."[57] In an effort to regain authority and influence, he attempted to go on the offensive. Allying with the Dominican archbishop, Valderrama and the Audiencia announced that the doctrinas (parishes currently served by the Franciscans) were to be taken from them and turned over to secular clergy.

Hoping to please the monarch, Valderrama and the Audiencia pursued the possibility of having encomiendas return to the Crown wherever there was no male heir. This last set of steps caused the encomenderos to become enraged and to flock to the young marquis, the son of Cortés, hoping he would lead them. The encomenderos lived with a great deal of power over the Indians in their lives, and they were a lengthy sea voyage away from the authority figures of Spain. Some began to say they should think of secession, that no one in New Spain needed anything from the mother country any longer. Don Martín, Malintzin's son, knew these young men well, so he was likely speaking truth when he said that none of them were capable of planning and executing a complex political coup, but were only strutting and shouting like boys. In any event, the talk soon quieted when no firm steps were taken to limit the power of the encomenderos.

In March of 1566, Valderrama, no longer trusted by the king, was pressured to depart in the same convoy that took Paquiquineo away. Valderrama had always liked the cocky young legitimate heir of Cortés. But now he was gone. Ceynos, the senior Audiencia judge, was fully in charge, and he did not like the young marquis at all. Within weeks, he moved against the Cortés brothers, accusing them of having committed treason a year earlier, during the middle months of 1565. They had purportedly planned an uprising, working hand in glove with the Franciscan friars and the Indians. "And when they were arrested," reported an indigenous commentator, "muskets were brought to the tecpan, to the central patio of the building, and a Spanish military guard was prepared, every one of them armed."[58] Ceynos was taking no chance of the Indians rioting in defense of the accused rebels—which he apparently believed they might do.

Then began the summary trials, the torture sessions, and the executions. The rapidity and harshness with which Ceynos dared to move against the scions of noble families—among them former playfellows of the king— would be mystifying, were it not for the context. All of New Spain knew that the year before, the Audiencia had faced a massive popular upheaval among the indigenous citizens of the city. Spaniards everywhere still shuddered when they thought of that terrifying Thursday in July 1564, when the Mexica had poured into the streets en masse, armed with anything they could lay their hands on.

Yet there was no genuine evidence that any of the would-be Spanish rebels had ever spoken to any of the Indians about their plans. The trials only revealed rumors that they had.[59] They certainly could not have been in regular consultation with don Luis Cipac, for indigenous records reveal that he had broken under the stress by that time. In April 1565, he had begun to experience delusions, and in May, he suffered a mental collapse: he climbed up to the roof in the middle of the night and began a sword fight with an imaginary enemy. He fell to the ground, breaking several bones as well as his spirit.[60] In August, as soon as he recovered, Ceynos arrested him for failure to pay a missing 170 pesos.[61] At first don Luis claimed he did not owe the state these funds, but several weeks later, in order to secure his release, he arranged to have the money paid. He emerged from prison a profoundly weakened man. In December, the legal charges against him and the cabildo were finally dismissed, but the news came too late to aid in don Luis's recovery. He died at the end of the month. Then for a long time, there was no gobernador at all. With him the line of Mexica kings descended from Acamapichtli came to an end; the indigenous recorded the event in their annals. In the critical period between 1565 and 1567, while the Spaniards experienced their own cataclysm, don Luis's people seem to have focused their energies not on fomenting further rebellion but on managing the fallout of the destructive new tax policies. Some worked hard at orchestrating and executing a new census, designed to demonstrate that the total tax bill, which was based on a head count, was too high and did not take into account the deaths in the most recent epidemics. Others worked on bridging the class- and neighborhood-based schisms that had surfaced during the 1564 crisis: the traditional ruling families partially gave way to allow other people to sit beside them on the cabildo.[62] The nobility, unable to agree on who among them should govern, eventually accepted the prospect of another eagle lord tlatoani. The gobernadors of Tenochtitlan would henceforth be outsiders, noblemen from other altepetls, appointed by the Spaniards.[63]

Still other men set about writing as complete a history of the disastrous events as they could. Just as in the performances of the old xiuhpohualli, the historical annals of years past, they made sure that different perspectives were given voice, one after another, although this time the record was in writing. They carefully transcribed the statements of men from different neighborhoods, which were still organized according to the old calpolli groupings. To them, truth was necessarily multiple; they knew that no single person could give a full account of an important moment. And they wanted posterity to understand the constraints they had faced and the reasons they had finally acquiesced. They filled dozens of pages, complete with dialogue, detail, anger, and hope.[64] The Spaniards still dreaded the mighty Aztecs, but the Mexicas' own fears in the night were of a different sort. After all the power they had once wielded, they feared that all true knowledge of the world they had inhabited would be lost. It was the prospect of oblivion that haunted them.

8

The Grandchildren

1570s–1620s

The bells were chiming six o'clock in the evening of Thursday, May 3, 1612, as people began to gather at the Royal Accounting Office.[1] The doors were unlocked. Inside the great stone chamber of the first floor, twenty-nine decapitated black bodies were piled. Relatives of the dead had been allowed to spread cloths over them earlier in the day, after they were cut down from the gallows from which they had been hanged and their heads placed on spikes, but the flies still swarmed around them. The people who had come now, at the hour spread about by word of mouth—black men and women and Spanish friars and a number of Indians, all of whom wanted to help—at first found themselves in shock. They said little. Don Domingo, or Chimalpahin, an Indian who worked at a nearby church, saw that they had no proper biers for so many, but the families had brought straw mats, taken from beds, floors, and walls, to help carry the bodies.[2] They began to walk towards the Hospital of Our Lady of Mercy, where they had been told they would be allowed to bury the dead. Perhaps to give expression to their feelings, perhaps to prevent any hostile Spaniards from stopping them, the friars in the procession began to sing. The Christian hymns carried in the evening air.

***

CHIMALPAHIN WAS a reserved and self-contained man, but he was none-theless an astute observer. He descended from a line of observers and social critics—it was a relative of one of his ancestors, Quecholcohuatzin, or

---

A grandmother speaks to her grandchildren. The Bodleian Libraries, the University of Oxford, Codex Mendoza, MS. Arch. Selden. A.1,folio 71r.

Flamingo Snake, who had come from Chalco to this very spot more than a century earlier to protest the treatment that the Mexica were meting out to the Chalca people.[3] The Chalca, despite being inhabitants of the central valley, had been treated like the most ordinary prisoners of war and sacrificed with little honor; his ancestors hadn't liked it and had come to sing a protest song. Now the Spaniards were behaving comparably: they were abusing the power fate had given them, apparently without any sense of shame. Once again, a song, a hymn, that said implicitly, "We know that this is wrong, and you do, too," was the only weapon available.

This was far from the first time that Chimalpahin, the Nahua, had walked side by side with a black man. As early as the 1570s, the decade in which he was born, the African slave trade to Mexico had emerged as a major phenomenon. Over the years, more and more enslaved people had been brought from the faraway continent. (The bookish Chimalpahin went to read about Africa in a popular almanac.)[4] In fact, until about 1600, more Africans were brought to Mexico than anywhere else in the New World.[5] They were auctioned off in the port of Veracruz. Most were sent to work in the silver mines or on sugar plantations, but a sizable number were sold to the elite of Mexico City or to the nearby secondary city of Puebla de los Angeles. By the early 1600s, Mexico City had become one of the wealthiest and most impressive metropolises in the world, and every powerful Spaniard wished to be attended by a string of liveried black servants. Even more importantly, as the indigenous population declined and struggled even to subsist, urban businessmen found they could use enslaved labor in the incipient shoemaking and textile workshops, as well as the booming iron foundries and construction trades (including brickmaking, tile work, and masonry).[6] An enormous and elegant baroque city was being built, and it required more labor than the beleaguered Indian population could provide. In the 1570s, there had been about as many African and African-descended men in the capital city as there were Spanish men— roughly eight thousand each.[7] The number of Spanish settlers increased proportionately as time went on, but because of the scale of the trade in those decades, the percentage of black urbanites nevertheless remained large. At the start of the seventeenth century, there were at least twelve thousand Africans and mulattoes in a city with perhaps three times that many Spaniards.[8]

Meanwhile, between the 1570s and the early 1600s, the indigenous population of Mexico City, like that of New Spain as a whole, had dropped precipitously. In 1570, there may still have been as many as sixty thousand Indian people in the city, but their resources were depleted after the tax law changes of the 1560s, leaving them more vulnerable than they had been. Then in

1576/77 a horrifying epidemic struck. Hemorrhagic smallpox caused people to bleed from all the orifices, even the eyes, and in its wake, other diseases spread rampantly in the weakened population. "There were deaths all over New Spain," Chimalpahin later wrote. "We Indians died, together with the blacks, but only a few Spaniards died."[9] The epidemic was followed by others. By 1610, there were only about twenty thousand to twenty-five thousand indigenous left in what once had been Tenochtitlan.[10] In short, the majority of the city's people were no longer indigenous.

On a daily basis, the shrinking Mexica population probably interacted more frequently with the laboring Africans on the streets and at work than they did with the more numerous Spaniards. In some ways, the Africans would have seemed to them a thriving group. They were quite visible as skilled workers; they worshipped at certain churches where they founded their own confraternities, associations through which they could work together to celebrate festival days or pay for the funeral of indigent comrades.[11] And not all of the Africans or African descendants were enslaved. In a large and cosmopolitan city, many black men were incentivized to work hard by being allowed the right to purchase themselves, or they chose to have children by free indigenous women, thus saving their offspring from slavery.[12] After an initial period of confusion, it was determined that children would follow the legal condition of the mother. For Chimalpahin and the other Indians, this was a new kind of slavery: the disaster that befell the mother when she was enslaved would be visited on her descendants forever. Before the conquest by the Spaniards, such a thing would have been unthinkable to them. But now they grew accustomed to the idea that *in tliltique* ("they who were black") were tied to the condition of slavery if they were born to an enslaved mother. The Mexica lived and worked with their new African neighbors, sometimes resenting them as individuals, sometimes respecting them, sometimes pitying them, sometimes loving them, but probably almost never questioning the new order that held them all in its grip.[13]

What Chimalpahin had learned a few years earlier was that the very vibrancy of the urban black subculture sometimes exacerbated its vulnerabilities. On Christmas Eve, 1608, many dozens of the city's black residents participated in a mock "coronation" of a black king and queen, giving them paper crowns and decorated thrones, and then partying through the night. This was in keeping with traditions of West Africa as well as Europe's widespread carnival. The frightened white population—which had long been nervous about the rising numbers of Africans in their midst—was not accustomed to the idea of anyone bowing to a local African king. They held an investigation, but could not prove that anyone had ever genuinely planned to initiate a *monarquía Africana*, except in fun.[14]

The Spaniards behind the investigation, however, did not let the matter drop. It was no accident that a few months later the ruling council of Mexico suddenly decided to organize a force to go out into the countryside and ferret out the so-called *maroon* communities. The word *cimarrón* had once referred to runaway cattle and other errant farm animals but was now shortened and applied to people. Over the years, first dozens and then hundreds of slaves on sugar plantations had run away and joined other escapees living in relatively unknown, unsettled lands, especially in the eastern lowlands. They made their living by robbing passersby on certain roads, hunting and trapping animals, and planting crops in tiny plots hidden in the wilderness. In the early months of 1609, the Spanish authorities decided to send a force out after maroons living near the city of Puebla. The patrol was composed of several hundred men, including conscripted rural Indians still armed with their traditional bows, the same kinds of allies usually brought by the Spaniards when they went to conquer new territories. After a few months chasing the fugitives about the countryside without result, the authorities decided to declare victory and grant the renegades the right to establish a small, permanent town, on the condition that they not allow any new runaways to join them. This was the Europeans' standard maneuver in such situations.[15]

Then in the waning days of 1611 an enslaved African woman in Mexico City who had been beaten and tormented by her owner for years was murdered by him. The owner was Luis Moreno de Monroy, from a famous and wealthy family; today we do not even know the brutalized woman's name. But the people knew her name then. The large black population—many of whose members had by now attained positions of great authority as supervisors and foremen—nearly rioted the day of her funeral. The organizers of the protest were said to be members of a black confraternity at the church of Nuestra Señora. Hundreds of people marched to the Royal Palace to demand that the murdered woman's master be held accountable for his deed and then marched on to Moreno de Monroy's house and shouted at him for several hours, but they hurt no one. The high court did not order an investigation of the woman's death as the people had demanded. Instead, the authorities decided to attempt to calm the white population's fears by ordering that the leaders of the protest be flogged. Fortunately for the latter, their powerful owners intervened and prevented the punishment from being carried out.[16]

The Spanish population of Mexico City continued to feel jittery. There remained angry blacks in the countryside and angry blacks in the city. Then on February 22, the viceroy, don fray García Guerra, died of an infection.[17] Without a highly responsible person in charge, the city was vulnerable to the manipulations of power-hungry and vicious men, just as it had been in the mid-1560s after don Luis de Velasco died unexpectedly. Members of the Audiencia, the ruling council that held supreme power in the absence of a viceroy, began to hear stories from whites who claimed to have overheard black people talking about an uprising, among them some Portuguese slave traders who said they could understand the Angolan language.[18] On Sunday, April 1, the council sent guards to the church of Our Lady of Mercy where they arrested a number of black worshippers on the grounds that they had been fomenting rebellion against their Spanish masters. Chimalpahin heard all the details from someone who was there. "The sermon was being preached when the officers came," he commented.[19] Two weeks later, several edicts were read aloud by town criers all over the city. Henceforth, no black man was to carry a sword or wear a Spanish-style collar; no black woman was to wear a veil. And Spaniards owning more than two black slaves were to sell them, so that no household would have more than two black residents. No sitting viceroy would have alienated the city's wealthiest white men in this way, but angry, lesser men were in power now. Finally, the council posted guards at all the major entries to the city, lest the maroons living to the east or west reenter the city to free their urban kin. Chimalpahin could see the guards stationed on the southern road from where he lived.[20]

Two days later, on Monday of Holy Week in 1612, another proclamation was made: there would be no further processions or any public celebration of Easter week. These precautions were taken because it was rumored that the blacks were going to rise up on Thursday of Holy Week. At this, Chimalpahin became seriously irritated. A close friend of his had recently petitioned for and organized a new church organization, an indigenous confraternity, among the Mexica living up in Tlatelolco, and they had spent many hours planning and preparing for a grand procession that would bring honor to the Tlatelolca people. "But it was ruined," Chimalpahin said.[21] It had been an utter waste of effort. (Later, Chimalpahin would note, the Indians—those in Mexico City proper—were the only ones in the city who kept the faith and took the usual papier-mâché figure of Jesus down from the little wooden cross where it was hanging and buried it according to custom. They had to do this secretly in the garden, inside the wall surrounding their indigenous chapel, not out in public, as all events were supposed to be canceled.)[22]

On Wednesday, the Spaniards worked themselves up into a frenzy of fear. Chimalpahin remembered: "It was very dark because of clouds, and it rained,

and it cannot be found out who went shouting all around the city of Mexico—
was it not some mischievous Spanish youth?—shouting to people and going
about saying at the corners of houses everywhere that the blacks had arrived,
that they were not far away, that everyone should get equipped for fighting. . . .
All night the Spaniards did not sleep and kept vigil."[23] Years later, a Spaniard,
not wanting to blame a practical jokester, would say it was some roving pigs
that had first frightened someone and generated the initial alarm.[24] Be that as
it may, Chimalpahin couldn't help laughing. "We indigenous were not at all
frightened by it but were just looking and listening, just marveling at how the
Spaniards were being destroyed by their fear and didn't appear as such great
warriors [after all]."

He probably would not have found humor in the situation, however, had
he known all that was going on. In the basement of the Royal Audiencia, dozens of the black men and women who had been arrested during Easter Week
were being tortured on the rack, as well as by water boarding, just as Malintzin's
son had been. Don Martín Cortés, however, had been better prepared for it,
and he still had his honor and high status left to lose, so he managed to refuse
to give his tormentors what they most desired. This time, many of the victims
apparently said what their torturers told them would bring an end to their
sufferings—that there had been a plot. No records of the fast-paced sessions
survive; probably none were kept. But we know how such events usually
went: the victims merely had to answer "yes" as their torturers fed them
details. In a final summary, the high court judge wrote that the blacks, free
and slave together, had worked out a scheme in which some of them were to
be given the titles of "duke" and "marquis," and they had planned to distribute
the Indian encomiendas among this new nobility. A woman named Isabel
was to be queen. (The accused woman may have been a healer, for the
Spaniards later said that witchcraft had also been involved.) Supposedly, the
Spanish men were all to be killed, and their wives and daughters distributed
among the black men—the same reversal so often feared by white enslavers,
male and female, throughout the hemisphere.[25]

As word of what had been "confessed" began to circulate among the
Mexica, the story took on a decidedly preconquest twist. It seemed the rebels
had imagined future crises, revolving around who an individual's mother was,
and whether her lineage was being given its due respect. The younger Spanish
women were purportedly to have been distributed among the victorious black
men, and the older Spanish women either killed or sent to convents. When
the Spanish women's children were born, the boys (but not the girls) were to
be taken away and killed. This would be necessary because "when the *moriscos*

[the mixed-ancestry children] increased in number, they might remember that their mothers, on the female side, were Spanish women who came from splendid stock, splendid lineages, more splendid than they were on the side of their fathers, the blacks, so that perhaps then they would prepare for war against them, perhaps they would kill their fathers, the blacks." Interestingly, the indigenous gossips also insisted that the blacks were going to keep the members of three religious orders alive as teachers—the humble Discalced (Barefoot) Carmelites and Discalced Franciscans, and the learned Jesuits. But even they, the scaremongers said, were to be castrated.[26]

Chimalpahin, however, does not seem to have believed any of it. Nothing indicates that he could not believe *in tliltique*, the blacks, to be angry.[27] He understood their anger. He simply could not believe that so many had participated in creating such a farfetched plot, or that they would have wanted to bring on an unwinnable war. Instead, he saw them as victims and began to refer to them by a word only he seems to have used, *in tliltzitzin*, something akin to "the poor blacks." In ordinary life, the suffix *-tzin* was not so much an honorific as an expression of empathy or affection. Technically, he should have said, *in tlilticatzitzin*, but since he had generated the word on his own, he could say whatever he liked. On Wednesday, May 2, after only a few weeks of investigation, twenty-eight men and seven women were hanged in one day. "It took three full hours to hang them," he said.[28] Eight new gallows were constructed for the occasion. He noticed that when the condemned faced death, even at the last moment, when they could have cursed the world that had been so cruel to them or, if the stories were true, gained a probable ticket to heaven by confessing, they did neither. They utterly denied having participated in a plot. "We do not know what we are accused of, what we are being punished for," they shouted. As they died, they "cried out to their redeemer our lord God."[29] The authorities' plan, Chimalpahin said, had been to quarter them all and leave their body parts on display on the roads radiating out of the city, but a group of priests and doctors went to remonstrate with the high court judges, reminding them that such a step would create a health hazard. That was the only reason, sniffed Chimalpahin, that they decided the next day to quarter only six of them. The decapitated bodies of the other twenty-nine were deposited in the nearby chambers of the Royal Accounting Office.[30]

On Thursday evening, Chimalpahin helped with the work of the burial at the Hospital of Our Lady of Mercy. Later he went home to his room at the church of San Antonio Abad, at the southern gate of the city. He wanted deeply to believe in the elemental goodness of the world in which he lived— he had largely put the conquest behind him, and was moving matter-of-factly toward the future—but on that day, when he had witnessed an atrocity committed in the name of the law, the name of the king, and the name of God, he had no choice but to doubt the justice of the laws as well as the morality of the men who enforced them. He made no impassioned statements, but in his writings he subtly made it clear to posterity that there was a limit to the moral authority he would accord the Europeans who ruled his world.

***

UNDERSTANDING THE REACTION of this observant Nahua—his ability to critique the Spaniards, and yet his hesitation to rage at them—requires a comprehension of the range of his life experiences from his childhood on. The infant Chimalpahin was born in the countryside on May 26, 1579.[31] His town, Amaquemecan, for many generations had been part of the greater altepetl of Chalco, which had been founded long before the Mexica established themselves on their reedy island. Chimalpahin's people were also Nahua migrants who had come down from the north, and they shared a language, religion, and many cultural sensibilities with the Mexica. However, they had been in the central valley longer, and in Chimalpahin's day, they still had not forgotten it. In the 1200s, they had come down from the north and conquered their kingdom on the south side of the great lake at the center of the valley, and they had defended it successfully against all comers until the 1460s, when the Mexica proved too much for them.

When Domingo—as the boy was christened—was growing up in the 1580s, the conquest of Chalco by the Mexica seems to have filled his imagination as much or more than the one by the Spaniards did. He was raised on stories of the old days, of the deep past as well as the recent past, for his family was proud of their noble lineage and counted backward nine generations to the time of their arrival in the region in the 1200s. Domingo's father was born in 1550, and his beloved grandmother in 1535,[32] just as the Spanish government was becoming fully established in the area. His grandmother apparently knew—almost certainly was related to—the Amaquemecan musician who was baptized "don Jerónimo" as an aging man in his sixties, the one who had been known before the conquest as Quecholcohuatzin, Flamingo Snake.[33] Chimalpahin loved to hear stories about this man who had been a famous drummer, singer, and dancer; he had helped Chalco speak back to power when Axayacatl was king. Sometimes the stories of the past were sad—like those of the adolescent children who left home during the great famine of the 1450s, but then died by the roadside and were picked apart by vultures. Even then, sad as they were, the stories spoke to him, and he remembered them.

At some point in his youth, he learned about the tradition of the xiuhpo-hualli, or year count, and in his head, he began to construct timelines with stories attached.[34]

Domingo grew up in a *doctrina* (or parish) run by the Dominicans, and it is likely that one of the friars became his teacher. Or perhaps he was taught by an indigenous man who had himself been educated by friars, for by now, the Roman alphabet circulated in the indigenous world independently of Europeans. The worlds of educated Spanish families and the indigenous nobility were by no means entirely separate: in fact, a man only a bit younger than Chimalpahin, who chose to become a Dominican, had a Spaniard as his father and the granddaughter of a notable Amaquemecan chief as his mother.[35] However Domingo came by his education, he learned fast and impressed those who knew him. By the time he was eleven, he had been sent to live in Mexico City, possibly with relatives, possibly with friars, but almost certainly in order to further his education and apprentice himself within the clerical world.[36] Judging from the record he kept at the time—less a diary than a xiuhpohualli—he lived from that young age near the center of town. He was a frequent visitor to the indigenous chapel of San Josef de los Naturales, near the Church of San Francisco, and he liked to go to the zoo at the indigenous community center. On Sunday, April 26, 1592, he reported that two jaguars who had lived there were taken to Spain, and on another day, that a horde of grasshoppers arrived at exactly four o'clock.[37]

Meanwhile, in 1591, as the city was growing rapidly, a new church was completed at the edge of the old Tenochtitlan, in the barrio of Xoloco, at the start of the road going south to Itztapalapan and then Chalco.[38] The road was at first a causeway, for it had to pass over the lake before continuing. The site was exactly the place where Moctezuma had walked out to meet the arriving Hernando Cortés. The church was named for San Antonio Abad (Saint Anthony of Egypt, who wandered in the desert), and its patron was don Sancho Sánchez de Muñón, a leading member of the cathedral council who in the 1580s had even served briefly as acting archbishop. Through the church's network, this prominent cleric heard of the promising young Indian boy; he could help him cope with the burgeoning tasks associated with running a busy place of worship. Two years after the church was consecrated, when Domingo was fourteen years old, he "entered the church of San Antonio Abad," as he put it. He would live and work there for many years. Not long after he got there, when he was about sixteen, he was made the *mayoral,* the general manager of all matters related to the indigenous congregation and probably of the physical plant as well. The church trusted this boy, who already behaved as a man. He became known as don Domingo de San Antón. Scholars later began to call him Chimalpahin, one of the family names he tacked onto his usual moniker, and the name stuck.

Domingo was still relatively new in the city when he experienced his first horrendous epidemic. It began in 1595. It was measles and would abate but then return. In 1597 the disease exploded even more virulently. "The epidemic raged terribly, there was a great deal of death. Infants who could already raise themselves up well and crawl, youths and maidens, grown men, mature men and women, and old men and women, all died."[39] In this time of sadness, Chimalpahin's language echoed the prayers of his people for generations. His words were reminiscent of those once addressed to Tlaloc in times of famine: "With pallid eyes live the babies, the children [of all ages]—those who totter, those who crawl, those who spend their time turning dirt and potsherds, those who live sitting on the ground."[40] Fortunately for Chimalpahin, as part of a well-funded church community, he received good care and good food. He survived this scourge and would survive numerous others.

Surely the young man often felt vulnerable, not only to sickness and death but also to the great fast-paced city in which he lived alone, without his blood family, who were in Chalco. At the same time, it is clear that he also felt profoundly empowered. He believed deeply in Christianity, in the radical equality of all souls before God, and he was proud to be part of the New World formed by the merger of his people with the worldwide kingdom of Christ. He saw himself as part of a far-flung network of brave Christian men who left their homes and traveled great distances to work on behalf of the souls of all the earth's people. He mentioned it in 1591 when hundreds of Tlaxcalans, who had taken it upon themselves since the conquest to be the Spaniards' ablest lieutenants, departed for the northern wildlands, from which point they would later aid in the conquest of New Mexico. They themselves did not want to go, and in their writings they raised a cry of suffering,[41] but Chimalpahin wrote optimistically, "The Tlaxcalans left for New Mexico. . . . People went out to meet them and feted them and encouraged them with good food."[42] He likewise wrote with delight in 1598 when the friars in the city received word of the successful founding of Santa Fe. Indeed, he knew personally three of the Indians who had gone north, two musicians and a lay brother. The latter was from his hometown of Amaquemecan.[43] A few months later, he reported with reverence on the deaths of some martyred Christians even farther away, in Japan:

Sunday, the 6th of the month of December of the year 1598, in the afternoon, was when the bones of the Discalced fathers who died in

Japan in the land of China arrived. It was afternoon when the friars arrived; they came carrying them enclosed in chests. All the religious who are here in Mexico went to meet them; when they reached [the church of] San Diego, the guns were discharged. How they died and what happened there was painted on four cloths which were hung at the [indigenous] church of San Josef; everyone saw and admired them, the Spaniards and we indigenous.[44]

In subsequent years, Chimalpahin reported avidly on all contacts the Spaniards made with Japan and the Philippines. There were many of these contacts as the Pacific trade grew. And to a great extent, he seemed to understand the political situation in that part of Asia. At one point, he even referred to the "indigenous" people of the Philippines, using the same word he used to indicate that his own people were indigenous.[45] He called them the *macehualtin*, which at one point had meant "commoners" but these days could be put to use to distinguish those who did not have the highest political power from those who did, separating lineages that were native to a land from lineages that were powerful newcomers or invaders. Perhaps Chimalpahin understood much of what he heard mentioned in Spanish churchmen's circles because he knew some Asians himself: in those years, there were many unfortunate souls from India and the Philippines who were kidnapped, sold in the Manila slave market, then brought to Mexico's western port of Acapulco. They were called *chinos*, and many hundreds of them labored in Mexico City as domestic servants. Some even staffed a monastery run by the Dominicans.[46]

Chimalpahin could not have believed that everything Christian people did as they spread throughout the world was a positive good. But he clearly did believe that the word of God was worth hearing. He was proud of all Christians, whatever color they were, who helped to spread it. He never thought that Spaniards or any other Europeans had a monopoly on the comprehension of God's truths; on the contrary, it was the universality of the human soul's worth that seems to have drawn him. He insisted repeatedly that all humans were the descendants of Adam and Eve; all were equally the purposeful creation of God. One of his favorite books was *The Confessions of Saint Augustine*. He liked Book 1 best, which closed, "The God who made me must be good, and all the good in me is his. I thank him and praise him for all the good in my life."[47]

It may seem surprising that a thoughtful indigenous man living about a century after the conquest found his life satisfying, often invigorating and exciting. But have any of the world's peoples ever allowed themselves to be flattened by crisis forever? Certainly the Native Americans did not. In the City of Mexico, Chimalpahin was surrounded by the Mexica—and other Indians who, like him, had migrated from the countryside—who spent their days working, laughing, and arguing, much as they had always done. There were fewer of them than there once had been—the devastating epidemics saw to that—and far more of them lived hand to mouth than had been the case before—extractive Spanish taxation policies guaranteed that—but neither the 1520s nor the 1560s, as hard as they had been, had turned out to be the end of all things. The people were still here, and they still knew how to seek happiness. There were even specific elements of the new life that they liked very much—chicken's eggs, cow's milk, wax candles, and boxes with locks, they sometimes said, for instance.[48] And there were more subtle winds of change that many liked—the new strands of music being played in the streets, from Africa and Europe, as well as the colors first seen on the silks brought from Asia on the Manila galleons.[49] Some must have liked the sense of being at the heart of things: an elegant city of monumental architecture was growing up all around them, its rulers in constant contact with the rulers of Europe and of Asia.

Yet Chimalpahin and his fellows did experience nostalgia and were often aware of a sense of loss. At the start of the year 1600, when Chimalpahin was not quite twenty-one years old, he suddenly came face-to-face with the past. Juan Cano de Moctezuma decided to stage a great pageant. He was a one-quarter Indian grandson of Moctezuma's daughter, Tecuichpotzin, as the people still referred to her,[50] or Isabel, as the Spaniards called her. The Spaniards wanted to mark the opening of a new century with a grand celebration, and Juan Cano the Younger in particular was glad to sponsor a show that would underscore his own family's remarkable history. He wanted a tableau of some sort surrounding the figure of the Moctezuma who had been in power a century earlier. To find someone to play the key role, he turned to surviving members of the royal family. Who could do this job and be taken seriously?[51]

Not since the downfall of don Luis Cipac had a member of that family been allowed to assume the role of tlatoani, but the family line still existed. In 1566, in the midst of the political crisis of the Spaniards, a son of the late governor don Diego Tehuetzquititzin named don Pedro Dionisio had put himself forward as a potential ruler, but he was immediately accused of having molested women and girls in his household.[52] In the midst of the chaos, the city folk decided to accept the rule of a quauhtlatoani, an outsider, a nobleman from the town of Tecamachalco, don Francisco Jiménez.

Other scions of the royal family still lived in the city, even though they no longer ruled. A number of them were descended from don Diego de Alvarado

Huanitzin, the first of the royal line to have been made gobernador, the nephew of Moctezuma who had been married to doña Francisca of Ecatepec—that daughter of Moctezuma who had been kept out of the view of the Spaniards. When Huanitzin died in 1541, he left behind a number of children. His youngest son could have been no more than a few years old at the time.[53] He was named Hernando (probably for Cortés) Alvarado (for his father) Tezozomoc (for his father's father, Moctezuma's brother, who was himself named for his grandfather, the son of Itzcoatl). In 1600, this junior Tezozomoc still lived in Mexico City and was at least sixty years old. He was famous in his day for being Moctezuma's grandson through his mother and his grand-nephew through his father. Juan Cano invited him to play the role of Moctezuma of the ancien régime, and he accepted. In full traditional regalia, he perched on a litter with a canopy and was carried through the streets. Before him went a troupe of musicians and dancers. They could no longer perform the old dances as deftly as people did in the 1560s at don Luis Cipac's wedding, for instance, but they used their talents and new ideas to improvise, and they impressed Chimalpahin and all the other spectators.[54]

What some in the audience undoubtedly thought, however, was that it had been eighty years since the fall of Tenochtitlan, which meant that suddenly there was almost no one left alive who could remember with clarity any of the comparable celebrations prior to 1519, or who had heard such great events described by their own parents. The people who knew about the old days were dead or dying. Even the first generation of young people who had worked with the friars and guided their people ever since were passing away. One of Huanitzin's younger daughters, for example, Tezozomoc's sister Isabel, had been married to a nobleman from Azcapotzalco named Antonio Valeriano, who had been one of the first friars' most talented students, known for his work in Spanish, Nahuatl, and Latin, as well as his musical compositions. He had worked at the school in Tlatelolco, and later became gobernador in the City of Mexico after don Francisco Jiménez left—an arrangement that satisfied everybody, for he was the perfect quauhpilli, eagle lord, if ever there was one—an outsider, true, but a nobleman from within the Triple Alliance, married to a daughter of Huanitzin, and a scholar beloved by the Spaniards. Now he was growing deaf and a little senile and had to have a young man aid him in all things.[55]

Years went by in which Chimalpahin continued much as usual. Then in 1606–7, a series of events occurred that seem to have convinced him that he should set about writing the history of the Nahua peoples. First, in 1606, typhus came to the central valley; thousands died. In July, the sickness took his father, and in October, his grandmother.[56] In the rainy season of 1607, overwhelming flooding began. The city, in the center of a geological basin, often experienced flooding problems, but that year the scale was far beyond what had been experienced before. In the downtown area, the waters rose about a foot above street level, making transporting goods and removing waste almost impossible. The common people living at the edges of town suffered most. "Adobe houses got soaked at the base, so that they fell inwards," explained Chimalpahin.[57] The people had to leave their homes and thus became wanderers in that filthy, watery world.

Faced with this emergency, the Spanish government decided to take steps toward the permanent drainage of the central basin.[58] This was work that the Indians would be required to do. Every altepetl would contribute materials, food, or labor. The massive project that became known as the "Desagüe (drainage) of Huehuetoca" began almost at once. First, the Spaniards demanded that thousands of people work on digging a great channel that would direct the melting snows from the surrounding mountaintops away from the city. It soon became evident, however, that the project was ineffective, and it was abandoned. Then the engineers conceived of a plan of excavating a massive, V-shaped ditch that would fill with excess water in certain years at certain seasons. As Chimalpahin described it, "There was an excavation so that the mountain was opened up, cut into, and a hole made in it. And they removed the bones of the dead from there; some of their bones resembled those who lived formerly here on earth. . . . So many indigenous people died there [at the drainage works], and some of the people from the various altepetl fell sick or got hurt."[59] It was rumored that thousands were dying. Once again, it seemed that the end had come for the indigenous peoples of Mexico.

As the death toll rose and Chimalpahin went about his work in the church, he came across two books that had just been printed in 1606 on one of the city's printing presses.[60] From 1539 on, friars in Mexico had been publishing books, generally for their own use in the field: indigenous-language dictionaries and grammars, as well as catechistic texts, including not only catechisms in indigenous languages but also confessional manuals and collections of sermons.[61] They wrote and edited these works with the help of Nahua assistants who often remained anonymous. There had been a slight tapering off later in the century, as the ideas of the Counter-Reformation gained sway, and the church fathers began to discourage the use of the vernacular, seeing it as too dangerous to the souls of the ignorant. But recently, such warnings almost seemed to have been forgotten, at least in Mexico. Although the first Anglo colony far to the north at Jamestown still consisted of a primitive fort, the colonists in Spanish America were in the midst of a new burst of publications.[62]

Two of the latest works impressed don Domingo. One was quite different from those by the religious authors that he was accustomed to reading. It was by a newly arrived Spaniard, Enrico Martínez, who used his knowledge of European almanacs and encyclopedias to write about his new home— *Reportorio de los tiempos e historia natural de esta Nueva España* ("Report on the History and Natural History of New Spain"). He included a little about everything—though his knowledge of the history of the Americas was quite limited compared to Chimalpahin's. The work was theoretically a compendium of knowledge about the New World, but it lacked an indigenous perspective. The other book was by a prolific (and to Chimalpahin, quite familiar) Franciscan friar Juan Bautista Viseo, and was called *Sermonario en lengua Mexicana* ("Sermons in the Mexican Language"). On its smooth pages where word after word was printed in Nahuatl, fray Juan gave credit in the introductory pages to the eight Nahuas who had worked with him, undoubtedly almost all known to Chimalpahin, among them don Antonio Valeriano.[63]

In 1608, Chimalpahin began the project of writing his people's history on a grand scale.[64] It would be a xiuhpohualli, or a collection of multiple xiuhpohualli, in the old tradition. He would record the history of the Mexica, of the Chalca people, and of anyone else for whom he could find sources, perhaps Azcapotzalco, Texcoco, and others. And he would do it before it was too late.

In some ways, Chimalpahin had been researching this project for years. He had always been interested in his people's past, and his friends and acquaintances often showed him materials or shared stories with him. It had probably started with his learning about the nine known generations of his family's heritage. When he began to write, he styled himself "don Domingo de San Antón Muñón Chimalpahin Cuauhtlehuanitzin." The "San Antón" and the "Muñón" were in honor of his church and its patron, but the last two names commemorated the family lines from which he was descended. "Chimalpahin" meant "Ran-with-a-Shield," and it was the name of a great-great grandfather on his father's side, the younger brother of a reigning tlatoani. Cuauhtlehuanitzin, or "Rises-Like-an-Eagle," was the name of the elder brother king himself, and don Domingo was descended from him through his mother's line.

Chimalpahin had long collected his family's genealogies and paid attention to stories that aging family members could recount to him, but he also sought written documents. In the final section of his great work, he wrote a great deal about where he had obtained them—for, he said, like the scholar that he was, he thought his readers might someday want to know.[65] A number of friends and relatives among the Amaquemecan nobility were able to give or loan him aging folios, documents created decades earlier when the use of the Roman alphabet was new and young students were eagerly writing down what their elders told them. The best of all came from don Vicente de la Anunciación, a cousin of his maternal grandfather. He had copied it from a book that had been in the possession of his father-in-law, don Rodrigo de Rosas Huecatzin. When don Rodrigo was a child, he had been among the very first generation to learn the alphabet, and in the 1540s, as a young adult, he became Amaquemecan's scribe. This turned out to be important, because the five subsections of the altepetl were squabbling about which of them, in this new postconquest world, should provide the altepetl's tlatoani. In 1547, the viceroy, don Antonio de Mendoza, sent an indigenous judge from Xochimilco to settle the dispute. The people held a great public meeting about the issue.

> In order that the judge could investigate all the ancient pronounce-ments of all five segments of the altepetl, those who were the noble elders deliberated over it in a great gathering and put forth certain ancient statements. And they put down in written form, in a book, how the five segments had been organized, so that they could present it to the judge. What the elders sought to present was really a true account, just like it had been, because it was impossible to lie before the others.[66]

Don Rodrigo was the scribe at this great event. Through him Chimalpahin had direct access to the rich, detailed language of the history performances of past times. Each section of the altepetl would have presented their remem-bered history, one after the other, as was traditional, but this time the statements were phonetically transcribed and preserved in a book. Thus Chimalpahin could step back in time to the 1540s, to the days of his grand-mother's childhood, and actually hear the elders speaking, giving him nearly unique access to the past.

Don Vicente had copied only part of the book. Realizing the value of what he had after speaking with Chimalpahin, he went back to his father-in-law's house where the book had been stored in the attic. But sadly, someone in the intervening years had disposed of the disintegrating and possibly worm-eaten object. All that remained of it was the part he had copied, which Chimalpahin now possessed.[67]

Meanwhile, in Mexico City, Chimalpahin let it be known among his many Mexica friends that he was working on a grand historical project and would be grateful to be allowed to borrow and copy any writings that the people had. He got word of numerous documents and copied them all tirelessly. Relatively early in the process, in 1609, he went to speak to Tezozomoc of the royal line, who had played the role of Moctezuma at the celebration of 1600.[68] Tezozomoc, too, was a bookish man, a history-keeper. In his head, and in rolls of paper in boxes and baskets, he held dozens of detailed, highly specific Mexica genealogies involving people of the sixteenth century both before and after the conquest. He knew what was solid information and where there were gaps. When he couldn't remember, for example, the name of someone's third daughter, or whom she had married, he said so, rather than making something up. He was also acquainted with stories, remote apocryphal tales that were significant in a different way, important for what they revealed about people's beliefs, even if they were not literally accurate. Some of what he knew he had already written down: "I, don Hernando de Alvarado Tezozomoc, write this on this day," he recorded occasionally. Tezozomoc was at least seventy years old, and he knew these papers needed a safe home where they would be recognized as valuable and useful. Other material still existed only in his head, and he needed an amanuensis who cared about historical memory.[69]

When Chimalpahin and Tezozomoc met, the two men must have looked with interest at each other. One was a scion of the Mexica royal household, a wealthy man in his own right, and the other a lesser nobleman from the once-subject state of Chalco, the mayoral of a local church. Their great-grandfathers had once been at war with each other. Quecholcohuatl from Amaquemecan had knelt in fear before Axayacatl. But those days were gone, and in that fact the two found their common purpose. Neither of them wanted the complex Nahua world of the central valley, as it had existed before the arrival of the Europeans, to be forgotten, or "erased," to use their grandfathers' word. In their writings, both men made passionate promises, almost certainly reiterating what used to be said on the days of great historical performances, using highly traditional metaphors. "It will never be forgotten," Chimalpahin said. "It will always be preserved. We will preserve it, we who are the younger brothers, the children, grandchildren, great grandchildren and great great-grandchildren, we who are the [family extensions]—the hair, eyebrows, nails—the color and the blood, we who are the descendants . . . we who have been born and lived where lived and governed all the precious ancient Chichimeca kings."[70] Tezozomoc murmured much the same. "What the ancestors came to do, what they came to establish, their writings, their renown, this history, their memory, will never perish, will never be forgotten in times to come. . . . We shall always keep them, we sons, grandsons, younger brothers, great- great-grandchildren, great- grandchildren, we their descendants . . . and those yet to live, yet to be born, will go on telling of them, will go on celebrating them."[71]

The religion of the two men's grandparents was premised on the notion of a carefully maintained record of a succession of imploding and renewing worlds, none of which was ever to be entirely forgotten. They themselves lived not in an original setting, but under a Fifth Sun, and since the fifth world's beginnings, people had been remembering the story of how it came to be and coping with changes in it by reiterating all that had passed before. They did this not just through oral retellings, but through oral history guided by writings. "Here it will be said and told, the relations about the ancient way of life, the painted words about the ancient kingships." It was a tradition that could not be broken without breaking faith with many generations past. "They left us, spoken and painted, their ancient words, the elder men and the elder women, the kings and nobles, our grandfathers and grandmothers, great-grandfathers and great-grandmothers, our ancestors who came to live here. Such is the relation that they made, that they left for us. This relation of the altepetl and of the altepetl's kingly lines, painted and written on paper in red and black, will never be lost, never be forgotten. It will be preserved forever."[72]

Perhaps the two men prayed together in this very way. Or perhaps they were too busy and too practical. But they understood each other nonetheless.

***

As Chimalpahin sat down to write his great work, he imagined an audience not of Spaniards or other Europeans but of Native Americans of the future. He envisioned readers who were indigenous and in danger of losing touch with their ancestors' experiences on earth. He said to his readers of the future that he knew, if they were reading his work, that they had become Christians, and he acknowledged that the Christians had brought a great deal of scientific and technological knowledge with them (mentioning eclipses, for instance). But their own people had had a wealth of knowledge, too, which they had preserved as best they could in the early days, and he would explain how he had come by these writings, "so that you the reader, you who are Christian, may not doubt or waver."[73] As he proceeded, on occasion, he would also explain terms and phenomena. For example, when he mentioned a god named Ome Tochtli (Two Rabbit), he knew that a seventeenth-century reader, even an indigenous one, might not know what he was talking about. He asked his readers to recall their school days and compared Ome Tochtli to the Roman god Bacchus.[74] He hoped that with this sort of scaffolding, his writings might be accessible. He would write only a little in Spanish; mostly the work would be in Nahuatl, the language of their people.

In his final compilation of his various works, he began at the beginning, with Adam and Eve. He could imagine some of his audience objecting that this was irrelevant, but he was adamant that this was the place to start:

> Even if it doesn't seem relevant to treat it here, it is necessary that all of us people here—we indigenous people from New Spain—that we know that what is called the first human generation was created from the earth, from the mud, and was created only one time. From it we all come and are born. From it all of us people on earth descend, even though there have been [two groups], gentiles and idolaters—[including] those who engendered us, we the people here in Mexico Tenochtitlan, and all the altepetls of New Spain.[75]

In the next section, Chimalpahin gave a brief synopsis of Old World history, drawing freely from Plato, the Bible, Saint Thomas Aquinas, Saint Augustine, and other foundational Western texts. He theorized that the peoples from the edge of Europe, from the Baltic, who had given the medieval Christians the most trouble in their conquest, might have been the Nahuas' ancestors.[76] Someone from the Old World, he was sure, had constructed boats and somehow made it to the (then unknown) New World. However it had happened, people had somehow ended up at Aztlan, at the Seven Caves, and from there had begun to wend their way south.

Now Chimalpahin could begin to write the histories he knew so well. Before long, Shield Flower was shouting at her captors, daring them to attempt to extinguish her. Her people, she warned them, including those yet unborn, would never waver. Individuals would perish, but her people would never die. They would experience loss, but it would never be permanent. Life was not easy, but it was nevertheless profoundly good. It was too simple to say that any enemies, including the Europeans, could ever bring pure evil or utter devastation to the land.

***

YET ONE MAY EVENING in 1612, Chimalpahin's steadiness of purpose and eternal optimism seem to have wavered. Even before the events that had ended in the brutal killing of thirty-five people, he had been struggling. In that period, the indigenous chapel of San Josef had as chaplain a vicious and corrupt man, fray Gerónimo de Zárate. He had tormented the city's indigenous people for years. Then one day in January 1612, the chaplain decided to extract money from the head of one of the confraternities, a man named Juan Pérez. "He stood him up against a stone pillar, naked and quite ill, where by the order of the priest they gave him a lashing. They left him almost dead, having fainted from the lashing. And [the chaplain] preached about him, saying in the pulpit that he dissipated much money that had been given to the confraternity. And then he had people take him to jail and lock him up, so that he would pay it back."[77] When Juan's wife learned what had happened, she went mad with rage and found the courage to go the office of the viceroy. Several others went after her and told their own awful stories about Zárate. Chimalpahin wrote of what he knew, summarizing, "[Zárate] thought nothing of the Mexica. He even thought nothing of some Spaniards, when they implored him on someone's behalf about something." Chimalpahin evinced the greatest admiration for Juan's wife. "The people thought [Zárate] very evil, but although the Mexica were angry about the priest because he treated them like this, they had patience, they kept it inside, no one dared to make it public and make complaint to the Royal Audiencia." These were remarkable words for the seventeenth century, a direct avowal of hidden feelings: *They kept it inside, no one dared to make it public.* And Chimalpahin added that it would have remained thus "if it hadn't been for María López, who was so bold as to accuse him before the lord judges." It took months before the chaplain was permanently ousted, and by the time he was, the viceroy had died and the arrests of the black city folk had begun, so there was little celebration.

In his writings, Chimalpahin had always fallen back on the idea that the world might be largely good, largely the work of a benevolent God, yet have within it certain evil individuals. That was how he thought of Zárate. "Let him alone give an accounting [of his actions] to our lord God." And he added, "Let him not be talked about."[78] By that phrase, "to be talked about," he meant "to be honored, to be known." He wanted Zárate erased from the people's memories; he counted on God to punish him in the hereafter, based on a full accounting of his deeds.

But in May 1612, Chimalpahin seemed to reach a kind of turning point. He was not satisfied simply to dismiss the high court judges who sentenced thirty-five black people to death in one day as people who were best forgotten. In a unique move for him, he very carefully listed the names of every single one of the fourteen Spanish royal officers who had condemned them, as if he wanted their names recorded so that justice could one day be done, before God if before no one else. The vertical column of names and titles was long, dominating the page. He ended his list: "These were the councilors who administered the law upon the thirty-five blacks, so that they were hanged on this day."[79] Chimalpahin, whose imagination was drenched in biblical imagery, would have remembered the haunting text from the book of Revelation: "I saw the dead, small and great, stand before God; and the books were opened, and another book was opened, which is the book of life: and the dead were judged out of those things which were written in the books, according to their works. And the sea gave up the dead which were in it; and death and hell delivered up the dead which were in them, and they were judged every man according to their works."[80]

***

YET CHIMALPAHIN MAY not have found sufficient comfort in keeping his book of records, for only a few years later, he ceased to work on it. The problem was deeper than the existence of certain evil individuals who would one day meet their maker and pay for their sins. The problem lay in the existence ever since the Spanish conquest of *extreme* power imbalances. In their daily lives, the Indians and the free blacks and mixed-ancestry people and even the enslaved could often live happily—loving each other, arguing, telling stories, laughing at a good joke. But when the Europeans in their lives chose to strike, the disempowered had almost no recourse. It could happen anytime, and fighting back could sometimes make the situation worse. So it was that "they kept it inside," as Chimalpahin said regarding the events surrounding the chaplain Zárate. It was an old story, as Chimalpahin the Chalcan knew, predating the arrival of the strangers, but it had grown worse due to the greater imbalances that now existed. Human sacrifice had ended, as had been promised, but other forms of abuse proliferated. In some ways, violence was even more pervasive than it had been, because a small group of people had the legal right—born of might—to denigrate so many.

Whether or not Chimalpahin ever thought this way on a conscious level, some Indians in the former Tenochtitlan definitely did. When Chimalpahin was a child, probably around the time he moved to the city, the remaining indigenous students at the school in Tlatelolco put on a play. There were few of them left, for public opinion had turned against the school since its early founding, and it was starved for funds.[81] The students wrote the play's dialogue themselves. One character commented, "According to the opinion of many, we the Indians of New Spain are shams, like magpies and parrots, birds that with great effort learn to talk, and soon forget what they have been taught."[82] The youthful playwright was angry, and he did not "keep it inside." Few others, however, gave voice to any rage they felt. It was safer not to. The closest Chimalpahin ever came, even in his private writing, was to say about certain mestizos: "They just try to be Spaniards, belittling us and mocking us, as some Spaniards do."[83] But then he concluded by reminding himself that whatever these arrogant people might think or do, Adam was father and Eve mother to all living people.

In 1624, Chimalpahin left San Antonio Abad after thirty years there. The church had been closed down. Its patron died, and a bitter legal fight over the inheritance ensued.[84] In the same period, the entire city was engulfed in what is now called "the tumult of 1624." Crop failures and rising deaths—especially of children—from a terrible epidemic of whooping cough sent people into the streets. The crisis brought political fissures at the highest levels to the fore; the viceroy and the archbishop found themselves very nearly at war with one another.[85] On top of this came serious flooding. One indigenous writer commented wryly that "the viceroy became a fish," as he had to travel around by boat.[86] We do not know what Chimalpahin thought of these events, for he had stopped keeping his record. Comments in the text of his great book of his people's ancient history indicate that he was still working on that project in the 1620s—his last dated comment there is made in 1631—but in 1615, Chimalpahin seems to have entirely given up keeping a record of current events.[87] Perhaps he did not have time and energy for both works. Perhaps he found the record of his own times depressing and the record of the Nahua past energizing.

From what Chimalpahin had written before, it is clear that he foresaw certain dangers and envisioned certain battles he wanted to see waged. Like some who had gone before him, he feared collective amnesia—the loss not just of the Nahuas' cultural knowledge but even of any genuine belief that his people had ever had a complicated history or experienced subtle and shifting reactions to it. To counteract this, he used his quill to transcribe and organize all the stories that he could find.

***

WHEN CHIMALPAHIN DIED, his papers passed into the hands of a direct descendant of king Nezahualpilli of Texcoco, in whose reign great poetry had been sung to rapt audiences. This was don Fernando de Alva Ixtlilxochitl (Eesh-tlil-SHO-cheet), whose name referenced an orchid-flowering vine. Like Chimalpahin, he had added an Aztec ancestor's name to the Christian one he had been baptized with as a youth. The ancestral Ixtlilxochitl had been the son of Nezahualpilli, the one who refused to be bought off by Tenochtitlan's preferred heir and who joined the Spaniards out of expedience. The living Ixtlilxochitl's mother was the great-granddaughter of that famous conquest-era figure. The living man's father, a Spaniard, was for a while the municipal overseer of Mexico City's construction projects. As a mestizo child of a wealthy Spanish man, Ixtlilxochitl lived largely in the Spanish world, yet he was deeply proud of his mother's antecedents and embraced them as his own. He, too, was a writer of history, but his work was in Spanish and addressed itself to a Spanish audience. He had long wanted to make a point to his Spanish-speaking tutors and schoolmates, explaining, "From my adolescence, I had a great desire to know the events that befell in this New World, which were not lesser than those of the Romans, Greeks, Meads and other Gentile republics famed to the world."[88] To educate himself, Ixtlilxochitl sought out texts from the still-vibrant world of Nahua intellectuals. Chimalpahin was the most prolific writer, but he was by no means the only one. Ixtlilxochitl collected all the texts he could and used them to produce multiple volumes of history.[89]

There is indirect evidence that Ixtlilxochitl and Chimalpahin—who were almost exactly the same age—knew each other personally, though they never mentioned each other in their writings, and one was fully indigenous and perceived as such and the other almost lived the life of a Spaniard. Chimalpahin said that he knew and liked Ixtlilxochitl's Spanish grandfather. The two men were both good friends of the Franciscan scholar fray Juan de Torquemada, and Ixtlilxochitl's children referred to Chimalpahin as "the good don Domingo." The existence of some sort of friendship between the two seems even likelier, given the fact that Ixtlilxochitl received Chimalpahin's papers at his death.[90]

Ixtlilxochitl's son, don Juan, lived entirely in the Spanish world, and when he died, his papers went to his longtime companion, the Spanish intellectual Carlos Sigüenza y Góngora. Through him, Chimalpahin's work came to be known to European scholars who soon began to delve into all things Aztec. They understood relatively little of the material and at first took whatever pieces they wanted from Chimalpahin's texts as well as Ixtlilxochitl's and others'. They used bits of the material to suit their own purposes, creating a vision of ancient Mexico that strayed widely from the reality.[91] It was in their hands that the story of Cortés having been mistaken for Quetzalcoatl, for instance, took on such sturdy life. Chimalpahin, had he known, might have made one of his dry comments. Yet it is possible that he would not have minded. He had a fine sense of irony and tended to remain relatively unflappable, except in the very worst of crises. He might well have told himself that as long as his works were cared for and protected, it did not matter for the time being if few people grappled with what they actually said. The papers would still be there when people were ready to hear what the ancient Nahuas themselves had to say about the world they once inhabited.

Then would Shield Flower cry aloud from her pyre once again and Itzcoatl reveal the political strategies of a rising altepetl. King Axayacatl and Flamingo Snake might yet dance and play the drum together in a moment of creativity and joy. Moctezuma would walk straight-backed toward a looming pyramid for a grisly ceremony, intent on frightening all others, while Malintzin called out a warning to him from a distance. The Mexicas' extraordinary efforts to defend their realm would be in vain, for the high king and his people would lose a great war. Then Moctezuma's daughter Tecuichpotzin would cry bitter tears, some for herself, some for the people running out of their burning houses, some for the newly arrived Africans. The next generation would do the best they could for posterity, doing everything possible to try to fend off the worst results of conquest, including a lasting, grinding poverty. Don Luis Cipac, the last tlatoani, and don Martín Cortés, son of the brilliant slave girl Malintzin, would both meet tragic ends, but their stories would survive and be handed down, albeit in fragmented pieces. Then Tezozomoc of the royal line and Chimalpahin of the conquered altepetl of Chalco would come together to create books of history—books that, contrary to all expectations, would defiantly remain a part of the world of the Fifth Sun for as long as it might last.

Epilogue

AT THE BEGINNING of the seventeenth century, Tezozomoc and Chimalpahin worried that posterity might not remember the Aztecs and their achievements. At the time, they were right to be concerned. All around them, the two men found young people who could no longer read the glyphs and possessed no alphabetic annals, who knew little of their own history and understood even less of that history's context. The situation grew even more dire after the deaths of Tezozomoc and Chimalpahin. By the end of the seventeenth century, only people from the place called Tlaxcala still understood clearly how a xiuhpohualli was supposed to be organized and could still write one in Nahuatl. The Tlaxcalans had the advantage as far as cultural survival was concerned because, as a reward for siding with Hernando Cortés early on, the Crown had ordered that they not be given out in encomienda, and relatively few Spaniards lived among them. Dozens of Tlaxcalans maintained traditional annals, and one author, don Juan Buenaventura Zapata y Mendoza, devoted much of his life to writing hundreds of pages. But they were the last of their kind. By the second half of the eighteenth century, virtually no one remembered how to write (or even read) a xiuhpohualli. Indeed, when an indigenous community needed papers with a flavor of "ye olden tyme" in order to protect their lands, they often had to pay a workshop to produce them. Many of those documents were very beautiful, and they were most certainly indigenous, but they bore almost no resemblance to the histories that

A bird takes flight. The Bodleian Libraries, the University of Oxford, Codex Mendoza, MS. Arch. Selden. A.1, folio 46r.

were once written. All detailed knowledge of a remarkable way of life and a style of complex thinking seemed to have disappeared.[1]

In a certain sense, one might ask, did it matter? The rest of the people who lived in the Americas crossed the ocean in order to get there, whether by choice or in chains. In neither case did their great-grandchildren understand much about the world of their ancestors, yet they remained proud of where their people came from.

The same was true of the Mexicans. On one level, it turned out that Chimalpahin and Tezozomoc had absolutely nothing to fear. Their people's sense of being indigenous never even came close to dying away. Throughout the colonial era, native people's sense of themselves thrived. The Spanish Crown established a system of "two republics": two self-governing entities, that of the creole Spaniards, and that of the indigenous. The native peoples were, in theory, to stay in their communities and contribute part of their labor to the Spanish world, at first through the encomienda, and later through other institutions and practices. Sometimes those duties grew onerous to the point of being devastating; at that point an indigenous family or two might take to the road, taking risks on behalf of their children in the hope of finding a place where they might live in peace and where their hard work would benefit them. Sometimes their paths led them to a city, sometimes to a private hacienda; in either place, if they stayed, they gradually became Hispanized. But the indigenous who remained in their villages numbered in the millions, and there they continued to speak the languages of their ancestors and to organize their mental worlds at least partly along traditional lines.[2]

In the City of Mexico, once Tenochtitlan, a sense of being specifically *Mexica* did fade among the majority, but a sense of being descended from a great empire full of vibrant people did not die away, even after numerous cultures came to call the city home. The indigenous population remained large and significant. Africans intermarried happily with Native Americans to such an extent that their own phenotype was mostly lost; their descendants, too, thought of themselves as largely Indian. Well-to-do indigenous men remained visible in the city, living as the neighbors of Spaniards. They sent some of their sons to the university to become priests and founded convents for their daughters.[3]

At the same time, the mestizo as well as the Spanish creole populations took pleasure in imagining their city as heir to the Aztec tradition. In the middle of the seventeenth century, pilgrimages to the Virgin of Guadalupe became a full-fledged phenomenon, and people told the story that she had first appeared to an Aztec Indian named Juan Diego in 1528 on the outskirts of the city. It didn't matter that the story was a relatively new invention; what mattered was that everybody, rich and poor, wanted it to be true. At the end of the seventeenth century, one of the greatest Mexican minds of the era, the nun Sor Juana Inés de la Cruz, took pride in writing some of her poetry in Nahuatl. Her grammar was dreadful, and it is clear she never spoke the language well, but her determination to try is intriguing, as is the delight that her Spanish-speaking readers took in such work.[4]

Arguably only in the wake of the War of Independence (1810–1821) did indigenous identity truly suffer. In one of the greatest ironies of history, it was the efforts of the humanitarian and progress-oriented liberals that struck a significant blow at Mexico's indigenous peoples. With all people suddenly equal in the eyes of the law, it seemed counterproductive to persist in encouraging indigenous peoples to speak their own language. No longer could a native person go to court and find a translator: that person would need to speak Spanish. No longer could a native person say she preferred to be educated by her parents in the old way: such a person would need to learn Spanish. No longer could native people say they preferred to own their land in common and let the chiefs decide how to distribute it: they were told it would be best if they owned individual family farms. If they needed to prove title, they could go to court—and do their business in Spanish.[5]

Under such circumstances, indigenous poverty grew in the nineteenth century. Eventually a government came to power that did not even pretend to care for the rights of ordinary people. And when resentments against the dictator Porfirio Díaz spread throughout the land, many indigenous people joined the fight against him and helped to bring him down. One of the great heroes of the Mexican Revolution was the Nahuatl-speaking Emiliano Zapata from Morelos. Photos of him leading his men to victory or convening a council where his people sat down to make their own laws, still grace the pages of textbooks and the walls of bars and restaurants. In the decades after the revolution, progress did not move in a straight line—but there *was* progress, and often native peoples were in the vanguard. The Maya who came out of the forest to protest NAFTA in the 1990s called themselves the Zapatistas after the revolutionary Emiliano Zapata. By the turn of the twenty-first century, Mexico's indigenous people were thoroughly engaged in their own struggles to seek out their history and define and protect their ancestral heritage, much like disempowered peoples elsewhere.

Today, more than a million Mexicans still speak Nahuatl. Among them are those who are promoting scholarship in Nahuatl; they have even written a Nahuatl-Nahuatl dictionary, for instance. They do not want all work with

Nahuatl texts to have as the only goal translation into a European language. They prefer to participate in creative and critical thinking in terms their own language allows for. Among the Nahuatl speakers there are not only scholars but also artists and writers. They have published plays, stories, and books, some written entirely in their own language, some with Spanish text as well. They write in workshops, and they write alone; they paint on traditional maguey-plant paper, or they type at keyboards, as they choose. Perhaps, say the poets, given all the changes, we have now embarked on life under the Sixth Sun.[6]

And yet, for every Nahuatl speaker who writes defiant poems, there is another who lives in poverty so oppressive that poetry is out of the question: for every person who is able to give a paper in Nahuatl at an international conference, there is another whose only hope is to leave home and try to start over somewhere else. He may move to a large town in Mexico, where at one time the Mexica founded a trading post at a merchant crossroads that later became a city. Or she may choose to go north, to the land of her remote ancestors, the forebears of Shield Flower and Itzcoatl, who came from the American Southwest, and hope that she may not be turned away. In either case, it can only be to the good for such people, and all who come to know them and respect them, to be acquainted with their deep history—a legible past that renders them human and envisions them as equals in the drama of the world's history.

How Scholars Study the Aztecs

FOR MANY YEARS, scholars accepted the idea that very limited sources were available for the study of ancient Native Americans. They examined the buildings and objects uncovered in archaeological digs,[1] as well as the words of Europeans who began to write about Indians almost as soon as they met them. Columbus, for instance, wrote in his log on the first day he met some Taino people in the Caribbean in October 1492, and Hernando Cortés in Mexico lost little time before he started sending letters home.[2] These sources weren't nearly enough, yet researchers made do because they thought they had no choice. These texts were what was available.

Over the years, two groups of scholars came closer than others to hearing what ancient Native Americans themselves had to say, at least in Mesoamerica. Mayanist epigraphers worked tirelessly, attempting to read the glyphs carved on ancient stelae and on buildings. Eventually they realized that certain elements were phonetic and that they would need to learn Mayan languages in order to make sense of the writing.[3] What had once been thought to be the highly individualized spiritual expressions of artists and priests turned out to be political narratives about the births, marriages, and deaths of kings and queens. One long statement began, for instance, "At 29 days, 14 yaxkin [on July 7, 674], she was born, Lady Katun Ahau, noblewoman from the place called *Man*."[4] Meanwhile, art historians and anthropologists carefully studied the sixteenth-century painted codices prepared by the Aztecs (and other Mesoamerican peoples), often at the request of curious Europeans and usually

with accompanying written text in Spanish.[5] These scholars, too, found political narratives of kings and conquests and detailed delineations of past pere-
grinations, as well as images of clothing people wore or the objects they used
before the Spaniards arrived. The texts also included answers to questions
posed by the newcomers. "Whom did you sacrifice, and when did you do it?"
the Spaniards would ask. And the Nahuas would respond, "This chapter tells
of the feasts and blood sacrifices which they made on the first day of the first
month," or "This chapter tells of the honors paid, and the blood offerings
made, in the second month."[6]

Neither the ancient, highly controlled carvings nor the sixteenth-century
codices prepared collaboratively with Spaniards gave vent to full, open-ended,
or spontaneous language. They offered no meandering and revealing tales,
and precious few poems, jokes, innermost fears, or flashes of anger. The texts
largely told what Mayan kings wanted posterity to know about their lineages
and what sixteenth-century Spaniards wished to believe about the people
whom they had conquered. Nevertheless, there was copious material for talented scholars to work with. They combined their knowledge of the codices
with studies of archaeology and of Spanish accounts, and produced impressive books about Mesoamerican peoples. Many of their works are highly
recommended.[7]

The Aztecs, however, did write a great deal more in the sixteenth century
after they learned the Roman alphabet from the Spaniards—and eventually,
beginning in the 1950s and 1960s, a number of scholars began to take those
writings seriously.[8] At first, scholars looked at the ways indigenous students
used the phonetic alphabet to answer questions put to them by the Spaniards
about their religion, or to help the friars invent Nahuatl phrases that could
be used to teach the people about Christianity (referring to the Virgin
Mary, for instance, as "forever an unmarried daughter") or to write such
things as Nahuatl-language confessional manuals and religious plays. It did-
n't take many years for scholars to look beyond the religious works and to
realize that native writers also helped their people with more mundane
tasks such as recording the public ceremonies held at the time of land trans-
fers, or writing down a dying man's perorations as to how his land was to be
divided among his children. Historians and anthropologists who learned
the Nahuatl language could read these sources; in the 1980s and 1990s they
began to produce insightful studies on how the indigenous people interacted with Christianity[9] and with the Spanish political system.[10] It had
previously been thought that the indigenous people were overwhelmed,
even devastated, by these two aspects of Spanish culture; once scholars

translated what the people actually said in the earliest generations' interactions with the newcomers, they learned that the indigenous took a rather pragmatic approach to change.

Yet even in the midst of all the revisionism, few asked what the Aztecs talked about in private—what they thought about their own history or dared to hope for when they considered their future. Who were they, in short, when there was no Spanish interlocutor? That project remained neglected. It wasn't for lack of sources, for there were documents in existence that revealed such things. The *xiuhpohualli*, or "yearly account," went back many generations, and examples were eagerly recorded by some of the young Nahuas who learned to manipulate the Roman letters. Dozens of those xiuhpohualli transcriptions survived and ultimately became part of libraries' rare book collections, where they were gradually discovered in the eighteenth, nineteenth, and twentieth centuries. From the beginning, scholars referred to these texts as "historical annals" as they bore a resemblance to a medieval European genre of that name. They were difficult to understand, and not always directly relevant to questions of interest to outsiders, so investigators rarely worked with them. In the multicultural world of the late 1990s and early 2000s, one might have expected that such sources would be rapidly seized upon, read aloud, and translated, and thus made to speak their secrets to the wider world. But this could not happen immediately. First, a major breakthrough was needed in outsiders' understanding of the relationship between clauses in this far from well-known language.[11] Next, scholars had to learn to read Nahuatl easily enough to be able to translate unpredictable and wide-ranging statements (different from repetitive wills or Christian texts); those scholars then had to read enough of the histories—written without any regard for Western conventions—in order to be able to understand what they were getting at. It took quite some time to make real headway.[12]

And there was another problem—namely, that even many academics seem to have thought that learning Nahuatl wasn't worth the trouble, that we already knew enough to render the work unnecessary. We had learned a great deal from looking at objects and images, and from listening to Spaniards or to Indians who were answering Spaniards' questions. We had in many ways already decided who the Aztecs were. Perhaps we didn't need to eavesdrop on their private conversations. Or that, at least, is what people said in an implicit sense. What they said explicitly is that it would be disrespectful, even imperialistic, to work with the few surviving, crystallized moments from what was once a vibrant, oral tradition. But since people did not stop talking about the Aztecs, and continued to rely on the former sources, the real reason may perhaps have had more to do with an unwillingness to challenge all that we thought we knew.[13]

* * *

WHAT SHOULD NOW BE CLEAR is that scholars themselves sometimes disagree about the best way to proceed with a difficult set of issues. They prioritize different subjects for research and have different understandings of what is visible in the existing sources. The study of any history is fraught with multiple tensions. "The past is a foreign country," the historian David Lowenthal titled his now-classic book.[14] When we go back in time, just as when we travel to far distant places, we face multiple cultural barriers, some that we are looking for, and some that are unexpected and therefore hard to recognize. We are all products of the culture or cultures to which we were exposed as young people and have difficulty envisioning other modes of thought. But what exactly does "have difficulty" mean? This is an area where historians often disagree. Some argue that peoples foreign to us in space and time are, and must always be, unknowably remote. We can struggle to understand them on their own terms, but to some extent we will always be trapped within our own worldview and unable to grasp theirs. Other scholars would argue that although people's cultures vary to an immense degree, we are all nevertheless human in the same ways; what makes us feel loved, for example, may vary, but the desire to be loved does not. Or what makes us feel afraid may differ, but the need to find some degree of security is a constant. In this book, I take it for granted that both schools of thought are absolutely right, and that good history explores the tension between them. The Aztecs I have come to know are both profoundly different from me and mine, and yet at the same time, deeply similar.[15]

Not only should historians explore the tension between these two different kinds of truth, but in their work they must decide what kind of reminders they themselves and their readers most need and then offer them frequently. If I were writing about the Founding Fathers of the United States, it might behoove me to nudge us all to remember that they lived and thought within a framework utterly different from our own, far more so than we often care to consider when we invoke them. However, I am not writing about a topic we have rendered familiar but rather about Moctezuma and his people. We are accustomed to being afraid of the Aztecs, even to being repulsed by them, rather than identifying with them. So perhaps we need to remind ourselves from time to time that they loved a good laugh, just as we do.[16]

The *writing* of history is in some ways as complex as the study of history. There are numerous registers within which historians work. At the one

extreme, in the written exchanges that unfold between scholars in their jour-
nals and monographs, historians talk to each other about their sources—
where they found them, how they interpret them, and how past interpretations
have been affected by prior assumptions that caused people to miss certain
elements. Scholars include not only a discourse (which offers knowledge about
a subject) but a great deal of metadiscourse (which gives an analysis of how it
is they know whatever they know about that subject). At the opposite extreme,
in the case of most textbooks and popular history books, historians tell a story
directly and authoritatively, including absolutely no "metadiscourse" whatsoever,
as if the present state of knowledge about a field has always existed. It is assumed
in such cases that this is not the place for thinking aloud about how we know
what we know. There is a value in both kinds of writing. In this book, I have
tried—as do many historians—to strike a balance between the two extremes.

Counterintuitively, perhaps, I have found that people have less tolerance
for a book without metadiscourse when they are reading about a topic they
themselves know little about. We tend to like a seamless, authoritative discourse better when we are reading about topics we think we know quite well
already and can determine whether to trust the author. On topics where we
do not have enough expertise to judge the discourse on our own, we need
signposts about the relative importance of different aspects and the larger reasons why certain elements must be tended to, or else we cannot follow the
argument or know whether to trust the speaker. In writing this book, I have
assumed that many of my readers know very little about the Aztecs, and that
if I tell their story in a purely textbook style, I will be ineffective. I have therefore tried to offer enough material about the sources we have and the ways in
which I read them, so as to be believed.

Yet at the same time I have tried not to spend so much time on such matters as to overwhelm the reader. Those who wish to know exactly where the
assertions of any particular paragraph come from can—and hopefully will—
turn to the notes, where I engage directly with difficult issues. At the end of
this essay is an annotated bibliography of the existing annals. These texts are
not mysterious "ancient documents" that ordinary readers have no way of
accessing. Each one is a real manuscript written in Nahuatl and stored in a
particular library or archive, and almost every one of them has been translated into a European language and published at least once. Some of the translations are better than others, and some editions are simply more accessible
than others; those are the ones I have listed.

There is one scholarly argument regarding the Aztecs that must be
addressed directly because I am taking a side on the matter on nearly every

page. While studies of the Aztecs traditionally were based only on archaeology and European sources, the partial and ad hoc inclusion of partly misunderstood Nahuatl histories did become a part of some works, especially in the second half of the twentieth century. Thus the use of Nahuatl-language annals has a history of its own. At first, scholars were delighted to be exposed to them and quoted large chunks of them as material to be taken quite literally, even if the annals were recounting events that had occurred several hundred years earlier or were telling obviously apocryphal stories. From there, the pendulum of scholarly opinion understandably swung away from taking such indigenous texts literally at all. In this view, they revealed cultural mindsets and propagandistic efforts but did not illuminate events.[17] It began to be thought that we have no way of knowing what actually occurred during the reign of the Aztecs, except what can be gleaned from the study of archaeology.

Today, however, some historians would argue that the Nahuatl annals tell a great deal about the hundred years or so prior to the conquest.[18] Ironically, while other scholars have sometimes discounted the Nahuatl annals as history, they have unselfconsciously continued to quote Spaniards (especially the friar Diego Durán) and Spanish-influenced texts (e.g., the *Florentine Codex*, the *Codex Mendoza*) with abandon. In fact, it is generally these Spanish-derived sources that are culturally dissonant and thus suspect. Yet we have drawn conclusions from them about the Nahuas' preconquest political patterns or cultural beliefs for which there is little to no Nahuatl-language evidence.[19] In the field of history, if we see contradictions between a source like Diego Durán and a set of Nahuatl annals, we often conclude that the sources confound us, and that there is no way to know what happened. But if we do not allow the Spanish sources to distract us and take notes only on what the sixteenth-century indigenous annals say, we find that they generally agree on the core points.

Sometimes the details do confound us. When the annals speak of Acamapichtli, the Aztecs' first ruler, for example, they tell of a woman in his life named Ilancueitl (ee-lan-CWEY-it, Elder Woman Skirt). Some said she was his mother, some his wife, some that she mothered his children, and some that she was barren. But we shouldn't get caught up in such minutiae: What all sources agree on was that she was from the area's most powerful town, the one that had to agree to allow the wandering Aztecs to establish their little settlement if it was to happen at all. Now we begin to understand something about the political process at play: an alliance was being established through a marriage. If we put this puzzle piece next to another comparable one, a comprehensible picture begins to emerge. Over the years, it has become abundantly clear to me that we can indeed recount a relatively accurate version of Aztec history from a few generations before the conquest, and I have done so here.

For very ancient times, I do not think we can tell the history, except from what we learn from archaeology and from a study of the cultural tendencies revealed by the annals. But I am convinced that careful study does bring forth a coherent narrative for approximately one hundred years prior to the arrival of the Spaniards. At each point, I have aligned all the indigenous annals that treat the era and were written within about eighty years after the conquest, and if I find consensus among them, I assume that we are learning something we can consider "real."[20] I do not take sides among them if one insists on the importance of a particular battle or marriage and others do not, but I may mention the matter if the difference of opinion is illuminating. For the pre-conquest period, I have carefully excluded Spanish sources, as they almost always introduce a different vision. For the years after the conquest, I often rely partly on Spanish sources but only where they are revelatory of events that occurred. For indigenous thoughts and perspectives, I continue to turn to Nahuatl-language sources from that era.

The payoff of many years of patient reading has been immense. Studying all the annals that still exist—or attempting to, as I undoubtedly missed some—has taught me much about the wider context of Aztec life, which can in turn sometimes help me make sense of the specifics mentioned in a particular set of annals. If we belittle these documents as sources, we will continue to miss a great deal. They are well worth examining. The following guide is intended to help readers launch their own investigations.

Annotated Bibliography of the Nahuatl Annals

Note: All major Nahuatl-language texts with substantial annals-like content are noted here, as well as a few early Spanish-language ones, which are in effect commentary on annals-like pictographic sources. The language is Nahuatl unless it is specifically noted as Spanish. Entries are listed alphabetically by author if the author is a well-known individual, otherwise by the title's first major term. (Ignore articles as well as the typical opening words that are part of the names of virtually all such texts—"history" or "historia," "book" or "libro," "annals" or "anales," and "codex" or "códice.") More information on all of these texts and on the attributions given here (several of which are based on new research) can be found in Camilla Townsend, *Annals of Native America: How the Nahuas of Colonial Mexico Kept Their History Alive* (New York: Oxford University Press, 2016).

Anónimo mexicano

This unsigned early eighteenth-century Nahuatl-language history describes waves of Nahua migrants arriving in central Mexico. It is written in European-style chapters rather than employing Nahuatl annals format. However, it draws its information from a number of Nahuatl sources, including the annals of don Juan Buenaventura Zapata y Mendoza. Despite its title, research has recently demonstrated that it is likely the work of don Manuel de los Santos Salazar, a man from an indigenous noble family of Tlaxcala who attended university and became a priest. It is housed in the Bibliothèque Nationale de France in Paris as Méxicain 254. A published edition is Richley Crapo and Bonnie Glass-Coffin, eds., *Anónimo Mexicano* (Logan: Utah State University Press, 2005).

Codex Aubin

Named for a French collector, this text should more properly be called something like *Annals of the Mexica*. An indigenous resident of the San Juan Moyotlan quarter of Mexico City wrote a combined pictorial and alphabetic text in the 1560s and 1570s. We know little about the author, but textual elements indicate that he was apparently an artisan plasterer, had a Spanish surname (López), and had been trained by the Franciscans (or possibly by someone trained by them). He does not seem to have moved in the noble circles of the writers of the *Annals of Juan Bautista*. He begins with the ancient history of the Mexica and then moves through to the history of his own day.

The original is held by the British Museum; they have made images of the beautifully colored pages freely available online. A printed facsimile and transcription, presented together with related documents, is Walter Lehmann and Gerdt Kutscher, eds., *Geschichte der Aztekan: Codex Aubin und verwandte Documente* (Berlin: Gebr. Mann, 1981). There are published Spanish translations, but a newer one is needed, as is a full translation into English. The best available at this point is probably Charles Dibble, ed., *Historia de la Nación Mexicana* (Madrid: Porrúa, 1963).

Bancroft Dialogues

In the 1570s, a highly educated resident of Texcoco transcribed a variety of formal speeches on different occasions—when a new chief took office, when a nobleman was married, when grandchildren came to visit their grand-mother. The text was almost certainly prepared for the benefit of a "philolog-ically-minded Franciscan stationed in Texcoco," to use the words of James Lockhart. Later, the text was put to use by the well-known Jesuit Horacio Carochi; the copy we have was probably his, as it bears a variety of his mark-ers. One might argue with justification that this text does not belong in a listing of annals-like sources; however, I would say that it belongs among them for two reasons: first, one of the speakers, an elderly woman, recounts certain historical events that she remembers as if she were offering dialogue at a xiuhpohualli performance, mixed with her own idiosyncratic commentary; and second, a number of the ceremonial speeches mark the type of occasion often included in annals (such as the seating of a chief or his marriage).

The manuscript is housed in the Bancroft Library at the University of California, Berkeley. A peerless edition is Frances Karttunen and James Lockhart, eds., *The Art of Nahuatl Speech: The Bancroft Dialogues* (Los Angeles: UCLA Latin American Center, 1987). Lockhart later made adjust-ments to his earlier translation, which are available in electronic form.

Cantares Mexicanos

In the 1560s, fray Bartolomé de Sahagún began to encourage the Nahuas to transcribe the lyrics of some of their songs. He abhorred the pagan nature of the songs, so presumably he wanted the task to be accomplished so that he and other linguists might study them and use them to undermine the old reli-gion. However, he could only go so far in that direction, as the songs were very difficult for him to translate (and they remain so for us today). Chimalpahin in his "Seventh Relation" explains that in the preconquest world, songs were recycled over the years; an old chestnut might be called up and reused with the names changed if its themes were applicable to a current event. Because the songs therefore occasionally reference *Dios* or the Virgin Mary or the name of a Spaniard, and because their transcription was inspired by a Franciscan, people who do not know the tradition well have often mistakenly assumed that they show deep Christian influence. However, nothing could be farther from the truth. There are no other Nahuatl texts in existence that show such a wide array of old forms in both a grammatical and metaphorical sense. Although the songs certainly are not annals, they are profoundly com-plementary in that they often were performed on the same occasions and often dealt with comparable themes—such as the rise and fall of particular leaders, pride in the altepetl, and concern for its future.

There are two manuscripts in existence—one known as the *Cantares Mexicanos*, in the Biblioteca Nacional in Mexico, and another dubbed the *Romances de los Señores*, in the Nettie Lee Benson Collection of the University of Texas at Austin. John Bierhorst has published excellent transcriptions of both, together with partially useable translations into English. See John Bierhorst, ed., *Cantares Mexicanos: Songs of the Aztecs* (Stanford, CA: Stanford University Press, 1985); and *Ballads of the Lords of New Spain; The Codex Romances de los Señores de la Nueva España* (Austin: University of Texas Press, 2009). Sadly, Bierhorst was convinced that the songs were of the same tradition as the ghost songs of the American Midwest and adjusted his translations accordingly whenever he needed to in order to retain that paradigm. Miguel León-Portilla has also published full transcriptions, together with translations into Spanish. See Miguel León Portilla, ed., *Cantares Mexicanos*, 3 vols. (Mexico City: UNAM, 2011). He follows Angel María Garibay, a mid-twentieth-century scholar, in assuming that the cantares should be divided into short lines, like western poetry, and that they were authored by individuals. Peter Sorenson is presently preparing a more up-to-date translation of key songs and a full study of the genre.

Cristóbal de Castillo

We know very little about this author of sixteenth-century Nahuatl histories. He used a chapter format, not a timeline, and mused aloud about the religious errors of his forebears, so he was certainly educated by friars. Yet much of his language reflects ancient Nahua traditions; political difference, for instance, is expressed through dialogue. His words at one point imply that his people came from Texcoco, yet most of his text concerns the Mexica. In short, though Castillo signs his name and says that he is finishing his work as an old man in July 1599, he reveals almost nothing about his background. All we have are copied-out fragments of his work housed in the Bibliothèque Nationale de France, Paris, as Méxicain 263 and others. An excellent study, transcription, and Spanish translation is Federico Navarrete Linares, ed., *Historia de la venida de los mexicanos y otros pueblos* (Mexico City: INAH, 1991).

Don Domingo de San Antonio Muñón Chimalpahin Quauhtlehuanitzin

The indigenous historian who styled himself "Chimalpahin" (after an ancestor) was known to others in his own day as don Domingo de San Antón. He was from a noble family of Amaquemecan, a sub-altepetl of Chalco, but as a young person in the 1590s he came to live in Mexico City and soon took a position as the manager of the church of San António Abad. He researched and wrote history in his spare time. His extensive works fall under four divisions:

1. The *Diario* or the *Annals of His Time*: a year-by-year record of events in Mexico City from the 1570s through 1615.
2. The *Eight Relations*, a set of detailed texts that should really be called Various Annals of Chalco and the Central Valley.
3. *Codex Chimalpahin*, a bound volume containing various works, some authored by him and some copied by him, which at one point was in the keeping of Ixtlilxochitl's family.
4. A full-length, annotated Nahuatl translation of a biography of Hernando Cortés written by his secretary.

Tragically, in the century after his death Chimalpahin's papers were scattered. Most of the *Diario* (or more properly, *Annals of His Time*) is now in the Bibliothèque Nationale de France (BNF), Paris, as Méxicain 220, but the opening pages are at the Instituto Nacional de Antropología e Historia (INAH), in Mexico City, as Colección Antigua 256B. The *Eight Relations* are also at the BNF as Méxicain 74. The writings contained in the *Codex Chimalpahin* surfaced in the 1980s at the British and Foreign Bible Society Library at Cambridge University; in 2014, Cambridge sold the volume to the INAH, where they are justly regarded as a national treasure. Rafael Tena has produced excellent Spanish translations of most of the work: see his edited editions of *Ocho relaciones y el memorial de Colhuacan*, vols. 1 and 2 (Mexico City: Conaculta, 1998); *El Diario de Chimalpahin* (Mexico City: Conaculta, 2001); and *Tres crónicas mexicanas: Textos recopilados por Domingo Chimalpahin* (Mexico City: Conaculta, 2012). Susan Schoeder has spearheaded translations of two of the major works into English; see James Lockhart, Susan Schroeder, and Doris Namala, eds., *Annals of His Time: Don Domingo de San Antón Muñón Chimalpahin Quauhtlehuanitzin* (Stanford, CA: Stanford University Press, 2006) and Arthur J. O. Anderson and Susan Schroeder, eds., *Codex Chimalpahin*, vols. 1 and 2 (Norman: University of Oklahoma Press, 1997). Currently there is no English translation of the *Eight Relations*. The surviving copy of Chimalpahin's translation of the biography of Cortés is located in the Newberry Library of Chicago; an excellent edition is Susan Schroeder, Anne J. Cruz, Cristián Roa-de-la-Carrera, and David Tavárez, eds., *Chimalpahin's Conquest: A Nahua Historian's Rewriting of Francisco*

López de Gómara's La conquista de México (Stanford, CA: Stanford University Press, 2010).

Codex Chimalpopoca

See *Annals of Cuauhtitlan*

Faustino Galicia Chimalpopoca

See J. F. Ramírez

Annals of Cuauhtinchan

See *Historia Tolteca Chichimeca*

Annals of Cuauhtitlan

Textual references within the *Annals of Cuauhtitlan* indicate that the work was composed in the 1560s and 1570s by someone living in Cuauhtitlan (just north of Mexico City) who was intimately familiar with the projects of fray Bernardino de Sahagún. There was indeed such a person—Pedro de San Buenaventura, a former student of Sahagún who moved to Cuauhtitlan and continued to correspond with him. He is probably the author. This extraordinarily detailed narrative weaves together the histories of peoples throughout the central valley, focusing particularly on Cuauhtitlan and Tenochtitlan.

A surviving copy of the *Annals of Cuauhtitlan* was formerly located in the Instituto Nacional de Antropología e Historia in Mexico City. The document was bound to another Nahuatl-language text, an origin story now known as the "Legend of the Suns," as well as a statement in Spanish labeled "Breve Relación de los dioses y ritos de la gentilidad" ("Brief relation of the gods and rites of the gentiles"). The handwriting and certain stylistic elements indicated that the documents were copies dating from the seventeenth century. On the inside of the binding appeared a genealogy of the Texcocan writer don Fernando de Alva Ixtlilxochitl, indicating that the volume was likely in his family's possession at some point. A note dated 1849 labeled the whole set of eighty-four pages the "Códice Chimalpopoca" (*Codex Chimalpopoca*) and that name has stuck in some circles. In the early 1940s, the Mexican scholar Primo Feliciano Velázquez took photographs of each page and then published a facsimile edition: *Códice Chimalpopoca: Anales de Cuauhtitlan y Leyenda de los soles* (Mexico City: Imprenta Universitaria, 1945). By 1949 the originals had been lost, so all further work with the text has depended on the facsimile. There is a recent edition in English (John Bierhorst, ed., *History and Mythology of the Aztecs: The Codex Chimalpopoca* [Tucson: University of Arizona Press, 1992]) and another in Spanish (Rafael Tena, ed., *Anales de Cuauhtitlan* [Mexico City: Cien de México, 2011]).

Florentine Codex

This is by far the most famous sixteenth-century Nahuatl-language source in existence. The work consists of an encyclopedic twelve-book effort to create an enduring record of Aztec culture; it was intended that the information be used to help proselytize indigenous people more effectively. The Franciscan provincial fray Francisco de Toral (see *Annals of Tecamachalco*) ordered fray Bernardino de Sahagún to begin the work in the 1550s. He started the project in Tepepolco, working with a number of indigenous aides, including a young man from Cuauhtitlan, Pedro de San Buenaventura (see *Annals of Cuauhtitlan*). Sahagún and members of his entourage continued to work on the codex for the next three decades—collecting information; organizing, editing, and copying; placing the material in columns to include translations or glosses; and adding illustrations. After the Council of Trent (1545–63), the work came to be seen as dangerous and was stopped; it was collected by the Crown and never published in its own day. There are annals-like elements in several of the books; and the second half of Book 12, about the experience of the conquest by the Spaniards, is a month-by-month account effectively in xiuhpohualli format.

In recent times, scholars have had heated arguments over the worth of the *Florentine Codex* as a source of information about Nahua culture. On the one hand, it is as a whole evidently the product of a European imagination and demonstrates the use of questionnaires and heavy editing by Sahagún. On the other hand, it is a richly detailed set of comments provided by dozens of Nahua people who still remembered the "old days" of forty years earlier. Sometimes the text includes statements that were obviously designed to satisfy Spanish expectations. (Did the bloodthirsty devil-gods demand excessive numbers of human sacrifice victims? Yes, indeed they did. Did your doctors engage in dreadful, superstitious practices? Yes, indeed they did.) But at other moments the text includes elements that no European could possibly have planned to elicit. Used judiciously and in conjunction with entirely Nahua-authored sources, the *Florentine Codex* is invaluable. It is only because so many scholars have relied almost entirely upon it as regards some subjects that it has become problematic.

The original text is in the Biblioteca Medicea Laurenziana in Florence (hence the work's modern-day name). There have been facsimiles published, but these became obsolete in 2012 when the text was placed in the World Digital Library. Because Sahagún included Spanish glosses, there has not been a serious effort to translate the Nahuatl text into Spanish; this is unfortunate, as the glosses only partially represent what the Nahuatl actually says and have frequently misled scholars. James Lockhart underscored this point by doing separate English translations of the Nahuatl and the Spanish of Book 12 in his *We People Here: Nahuatl Accounts of the Conquest of Mexico* (Berkeley: University of California Press, 1993*).* A full translation of the Nahuatl into English is Bernardino de Sahagún, ed., *General History of the Things of New Spain: The Florentine Codex*, vols. 1–12, edited by Arthur J. O. Anderson and Charles Dibble (Salt Lake City: University of Utah Press, 1950–82). Anderson and Dibble inject a "high" tone, using "thee" and "thou" in their translation, terms that do not exist in Nahuatl, but their work is nevertheless mostly excellent. Many of the earlier notes collected by Sahagún and his aides still exist in the Libraries of the Real Academia and Real Palacio, both in Madrid. A partial facsimile of this early material—which is itself rare—is Francisco del Paso y Troncoso, ed., *Historia de las Cosas de Nueva España: Códices matritenses*, 3 vols. (Madrid: Hauser y Menet, 1906–7). A small part of the earlier work, including all the pictorial images but not most of the written text, has been published in Thelma Sullivan et al., eds. *The Primeros Memoriales* (Norman: University of Oklahoma Press, 1997).

Libro de los Guardianes

The full title of this work is *Libro de los guardianes y gobernadores de Cuauhtinchan*. In the late nineteenth century this text was discovered in Cuauhtinchan's municipal archives in an old rawhide binding, and after a period of private ownership, it was donated to the Instituto de Investigaciones Jurídicas at the Universidad Nacional Autónoma de México, in Mexico City, where it remains. This is an original set of annals begun in the second half of the sixteenth century by people known to the writers of the *Historia Tolteca Chichimeca*, and then maintained by a series of people (with different handwritings) mostly in Nahuatl but sometimes in Spanish, continuing until the 1630s. A transcription and Spanish translation can be found in Constantino

Medina Lima, ed., *Libro de los guardianes y gobernadores de Cuauhtinchan (1519–1640)* (Mexico City: CIESAS, 1995).

Don Fernando de Alva Ixtlilxochitl

Born ca. 1580 to a Spanish father and a noble Texcocan mother, the young don Fernando grew up bilingual in Spanish and Nahuatl. He was well educated and as an adult made it his mission to write extensive histories in Spanish (with an eye to a Spanish audience) about the history of Texcoco. Although some scholars have taken him at his word and simply call him "indigenous," and others imply that he was in effect a Spaniard and thus a fraud, the reality was complex: he was truly proud of his indigenous heritage, lived partly within its traditions, and collected all the indigenous pictorial and Nahuatl-language sources he could. (For a detailed study of what is known about his life, see Camilla Townsend, "The Evolution of Alva Ixtlilxochitl's Scholarly Life," *Colonial Latin American Review* 23, no. 1 [2014]: 1–17.) Scholars have recently taken to calling him "Alva" on the understanding that it was his patronymic, but in fact, it, too, was a taken name, added later in life in honor of a godparent; his father's surname was actually Paraleda. The man clearly wished to be called Ixtlilxochitl, and we should respect that, just as we do Chimalpahin's choice of name.

Ixtlilxochitl's writings, like the *Florentine Codex*, are very useful if approached with caution. When he says that an old king with dozens of wives died with only one possible heir, we know that he is adjusting matters to distract Spanish readers from his ancestors' practice of polygyny. On the other hand, when he mentions, for instance, the ferocity of a certain war in particularly evocative language, we have no reason to doubt that he is looking at an old source or has heard it mentioned in such terms. Ixtlilxochitl also left posterity the most impressive pictorial Nahua history in existence, the *Codex Xolotl*. Normally it has been thought that his writings were profoundly influenced by it. Yet the text is so unusual—so different from the traditional timelines generally employed by the Nahuas—and Ixtlilxochitl was so clearly a promoter of his people, that one is left wondering if he created it himself: choosing to use old-style glyphs in brilliantly creative ways to narrate events he knew (or thought he knew) from prior studies. On the Project Xolotl, see Jerome Offner, "Ixtlilxochitl's Ethnographic Encounter: Understanding the Codex Xolotl and Is Dependent Alphabetic Texts," in *Fernando de Alva Ixtlilxochitl and His Legacy*, edited by Galen Brokaw and Jongsoo Lee (Tucson: University of Arizona Press, 2016).

For centuries, the whereabouts of Ixtlilxochitl's original manuscripts were unknown; scholars worked only with copies that had been found in various libraries. Then in the 1980s the originals surfaced in England, along with some collected writings of Chimalpahin (see *Chimalpahin*). They have now been repatriated to Mexico, to the Instituto Nacional de Antropología e Historia. Remarkably, an earlier edition based on the known copies has proven to be quite reliable; it includes only a few errors and continues to be in widespread use by scholars: Don Fernando de Alva Ixtlilxochitl, *Obras Históricas*, 2 vols., edited by Edmundo O'Gorman (Mexico City: UNAM, 1975–77). An English translation of one of Ixtlilxochitl's more remarkable narrations is Amber Brian, Bradley Benton, and Pablo García Loaza, eds., *The Native Conquistador: Alva Ixtlilxochitl's Account of the Conquest of New Spain* (University Park: Penn State University Press, 2015).

Annals of Juan Bautista

This extraordinary history provides an unusually direct window into Mexica thinking. In the 1560s, the Tenochca residents of Mexico City were struggling to avoid having to accept a new head tax to be levied on all of them, in effect reducing them to a fully conquered people. In traditional annals performance format, the authors placed side by side the views and memories of different segments of San Juan Moyotlan (the quarter of Mexico City where the royal family had once predominated). The language is rich and evocative, not terse at all. The writers were scribes and artisans who worked for the friars—they had been children at the right age for training in the 1520s and 1530s—but they clearly had no intention of showing this document to their ecclesiastical supervisors. It was evidently intended for their own posterity, so they would be forgiven for having failed to fend off the change in their legal status. "Juan Bautista" is a misnomer; that was the name of the owner of a tax collector's notebook, which was repurposed to copy out this set of annals.

The original is located in the archive of the Biblioteca Lorenzo Boturini of the Basilica of Guadalupe in Mexico City. A facsimile edition with Spanish translation is Luis Reyes García, ed. ¿*Cómo te confundes? ¿Acaso no somos conquistados? Anales de Juan Bautista* (Mexico City: CIESAS, 2001). A complete English translation and full study of this remarkable work is in preparation by Celso Mendoza.

Legend of the Suns

This is not primarily a set of annals but rather an origin story describing the eras of the five suns; yet it ends in an annals-like segment on the Mexica kings. It is an important and oft-cited text. However, it may have been written later than is often assumed; its style is frequently truncated, as though the writer had somewhat lost touch with earlier oral performances. Richer versions of several segments of the narrative can be found in the *Florentine Codex*. On its whereabouts, see the *Annals of Cuauhtitlan*.

Codex Mendoza

In the 1540s or 1550s, someone within the state apparatus of the Audiencia of New Spain requested that the city's indigenous people create a sort of visual encyclopedia of their past lives that would be annotated in Spanish and then sent to Spain with the annual spring convoy for the Crown's perusal. The Spanish-language text called the *Codex Mendoza* came into being as a result of that endeavor. It has traditionally been assumed that the viceroy (who was Antonio de Mendoza until 1549) made the initial request, but there is no documentary evidence for that. The second of three sections portrays in exquisite images the tribute that the Mexica king received from each conquered region, using preconquest-style glyphs; the third section provides a sort of anthropological guide to different categories of people in the old regime, calling to mind European genres rather than indigenous ones. The first section, however, is in effect a set of annals. A repeating timeline bearing glyphic representations of the years runs along the left margin. Each Mexica king is portrayed next to the year in which he attained power, and there follows a glyphic representation of each and every altepetl conquered in his reign. This segment provides a marvelous tutorial on the pictorial system once in use. Occasionally some additional drama is introduced beyond the listing of defeated towns: Moquihuixtli falls from the pyramid at Tlatelolco, or an army of canoes approaches from the four altepetls of Chalco. The original is housed in the Bodleian Library at Oxford, which has made this beautiful text accessible online. A full study of the document is in preparation by Daniela Bleichmar.

Annals of Puebla

In the 1670s and 1680s, an indigenous craftsman named don Miguel de los Santos wrote the zestiest set of Nahuatl annals still in existence. He was a

Tlaxcalan-descended resident of the city of Puebla de los Angeles; as such, he was intimately familiar with both high Nahua culture as it survived among Tlaxcalans (See *Annals of Tlaxcala*) and with the Spanish baroque culture that flourished in his city (in the form of music, art, preaching, and bookmaking). His text reflects both worlds: the material from the 1680s is a uniquely vivid record.

After don Miguel died, apparently in the epidemic that swept Mexico in 1692, numerous relatives or other connections copied his work. Four of their versions survive as nineteenth-century copies (see Ramírez) and two as originals. One is under the protection of the archive of the Institute Nacional de Antropología e Historia as GO 184 (it has been moved to the national vault), and one is conserved in the archive of the Venerable Cabildo of the Cathedral of Puebla, vol. 6 of Colección de Papeles Varios. The former has been transcribed and translated into English in Camilla Townsend, ed., *Here in This Year: Seventeenth-Century Nahuatl Annals of the Tlaxcala-Puebla Valley* (Stanford, CA: Stanford University Press, 2009); the latter is reproduced as a facsimile in Lidia Gómez García, Celia Salazar Exaire, and María Elena Stefanón López, eds., *Anales del Barrio de San Juan del Río* (Puebla: Benemérita Universidad Autónoma de Puebla, 2000). The first has longer and richer text, the latter more impressive visual elements.

José Fernando Ramírez

This nineteenth-century director of the Museo Nacional de Antropolgía e Historia collected annals that had been copied out by the indigenous scholar Faustino Galicia Chimalpopoca. He placed them in a massive volume he titled *Anales Antiguos de México y Sus Contornos*. The material is still found in the library of the Instituto Nacional de Antropología e Historia. Because the annals are nineteenth-century copies (and sometimes copies of copies), part of the material is riddled with errors or inexplicable elements. However, most of the sets of annals appear to be relatively complete and seem to be products of the eras that they reference. Several of the documents have been printed in Mexican publications, but these versions are even further removed from the originals.

Annals of Tecamachalco

This set of annals was written by don Mateo Sánchez, a nobleman from Tecamachalco, near Cholula (east of the central basin), over the course of his lifetime and then continued by younger relatives. Don Mateo was born a few years after the conquest and educated by the Franciscans; he had a close connection with fray Francisco Toral. Because the annals cover many years from the perspective of one man, the document offers unique insight into such things as a surviving individual's experience of loss over the course of the sixteenth-century epidemics.

The original text is held by the Nettie Lee Benson Collection of the University of Texas at Austin. A facsimile and Spanish translation is available in Eustaquio Celestino Solís and Luis Reyes García, eds., *Anales de Tecamachalco, 1398–1590* (Mexico City: CIESAS, 1992). An English translation of key passages can be found in Townsend, *Annals of Native America*, 99–105.

Codex Telleriano-Remensis

In the years after the conquest, Mexica writers and artists produced a number of glyphic timelines with brief accompanying written commentary in Nahuatl or Spanish, sometimes on their own initiative and sometimes at the behest of Spaniards. These works (e.g., *Codex Azcatitlan, Codex Mexicanus, Codex en Cruz*) have been well studied by art historians. The *Telleriano-Remensis*, as the most extensive, is the only example included in this bibliography. It was completed about 1560, just before the political cataclysm that rocked the Mexica world. (See *Annals of Juan Bautista*.) Following two calendrical sections, this work contains a substantial annals segment (twenty-three folios, front and back). The images are fascinating. However, the commentary is in Spanish, demonstrating that the work was designed for a Spanish patron, and it offers only truncated explanations, nothing like the complex history found in Nahuatl alphabetic annals. Still, because the written text is simple and in Spanish, and the illustrations quite rich, the Telleriano-Remensis provides a good entrée for beginners. It is suggestive of the kind of painted timelines narrators once used as mnemonic devices in giving historical performances. The original is in the Bibliothèque Nationale de France, Paris, as Méxicain 385. A full facsimile with commentary is Eloise Quiñones Keber, ed., *Codex Telleriano-Remensis: Ritual, Divination, and History in a Pictorial Aztec Manuscript* (Austin: University of Texas Press, 1995).

Texcoca Accounts of Conquest

Among the material collected by Chimalpahin there are some invaluable mid-sixteenth-century statements authored by people from Texcoco. They include detailed statements of events as they unfolded during the period of the Spanish conquest, replete with the complexities faced by the divided altepetl as well as a letter by a disinherited nobleman, don Juan de San Antonio. A classic set of annals was written by the Texcocan nobleman don Gabriel de Ayala, but he was a resident of Mexico City and his work actually focuses on the Tenochca. See *Codex Chimalpahin* under "Chimalpahin."

Don Hernando Alvarado Tezozomoc

Tezozomoc was a scion of the Mexica royal family. He was the son of don Diego Huanitzin, chosen as the first postconquest indigenous governor of Mexico City; through his mother he was a grandson of Moctezuma. He wrote (or possibly dictated) detailed genealogies of the Mexica royal family, which he then gave into the keeping of Chimalpahin for use in his work. After the posthumous dispersal of Chimalpahin's papers, the segment that Tezozomoc narrates in the first person was copied out as the *Crónica Mexicayotl* (the title is an odd mixture of Spanish and Nahuatl); in 1949 Adrián León published a well-known edition of the work that solidified the sense of Tezozomoc's authorship. Later, in the 1980s, the original version of the same text, embedded seamlessly in a longer work drawn together by Chimalpahin, was found in England. Today there is debate among scholars about which man should have authorship ascribed to him. It is clear that Tezozomoc wrote or narrated a statement, but we cannot know how much of the overall work is his; moreover, it is pointless to try to pull out of Chimalpahin's work every embedded statement initially authored by someone else, since it was his modus operandi to weave together various accounts, in keeping with ancient Nahua tradition. See Susan Schroeder, "The Truth About the Crónica Mexicayotl," *Colonial Latin American Review* 20 (2011): 233–47. For the text's venues of publication, see *Codex Chimalpahin* under "Chimalpahin."

Annals of Tlatelolco

This was probably the first set of Nahuatl annals recorded in the Roman alphabet. It has sometimes been dated to 1528, as that year appears on a surviving copy (in another, later handwriting). However, that date cannot possibly be accurate, as the friars had not yet fully learned the Nahuatl language nor had they begun to train a cadre of students systematically; that date must have been the later copyist's guess. A great deal of circumstantial evidence puts the creation of the text in the 1540s. It was clearly authored by students at the Franciscan school in Tlatelolco, or perhaps by other Tlatelolcans who were taught to write by them, but more than that has been impossible to deduce. It contains highly traditional language and material, and also reveals close knowledge of Spanish concepts and objects (the Spanish term "espada" is used to refer to a sword, for instance).

There are two extant copies, both in the Bibliothèque nationale de France in Paris, cataloged as Méxicain 22 and Méxicain 22bis. Méxicain 22 is written out on indigenous paper and is the only set of annals for which that is true. Méxicain 22bis is clearly a copy, and the handwriting is seventeenth-century in style. It includes additions not found in the older work. A facsimile edition of both versions is Ernst Mengin, ed., *Unos annales [sic] de la nación Mexicana* (Copenhagen: Einar Munksgaard, 1945). A recent Spanish edition is Rafael Tena, ed., *Anales de Tlatelolco* (Mexico City: Conaculta, 2004). James Lockhart transcribed and translated into English the section about the Spanish conquest in Lockhart, ed., *We People Here: Nahuatl Accounts of the Conquest of Mexico* (Berkeley: University of California Press, 1993). In his introduction to that work, Lockhart included a thorough discussion of the dating of the older manuscript.

Annals of Tlaxcala

The region around Tlaxcala, east of the central valley, boasted a particularly vibrant community of indigenous scholars who maintained annals throughout the sixteenth and seventeenth centuries. Don Juan Buenaventura Zapata y Mendoza (see Zapata) was the only writer who signed his work, but many other men (and conceivably some women) exchanged annals with each other, copying and adding as they saw fit. There are twenty-three known texts from the greater area, eight of them from Tlaxcala itself. All eight of these texts share a large proportion of their entries up to the year 1538, so there was probably one author who launched the tradition not too long after conquest. Besides Zapata's text, there are six works that survive as nineteenth-century copies (see Ramírez) and one other that exists in its original form in the archive of the Institute Nacional de Antropología e Historia, Colección Antigua 872. That one has been transcribed and translated into English in Camilla Townsend, ed., *Here in This Year: Seventeenth-Century Nahuatl Annals of the Tlaxcala-Puebla Valley* (Stanford, CA: Stanford University Press, 2009).

Historia Tolteca-Chichimeca

This rich and aesthetically beautiful text contains a number of genres within it, including an origin story and a record of town boundaries, but it is primarily a set of annals from Cuauhtinchan (an altepetl east of the central basin) spanning more than four hundred years. The project was orchestrated in the 1550s by a Cuauhtinchan nobleman, don Alonso de Castañeda (his indigenous name was Chimalpopoca), who had a son or other young relative who attended the Franciscans' school at Tlatelolco. A 1540s experience in a Spanish courtroom seems to have convinced him of his people's need to record their past using a phonetic transcription system. He also included in this text some extraordinary artwork, largely but not entirely in indigenous style.

The original is housed in the Bibliothèque Nationale de France, Paris, as Méxicains 46–50, 51–53, and 54–58. A facsimile and Spanish translation can be found in Paul Kirchoff, Lina Odena Güemes, and Luis Reyes García, eds., *Historia Tolteca Chichimeca* (Mexico City: INAH, 1976). An excellent study of the work from an art historian's perspective is Dana Leibsohn, *Script and Glyph: Pre-Hispanic History, Colonial Bookmaking and the Historia Tolteca Chichimeca* (Washington, DC: Dumbarton Oaks, 2009).

Annals of Tula

This text is a timeline with traditional year-glyphs running from 1361 to 1521. More glyphs as well as western-style illustrations occasionally appear above and below the line, as does text in Nahuatl explaining what happened in that year. In effect, this set of annals correctly documents the ties between Tula's ruling family and Itzcoatl (of Tenochtitlan) and Nezahualcoyotl (of Texcoco), as they made a successful bid for power in the early fifteenth century. Both the images and the written content indicate the influence of Franciscan training on the creator.

The document is in the archive of the Instituto Nacional de Antropología e Historia. A transcription and Spanish translation, together with select images, were published by Robert Barlow, "Anales de Tula, Hidalgo, 1361–1521," *Tlalocan* 3, no. 1 (1949): 2–13.

Codex Xolotl

See Don Fernando de Alva Ixtlilxochitl

Don Juan Buenaventura Zapata y Mendoza

Born to a Tlaxcalan noble family in the early seventeenth century, Zapata began to write a detailed set of annals in the 1650s. He started his text in the ancient period, using various Nahuatl-language sources at his disposal through family connections, and then maintained the record in some depth during the period of his own life and work on the indigenous cabildo of his altepetl. Probably because relatively few Spaniards settled in Tlaxcala, aspects of traditional Nahua high culture, including knowledge of the xiuhpohualli, seem to have lasted longer in this region than was generally the case. After Zapata died, his work passed to a young family friend, don Manuel do los Santos Salazar, an indigenous priest. He added certain elements, including a frontispiece with the title "Chronología de la Muy Insigne Noble y Leal Ciudad de Tlaxcala."

Zapata's two-hundred-page book is held at the Bibliothèque Nationale de France, Paris, as Méxicain 212. A published transcription and Spanish translation is *Historia cronológica de la noble ciudad de Tlaxcala*, edited by Luis Reyes García and Andrea Martínez Baracs (Tlaxcala: Universidad Autónoma de Tlaxcala, 1995). A sample two-year period (1675–76) has been translated into English in Townsend, *Annals of Native America*, 175–180.

Notes

Prelims

1. Geologically speaking, a ring of mountains surrounds an actual basin, without egress for water. However, many of the sources refer to the area as a valley, and I will sometimes do the same.

2. For a brief introduction to colonial-era Nahuatl, see James Lockhart's textbook *Nahuatl as Written* (Stanford, CA: Stanford University Press, 2001). To launch a serious study of the language as an outsider, consult John Sullivan through his language school, El Instituto de Docencia e Investigación Etnológica de Zacatecas (IDIEZ), which offers classes in the United States, Mexico, and online (http://www.macehualli.org)

Introduction

1. Fray Bernardino de Sahagún, *The Florentine Codex: General History of the Things of New Spain*, ed. Arthur J. O. Anderson and Charles Dibble (Salt Lake City: School of American Research and University of Utah Press, 1950–1982), 7:4–7.

2. A work dedicated to the study of these remarkable sources is Camilla Townsend, *Annals of Native America: How the Nahuas of Colonial Mexico Kept Their History Alive* (New York: Oxford University Press, 2016).

3. The appendix ("How Scholars Study the Aztecs") gives a sense of the range and depth of previous scholarly work and is intended as a guide to the secondary literature. Readers will find an overview of the kinds of studies that have been done, with specific titles listed in the notes.

Chapter 1

1. The story is found in nearly all surviving sixteenth-century Mexica annals that cover the period. The most detailed rendition is found in what is probably the

oldest set, the *Annals of Tlatelolco* (fol. 8 and 8v), in *Unos annales [sic] de la nación Mexicana,* ed. Ernst Mengin (Copenhagen: Einar Munksgaard, 1945). Other versions of the story appear in the *Codex Aubin,* ed. Charles Dibble, *Historia de la Nación Mexicana* (Madrid: Porrúa, 1963), 32; and in *Codex Chimalpahin,* ed. Arthur J. O. Anderson and Susan Schroeder (Norman: University of Oklahoma Press, 1997), 2:76. The latter two share some material verbatim. For more on all three texts, see the annotated bibliography of extant annals in the appendix.

2. There is evidence in the annals that this was a very old association. However, it is also possible that it was retroactively applied, as a severe drought in the mid-fifteenth century seems to have begun in a year of that name. It is definite that different history tellers adjusted the year when they assumed certain events occurred in order to have them resonate better with audience expectations.

3. This story appears in the Spanish text of fray Diego Durán. Durán spoke Nahuatl but was not a Nahua, and some of what he says bears little relation to Nahua cultural expectations. See Fray Diego Durán, *The History of the Indies of New Spain*, ed. Doris Heyden (Norman: University of Oklahoma Press, 1964), 37.

4. For an entrée into the scholarship on this material, see Hanns Prem, *The Ancient Americas: A Brief History and Guide to Research* (Salt Lake City: University of Utah Press, 1997 [1989]). An excellent synthesis of the state of archaeological knowledge on the topic is Susan Toby Evans, *Ancient Mexico and Central America* (New York: Thames and Hudson, 2013).

5. There has been extensive debate about the Monte Verde site among archaeologists, but almost all now believe that the ancient dating is accurate, and that some fisher peoples moved down the coast of the continent before the land bridge existed. See David Metzer, *First Peoples in a New World: Colonizing Ice Age America* (Berkeley: University of California Press, 2009).

6. The people then knew nothing of cells or the amino acids that formed their component parts, but they did not need to know anything about biology to know when their diet was providing adequate sustenance.

7. These arguments are presented for laypeople in Jared Diamond, *Guns, Germs and Steel* (New York: Norton, 1997). There has been a great deal of debate about some aspects of Diamond's work among historians. Diamond is a biologist who examined the radio carbon dating of food plants and drew important conclusions; here I present what I believe is scientifically incontrovertible.

8. The people could not have known that corn is missing two of the amino acids essential to form a complete protein and that beans contain the missing amino acids.

9. Evans, *Ancient Mexico.* For a good introduction to Mesoamerican agriculture in the preconquest period, start with Robert West and John Augelli, *Middle America: Its Land and Peoples* (New Jersey: Prentice Hall, 1989 [1966]).

10. See Richard Diehl, *The Olmecs: America's First Civilization* (New York: Thames and Hudson, 2004). On the important work that has been done on the writings

of the Olmecs' descendant cultures, see John Justeson and Terrence Kaufman, "A Decipherment of Epi-Olmec Hieroglyphic Writing," *Science* 259 (1993): 1703–11.

11. Some scholars have begun to doubt the importance of Olmec influence, and have underscored the creativity and verve of cultural motifs originating elsewhere. (For instance, the very first writing may have occurred in western Mexico.) However, Susan Toby Evans and others underscore that there are countless instances of Olmec influence found both east and west, and relatively few instances of the the surrounding areas influencing the Olmec region. In the big picture, it seems to me that the Olmecs must remain central to our understanding of Mesoamerican history.

12. Dennis Tedlock, *2000 Years of Mayan Literature* (Berkeley: University of California Press, 2010). Tedlock argues eloquently at this point for using the term "translating" rather than "deciphering" when we speak of the Maya glyphs. However, for the necessary preliminary step of what was in fact decipherment, see Michael Coe's *Breaking the Maya Code* (New York: Thames and Hudson, 1992).

13. See Evans, *Ancient Mexico*. Some readers may be interested in a foundational work, a more technical book by a team of archaeologists: William Sanders, Jeffrey Parsons, and Robert Santley, *The Basin of Mexico: Ecological Processes in the Evolution of a Civilization* (New York: Academic Press, 1979).

14. The etymology of place names is often uncertain, and so it is in this case. "Teotihuacan" is often interpreted as the passive construction of *teoti* ("to become a god") and hence "the place where people become gods" or "the place where gods are made." However, a place name coming from an impersonal verb should end in *yan* not *can*. I believe it should be translated as "the place of those who had great gods." The embedded noun is *teotiuhtli* (elder god, or great god), and then we see the possessive *hua* and the "place of" suffix *can*. For a detailed exposition of the formation and the most common errors, see Richard Andrews, *Introduction to Classical Nahuatl* (Norman: University of Oklahoma Press, 2003), 498.

15. Fray Bernardino de Sahagún, *Florentine Codex: General History of the Things of New Spain,* ed. Arthur Anderson and Charles Dibble (Salt Lake City: School of American Research and the University of Utah, 1950–1982), 7:4. A more truncated version of the story is found in Legend of the Suns (see appendix), published in *Códice Chimalpopoca,* ed. Primo Feliciano Velázquez (Mexico City: Imprenta Universitaria, 1945).

16. See Esther Pasztory, *Teotihuacan: An Experiment in Living* (Norman: University of Oklahoma Press, 1997; and Geoffrey Braswell, *The Maya and Teoitihuacan: Reinterpreting Early Classic Interaction* (Austin: University of Texas Press, 2003).

17. See Michael Foster and Shirley Gorenstein, eds., *Greater Mesoamerica: The Archaeology of West and Northwest Mexico* (Salt Lake City: University of Utah, 2000). Within that volume, Michael Spence's chapter "From Tzintzuntzan to Paquime: Peers or Peripheries in Greater Mesoamerica?" outlines the resistance that some archaeologists of the region have evinced in accepting central Mexico's

influence. They argue, for example, that refugees from Teotihuacan could have been the source of the architectural similarities we see. That seems willful thinking, however; powerless fugitives are not usually the shapers of culture, as Spence acknowledges.

18. The extraordinary, multilayered influence of Teotihuacan even after the dissolution of its polity is testified to in David Carrasco, Lindsay Jones, and Scott Sessions, eds., *Mesoamerica's Classic Heritage: From Teotihuacan to the Aztecs* (Boulder: University of Colorado Press, 2000).

19. A key article on this topic is John Blitz, "Adoption of the Bow in Prehistoric North America," *North American Archaeologist* 9 (1988): 123–45.

20. Conquest-era annals from Tlaxcala were recorded first in the sixteenth century and then copied in the seventeenth century by the indigenous historian don Juan Buenaventura Zapata y Mendoza; see *Historia cronológica de la noble ciudad de Tlaxcala,* ed. Luis Reyes García and Andrea Martínez Baracs (Tlaxcala: Universidad Autónoma de Tlaxcala, 1995), 84–85.

21. The descendants of Xolotl settled the Texcoco region. Some of their histories were written in Spanish by don Fernando de Alva Ixtlilxochitl, a mestizo scholar who identified with his maternal ancestors. For an entrée into the substantial literature on this colonial writer, see the special issue of *Colonial Latin American Review* 23, no. 1 (2014).

22. Readers may find the latest research on the most impressive ruins in North America in Carrie Heitman and Stephen Plog, *Chaco Revisited: New Research on the Prehistory of Chaco Canyon, New Mexico* (Tucson: University of Arizona Press, 2015); for the best overview of what is known so far, see Stephen Lekson, ed., *The Archaeology of Chaco Canyon: An Eleventh-Century Pueblo Regional Center* (Santa Fe: School of American Research, 2006). Within that volume, see especially Ben Nelson, "Mesoamerican Objects and Symbols in Chaco Canyon Contexts," for a thoughtful and subtle analysis of the question of influence.

23. Both the basic commonalities and the subtle differences found from region to region are explored in Munro Edmonson, *The Book of the Year: Middle American Calendrical Systems* (Salt Lake City: University of Utah Press, 1988).

24. As Mexican corn and beans spread up the Mississippi, the mound culture definitely went with the new agricultural complex. However, some scholars maintain that the ritualistic games that were present developed independently and were not part of the exported culture complex. Needless to say, we will never be able to be certain about this.

25. Those who wish to see charts of the contents of the surviving annals, including all variations, should consult Federico Navarrete Linares, *Los orígenes de los pueblos indígenas del valle de México: Los altepetl y sus historias* (Mexico City: Universidad Autónoma de México, 2015). In English, some of this material is covered in Elizabeth Hill Boone, *Stories in Red and Black: Pictorial Histories of the Aztecs and Mixtecs* (Austin: University of Texas Press, 2000).

26. Readers may find the linguistics literature to be highly technical. A good beginning would be Terrence Kaufman, "Native Languages of Mesoamerica," in *Atlas of the World's Languages* (New York: Routledge, 1994).

27. A good discussion of the complications surrounding the use of the terms "Tula" and "Toltec" is found in Hanns Prem, *The Ancient Americas.*

28. *Historia Tolteca Chichimeca*, folio 2, in *Historia Tolteca Chichimecca* ed. Paul Kirchoff, Lina Odena Güemes and Luis Reyes García (Mexico City: Instituto Nacional de Historia e Antropología, 1976). See the annotated bibliography of extant annals in the appendix for more on this source.

29. *Annals of Tlatelolco*, folios 8 and 9, in Mengin, *Unos annales.* (More truncated versions of the story are found in other sixteenth-century sets of annals as well.)

30. The root is probably "nochtli," the prickly pear cactus fruit, although "tenochtic" means "something painted, colored." Both etymologies involve grammatical problems, so we cannot be certain of the provenance. Other theories have been offered but likewise cannot be proven.

Chapter 2

1. The event described in this paragraph could actually have occurred anywhere between 1428 and 1432. The histories told in the annals are not perfectly aligned with each other as different villages began keeping the calendar at different times (in one, One Reed might be our 1424, and in another, our 1425, for example), and in some cases, different history tellers may simply have been in error. Nonetheless, the histories are generally consistent within themselves. In the case of this set of events, for example, Itzcoatl is understood to have felt secure in his power within about four years after the death of Tezozomoc of Azcapotalco (whose story will be told in this chapter). Since most sources place Tezozomoc's death in our 1426, I have, too. It doesn't matter if it actually occurred a year earlier or later in our calendar count: what is important is that the book-burning occurred a few years later.

2. Fray Bernardino de Sahagún, *Florentine Codex: General History of the Things of New Spain,* ed. Arthur J. O Anderson and Charles Dibble (Salt Lake City: School of American Research and the University of Utah Press, 1950–1982), 10:191. The *Codex* itself tells us only of the event. One needs to learn more about Itzcoatl's history and that of the Mexica to understand why he would do this; this chapter will render it clear.

3. See Elizabeth Hill Boone, "The Physicality of the Painted Books," in *Stories in Red and Black: Pictorial Histories of the Aztecs and Mixtecs* (Austin: University of Texas Press, 2000), 23–24.

4. *Florentine Codex*, 6:239.

5. This perspective is laced throughout the statements of the colonial-era writer, Tezozomoc, a descendant of Tlacaelel's branch of the royal family. See don Domingo Chimalpahin, *Codex Chimalpahin,* ed. Arthur J. O. Anderson and Susan

Schroeder (Norman: University of Oklahoma Press, 1997), e.g., 1:40–47 and 2:36–37. For the full story of Tlacaelel, see Susan Schroeder, *Tlacaelel Remembered: Mastermind of the Aztec Empire* (Norman: University of Oklahoma Press, 2016).

6. *Codex Chimalpahin* 1:36–37, 112–17, 206–9; 2:90–91, 82–83. There are slight variations on the story in other annals, but in effect they all tell the story I have distilled here, even though the timing varies. The story is alluded to in the *Annals of Cuauhtitlan* as having occurred in the 1370s.

7. Song XXXIII, in *Cantares Mexicanos*, ed. John Bierhorst (Stanford, CA: Stanford University Press, 1985), 202–3. Translation amended. It could possibly mean that the bird flew "over a field in a place unknown." In either case, the "place unknown" refers to the land of the dead.

8. Susan Toby Evans in *Ancient Mexico and Central America* (New York: Thames & Hudson, 2013), 464, diagrams and charts the building phases of what would ultimately become the great Templo Mayor.

9. Western-influenced sources have traditionally described the Aztecs as having held "elections" to choose the next chief after the death of the old one. There is a kernel of truth here. The Nahuatl annals refer to period ranging from a few days up to (in the worst case) a few years, during which time negotiations and dickering took place before consensus was reached. But we must understand that long before an old chief died, there would generally have been a sense of who the most likely contender would be.

10. All the sources refer in vague terms to his having been what would be called "illegitimate" in Western terms. Chimalpahin is explicit: *Codex Chimalpahin* 1:36–37. The Nahuas had no word for "illegitimate," but there were various words referring to conjugal and sexual relations, and those terms denoted differences regarding the fate of the offspring.

11. See Camilla Townsend, "Slavery in Pre-Columbian America," in *The Cambridge World History of Slavery,* vol. 2, ed. Craig Perry, David Eltis, et al. (Cambridge: Cambridge University Press, forthcoming 2020).

12. On the political complexities of marriage relationships, see Pedro Carrasco, "Royal Marriages in Ancient Mexico," in *Explorations in Ethnohistory: The Indians of Central Mexico in the Sixteenth Century*, ed. H. R. Harvey and H. Prem (Albuquerque: University of New Mexico Press, 1984); and Camilla Townsend, "'What in the World Have You Done to Me, My Lover?': Sex, Servitude, and Politics among the Pre-Conquest Nahuas as Seen in the *Cantares Mexicanos,*" *Americas* 62 (2006): 349–89.

13. The central image of just such a shield appears on the cover of this book. See Renée Riedler, "Materials and Technique of the Feather Shield Preserved in Vienna," in *Images Take Flight: Feather Art in Mexico and Europe, 1400-1700* (Florence, Italy: Kunsthistorisches Institut in Florenz, 2015). There is a strand of humor or irony in much Pre-Columbian art.

14. *Codex Chimalpahin*, 1:118–25.

15. Other parts of Chimalpahin's annals, and indeed almost all annals as well as Spanish sources, mention a long war against Cuernavaca, the cotton country. It began even before Huitzilihuitl's reign.

16. The trope of a swallowed stone leading to pregnancy appears in other Mesoamerican stories as well. See, for instance, the *Annals of Cuauhtitlan*, ed. Rafael Tena (Mexico City: Cien de México 2011), 36–37. The idea of a magic pit or stone impregnating a girl is found as far south as Peru, in a document known as the Huarochirí Manuscript.

17. The Nahuatl name is actually Moteuczoma, or "Frowns like a Lord," but given that the Spanish version has become nearly universal, I use the moniker that has become familiar. (The English later adjusted even that name, rendering it Montezuma.)

18. Susan Schroeder beautifully analyzes the story in this way in her article "The First American Valentine: Nahua Courtship and Other Aspects of Family Structuring in Mesoamerica," *Journal of Family History* 23 (1998).

19. The dominance of the Tepanec town of Azcapotzalco is made clear in a wide variety of sources. The best stories from the Tepanec perspective are found in the *Annals of Cuauhtitlan*.

20. *Codex Chimalpahin*, 1:118–19, 122–23; 2:44–45, 82–85.

21. *Florentine Codex* 8:64. A comparable postconquest seating of a nobleman as gobernador, with similar language, appears in the *Bancroft Dialogues* (see annotated bibliography of extant annals).

22. Townsend, "What in the World Have You Done to Me, My Lover?," 385.

23. For a detailed study of this subject, see Camilla Townsend, "Polygyny and the Divided Altepetl: The Tetzcocan Key to Pre-conquest Nahua Politics," in *Texcoco: Prehispanic and Colonial Perspectives*, ed. Jongsoo Lee and Galen Brokaw (Boulder: University Press of Colorado, 2014): 93–116.

24. All the annals refer directly or indirectly to the idea that Maxtla had been given Coyoacan to rule, but then chose to return to Azcapotzalco and usurp his brother's place.

25. *Codex Chimalpahin* 1:128–31. In another version, Chimalpopoca was not tricked but tried to defend the Tlacopan nobility of Azcapotzalco. See *Annals of Cuauhtitlan*, 136–39.

26. *Codex Chimalpahin* 1:128–29, 2:94–95.

27. See Schroeder, *Tlacaelel Remembered*, for a full biography.

28. The Nahuatl-speaking historian don Fernando de Alva Ixtlilxochitl provides us with a detailed narrative of Texcocan history. Ixtlilxochitl wrote in Spanish, for a largely Spanish audience, so he does sometimes confound issues. Nevertheless, he worked with many Nahuatl sources. See Amber Brian, *Alva Ixtlilxochitl's Native Archive and the Circulation of Knowledge in Colonial Mexico* (Nashville, TN: Vanderbilt University Press, 2016). When placed thoughtfully in juxtaposition to Nahuatl annals, as will be done throughout, his work can be very helpful to us.

29. Fernando de Alva Ixtlilxochitl, *Obras completas*, ed. Edmundo O'Gorman (Mexico City: Universidad Nacional Autónoma de México, 1975–77), 2:326, 371. Ixtlilxochitl possessed a visual source, the *Codex Xolotl*, which portrays the situation graphically: two lines of descent stretch forth from the image of the king Huehue Ixtlilxochitl.

30. *Annals of Cuauhtitlan*, 140–43.

31. *Annals of Cuauhtitlan*, 142–43.

32. *Annals of Cuauhtitlan*, 134–35.

33. *Codex Chimalpahin* 2:92–93.

34. Ixtlilxochitl, *Obras*, 2:332–33. The battle is portrayed graphically in the *Codex Xolotl*. Many of the pictorial sources, as well as the *Annals of Juan Bautista*, remind us of the importance of the artistry displayed on shields, including the scene as described here.

35. Elements of this story are found in Ixtlilxochitl, often with great embellishment. Enough are found in the *Annals of Cuauhtitlan* for us to be certain of the gist. There, in Nezahualcoyotl's years of wandering, he maintains ties with Maxtla and his people, though as a derided supplicant. That part of the story is probably apocryphal.

36. Ixtlilxochitl, *Obras*, 2:343. This story, found nowhere else, at first seems suspect, and one wonders if it stems from the classical literature the highly educated Ixtlilxochitl knew so well. However, scholars in that field have not been able to find a source, so it is likely that Ixtlilxochitl came by it as he said he did.

37. *Annals of Cuauhtitlan*, 164–71. Chimalpahin, "Tercera Relación" in *Ocho relaciones y el Memorial de Colhuacan*, ed. Rafael Tena (Mexico City: Conaculta, 1998), 1:241–44.

38. Scholars have recently begun to doubt the traditional use of the word "empire" to describe the Aztec state, and to note that no one then ever spoke of a "Triple Alliance," but we should not reject the notion of Aztec power by any means, nor of the state's key alliances. Pedro Carrasco does an excellent job of explaining the real nature of the Mexicas' power, in his *Tenochca Empire of Ancient Mexico: The Triple Alliance of Tenochtitlan, Tetzcoco, and Tlacopan* (Norman: University of Oklahoma Press, 1999). For an updated discussion, allowing for a critique of colonial sources without discarding the idea of the existence of a major alliance, see Jongsoo Lee, "The Aztec Triple Alliance: A Colonial Transformation of the Prehispanic Political and Tributary System," in *Texcoco: Prehispanic, and Colonial Perspectives*, ed. Jongsoo Lee and Galen Brokaw (Boulder: University Press of Colorado, 2014).

39. The best overview of local Nahua politics as the system existed in the early colonial period, stretching back into time immemorial, is James Lockhart, *The Nahuas After the Conquest* (Stanford, CA: Stanford University Press, 1992), esp. chap. 2, "Altepetl."

40. Inga Clendinnen, *Aztecs: An Interpretation* (Cambridge: Cambridge University Press, 1992), 25. Spanish sources bandied about careless statements concerning the relationships between subservient polities and Tenochtitlan in these regards; many

of their authors were intent on making an implicit comparison with Rome, a subject about which they knew a great deal due to their classical education. To get to the truth, it is necessary to find moments where such matters were referred to unselfconsciously by Nahuas themselves in the course of addressing other matters, and also to consult the archaeological record. It does seem that in this period, there was little effort to integrate conquered communities into a greater polity; but, as we shall see in chap. 3, that began to change as time progressed.

41. For more on this, see Ross Hassig, *Time, History, and Belief in Aztec and Colonial Mexico* (Austin: University of Texas Press, 2001).

42. Almost all of the annals refer at one point or another to the idea that a responsible chief is one who cares for his people and prevents too many deaths, so that the life of the altepetl will continue; he cannot be rash or careless. For a treatment of this subject, see Camilla Townsend, *Malintzin's Choices: An Indian Woman in the Conquest of Mexico* (Albuquerque: University of New Mexico Press, 2006) 102–6. An explicit belittling of a chief as a "child," for instance, is found in *Annals of Tlatelolco*.

43. Fray Diego Durán, *History of the Indies of New Spain*, ed. Doris Heyden (Norman: University of Oklahoma Press, 1994 [1964]), 165. Durán is explicit about the violence in ways that the writers of annals did not find it necessary to be, so I quote him here, rather than one of the annals. For the Nahua historians, merely the use of the verb *polihui*, for example, implied utter destruction (Stephanie Wood, personal communication). Alternatively, they would often say tersely, "No one was left alive."

44. For an overview of the economy and the structure of households, see also Lockhart, *The Nahuas*, especially chaps. 3 ("Household") and 5 ("Land and Living").

45. The chronicles of the conquistadors tell us how the built environment intensified as they approached Tenochtitlan.

46. See Townsend, "Slavery."

47. Ronald Hutton, *Blood and Mistletoe: The History of the Druids in Britain* (New Haven, CT: Yale University Press, 2009).

48. *Florentine Codex,* 2:129 and 132; and 9:67 and throughout. The *Florentine Codex* describes the ceremonies as they were enacted on the eve of conquest. Although I assume that in their essence these ceremonies were very old (e.g., that people had long watched, gravely holding the proper flower in their hands), I also assume that in their specifics they were a product of their time (e.g., that the Aztecs certainly could not have sacrificed on the scale described when their settlement was new, and they were still far from the most powerful group in the valley). David Carrasco explores the moral implications of this part of Aztec life in *City of Sacrifice* (Boston: Beacon Press, 1999). See chap. 3 for a treatment of human sacrifice at the height of Aztec power.

49. Miguel León Portilla, ed., *Coloquios y doctrina Cristiana* (Mexico City: Universidad Nacional Autónoma de México, 1986).

50. For a fine exploration of the nature of one Aztec god, see Guilhem Olivier, *Mockeries and Metamorphoses of an Aztec God: Tezcatlipoca, "Lord of the Smoking Mirror"* (Boulder: University Press of Colorado, 2003). In general, it is extremely difficult for us today to attain a glimmer of real understanding of these gods: the Spaniards frowned on discussion of them, except under their auspices and based on leading questions they posed. Thus genuine knowledge of the old religion was gradually suppressed, even as a westernized pantheon was created. See David °Colmenares, "How the Aztecs Got a Pantheon: The Creation of Ancient Religion in New Spain," PhD diss., Columbia University, 2019. Nahuas highly educated in western traditions were only too happy to participate in this project. Today, those who wish to explore Aztec notions of divinity must ultimately focus largely on archaeological, rather than alphabetic, texts; thus we can rarely hear the gods themselves speak. For a reader wishing to begin a study, I suggest Rafael Tena, *La religión mexica* (Mexico City: INAH, 1993); Mary Miller and Karl Taube, *An Illustrated Dictionary of the Gods and Symbols of Ancient Mexico and the Maya* (London: Thames & Hudson, 1993); and Leonardo López Luján, *The Offerings of the Templo Mayor of Tenochtitlan* (Boulder: University Press of Colorado, 1994). It is even more difficult to grasp spiritual concepts in the Nahua world due to the limited nature of the evidence. Many have made assertions, but recent work indicates how dangerous such guesswork often has been. See Justyna Olko and Julia Madajczak, "An Animating Principle in Confrontation with Christianity? De(Re)constructing the Nahua 'Soul,'" *Ancient Mesoamerica* 30 (2019): 1–14.

51. 1 Kings 16:34 and Monmouth's *History of the Kings of Britain*, ed. Lewis Thorpe (London: Folio Society, 1969). For a study of this theme, see Paul G. Brewster, "The Foundation Sacrifice Motif in Legend, Folksong, Game, and Dance," *Zeitschrift für Ethnologie* 96 (1971): 71–89. For a study of the influence that Geoffrey of Monmouth (or a comparable text) seems to have had on Ixtlilxochitl, see Pablo García Loaeza, "Deeds to be Praised for All Time: Alva Ixtlilxochitl's *Historia de la nación chichimeca* and Geoffrey of Monmouth's *History of the Kings of Britain*," *Colonial Latin American Review* 23 (2014): 53–69.

52. See Salvador Guilliem Arroyo, "The Discovery of the Caja de Agua of Tlatelolco: Mural Painting from the Dawn of New Spain," *Colonial Latin American Review* 22 (2013): 19–38. For a selection of poetry, see Miguel León Portilla, ed., *Fifteen Poets of the Aztec World* (Norman: University of Oklahoma Press, 1992). For more on these subjects, see chap. 3.

53. Paul Veyne, *Did the Greeks Believe in Their Myths? An Essay on the Constitutive Imagination* (Chicago: University of Chicago Press, 1988).

54. *Florentine Codex*, 6:101. In the *Bancroft Dialogues*, we find similarly strict admonishments delivered to the young in a postconquest family ceremony.

55. These images are found throughout the Nahuatl corpus. There are excellent examples in the *Florentine Codex*, vol. 6, as well as in the *Bancroft Dialogues*.

56. There is a substantial literature on this subject. Readers should begin with Louise Burkhart, "Mexica Women on the Home Front: Housework and Religion in Aztec Mexico," in *Indian Women of Early Mexico*, ed. Susan Schroeder, Stephanie Wood, and Robert Haskett (Norman: University of Oklahoma Press, 1997); and Clendinnen, *Aztecs*, chaps. 4–8. Another important work is Lisa Sousa, *The Woman Who Turned into a Jaguar, and Other Narratives of Native Women in Archives of Colonial Mexico* (Stanford, CA: Stanford University Press, 2017).

57. Charles Gibson, *Tlaxcala in the Sixteenth Century* (New Haven, CT: Yale University Press, 1954). The concept of the "Flower Wars" has long been treated in the literature (see chap. 4, n. 41). It is perhaps due for another treatment, this time based purely on Nahuatl sources. They definitely reveal the existence of a notion of "xochiyaoyotl" as a desultory form of warfare practiced when neither group really wanted to commit itself to the destruction of the other. See, for example, the skirmishing between the Mexica and the Chalca in *Annals of Cuauhtitlan*, 118–19.

58. An excellent summary of the Mesoamerican "World System" is Robert Carmack's "The Mesoamerican World at Spanish Contact," in *The Legacy of Mesoamerica: History and Culture of a Native American Civilization,* ed. Robert Carmack et al. (Albany, NY: Institute for Mesoamerian Studies, 1996).

59. Almost all the annals refer to Tlacaelel. See Schroeder, *Tlacaelel Remembered.* However, only the accounts that come to us from Huitzilihuitl's descendant, Tezozomoc, via Chimalpahin, insist on his paramount place. On the question of the significant of titles of governing men, there is unfortunately little to be said: there was clearly widespread knowledge of the meaning of different titles of men who acted as counselors, not only of the Cihuacoatl, as the titles appear widely; and in nearly all the annals, not only of the Mexica but also of other Nahuas. Today, however, a deep understanding of these matters is lost to us.

60. The annals do not say all this explicitly. But a familiarity with the family tree of Acamapichtli's descendants, combined with knowledge of the events that transpired, tells us what we need to know. María Castañeda de Paz was the first to spot the pendulum of power swinging between the two branches of the family. See her "Historia de una casa real. Origen y ocaso del linaje gobernante en México-Tenochtitlan," *Nuevo Mundo Mundos Nuevos* (2011): 1–20.

61. *Florentine Codex*, 6:35–36 (translation changed). Michel Launey first alerted me to the fact that Dibble and Anderson's translation of this passage misses key elements (personal communication, 1998); more recently, Louise Burkhart improved my translation significantly and showed me that the paragraph reflects a common understanding among the Nahuas of the three stages of early childhood: those who are trapped in cradles then become children who can be left on the ground to play with the dirt; they then become those who are mobile (personal communication, 2018).

62. Chimalpahin, Third Relation in *Ocho Relaciones.* Almost all the annals refer to the famine of the 1450s.

63. Chimalpahin, whose home it was, explains that the name comes from a truncated version of the word *chalchihuitl* ("jade," referencing the blue-green waters).

64. *Annals of Cuauhtitlan,* 186–87 ("onca onpeuh ynic quauhtlatolloc chalco çenpo- hualxihuitl ozçe yn quauhtlatolloya"). It actually refers to rule by "eagle" lords, or those who were not of Chalco's royal line, being either Mexica or commoners imposed by the Mexica. (For more on the subject of eagle lords, see later chapters of this book, esp. chap. 7.) Naturally, Chimalpahin's Chalcan annals and stories tell of these events in much greater detail, complete with dialogue between the leaders and tales of mutual spying, sometimes with the help of a little magic.

Chapter 3

1. This section comes from the work of Chimalpahin, who opened the introduction. It is found in his "Seventh Relation," folios 175–76, in his *Ocho Relaciones* (see annotated bibliography of extant annals in the appendix). This story is transcribed and translated into English in Camilla Townsend, *Annals of Native America: How the Nahuas of Colonial Mexico Kept Their History Alive* (New York: Oxford University Press, 2016), 141–43.

2. On the symbolism associated with Aztec costuming, see Justyna Olko, *Insignia of Rank in the Nahua World: From the Fifteenth to the Seventeenth Century* (Boulder: University Press of Colorado, 2014).

3. Chimalpahin, "Seventh Relation," *Ocho Relaciones,* folio 176. For more on Chimalpahin and don Jerónimo, see chap. 8. Both Chimalpahin's grandmother and don Jerónimo were of the noble class and both belonged to Amaquemecan, a sub-altepetl of Chalco. It would thus have been impossible for them not to have known each other, and the details of Chimalpahin's text indicate that he had access to the behind-the-scenes story.

4. Fray Bernardino de Sahagún, *Florentine Codex: General History of the Things of New Spain,* ed. Arthur J. O Anderson and Charles Dibble (Salt Lake City: School of American Research and University of Utah Press, 1950–1982), 8:55.

5. For more on this history of Chalco, see Susan Schroeder, *Chimalpahin and the Kingdoms of Chalco* (Tucson: University of Arizona Press, 1991).

6. At least two versions of the song were transcribed in the mid-sixteenth century. A transcription, translation, and analysis are found in Camilla Townsend, "'What in the World Have You Done to Me, My Lover?' Sex, Servitude, and Politics among the Pre-conquest Nahuas as Seen in the *Cantares Mexicanos,*" *Americas* 62 (2006): 349–89. We know the song was popular and remained so, because in *The Annals of Juan Bautista* there is a reference to its being sung in the political upheavals of the 1560s.

7. Townsend, "'What in the World Have You Done to Me,'" 384.

8. Townsend, "'What in the World Have You Done to Me,'" 385.

9. The idea that the drums "spoke" or "called out" is found repeatedly in the annals and the cantares. For more on Aztec music, see Gary Tomlinson, *The Singing of the New World: Indigenous Voice in the Era of European Contact* (New York: Cambridge University Press, 2007).

10. This comes from Chimalpahin and is eminently believable, for in the *Florentine Codex*, there are numerous references to the importance of the king's joining a dance as a sign of favor or agreement. See, for example, *Florentine Codex* 2:95 or 8:27. This is also evident throughout the *Cantares Mexicanos*.

11. Again, this comes from Chimalpahin, but the details of exactly what the female nobility wore on such occasions come from the *Florentine Codex*, 8:47.

12. From Chimalpahin, but the gesture of "eating earth" is mentioned in a variety of annals and several conquistadors' chronicles, including the letters of Hernando Cortés.

13. For fascinating examples of polite social reversal dating to the late preconquest period, see Frances Kartunnen and James Lockhart, eds., *The Art of Nahuatl Speech: The Bancroft Dialogues* (Los Angeles: UCLA Latin American Center Publications, 1987).

14. Chimalpahin, "Seventh Relation," *Ocho Relaciones*, folio 175.

15. See Peter Sigal, "Queer Nahuatl: Sahagún's Faggots and Sodomites, Lesbians and Hermaphrodites," *Ethnohistory* 54 (2007): 9–34; and "The Cuiloni, the Patlache and the Abominable Sin: Homosexualities in Early Colonial Nahua Society," *Hispanic American Historical Review* 85 (2005): 555–94. On practices as investigated by the Spaniards in Morelia in the early years after conquest, see Zeb Tortorici, "'Heran Todos Putos:' Sodomitical Subcultures and Disordered Desire in Early Colonial Mexico," *Ethnohistory* 54 (2007): 35–67.

16. *Annals of Puebla*, entry for 1689, in *Here in This Year: Seventeenth-Century Nahuatl Annals of the Tlaxcala-Puebla Valley,* ed. Camilla Townsend (Stanford, CA: Stanford University Press, 2010), 144–45. There are several comparable incidents of men being punished for homosexual relations which are found in the annals originating in the Puebla region.

17. The *Florentine Codex* demonstrates that a number of religious rituals ended in sex. At least twice there is an implication that men sometimes had sex with each other (*Florentine Codex* 2:14 and 103), but the *Codex* does not discuss the subject explicitly. Sigal in "Queer Nahuatl" recounts the shock he experienced when he realized that even in that Spanish-influence source, the informants sometimes referred to a powerful deity as a "cuiloni," or faggot, clearly without self-consciousness. What the range of the Nahuas' sexual imagination might have been revealed to be, had the speakers been at liberty to express all that they felt or experienced, is impossible to say.

18. *Annals of Cuauhtitlan ,* ed. Rafael Tena (Mexico City: Cien de México, 2011), 146–47. The importance of gifting (especially on the part of chiefs) is omnipresent in indigenous sources.

19. The text says that they exchanged raucous greetings with those who had been most afraid.

20. *Florentine Codex* 8:44.

21. For a fine study of late preconquest Tenochtitlan (as well as its evolution after the conquest), see Barbara Mundy, *The Death of Aztec Tenochtitlan, the Life of Mexico City* (Austin: University of Texas Press, 2015).

22. *Florentine Codex* 8:44. For more on the architectural remains left by each monarch, see Ross Hassig, *Time, History, and Belief in Aztec and Colonial Mexico* (Austin: University of Texas Press, 2001).

23. Matthew Restall has effectively analyzed Moctezuma's collections of animals, birds, and even people as a display of his political power in *When Montezuma Met Cortés: The True Story of the Meeting that Changed History* (New York: Harper Collins, 2018).

24. *Florentine Codex* 5:151, 161–63. In keeping with this, in the *Cantares Mexicanos*, animals call out at significant moments.

25. *Florentine Codex* 8:37–40. Some of these dishes were later commented upon by the Spaniards.

26. There are references to the bird gardens in *Florentine Codex* 8:46 and perhaps 9:83, where it is mentioned that feather work became a more prominent craft under Moctezuma the Younger, as that is when more feathers became available, through live birds received as tribute and in trade, and later farmed there in the city. Domingo Chimalpahin, *Codex Chimalpahin,* ed. Arthur J. O. Anderson and Susan Schroeder (Norman: University of Oklahoma Press, 1997), 2:54–55 offers an example of birds being tied to magic in the Chalcan imagination. "They came just to the edge of the forest and looked about behind them as if sorcerers lived in the light....It was dawn; the birds were already calling out." On the night sky being compared to popcorn, see *Florentine Codex* 6:237. It is the conquistadors, like Bernal Díaz, who tell us the overall effect the city had on those who first beheld it.

27. Over the years, there have been many wild exaggerations of Tenochtitlan's population, the most common assertion being 250,000. The archaeologist Susan Toby Evans offers an excellent discussion of the matter in her *Ancient Mexico and Central America,* "How Many People Lived in Tenochtitlan?" (New York: Thames & Hudson, 2014), 549. The footprint of the city at that time enclosed 5.4 square miles. To hold 250,000 people, there would have had to be 48,000 inhabitants per square mile. Modern Manhattan has a population density of about 67,000, so the proffered number is patently impossible; 50,000 people is absolutely as many as 5.4 square miles could contain in what were mostly single-story houses.

28. See Louise Burkhart, "Mexica Women on the Home Front: Housework and Religion in Aztec Mexico," in *Indian Women of Early Mexico,* ed. Susan Schroeder, Stephanie Wood, and Robert Haskett (Norman: University of Oklahoma Press, 1997); and Susan Kellogg, "The Woman's Room: Some Aspects of Gender Relations in Tenochtitlan in the Late Pre-Hispanic Period," *Ethnohistory* 42 (1995): 563–76.

29. Evans, *Ancient Mexico*, discusses the evolution of the city as evident in the great temple (462–65), and Frances Berdan draws together all material on the aqueduct and other hydrologic projects in *Aztec Archaeology and Ethnohistory* (Cambridge: Cambridge University Press, 2014), 76–80.

30. *Codex Chimalpahin*, 1:136–37. Of course, it is possible that this comment encapsulates a rumor campaign, rather than reflecting what the two actually uttered in public.

31. The Spanish sources all declare that kings were chosen at a grand council of Mexica nobility, which is to a large extent true. What the Spanish sources miss is that it wasn't simply a candidate's charisma or policies that won him that successorship. Rather, only the sons of certain royal wives were ever in contention (except in moments of crisis, as with Itzcoatl), and there was a general understanding that the pendulum of power must swing back and forth between family lines in order to maintain overall stability. Even the specific outcome of the election of a certain son within a group of brothers probably came as a result of years of politicking as much as personal attributes. The Nahuatl annals do not say all this explicitly, but rather implicitly. They tell us if there was much disagreement in each case, and how long it took for the group to arrive at consensus; the context generally offers explanations for the tension. The family tree demonstrates that power was handed back and forth regularly. And this is all in perfect keeping with what James Lockhart deduced about early postconquest political control rotating among "cells" of the whole body politic according to highly traditional modes. On the specific succession of the figures mentioned in this paragraph, the Spanish sources must be ignored altogether, as they assume that all three brothers had the same mother. *Codex Chimalpahin* 1:135–37, 2:97, and elsewhere, leads one to believe that they did not have the same mother, and that there had been another primary wife at first, creating strong tensions between elder siblings and younger ones. The *Annals of Tlatelolco* tell us that the first wife was Tlatelolcan, which makes perfect sense, given both the political context in Tezozomoc's youth and later events.

32. Indeed, it may well have been the issue of the rulership that broke them apart in the first place; these may have been "die hard" Mexica who did not want to bring in a tlatoani from Culhuacan, which most of the Tenochtitlan people were willing to do in order to get recognition as a kingdom. Or perhaps the Tlatelolca wished to bring in a different outsider tlatoani, one who whose family had intermarried with their own noble family. The records do not tell us what the trouble was, but such things were common causes of fissures.

33. The *Annals of Cuauhtitlan* and *Annals of Tlatelolco* agree on all of this. Chimalpahin references the split as well, but because his sources are Tenochca, he casts the Tlatelolca in a negative light, as troublemakers from the beginning. On Tlatelolco's relationship with the Toluca valley, see René García Castro, *Indios, territorio y poder en la provincia Matlatzinca* (Toluca: Colegio Mexiquense, 1999). On Tlatelolco's relationship with Cuauhtinchan, see Luis Reyes García, *Cuauhtinchan del Siglo XII al XVI* (Wiesbaden, Germany: Franz Steiner, 1977).

34. The Tlatelolcans in their annals say as little as possible about this war, which was, for them, disastrous. However, Chimalpahin, with his Tenochca sources, tells the story in various ways with great gusto and plenty of dialogue. See *Codex Chimalpahin* 1:137–39, 2:43–51 and 93–95, as well as "Third Relation" and "Seventh Relation" in don Domingo Chimalpahin, *Ocho relaciones y el Memorial de Colhuacan*, 2 vols., ed. Rafael Tena (Mexico City: Conaculta, 1998).

35. *Codex Chimalpahin* 2:45.

36. This comes to us from a Spanish source: Fray Diego Durán, *The History of the Indies of New Spain,* ed. Doris Heyden (Norman: University of Oklahoma Press, 1994 [1964]), 260. This incident seemed uncharacteristic and thus doubtful, until I found a similar reference in the *Annals of Tlatelolco* at the moment of Spanish conquest. Lisa Sousa treats this topic thoroughly in *The Woman Who Turned Into a Jaguar and Other Narratives of Native Women in Archives of Colonial Mexico* (Stanford, CA: Stanford University Press, 2017), 264–65.

37. *Codex Chimalpahin* 2:93 and less clear references elsewhere. This aspect of the drama made it into Spanish accounts as well (such as that of Diego Durán).

38. *Codex Mendoza*, entry for 1473. See annotated bibliography in the appendix for a discussion of this source.

39. *Codex Aubin*, entry for 1473. See annotated bibliography in the appendix for a discussion of this source.

40. Fray Juan de Torquemada was the friar who promulgated this story. For a detailed study of these events and the sources that help us disentangle the truth from the Spanish accounts, see Camilla Townsend, "Polygyny and the Divided Altepetl: The Tetzcocan Key to Pre-conquest Nahua Politics," in *Texcoco: Prehispanic and Colonial Perspectives*, ed. Jongsoo Lee and Galen Brokaw (Boulder: University Press of Colorado, 2014): 93–116.

41. Townsend, "Polygyny and the Divided Altepetl." The material comes from a judicious reading of Ixtlilxochitl's works side by side with the *Annals of Cuauhtitlan*.

42. Chimalpahin, "Seventh Relation" in *Ocho Relaciones*. Chimalpahin seems to be getting this material from individual stories told by people in his grandmother's generation.

43. All of the king lists in all the annals agree on these facts.

44. In the *Bancroft Dialogues,*155, an elderly narrator mentions the communal houses where representatives of other altepetls lived. (She says residents gathered on the roof of the Cholulans to see a grisly execution. The human exchange went two ways. In the sixteenth century, the *Historia Tolteca Chichimeca* indicates that Mexica people had come to live in the Cholula region. Likewise, numerous residents of the Toluca valley referred to Mexica settlers coming to live among them in the preceding century, who they said still retained their lands. See García Castro, *Matlatzinca*. The example of the neighborhoods cited here comes from Tepemaxalco, near Toluca. In the seventeenth century, the apparent descendants of the Nahuatl-speaking settlers still lived there and the members of one leading family wrote

extensively. Caterina Pizzigoni and Camilla Townsend, "Indian Life After the Conquest: The De la Cruz Family Papers from Colonial Mexico," unpublished manuscript.

45. The *Florentine Codex* tells us something about Moctezuma's communication systems in both merchant trade and the military apparatus, and a preponderance of the surviving sixteenth-century pictorials delineate borders and rulerships.

46. The archaeologist Michael Smith did a great service to the field in choosing to investigate ordinary rural villages and towns rather than great urban centers and temples. See Michael Smith, *The Aztecs* (London: Blackwell, 1996), and more recently *At Home with the Aztecs: An Archaeologist Uncovers Their Daily Life* (New York: Routledge, 2016).

47. See Hassig, *Time, History and Belief*, and, for examples of what tribute lists looked like, the *Codex Mendoza*.

48. Inga Clendinnen, *The Aztecs: An Interpretation* (New York: Cambridge University Press, 1992) revolves in significant sections around the experiences of traveling merchants, who told their story to the creators of the *Florentine Codex* (especially in book 9). Aztec-era luxury arts are treated in the extraordinary exhibit catalog: Joanne Pillsbury, Timothy Potts, and Kim Richter, eds., *Golden Kingdoms: Luxury Arts in the Ancient Americas* (Los Angeles: Getty Publications, 2017).

49. These are all matters that have been extensively studied. We have useful sources: the early Spanish conquerors and explorers, interested in establishing government control and taxation, wrote about them, and early legal transactions among the Nahuas illustrate some of the principles traditionally at work.

50. James Lockhart, *The Nahuas After the Conquest* (Stanford, CA: Stanford University Press, 1992).

51. *Codex Chimalpahin* 1:134–35.

52. *Bancroft Dialogues*, 147

53. Chimalpahin, "Eighth Relation," in *Ocho Relaciones*, 2:331–49. Fray Diego Durán speaks at length about a phenomenon he does not really understand, arguing that Moctezuma attempted a sort of "aristocratic revolution" in which commoners were excluded from aristocratic privilege. He had undoubtedly misunderstood references to a period of specifying who could count as a noble in a proliferating population of potential pipiltin. In the *Annals of Juan Bautista*, created in the mid-sixteenth century by men who had been children at the moment of the Spaniards' arrival, there are numerous references to tensions between pipiltin and macehualtin.

54. *Florentine Codex* 8:41–43, 54–55. This tells us how the court functioned, not what the principles of law or right vs. wrong were. These we can learn of through the facts of the stories recounted in the annals (e.g., that a man was not an adulterer unless he had relations with a married woman). A study of legal principles that seem to have held in Texcoco, based on Spanish sources, is Jerome Offner, *Law and Politics in Aztec Texcoco* (New York: Cambridge University Press, 1983).

55. *Florentine Codex* 8:63–65.

56. Bernal Díaz, *The Conquest of New Spain* (London: Penguin, 1963), 232.

57. It was the non-food items that most impressed the Spaniards. Bernal Díaz and Hernando Cortés both described what was sold, and they are implicitly corroborated in the *Florentine Codex* and other indigenous sources.

58. It was the food selection that most interested the Nahuas describing the market years later; *Florentine Codex* 8:68–69.

59. The *Florentine Codex* is an excellent source on the activities of the *ticitl*, the doctor, as long as one approaches the text cautiously. Some distinctions are made which were obviously introduced by the European friar-editor—for instance, that "good" doctors dealt in setting bones and pulling teeth and other "legitimate" activities, and that "bad" doctors dabbled in potions and spells.

60. Díaz, *Conquest*, 233.

61. *Florentine Codex* 6:93–103, 209–18, and 8:71–77. The *Bancroft Dialogues* also include extensive material on how students and teachers addressed each other and what information and subject matters were taught. A great deal of work has been done on the educational system of the Aztecs relying mostly on the *Florentine Codex* and the *Codex Mendoza*; some of the studies present the charming and idealized vision that the Nahua informants were happy to offer the Spaniards. The period after conquest has received somewhat more careful attention. See, for example, Pilar Gonzalbo Aizpuru, *Historia de la educación en la época colonial: El mundo indígena* (Mexico City: El Colegio de México, 1990).

62. *Florentine Codex* 6:93–103, 209–18, and 8:71–77.

63. We do not really know exactly how the system worked. Several sources refer to the weakness or cowardice of burden bearers, but this may possibly be because of the role's association with slavery, a dishonored status. It seems highly unlikely that a brilliantly talented young artisan from a lapidary family would really have to spend his life with a heavy bundle tied to his back if he failed to take captives, whereas it does seem possible that an algae collector might find an especially inept son marked out to be a salt-bearer.

64. The idea of the *quauhpilli* permeates both the annals and the cantares; it seems that it was a high compliment to a warrior to describe him thus. Years later, Chimalpahin and don Juan Zapata (in Tlaxcala) commented when someone was "not a pilli" but nevertheless held a position of authority.

65. *Florentine Codex* 7:17–18. There is more on the calmecac in 3:49–56.

66. Scholars primarily rely on the *Florentine Codex,* book 2 ("The Ceremonies"), for their discussions of Aztec human sacrifice. The informants for the *Florentine Codex*, however, were describing the situation on the eve of the Spanish conquest, when Mexica power was at its peak. Since the testimony may have contained exaggerated accounts, it is also important to consider archaeological evidence. Recently, a major discovery was made in Mexico City of the largest skull rack ever unearthed, with its two associated skull towers. It has thus far not been possible to determine how long

it took to fill the towers, but it was probably the work of decades. Fine tuning the dating will remain difficult. Thus far, the clearest presentation of the findings can be found in Lizzie Wade, "Feeding the Gods: Hundreds of Skulls Testify to the Monumental Scale of Human Sacrifice in the Aztec Capital," *Science* 360 (2018): 1288–92. For thoughtful explorations of the issues, see Clendinnen, *The Aztecs,* and David Carrasco, *City of Sacrifice* (Boston: Beacon Press, 1999).

67. *Florentine Codex* 2:53.

68. *Bancroft Dialogues,* 154–55. These events are also referenced in Ixtlilxochitl and the *Annals of Cuauhtitlan.* The former exaggerates markedly, but when the sources are considered together, it is quite clear that the executions took place, and that a particular wife and her cohort had lost power. For more discussion, see Townsend, "Polygyny and the Divided Altepetl." For the punishment in the context of other, comparable incidents, see Sousa, *Woman Who Turned Into a Jaguar,* 158–63, where the author creates a highly illuminating chart.

69. I am not merely gleaning this from context. The mestizo Juan Pomar said this explicitly. See "Relación de Tetzcoco," in *Relaciones de Nueva España,* ed. Germán Vázquez (Madrid: *Historia* 16), 91.

70. Ixtlilxochitl contradicts himself as to this lady's name and position, uncertain if she was from Azcapotzalco or Atzacualco or if her name was Azcaxochitzin. Presumably Ixtlilxochitl or his informant couldn't read the glyphs, as often was the case with him (Gordan Whittaker, personal communication), but his informant could name the eleven children specifically. They were probably alive when he was a child. See Ixtlilxochitl, *Obras Históricas,* ed. Eduardo O'Gorman (Mexico City: Universidad Nacional Autónoma de México, 1975–77), 2: 408, 449, 549. Furthermore, in legal documents created in Texcoco in the 1560s by a descendant of one of the brothers, Cuauhtliztactzin, it is specified in no uncertain terms that she was a Tenochca from Atzacualco, which makes perfect sense: a junior Tenochca wife would have had the ability to make a bid for power, especially with such a brood of sons. See Juan de San Antonio's Letter in *Codex Chimalpahin* 2:209–17 and 235.

71. *Bancroft Dialogues,* 157; Pomar, "Relación," 58, Ixtlilxochitl in "Historia de la Nación," 186, 200. On women speaking or singing in public, see Katarzyna Szoblik, *Entre los papeles de ocelote entono mi canto, yo Quetzalpetlatzin: El lugar de la mujer dentro de lo oralidad nahua* (Mexico City: Centro de Estudios de Antropología de la Mujer, 2016); Stephanie Wood, "Nahua Women Writing and Speaking," (paper presented at the Northeastern Nahuatl Studies Group, Yale University, New Haven, CT, May 2016).

72. On the multiplicity of voices at performances, see Camilla Townsend, "Glimpsing Native American Historiography: The Cellular Principle in Sixteenth-Century Nahuatl Annals," *Ethnohistory* 56 (2009):625–50. None of the available sources speak explicitly of the pair's break with tradition. However, were it not the case, the events that ensued could not have happened.

73. Chimalpahin is explicit that singers altered songs as they liked in the segment of his Seventh Relation cited in n. 1. We can also see that this must have been the case, given the surviving transcriptions of many songs: often the same song (or section of a song) appears multiple times, with only a few specific changes.

74. Song XI, in *Cantares Mexicanos,* ed. John Bierhorst (Stanford, CA: Stanford University Press, 1985), 148–49.

75. Song XXXIII, in Bierhorst, *Cantares Mexicanos,* 202–3. Translation amended.

76. The *Telleriano-Remensis,* folio 17, in *Codex Telleriano-Remensis,* ed. Eloise Quiñones Keber (Austin: University of Texas Press, 1995), 37.

77. *Bancroft Dialogues,* 157. On the bitterness left over from these events, see Juan de San Antonio's Letter, in Texcoco Accounts of Conquest, in *Codex Chimalpahin* 2:209–17 and 235. It would be the brother called Ixtlilxochitl who would rapidly choose to side with the Spaniards and arrange to have Cacama ousted. For a full study, see Townsend, "Polygyny and the Divided Altepetl."

78. *Florentine Codex* 8:56–57. This comes from a long and noteworthy section, conveying the opposite of the famous image of Moctezuma (concocted toward the end of the century) that he had somehow been foolish and uncaring. Similar imagery of a responsible chief "worrying in the night" is found in the *Annals of Juan Bautista.*

79. The *Florentine Codex,* book 12, and the accounts written by Hernando Cortés and Bernal Díaz corroborate each other regarding these very early interactions. On the indigenous words and concepts used to label European introductions (such as *mazatl* or "deer" for "horse"), see Lockhart, *The Nahuas,* chap. 7.

Chapter 4

1. This paragraph captures a moment in the life of the woman we now know as Malinche, or doña Marina, a slave who was given to Cortés and became his translator and mistress. Because she left no letters or diaries of her own, it is difficult to piece together her biography, but it has been done, triangulating between her actions, the records of the Spaniards, and the comments made by other Nahuas. For the full story, as well as discussion of the limited sources available to us, see Camilla Townsend, *Malintzin's Choices: An Indian Woman in the Conquest of Mexico* (Albuquerque: University of New Mexico Press, 2006).

2. For a range of names found in mundane sources recording ordinary aspects of life in the early years after conquest, see James Lockhart, *The Nahuas After the Conquest* (Stanford, CA: Stanford University Press, 1992), 118–22. "Little Old Woman" for instance was the name of a five-year-old child in one document. The girl from Coatzacoalcos could also have been given a calendrical name related to her birth, but this was uncommon in that area. See France V. Scholes and Ralph L. Roys, *The Maya Chontal Indians of Acalan-Tixchel: A Contribution to the History and Ethnography of the Yucatan Peninsula* (Norman: University of Oklahoma, 1968 [1948]), 61–63.

3. Bernardino de Sahagún, *Florentine Codex: General History of the Things of New Spain,* ed. Arthur J. O Anderson and Charles Dibble (Salt Lake City: School of American Research and University of Utah Press, 1950–1982), 6:172. This is from a Mexica source, but the attitude was typical of Nahuas in general. On the commonality of basic shared aspects of gender constructs in central Mexico, see Lisa Sousa, *The Woman Who Turned Into a Jaguar and Other Narratives of Native Women in Archives of Colonial Mexico* (Stanford, CA: Stanford University Press, 2017). On the importance of women's metaphorical association with the home, see Louise Burkhart, "Mexica Women on the Home Front: Housework and Religion in Aztec Mexico," in *Indian Women of Early Mexico*, ed. Susan Schroeder, Stephanie Wood, and Robert Haskett (Norman: University of Oklahoma Press, 1997).

4. On women's experience of enslavement through warfare or processes of appeasement, see Camilla Townsend, "'What Have You Done to Me, My Lover?': Sex, Servitude and Politics among the Pre-conquest Nahuas," *Americas* 62 (2006): 349–89. On the annual purchase of children to be sacrificed to Tlaloc, see *Florentine Codex* 2:42. Archaeology teaches us that these children were probably either captive slaves themselves or the children of abused slaves, for their remains demonstrate that they suffered from malnutrition. See Ximena Chávez Balderas, "Sacrifice at the Templo Mayor of Tenochtitlan and Its Role in Regard to Warfare," in *Embattled Bodies, Embattled Places: War in Pre-Columbian Mesoamerica and the Andes*, ed. Andrew Scherer and John Verano (Washington, DC: Dumbarton Oaks, 2014).

5. Scholes and Roys, *Maya Chontal Indians*, 27–35; and Anne Chapman, "Port of Trade Enclaves in Aztec and Maya Civilizations," in *Trade and Market in the Early Empires,* ed. Karl Polyani, Conrad Arensberg, and Harry Pearson (Glencoe, IL: Free Press, 1957), 129–42.

6. The *Florentine Codex* alludes to the trade in women and children being sent eastward from the war zones where they were captured. See *Florentine Codex* 9:17–18. Scholars who have studied this trade include Scholes and Roys, *Maya Chontal Indians*, 28–30, 56–59; Chapman, "Port of Trade Enclaves," 125–26; and Frances Berdan, "Economic Alternatives under Imperial Rule: The Eastern Aztec Empire," in *Economies and Polities of the Aztec Realm*, ed. Mary G. Hodge and Michael E. Smith (Albany: State University of New York Press, 1994). Archaeologists have revealed that high concentrations of spindle whorls moved east as Mexica power grew and the labor-intensive activities of spinning and weaving were pushed outward. See Elizabeth Brumfiel, "Weaving and Cooking: Women's Production in Aztec Mexico," in *Engendering Archaeology: Women and Prehistory*, ed. J. M Gero and M. W. Conkey (New York: Cambridge University Press, 1991), 232–33.

7. There is a substantial literature on Mesoamerican women and weaving. See Gabrielle Vail and Andrea Stone, "Representations of Women in Postclassic and Colonial Maya Literature and Art," and Marilyn Beaudry-Corbett and Sharissse

McCafferty, "Spindle Whorls: Household Specialization at Ceren," both in *Ancient Maya Women,* ed. Traci Ardren (Lanham, MD: Rowman & Littlefield, 2002).

8. See the account of the ship's friar, Juan Díaz, in *The Conquistadors: First Person Accounts of the Conquest of Mexico,* ed. Patricia de Fuentes (Norman: University of Oklahoma Press, 1993) and of Bernal Díaz, *The Conquest of New Spain* (London: Penguin, 1963). Fray Juan wrote a report immediately after the expedition's return, whereas Bernal Díaz wrote as an old man in his eighties and included far less detail. (Indeed, some scholars believe he wasn't really on that expedition and wrote his report based on stories heard from others.) The Spanish chroniclers are rarely in full agreement, each having their own specific agenda and their own lapses of memory and interpretation. However, reading them together certainly gives a sense of what happened. I would not presume to continue to tell the story in such detail, because there is too high a chance of transforming the narrative into fiction. But for a brief period, I mention some of the details the chroniclers included, to give the reader a sense of their experience as well as insight into what the indigenous specifically observed.

9. We cannot really know exactly what the indigenous were thinking. The exchange I paint here I deduce must have occurred from comments made by the Spaniards about the Indians' apparent concerns and questions (as articulated by the captive interpreter), and the Indians' own actions, both then and later.

10. It is the Spaniards who repeatedly tell us that in their expeditions along the coast, the Indians always knew they were coming. Their statements to this effect fit perfectly with what we know of Chontal culture—namely, that is was based on rapid canoe travel.

11. Díaz, *The Conquest,* 70.

12. Hernando Cortés tells largely the same story as Díaz about this battle—albeit less colorfully—in his First Letter. See Hernán Cortés, *Letters from Mexico,* ed. Anthony Pagden (New Haven, CT: Yale University Press, 1986), 19–23.

13. This is not merely my own deduction. Cortés's secretary later said they told him that their position depended on their being perceived as stronger than all others in the region. Francisco López de Gómara, *Cortés: The Life of the Conqueror by His Secretary,* ed. Lesley Byrd Simpson (Berkeley: University of California Press, 1965), 50. Cortés initially mentioned (in the First Letter) that the number of indigenous bodies they could see out on the field was about 220. Later, his secretary raised this number, and Díaz did so even more (mentioning 800). I think we should go with the initial estimate, which is high enough from an indigenous perspective.

14. All sources, indigenous and Spanish, agree that this was the moment when the future translator was transferred to Spanish power. A few sources say she was presented with a very small group of other girls, but the preponderance of the evidence suggests that there were twenty of them, as the Chontal were trying to make a definitive statement about submission, and twenty was a culturally significant number for them, as well as for the Nahuas.

15. Some modern authors have liked to think that the Spaniards might have been inspired to give her the name "Marina" because her indigenous name was "Malinalli," but there is no evidence for this. The Spaniards never asked captives what their "real" names were before they selected a Christian name for them, nor did the Nahuas give the name "Malinalli," because it boded bad luck.

16. For more on the relationship between Cortés and Puertocarrero, see Ricardo Herren, *Doña Marina, la Malinche* (Mexico City: Planeta, 1992), 26–27, as well as any of the major biographies of Cortés.

17. Frances Kartunnen comments on the jarring effect on our modern sensibilities when we read of the women's baptisms immediately prior to their being distributed as concubines. See her "Rethinking Malinche" in *Indian Women in Early Mexico*.

18. There is a great deal of misinformation available about this important figure. On Jerónimo de Aguilar and on research materials that illuminate his life, see Townsend, *Malintzin's Choices*, 37 and 239.

19. We have no actual record of what Aguilar conveyed to Malintzin, but her later choices and actions render it absolutely clear that she had been informed of the larger political context relatively early on.

20. Louise Burkhart, *Before Guadalupe: The Virgin Mary in Early Colonial Nahuatl Literature* (Albany, NY: Institute for Mesoamerican Studies, 2001), 3, 17. Burkhart is here translating a segment of Pedro de Gante's Nahuatl text, *Doctrina cristiana en lengua Mexicana* (1553).

21. Díaz and Cortés both mention the extraordinary rapidity with which the emissaries made their appearance, and the *Florentine Codex,* book 12, tells us that Moctezuma had had certain spots on the coast watched for a year; thus Spanish and indigenous sources confirm each other. For a fascinating study of the way sources of a "nonliterate" people and sources left by European colonizers can sometimes illuminate each other, see Richard Price, *Alabi's World* (Baltimore: Johns Hopkins University Press, 1991).

22. Cortés in his initial letters to the king barely mentions Marina, not wishing to give her much of the credit for the enterprise. By the time his secretary wrote his biography of his employer, the issue had to be dealt with as the public wanted to know how they had come by their by-then famous translator. It is he who tells the story (though he assumes Marina acted as she did in order to become rich); Gómara, *Life*, 56.

23. James Lockhart explores the use of the phrase in the introduction to *We People Here: Nahuatl Accounts of the Conquest of Mexico* (Stanford, CA: Stanford University Press, 1993).

24. Again, the Spanish chroniclers and the *Florentine Codex* confirm each other.

25. For a full scholarly study of this subject, see Camilla Townsend, "Burying the White Gods: New Perspectives on the Conquest of Mexico," *American Historical Review* 108 (2003): 659–87.

26. *Florentine Codex*, book 12, in Lockhart, *We People Here*, 94.

27. Díaz, *Conquest*, 222.

28. Fray Toribio de Benavente, also known as Motolonia, *Historia de los Indios de la Nueva España* (Madrid: Alianza, 1988), 107–8.

29. For a detailed study, see Camilla Townsend, *Pocahontas and the Powhatan Dilemma* (New York: Hill & Wang, 2004).

30. Felipe Fernández Armesto, "Aztec Auguries and Memories of the Conquest of Mexico, "*Renaissance Studies* 6 (1992). See also Stephen Colston, "'No Longer Will There Be a Mexico': Omens, Prophecies and the Conquest of the Aztec Empire," *American Indian Quarterly* 5 (1985).

31. *Florentine Codex*, book 12, in Lockhart, *We People Here*, 188.

32. *Florentine Codex*, book 12, in Lockhart, *We People Here*, 59.

33. This is one of the major aspects of the work of Susan Gillespie, *Aztec Kings: The Construction of Rulership in Mexica History* (Tucson: University of Arizona Press, 1989). I have studied the evolution of the treatment of the subject in the works of certain European-influenced indigenous historians; see, for instance, Camilla Townsend, "The Evolution of Alva Ixtlilxochitl's Scholarly Life," *Colonial Latin American Review* 23 (2014): 1–17.

34. This document is available in print: José Luis Martínez, ed., *Documentos cortesianos* (Mexico City: Fondo de Cultura Económica, 1990), 1:265–71. Part of the original survives in the Archivo General de Indias in Seville.

35. For more on this, see Lockhart, introduction to *We People Here*, and Townsend, "Burying the White Gods."

36. Pedro de San Buenaventura, a former student of fray Bernardino de Sahagún's at the school at Tlatelolco, either wrote or heavily influenced the writing of the *Annals of Cuauhtitlan* in the 1570s, and there he partially embraced the story, albeit with qualifiers. Later, Chimalpahin also partially embraced the story in the early 1600s, though he seems to have done so after reading the work of Ixtlilxochitl, who was himself influenced by the Franciscan fray Juan de Torquemada (see n. 33). See Camilla Townsend, *Annals of Native America: How the Nahuas of Colonial Mexico Kept Their History Alive* (New York: Oxford University Press, 2016), chaps. 3 and 4.

37. It is Bernal Díaz who tells us that the Indians began to refer to Cortés as Malinchi or Malinche. Nahuatl speakers interested in the unusual form of the vocative should consult Horacio Carochi, *Grammar of the Mexican Language*, ed. James Lockhart (Stanford, CA: Stanford University Press, 2001 [1645]), 44–45. The usage ("Malintze") is repeatedly attested in the *Annals of Tlatelolco*.

38. Later court cases about other matters indirectly reveal these facts. For their enumeration and analysis, see Townsend, *Malintzin's Choices*, 243 (n. 11).

39. The most penetrating analysis of Cortés's background and of his choices in this moment remains J. H. Elliott's introduction to Hernán Cortés, *Letters from Mexico*, ed. Anthony Pagden (New Haven, CT: Yale University Press, 1986).

40. Traditionally, it was asserted that Cortés actually "burned his ships" to prevent returns. Serious historians knew this to be false, but we did believe that he was

purposely leaving them scuttled at the shore. Matthew Restall has recently proven that in fact the ships were already in need of repair and were simply brought onto the beach where they could be repaired later. See Matthew Restall, *When Montezuma Met Cortés* (New York: HarperCollins, 2018).

41. This part of the story, in which the Tlaxcalans fought against the Spaniards with extraordinary determination, is not often recounted in narratives of the conquest, which tend to focus on the alliance the Tlaxcalans later proffered. But it is important to understand that the Mexica's enemies did not immediately rally around the Europeans. They did so only when it became clear that it was their best option in a military sense. The details in all the available Spanish chronicles corroborate this. For Flower Wars, see also chap. 2, n. 57.

42. Cortés, "Second Letter" in *Letters from Mexico*, 60. (This segment of Cortés's report is extremely detailed and continues for many pages.)

43. Díaz, *Conquest*, 149.

44. Cortés, "Second Letter," 61. Cortés says that he "cut off their hands." Matthew Restall in *When Montezuma Met Cortés* explains that the Europeans meant that they cut off the fingers; otherwise, the victims would have died immediately.

45. Cortés, "Second Letter," 62. It is Díaz who tells us that the translator was brought into the midst of the battles with them.

46. Tlaxcalan annals as found in don Juan Buenaventura Zapata y Mendoza, *Historia cronológica de la Noble Ciudad de Tlaxcala*, ed. Luis Reyes García and Andrea Martínez Baracs (Tlaxcala: Universidad Autónoma de Tlaxcala, 1995), 94–95. The best study of preconquest Tlaxcala remains Charles Gibson, *Tlaxcala in the Sixteenth Century* (Stanford, CA: Stanford University Press, 1967 [1952]), chap. 1.

47. For my own analysis of the Tlaxcalan conquest pictorials, see Townsend, *Malintzin's Choices*, 63–76. For a full study, see Travis Kranz, "The Tlaxcalan Conquest Pictorials," PhD diss., UCLA, Department of Art History, 2001.

48. For a study of the extraordinary difference the existence of indigenous allies made, see Michel Oudijk and Matthew Restall, "Mesoamerican Conquistadors in the Sixteenth Century," in *Indian Conquistadors: Indigenous Allies in the Conquest of Mesoamerica*, ed. Laura Matthew and Michel Oudijk (Norman: University of Oklahoma Press, 2007).

49. For more on this, see Townsend, "Burying the White Gods" as well as Matthew Restall, *Seven Myths of the Spanish Conquest* (New York: Oxford University Press, 2003). Inga Clendinnen promoted the idea that the Aztecs did not like to fight to the death in her article "'Fierce and Unnatural Cruelty': Cortés and the Conquest of Mexico," *Representations* 33 (1991): 65–100. Tzvetan Todorov contributed the notion that the indigenous participated primarily in man–god communication in his *The Conquest of America: The Question of the Other* (New York: Harper, 1984).

50. These were the words of Andrés de Tapia, printed in Fuentes, *The Conquistadors*, 36. For the best treatment of the battle in Cholula, see Ross Hassig, "The Maid of the

Myth: La Malinche and the History of Mexico," *Indiana Journal of Hispanic Literatures* 12 (1998): 101–33.

51. Díaz, *Conquest,* 214–15.

52. Cortés, "Second Letter," 84–85.

53. Cortés says little about what the monarch and his retainers wore; Díaz tells us more, in describing the canopy, for instance, referring to gold, silver, pearls, and jade suspended from a fan of green feathers. "It was a marvelous sight," he rhapsodized (*Conquest*, 217). I do not assume he is necessarily accurate in all the details he presents, merely that the monarch did indeed walk beneath a highly symbolic construction. See Justyna Olko, *Insignia of Rank in the Nahua World: From the Fifteenth to the Seventeenth century* (Boulder: University Press of Colorado, 2014). It is possible that Díaz either could not see well from a distance or misremembered the event, and that what he saw was actually a headdress worn on a back frame and thus suspended above Moctezuma, as such an arrangement was very typical.

Chapter 5

1. *Florentine Codex,* book 12 (best translation in *We People Here: Nahuatl Accounts of the Conquest of Mexico,* ed. and trans. James Lockhart [Los Angeles: UCLA Press, 1993], 181–82) describes the smallpox epidemic that struck not long after the Spaniards were forced to leave the city. The narrators mention the experience of lying immobilized on the soiled sleeping mats and emphasize that so many deaths occurred because there were not enough healthy people to care for the ill. "Starvation reigned, and no one took care of others any longer." The word *miccatzintli* for the corpse of someone known and loved appears in other annals. We have relatively little testimony about the experience of illness on the part of the Mexica. However, historians have been able to explore other smallpox epidemics in an experiential sense. See, e.g., Elizabeth Fenn, *Pox Americans: The Great Smallpox Epidemic of 1775–82* (New York: Hill & Wang, 2001). Both indigenous and Spanish sources (see nn. 2 and 3 this chapter) agree that there were three daughters of Moctezuma in Spanish custody who were given Spanish baptismal names; they remained in Tenochtitlan when the Spaniards retreated, and they survived the ensuing epidemic. Two were married to Spaniards after the conquest, and one died shortly after the war. (Cortés ceased referring to the one called María between 1522 and 1526, and the indigenous source says that María died "as an unmarried girl.") The Nahuatl verb *polihui* is to perish or to disappear.

2. A highly specific genealogical list of Moctezuma's children, which includes mentions of their deaths, does not specifically record any deaths by smallpox in the first great epidemic, so the royal line apparently fared relatively well in that regard. On the other hand, the list stops with children who were of marriageable age at the time of the conquest, as though Moctezuma had no younger children at the time,

which makes no sense in a polygynous context until we consider that child mortality would have been higher than adult mortality in the epidemic. See don Domingo Chimalpahin, *Codex Chimalpahin*, ed. Arthur J. O. Anderson and Susan Schroeder (Norman: University of Oklahoma Press, 1997), 1:158–65.

3. Mexica records assert that two sons were killed at the Tolteca canal because they were held hostage and were forced to flee with the withdrawing Spaniards (*Codex Chimalpahin*, 158–59; and *Florentine Codex*, book 12, in Lockhart, *We People Here*, 156). Cortés in his initial report asserted that one son was killed. (He assumed at the time of writing that the daughters were killed as well, but in fact they had been successfully rescued by their people, as he later learned.) He apparently was purposely undercounting, so as not to upset his king; besides referring to only one son, Cortés mentioned two daughters, when he would have known that he had had three in his custody. (See "Second Letter" in Hernán Cortés, *Letters from Mexico*, ed. Anthony Pagden [New Haven, CT: Yale University Press, 1986], 138–39.) Later legal documents reveal more about his dealings with three daughters, which is in keeping with the indigenous record. See Donald Chipman, *Moctezuma's Children* (Austin: University of Texas Press, 2005), 75–76.

4. Indigenous annals are consistent here; the Spaniards are also consistent in reporting that his own people hit him with a rock when he demurred from fighting back against the foreigners. The former is far more likely to have been true; in either case it is certainly what Tecuichpotzin would have been told.

5. Her age comes to us from Spanish documents (see Chipman, *Moctezuma's Children*); what the documents assert is highly believable; if she were much older, she would have been married before the Spaniards arrived, and if much younger, she would not have been considered of marriageable age.

6. On sweeping, see Louise Burkhart, "Mexica Women on the Home Front: Housework and Religion in Aztec Mexico," in *Indian Women of Early Mexico*, ed. Susan Schroeder, Stephanie Wood, and Robert Haskett (Norman: University of Oklahoma, 1997). The *Florentine Codex*, book 12, describes the great cleansing and repairing that took place, beginning the day the Spaniards left.

7. The meeting on the causeway is described in Cortés's letter and in the *Florentine Codex* (as well as in many other derivative accounts). For an analysis, see Matthew Restall, *Seven Myths of the Spanish Conquest* (New York: Oxford University Press, 2003), 95–99.

8. See J. H. Elliott's introduction to Hernán Cortés, *Letters from Mexico*, ed. Pagden.

9. Cortés, "Second Letter," 107; Díaz, *Conquest*, 276.

10. Fray Francisco de Aguilar in Patricia Fuentes, ed., *The Conquistadors: First Person Accounts of the Conquest of Mexico* (Norman: University of Oklahoma Press, 1993), 148. Statements by other chroniclers sound equally odd, as if they were trying to keep their story straight.

11. Restall, *Seven Myths*, 97–98. The attributed speech is in the *Florentine Codex*, book 12, in Lockhart, *We People Here*, 116. Restall also discusses the wide-ranging myths

surrounding this famous meeting in *When Montezuma Met Cortés* (New York: HarperCollins, 2018).

12. Francis Brooks wrote an essential article on this topic. See his "Motecuzoma Xocoyotl, Hernán Cortés, and Bernal Díaz del Castillo: The Construction of an Arrest," *Hispanic American Historical Review* 75 (1995). The *Annals of Tlatelolco*, the earliest set of annals to cover this period, written before the story of Quetzalcoatl and the Indians' wide-mouthed awe had been taken up, makes it clear that the indigenous peoples provided food for those who were their guests, just as we would expect.

13. A comparable scene had unfolded in Tlaxcala when the Spaniards were there, and the indigenous memorialized it in a pictorial text now called "the Texas Fragment," in the Nettie Lee Benson Collection of the University of Texas at Austin. For an analysis, see Camilla Townsend, *Malintzin's Choices: An Indian Woman in the Conquest of Mexico* (Albuquerque: University of New Mexico Press, 2006), 68–74.

14. *Codex Chimalpahin*, 1:142–43, 162–63; 2:108–9.

15. There has been confusion among historians as to who Isabel's mother was: Spanish documents first said she was named Teotlalco (which would not be a person's name in Nahuatl) and came "from Tecalco," and only later mentioned that she was a daughter of Ahuitzotl (see Chipman, *Moctezuma's Children*). There is no need for confusion on this point, however, as the use of *teccalco* might simply mean that she was from a settlement surrounding any royal household, "the place where the royals live." The Nahuatl genealogies all agree that she was Ahuitzotl's daughter by a Tepanec wife, which would certainly explain her status. (See *Codex Chimalpahin* 1:52–53, 154–55, 163–63; 2:86–87.)

16. This was doña Francisca of Ecatepec (see chap. 8). I have deduced the probable reasons for the silence around her, but there exists direct commentary on the reasons for keeping the existence of a younger half brother of hers a secret from the Spaniards at that time. See Anastasia Kalyuta, "El arte de acomodarse a dos mundos: la vida de don Pedro de Moctezuma Tlacahuepantli según los documentos del Archivo General de la Nación (México, D.F.) y al Archivo General de Indias (Sevilla)," *Revista Española de Antropología Americana* 41, no. 2 (2010): 471–500.

17. The latter actually went by "Leonor" by the late 1520s. She first married Juan Paz, then Cristóbal de Valderrama.

18. Restall, *When Montezuma Met Cortes*, 286–87.

19. Cortés, Díaz, and Andrés de Tapia all mention this. Indeed, there would have been no other way for Cortés to learn the news (but in his letter, Cortés claimed that he also heard of it through his own Spanish messengers, implying that his men roamed freely and knowledgeably through the countryside though we know this was not the case).

20. These matters have been extensively treated in biographies of Hernando Cortés. Dürer's diary is quoted in Benjamin Keen, *The Aztec Image in Western Thought* (New Brunswick, NJ: Rutgers University Press, 1971), 69. On the remarkable speed

with which news about indigenous peoples of the New World traveled via European print texts, see John Pollack, "Native American Words, Early American Texts," PhD diss., University of Pennsylvania, Department of English, 2014.

21. Almost all Spanish accounts agree on this. Only Cortés in his letter differs, recounting an intimate conversation in which he took a sympathetic Moctezuma into his confidence, but by the time Gómara wrote his biography, he, too, acknowledged that orders coming from Moctezuma's household clearly became more hostile to the strangers at this point. Francisco López de Gómara, *Cortés: The Life of the Conqueror by His Secretary*, ed. Lesley Byrd Simpson (Los Angeles: University of California Press, 1965). Contrast Cortés, "Second Letter," 119, with Gómara, *Life*, 188–89.

22. See Brooks, "The Construction of an Arrest," 181. We cannot be exactly certain when Moctezuma was placed under house arrest, given the contradictory statements.

23. The tactics of the conquest are put into perspective in James Lockhart and Stuart Schwartz, *Early Latin America* (New York: Cambridge University Press, 1983), 80–83.

24. All the chroniclers agree that they took him in a sudden strike and bound him. They claimed to have done this early on, when in fact, as Brooks demonstrates (see n. 22), they actually did so when other Spaniards arrived and they had to take action.

25. Cortés, "Second Letter," 128. Historians have written at length on this period of the campaign, sometimes taking the chroniclers' writings too literally, rather than looking for commonalities in their statements and considering what makes most sense in context. For a summary of my sifting of the evidence, see *Malintzin's Choices*, 99–101.

26. Cortés, "Second Letter," 128–29.

27. At the time, the place where these people were captured was called Zoltepec ("Old Hill"); the site was home to an ancient temple dedicated to Ehecatl, the wind god. Thereafter, it became known as Tecoaque ("People Were Eaten"), and has retained that name ever since. An archaeological excavation under the auspices of the Instituto Nacional de Antropología e Historia has revealed that the prisoners were sacrificed a few at a time, including the children. The site, between Mexico City and Tlaxcala, is an important one, as it is the only known archaeological record of direct interactions between Europeans, Africans, and indigenous in the years of the war of conquest. It was nominated as a UNESCO World Heritage Site in 2004.

28. We can gain insight into this period from the records of a 1529 investigation of the conduct of Pedro de Alvarado. These are available in print: Ignacio López Rayón, ed., *Proceso de residencia instruida contra Pedro de Alvarado y Nuño de Guzman* (Mexico City: Valdes y Redondas, 1847). Book 12 of the *Florentine Codex* (in Lockhart, *We People Here*, 140–42) reveals that people who did business with the Spaniards, or who were even suspected of doing so, were killed. This unfortunately included many of the palace servants.

29. *Florentine Codex,* book 12, in Lockhart, *We People Here,* 132–34.

30. Lockhart, *We People Here,* 142.

31. Lockhart, *We People Here,* 138–39. The *Annals of Tlatelolco* also remembers Moctezuma as working to calm the situation. Cortés makes the same claim.

32. See Townsend, *Malintzin's Choices,* 104–5. See also chap. 4.

33. Cortés, "Second Letter," 134–35.

34. First the speaker said *çan tlacapan* ("right on top of people") and then he grew more specific, saying *çan nacapan* ("right on top of flesh, of bodies"); see book 12 of the *Florentine Codex* in Lockhart, *We People Here,* 156. Cristobal Castillo shares a similar memory, focusing on the bodies of highborn indigenous women who were drowned.

35. Cortés, "Second Letter," 139. Cortés also made the spurious claim that only 150 Spaniards had died, but historians have been able to use other Spanish documents to ascertain the true number. We cannot do the same for the Indians. If we assume that he used the same multiplier, then about 8,000 Tlaxcalans died. However, that number seems implausible to me. The Tlaxcalans could not have spared such a large proportion of their population for so long; nor could Tenochtitlan have fed so many guests for six months.

36. Díaz, *Conquest,* 299.

37. *Florentine Codex,* book 12, in Lockhart, *We People Here,* 156. For more on this, see n. 3.

38. The literature on disease in the conquest of the New World is immense. A fine book, which reviews the literature, takes the disease factor extremely seriously and yet does not attempt to ascribe all that happened to that factor alone is Suzanne Alchon, *A Pest in the Land: New World Epidemics in a Global Perspective* (Albuquerque: University of New Mexico Press, 2003).

39. See Charles Gibson, *Tlaxcala in the Sixteenth Century* (New Haven, CT: Yale University Press, 1952).

40. Cortés, "Second Letter," 154–58.

41. Cortés, "Third Letter," 207.

42. Cortés, "Third Letter," 207, 221, 247. *Annals of Tlatelolco,* in Lockhart, *We People Here,* 268–69.

43. Cortés, "Third Letter," 220–21. To understand why Ixtlilxochitl would do this, see chapter 2's discussion of polygyny-induced factionalism. Bradley Benton has a chapter on the events of the 1510s in *The Lords of Tetzcoco: The Transformation of Indigenous Rule in Postconquest Central Mexico* (New York: Cambridge University Press, 2017).

44. See Don Juan Buenaventura Zapata y Mendoza, *Historia chronológica de la Noble y Leal Ciudad de Tlaxcala,* ed. Luis Reyes García and Andrea Martínez Baracs (Tlaxcala: Universidad Autónoma de Tlaxcala, 1995).

45. Several extant king lists mention his short reign. *Codex Chimalpahin* (1:165) and *Codex Aubin* say explicitly that he died "of the blisters," meaning smallpox.

46. The *Annals of Tlatelolco* mention this relationship, but that alone would not constitute proof, as the authors might have been guilty of wishful thinking. However, the most specific Mexica genealogical source verifies this statement (*Codex Chimalpahin* 2:79, 99). Later events, in which Tlatelolcans give Cuauhtemoc undivided loyalty, offer further proof.

47. All the indigenous annals agree that these events did occur. Only the Tlatelolcans seemed to see Cuauhtemoc as blameless. See *Codex Chimalpahin* 1:159, 167 (on the names of the assassinated brothers); *Codex Aubin* in Lockhart, *We People Here,* 277 (on the story of Cuauhtemoc having killed his own half brother), *Annals of Tlatelolco* in Lockhart, *We People Here,* 261 (for the quotation on the need for the actions). See also Kalyuta, "Don Pedro."

48. On the symbolic importance of the female consort as a legitimator, see Susan Gillespie, *Aztec King: The Construction of Rulership in Mexica History* (Tucson: University of Arizona Press, 1989), and specifically of Malintzin and Isabel being understood to be such a consort by Cortés's side, see Townsend, *Malintzin's Choices,* 77–78. A full exploration of the theme of legitimacy passing through the female line in Western myth is found in Alejandro Carrillo Castro, *The Dragon and the Unicorn* (Mexico City, 2014 [1996]).

49. There is a subgenre of such songs in the *Cantares Mexicanos,* some of them specifically about the war with the Spaniards.

50. *Florentine Codex,* book 12, in Lockhart, *We People Here,* 186. The *Annals of Tlatelolco* tell a similar story.

51. Lockhart, *We People Here,* 218.

52. Lockhart, *We People Here,* 222. Such moments also figure in the *Cantares Mexicanos.*

53. Lockhart, *We People Here,* 146.

54. Lockhart, *We People Here,* 224.

55. Cortés, "Third Letter," 257.

56. *Florentine Codex,* book 12, in Lockhart, *We People Here,* 230.

57. Lockhart, *We People Here,* 80, 90, 96, 110, and elsewhere.

58. Lockhart, *We People Here,* 74, 86, 98, 116, and elsewhere.

59. Cortés, "Third Letter," 246–47.

60. *Annals of Tlatelolco* in Lockhart, *We People Here,* 267 and 313. A clear explanation of the way in which this passage was partly mistranslated by Angel Garibay, then by Miguel Leon Portilla, and eventually altered yet again in the translation from Spanish to English, yielding the famous book title, "The Broken Spears," which exists nowhere in the original passage, can be found in John Schwaller, "Broken Spears or Broken Bones? The Evolution of the Most Famous Line in Nahuatl," *Americas* 16, 2 (2009): 241–52.

61. Cortés said he took him unawares, but the indigenous annals all say he went to give himself up. Indeed, it would be hard to imagine the Spaniards taking the tlatoani of the Mexica off guard in his own city.

62. *Florentine Codex,* book 12, in Lockhart, *We People Here,* 246–48.

Chapter 6

1. These events are mentioned in a sixteenth-century set of annals from Cuauhtinchan published as *Libro de los guardianes y gobernadores de Cuauhtinchan*, ed. Constantino Medina Lima (Mexico City: Centro de Investigaciones y Estudios Superiores en Antropología Social [CIESAS], 1995), 50. Spanish records confirm that the Franciscans took the lead in organizing the *congregación*, or resettlement.

2. A full study of Chimalpopoca, or don Alonso de Castañeda, appears in Camilla Townsend, *Annals of Native America: How the Nahuas of Colonial Mexico Kept Their History Alive* (New York: Oxford University Press, 2016), chap. 1. He and his family members authored two sets of annals and appeared in several court cases, providing a rare opportunity to piece together the life of one man before and after conquest. In other sixteenth-century annals, older men born before the conquest are sometimes quoted, but this source is special in being prepared by such a man.

3. Chimalpopoca was one of the narrators of what is probably the earliest and most beautiful set of annals in existence, the *Historia Tolteca Chichimeca*. See annotated bibliography of extant annals in the appendix for a discussion of this source. It will be treated in depth later in this chapter.

4. Due to the existence of several sets of annals and an important court case, scholars have been able to reconstruct the preconquest history of Cuauhtinchan. For the story in detail, see Luis Reyes García, *Cuauhtinchan del Siglo XII al XVI* (Wiesbaden: Franz Steiner, 1977).

5. *Historia Tolteca Chichimeca*, ed. Paul Kirchoff, Lina Odena Güemes, and Luis Reyes García (Mexico City: Instituto Nacional de Historia e Antropología, 1976), 228–29.

6. *Historia Tolteca Chichimeca*, 230. The record states only that he died. Since this was in the time of the smallpox epidemic and the war had not yet come to Cuauhtinchan, it is relatively safe to assume that the pestilence killed Tecuanitzin. It is, however, theoretically possible that he joined with others in early forays made against the Spaniards and died in battle or from some other injury or illness.

7. Michel Oudijk and Matthew Restall, "Mesoamerican Conquistadors in the Sixteenth Century," in *Indian Conquistadors: Indigenous Allies in the Conquest of Mexico*, ed. Laura Matthew and Michel Oudijk (Norman: University of Oklahoma Press, 2007).

8. *Historia Tolteca Chichimeca*, 230. The narrator refers only to the Atoyac, which later became a full-fledged creek. An environmental historian has demonstrated that the Atoyac was at that time a wetland containing discontinuous streams, which explains this statement. See Bradly Skopyk, "Undercurrents of Conquest: The Shifting Terrain of Agriculture in Colonial Tlaxala (PhD diss., York University, Department of History, 2010). On the choice of the word *polihui*, see Stephanie Wood, "Nahuatl Terms Relating to Conquest," paper presented at the American Historical Association, New York City, January 2015.

9. *Historia Tolteca Chichimeca*, 230. The record does not directly refer to back-and-forth negotiations, but the high degree of specificity is indicative of the fact that details were carefully worked out.

10. *Annals of Tlatelolco* in *We People Here: Nahuatl Accounts of the Conquest of Mexico,* ed. and trans. James Lockhart (Los Angeles: UCLA Press, 1993), 272–73.

11. Lockhart, *We People Here*, 271–73. On Malinche's participation, see book 12 of the *Florentine Codex* in Lockhart, *We People Here*. A full discussion is found in Stephanie Wood, *Transcending Conquest: Nahua Views of Spanish Colonial Mexico* (Norman: University of Oklahoma Press, 2003), chap. 3. There is one indigenous pictorial in which Malintzin seems to watch as the Spaniards unleash their mastiffs on defenseless indigenous people.

12. Indigenous annals (both book 12 of the *Florentine Codex* and the *Annals of Tlatelolco*) refer to the branding of prisoners for enslavement and to Spanish men seizing women. However, the extent of the two phenomena becomes clear in Spanish records listing goods being sent back to Spain and in correspondence from the king, such as "Instrucciones de Carlos V a Hernando Cortés sobre Tratameinto de los Indios, Valladolid, 26 junio 1523." These records are presently in the Archivo General de Indios, in Seville, Spain. For some discussion of them, see Camilla Townsend, *Malintzin's Choices: An Indian Woman in the Conquest of Mexico* (Albuquerque: University of New Mexico Press), 254–55 (nn. 3 and 4). For fuller discussion of this painful issue, see Matthew Restall, *When Montezuma Met Cortés: The True Story of the Meeting that Changed History* (New York: HarperCollins, 2018).

13. On the transformation of the city, see Barbara Mundy's *The Death of Aztec Tenochtitlan, The Life of Mexico City* (Austin: University of Texas Press, 2015).

14. *Annals of Tlatelolco*, in Lockhart, *We People Here*, 273.

15. For more on the political and economic organization of the colony, see James Lockhart and Stuart Schwartz, *Early Latin America* (New York: Cambridge University Press, 1983).

16. On Juan Pérez de Arteaga, see Townsend, *Malintzin's Choices*, 141, 184–85. On individual conquistadors, see Robert Himmerich y Valencia, *The Encomenderos of New Spain* (Austin: University of Texas Press, 1991).

17. See Townsend, *Malintzin's Choices*, 129–32, as well as "Polygyny and the Divided Altepetl: The Tetzcocan Key to Pre-conquest Nahua Politics," in *Texcoco: Prehispanic and Colonial Perspectives,* ed. Jongsoo Lee and Galen Brokaw (Boulder: University Press of Colorado, 2014). For more on Texcoco in this era, see Bradley Benton, *The Lords of Tetzcoco: The Transformation of Indigenous Rule in Postconquest Central Mexico* (New York: Cambridge University Press, 2017).

18. "Ordenanzas de Buen Gobierno Dadas por Hernando Cortés," March 20, 1524, in *Colección de documentos inéditos relativos al descubrimiento, conquista y colonización de las posesiones españoles en América y Oceania,* ed. Joaquín Pacheco, 42 vols. (Madrid: Manuel Bernaldos de Quirós, 1864–1884), 26:135–45.

19. In 1933, Robert Ricard published *La conquête spirituelle du Mexique* in France; after World War II his ideas percolated in scholarly circles, and the work was eventually published in English as *The Spiritual Conquest of Mexico* (Berkeley: University of California Press, 1966). Decades later, it was the work of Louise Burkhart and James Lockhart (see nn. 20 and 21), followed by that of their students, that forever laid to rest the idea that the indigenous really had changed their religious views so completely.

20. Louise Burkhart, *The Slippery Earth: Nahua-Christian Moral Dialogue in Sixteenth-Century Mexico* (Tucson: University of Arizona Press, 1989), 40–42. Recent work delving into such questions includes, for example, Elizabeth Hill Boone, Louise Burkhart, and David Tavárez, eds., *Painted Words: Nahuatl Catholicism, Politics and Memory in the Atzacualco Pictorial Catechism* (Washington, DC: Dumbarton Oaks, 2017).

21. James Lockhart, "Some Nahua Concepts in Postconquest Guise," *History of European Ideas* 6 (1985): 465–82.

22. This is the document known as the *Coloquios* (colloquies) of fray Bernardino de Sahagún. Both the Spanish and Nahuatl texts are published in Miguel León Portilla, ed., *Coloquios y doctrina christiana* (Mexico City: Universidad Nacional Autónoma de México, 1986). On the scholarly debate on the creation of the document, see Lockhart, *The Nahuas*, 205–6; and Jorge Klor de Alva, "La historicidad de los coloquios de Sahagún," *Estudios de Cultura Náhuatl* 15 (1982): 147–84.

23. The *Coloquios*, as translated into English in Kenneth Mills, William B. Taylor, and Sandra Lauderdale Graham, eds., *Colonial Latin America: A Documentary History* (Wilmington, DE: Scholarly Resources, 2002), 20–22.

24. Mills, Taylor, and Graham, *Colonial Latin America*.

25. Luis Reyes García, ed., *Anales de Juan Bautista* (Mexico City: CIESAS, 2001), 280–81.

26. Fray Toribio de Benavente Motolinia, who was present, later wrote this in *Historia de los Indios de la Nueva España* (Madrid: Alianza, 1988), 66.

27. Townsend, *Malintzin's Choices*, especially chap. 6. It is the testimony of later court cases that gives us these details, even down to the way she dressed in this period.

28. Townsend, *Malintzin's Choices*, especially chap. 7.

29. Townsend, *Malintzin's Choices*, 150–57. Traditionally it has been assumed that Cortés tossed Malinche to one of his aides because he was tired of her. This interpretation makes little sense, since he did not have to rid himself of her in order to bed another woman, and when the marriage occurred, he was still desperately dependent on her. *Malintzin's Choices* analyzes all extant evidence and concludes that what dozens of witnesses later swore in court was in fact true—that is, that Malinche chose to marry Jaramillo and received her natal village of Olutla as a wedding gift.

30. Bernal Díaz del Castillo, *Historia Verdadera de la conquista de la Nueva España* (Mexico City: Porrúa, 1960), 460. Díaz presumes to quote Malinche in speaking to

her family, saying that she forgave them, but since much of the personal history he gave for her was obviously invented, I do not think we should assume that he actually heard her private conversations with her relatives, and I do not quote him here. (The Penguin English edition of Díaz's text does not include this segment. Interested readers will need to consult the Porrúa Spanish edition.)

31. Accounts of these events left by Nahuas, Mayas, and Spaniards contradict each other to a certain degree: for instance, it is not certain how many others were ultimately hanged with Cuauhtemoc. For the best comparative analysis of the sources describing this affair, see Matthew Restall, *Seven Myths of the Spanish Conquest* (New York: Oxford University Press, 2003), 147–57.

32. We glean our knowledge of the basic events of this expedition from Cortés's "Fifth Letter," printed in *Letters from Mexico*, ed. Anthony Grafton (New Haven, CT: Yale University Press, 1986). However, Cortés does not mention to the king his actions regarding the enslavement of hundreds of people for his own profit. We learn of this only in archival documents presently in the Archivo General de Indias in Seville and in the Manuscripts Division of Yale University Library. See Townsend, *Malintzin's Choices*, 261 (nn. 22–24), and Restall, *When Montezuma Met Cortés*.

33. A number of historians have written about Isabel de Moctezuma. The most complete work on her is Donald Chipman, *Moctezuma's Children: Aztec Royalty Under Spanish Rule, 1520–1700* (Austin: University of Texas Press, 2005).

34. Cortés to his father, Martín Cortés, September 26, 1526, printed in *Cartas y otros documentos de Hernán Cortés,* ed. Mariano Cuevas (Seville: F. Díaz, 1915), 29.

35. Cortés made this claim in the document conceding an encomienda to doña Isabel. It is housed in the Archivo General de Indias and has been printed in Amada López de Meneses, "Techuichpotzin, hija de Moteczuma," in *Estudios cortesianos* (Madrid: Consejo Superior de Investigaciones Científicas, 1948).

36. Ordás to Francisco Verdugo, June 2, 1530, in Enrique Otte, "Nueve Cartas de Diego de Ordás," *Historia Mexicana* 14 (1964): 328.

37. We know this from the timing of the husband's death and the birth of the child, Leonor. We also know the child belonged to Cortés from both Spanish documents (such as the wills of Cortés and doña Isabel) and Nahuatl genealogies which included the child as Tecuichpotzin's firstborn and named the conqueror as the father. (See *Codex Chimalpahin* 1:163 and 2:87.)

38. Townsend, *Malintzin's Choices*, especially chap. 9.

39. *Florentine Codex* 6:160. (See also 161–67.) On Mexica motherhood, see Inga Clendinnen, *Aztecs: An Interpretation* (New York: Cambridge University Press, 1991).

40. Leonor Cortés Moctezuma later married Juan de Tolosa, governor of Zacatecas, where fabulously rich silver mines were discovered. Her children entered the highest ranks of Mexican society. For more on her, see Chipman, *Moctezuma's Children*.

41. Isabel's favoring of her firstborn son over those by her still-living husband of more than twenty years is evident in her will. See Chipman, *Moctezuma's Children*, 65–70. After her death, a lengthy lawsuit ensued.

42. Chimalpahin spoke of her this way in the record he kept of his own era, *Annals of His Time*, ed. James Lockhart, Susan Schroeder, and Doris Namala (Stanford, CA: Stanford University Press, 2006)

43. Donald Chipman, "Isabel Moctezuma," in *Struggle and Survival in Colonial America,* ed. David Sweet and Gary Nash (Berkeley: University of California Press, 1981).

44. On the dating of Malintzin's death using archival Spanish documents, see Townsend, *Malintzin's Choices*, 263, n. 40. Mexico City's Actas de Cabildo refer to her as being deceased by January 1529. Malintzin is mentioned as having translated in Chalco around 1530 inChimalpahin's Seventh Relation, *Ocho relaciones*, but she was already dead by then. Either his source misremembered when the events requiring translation occurred, or else, more likely, Malinche had translated in Chalco as late as 1528, and when mentioning an event in the early 1530s it was assumed by people years later that she was the one who had been present. At the time of Malintzin's death, her son was in Spain. Her little daughter was raised by her father, Juan Jaramillo, who married a Spanish woman of "good family." Later, the stepmother attempted to disinherit her, and a lengthy lawsuit followed.

45. *Historia Tolteca Chichimeca*, 231.

46. On the importance of malnutrition in rendering the indigenous more susceptible to disease, see Suzanne Alchon, A *Pest in the Land* (Albuquerque: University of New Mexico Press, 2003).

47. See Ida Altman, *The War for Mexico's West: Indians and Spaniards in New Galicia, 1524–1550* (Albuquerque: University of New Mexico Press, 2010).

48. Benton, *Lords of Tetzcoco*, 35.

49. A related nobleman and friend of Chimalpopoca's later swore that he himself had received baptism in 1529. See testimony of don Diego Ceynos in "Manuscrito de 1553," in *Documentos sobre tierras y señoríos en Cuauhtinchan*, ed. Luis Reyes García (Mexico City: Instituto Nacional de Antropología e Historia, 1978), 80. Chimalpopoca referred to himself by a Christian name (don Alonso) by 1532 (see "Donación de Tierras," in *Documentos sobre tierras*, 101).

50. *Libro de Guardianes*, 36.

51. *Libro de Guardianes*, 34 and 38. A surviving 1540s census from another region demonstrates that even leading Christian noblemen simply kept their multiple wives. See S. L. Cline, ed., *The Book of Tributes: Early Sixteenth-Century Nahuatl Censuses from Morelos* (Los Angeles: UCLA Latin American Center Publications, 1993).

52. "Donación de Tierras" in *Documentos sobre tierras*, 101–2. This document, dated 1532, is a remarkably early extant example of the use of the Roman alphabet by Nahuas in their own public proceedings. It survived only because someone submitted the document in 1554 as evidence in a legal case unfolding in Mexico City.

53. *Documentos sobre tierras*, 101–2. The scribe called himself "Simón Buenaventura." He appears in other documents in the 1550s. In 1532, he would still have been young, probably a recent student of the friars at Tepeaca.

54. *Historia Tolteca Chichimeca*, 231.

55. *Libro de Guardianes*, 36. This indigenous account accords well with that found in the Annals of Tecamachalco, printed in *Los Anales de Tecamachalco, 1398–1590*, ed. Eustquio Celestino Solís and Luis Reyes García (Mexico City: CIESAS, 1992), 21–22. The Franciscans, notably Gerónimo de Mendieta, focus on other elements in their treatment of the subject.

56. A rich literature has emerged on the persistence of indigenous religious beliefs. See, for instance, Patricia Lopes Don, *Bonfires of Culture: Franciscans, Indigenous Leaders, and Inquisition in Early Mexico, 1524–1540* (Norman: University of Oklahoma Press, 2010); David Tavárez, *The Invisible War: Indigenous Devotions, Discipline, and Dissent in Colonial Mexico* (Stanford, CA: Stanford University, 2011); and Eleanor Wake, *Framing the Sacred: The Indian Churches of Colonial Mexico* (Norman: University of Oklahoma Press, 2010).

57. *Historia Tolteca Chichimeca*, 232. For an analysis of the succeeding structure, built in the 1550s, in which indigenous forms have survived, see Pablo Escalante Gonzalbo, "El Patrocinio del arte indocristiano en el siglo XVI. La iniciativa de las autoridades indígenas en Tlaxcala y Cuauhtinchan," in *Patrocinio, colección y circulación de las artes,* ed. Gustavo Curiel (Mexico City: UNAM, 1997). On inter-altepetl competition in the colonial period, see James Lockhart, *The Nahus After the Conquest* (Stanford, CA: Stanford University Press, 1992).

58. *Libro de Guardianes*, 40.

59. This is the only place in the book where I make use of poetic license. Here are the facts of which I can be absolutely certain: (1) in the 1580s, a highly literate man named Cristóbal de Castañeda appears in the record as clerk of the indigenous cabildo; (2) an extant will proves that this Cristóbal was in don Alonso's direct line of descent, but he could have been a grandson or other relative, rather than a son; and (3) there is overwhelming evidence that a young member of don Alonso's family attended the school at Tlatelolco; even though it was most likely don Alonso's son, it could have been a young cousin or other relative. (See Townsend, *Annals of Native America*, chap. 1.) Thus in writing about the Castañeda family member who was a student at the school, I should technically refer to "the boy who was probably a son and probably named Cristóbal, but could have been some other young relative and/or could have had some other Christian baptismal name." I hope readers will forgive me for simply discussing "Cristóbal" and including this note by way of full disclosure.

60. On the reception of the boys and the goods they brought with them, see fray Juan de Torquemada, *Monarquía Indiana* (Mexico City: Porrúa, 1969), 3:113.

61. We do not know much about how the young indigenous students perceived their education or their educators, since none left us any commentary. It is clear, however, that the students were by no means deracinated or demeaned in the same way North American indigenous students were in the nineteenth- and twentieth-century boarding schools. Given the later activities of some of them, it seems safe to say that they were energized by what they learned and hoped to (and often did) use

their literacy to help their people. See the discussion of the "trilinguals" (speaking Spanish, Latin, and Nahuatl) and of their greatest teacher in Miguel León-Portilla, *Bernardino de Sahagún: First Anthropologist* (Norman: University of Oklahoma Press, 2002). The first alphabetic primer printed by the friars is available in facsimile: Emilio Valton, ed., *El Primer Libro de alfabetización en América* (Mexico City: Robedo, 1949 [1569]). There is no reason to think that students wouldn't have learned as quickly from the primer as modern kindergartners do from similar materials prepared for them. Lists of the inspiring texts in the Tlatelolco school library—such as the works of Cicero and Erasmus—have been printed in Joaquín García Icazbalceta, ed., *Nueva colección de documentos para la historia de México,* vol. 3 (Liechtenstein: Kraus Reprints, 1971 [1886]). For a glimpse of both the condescending commentary by teachers about the students' early artwork and the pride they took in some of their students' accomplishments, such as their joyous singing, see Motolinia, *Historia de los Indios,* 273.

62. Sahagún spoke Nahuatl well and bemoaned what the young people sometimes said to each other, without the full understanding of most of the friars who supervised them. See *Florentine Codex: General History of the Things of New Spain,* ed. Arthur J.O. Anderson and Charles Dibble (Salt Lake City: School of American Research and University of Utah Press, 1952), vol. 1, commentary on books 2 and 5.

63. *Libro de Guardianes,* 40–42. The writer also commented on the rebelliousness of the [newly Protestant] city of Geneva. He did not comment on the "bad behavior" of his own polygamous ancestors, but the friars did that often enough in their writings for us to be certain that they shared those opinions with their students.

64. See the facsimile of the *Historia Tolteca Chichimeca.*

65. *Libro de Guardianes,* 28.

66. "Manuscrito de 1553," in *Documentos sobre tierras,* 94.

67. Several sets of annals mentioned the number of deaths as 800,000. The *Libro de Guardianes* also repeated this. Remaining descriptions do not tell us which disease was the major culprit; it was probably smallpox hitting at the same times as other sicknesses.

68. This case is reproduced in full in "Cuauhtinchan contra Tepeaca por los linderos establecidos en el año de 1467, 1546–47," in *Documentos sobre tierras.*

69. *Documentos sobre tierras,* 13 and 28. They directly complained about the cost of boarding in the city.

70. *Documentos sobre tierras,* 11–14. The court recorder specifically mentions that don Alonso nodded his ascent.

71. In effect, don Alonso was facing the same conundrum that users of the largely pictographic cuneiform along the Mediterranean rim had faced centuries earlier when they first came across the sound-based alphabet of the Phoenicians. Should they perhaps relinquish their pictographic writing system in favor of this highly efficient recording of sound? Over time, many decided—consciously or unconsciously— that they would. The most complete encyclopedia of world writing-systems is Peter

Daniels and William Bright, eds., *The World's Writing Systems* (New York: Oxford University Press, 1996). For a fascinating treatment of the beginnings of writing in the ancient Mediterranean world, see two works by Denise Schmandt-Besserat: *How Writing Came About* (Austin: University of Texas Press, 1996), and *When Writing Met Art: From Symbol to Story* (Austin: University of Texas Press, 2007). For a discussion of the decline of cuneiform in the context of the phenomenon of the extinction of other writing forms, see Stephen Houston, John Baines, and Jerrold Cooper, "Last Writing: Script Obsolescence in Egypt, Mesopotamia and Mesoamerica," *Comparative Studies in Society and History* 45, 3 (2003): 430–79. Cuneiform was in fact partly phonetic—as were all Mesoamerican writing systems—but not nearly to the extent that the Phoenician alphabet or its descendants were.

72. The extraordinary manuscript now called the *Historia Tolteca Chichimeca* displays all these characteristics. Don Alonso orchestrated the project, as an in-text reference makes explicit, and his younger family members helped him, as circumstantial evidence makes clear. For a full study, see Townsend, *Annals of Native America*, chap. 1. For a thorough study of the images and the intent of the producers, see Dana Leibsohn, *Script and Glyph: Pre-Hispanic History, Colonial Bookmaking and the Historia Tolteca Chichimeca* (Washington, DC: Dumbarton Oaks, 2009).

Chapter 7

1. Documents relating to the investigation of don Martín Cortés and his half brother, the Marquis del Valle, are preserved in the Archivo General de Indias in Seville, Spain. Many of them were printed in Manuel Orozco y Berra, ed., *Noticia histórica de la conjuración del Marqués del Valle, años 1565–1568* (Mexico City: R. Rafael, 1853). For the record of the torture session, see 228–33.

2. For more on his life and character, see Ana Lanyon, *The New World of Martín Cortés* (New York: Da Capo, 2003), as well as Camilla Townsend, *Malintzin's Choices: An Indian Woman in the Conquest of Mexico* (Albuquerque: University of New Mexico Press, 2006), especially chap. 9.

3. The events are described or alluded to in several Nahuatl histories: *Annals of Juan Bautista*, *Codex Aubin*, and *Annals of Tecamachalco*.

4. The bull from Clemente VII is dated April 16, 1529. A copy was preserved when Cortés asked to have his newly legitimized son received into the Order of the Knights of Santiago. Those records are preserved in the Archivo Histórico Nacional in Madrid and have been published as "Expediente de Martín Cortés, niño de siete años, hijo de Hernando Cortés y la India Marina, Toledo, 19 Julio 1529," in *Boletín de la Real Academia de Historia* 21 (1892): 199–202.

5. Hernando Cortés to Francisco Nuñez, June 20, 1533, in Mario Hernández Sánchez-Barba, ed., *Hernando Cortés: cartas y documentos* (Mexico City: Porrúa, 1963), 514–23.

6. For many years, historians (myself included) believed that don Martín did not return to Mexico until he was in his forties. Recently, the careful research of María del Carmen Martínez Martínez unearthed several references to an earlier visit. She consulted the pay records of the royal court and was able to pinpoint exactly when Martín absented himself to visit the New World. See Martínez Martínez, *Martín Cortés: Pasos recuperados (1532–1562)* (León, Spain: Universidad de León, 2018), 33–40. (This is a biographical study of the legitimate don Martín, not Malintzin's son, but the author's research encompassed the latter.) A summary of the later years is found in a Probanza submitted by don Martín's son, Fernando, and preserved at the Archivo General de Indias, Patronato 17, R.13.

7. On the relations between the brothers, see Townsend, *Malintzin's Choices*, chap. 9. María del Carmen Martínez Martínez takes a view more sympathetic to the heir, whose documentary trail she knows intimately. She asserts that the constant litigation was simply part of life for people of this class and did not necessarily hurt their relationships with one another. She notes that Martín the heir had many onerous responsibilities, and that Martín the mestizo was perfectly capable of displaying temper. See her *Martín Cortés,* 77–79, 121, 141, 167–82. Undoubtedly the truth was complicated. To my mind, however, the mother's view of her son (the legitimate Martín) settles the question of his character, not to mention later events.

8. "Por Marina, soy testigo / ganó esta tierra un hombre, / y por otra deste nombre / la perderá quien yo digo," from a 1589 text by Juan Suárez de la Peralta, *Tratado del descubrimiento de las Indias y su conquista*, ed. Giorgio Perissinotto (Madrid: Alianza, 1990), 195.

9. Such details came out in the investigation of don Martín's conduct in the years leading up to the supposed conspiracy (see n. 1). Material on the life and death of María Jaramillo is found in the legal case (Archivo General de Indias, Justicia 168, Autos entre partes) she and her son waged to defend their inheritance against her stepmother. For more on this subject, see Townsend, *Malintzin's Choices*, chap. 8.

10. Archivo General de Indias, Pasajeros, L.4, E 3955, Bernardina de Porres.

11. Spanish and indigenous records corroborate each other. See Luis Reyes García, ed., *Anales de Juan Bautista* (Mexico City: CIESAS, 2001), 218–19, and France Scholes and Eleanor Adams, eds., *Cartas de Valderrama* (Mexico City: Porrúa, 1961), 11, 338.

12. A sense of the city's reaction comes not from the records of the investigation but from Suárez de la Perralta, *Tratado*.

13. This was the thrust of a 1532 petition in Spanish submitted by five Mexica noblemen, including Moctezuma's son and nephew, Nezahualtecolotl, and Huanitzin. See "Una petición de varios principales de la Ciudad de México al emperador Carlos V," in *La Nobleza Indígena del cento de México después de la conquista,* ed. Emma Pérez-Rocha and Rafael Tena (Mexico City: Instituto Nacional de Antropología e Historia, 2000), 99–102. Of course, the petitioners had reason to exaggerate the increasing difficulty of their plight, as they were petitioning to receive encomiendas or other sources of wealth, but what they say is indeed believable,

given what we know of the context. At the end of the document, several Audiencia judges added their own opinions that these men could not continue to function as social leaders if something weren't done. The petitioners did not explain "el oprobio en que estamos de nuestros naturales," but it becomes clear in *The Annals of Juan Bautista* that blame for the war with the Spaniards was still under discussion, even then.

14. For the sixteenth-century reorganization of the altepetl under Spanish rule, see James Lockhart, *The Nahuas After the Conquest* (Stanford, CA: Stanford University Press, 1992), esp. 28–44.

15. On the gossip about the cause of death of this son of Moctezuma, see don Domingo Chimalpahin, *Codex Chimalpahin,* ed. Arthur J. O. Anderson and Susan Schroeder (Norman: University of Oklahoma, 1997), 1:160–61. For a careful listing of the known documentary record pertaining to Nezahualtecolotl, see Emma Pérez Rocha and Rafael Tena, introduction to *La Nobleza Indígena*, 38–39. Pérez and Tena note that the story cannot be true, given the death date of the accused quauhtlatoani. The last recorded mention of Nezahualtecolotl is in 1536, when he received a coat of arms. Presumably, he died about that time.

16. This statement was made later in a legal case pursued in the 1560s and is cited in a thorough and highly illuminating article: Anastasia Kalyuta, "El arte de acomodarse a dos mundos: la vida de don Pedro de Moctezuma Tlacahuepantli" *Revista Española de Antropología Americana* 41, no. 2 (2011), 478.

17. See Don Domingo de San Antón Muñón Chimalpahin Quauhtlehuanitzin, *Annals of His Time,* ed. James Lockhart, Susan Schroeder, and Doris Namala (Stanford, CA: Stanford University Press, 2006), 132–33 and 136–37. Chimalpahin consulted with Tezozomoc, the son of Huanitzin, about the time he wrote of Huanitzin's having been held in Coyoacan and tortured, so he was probably repeating a family story. Given the context, the story is believable. In his petition to the Spanish monarch (see n.13), Huanitzin naturally did not mention the latter elements but spoke only of the trip to Honduras.

18. On Huanitzin having "elsewhere begot" children, see *Codex Chimalpahin,* 2:101; and on his marriage to doña Francisca, 1:165.

19. In the 1532 petition to the crown, the statement of Moctezuma's then-living son don Martín Nezahualtecolotl appears first, then—braiding the two family lines togetherin accordance with cultural norms—that of the leading member of Itzcoatl's family line, then that of Huanitizin, then that of a quauhtlatoani whose father had served as interim governor, and another relative. Though the Spaniards could not have known this, the order of statements or contributions was considered extremely important.

20. The Nahuatl record gives varying dates in the late 1530s for Huanitzin's enthronement as royal gobernador. See María Castañeda de la Paz's thorough study of the royal family in "Historia de una casa real: Origen y ocaso del linage gobernante en México Tenochtitlan," *Nuevo Mundo Mundos Nuevos* (2011), http://nuevomundo.

revues.org. Most likely, there was a series of interrelated steps that unfolded over the course of several years, rather like the founding of a town.

21. The best treatment of Huanitzin's period of rule is Barbara Mundy, *The Death of Aztec Tenochtitlan, the Life of Mexico City* (Austin: University of Texas Press, 2015), chap. 5. She includes a fine treatment of the feather-work gift. For the interest that Europeans grew to have in Mexico's feather work tableaux, see Alessandra Russo, Gerhard Wolf, and Diana Fane, eds., *Images Take Flight: Feather Art in Mexico and Europe, 1400–1700* (Florence, Italy: Kunsthistorisches Institut in Florenz, 2015).

22. Mundy, *Death of Aztec Tenochtitlan*, 156–60. Included in Mundy is a thorough discussion of the documentary evidence for the tlatoani's struggle to protect resources of both the community and his family. See also the brief but significant comment of Castañeda de Paz, "Historia de una casa real," 6.

23. Documents recording the debate on this issue among Spaniards are collected in France Scholes and Eleanor Adams, eds., *Sobre el modo de tributar los indios de Nueva España a Su Majestad, 1561–64* (Mexico City: Porrúa, 1958).

24. Modesto Ulloa, *La hacienda real de Castilla en el reinado de Felipe II* (Madrid: Seminario Cisneros, 1986).

25. *Cartas de Valderrama*, 65–66.

26. "Auto proveido por el virrey," in *Sobre el modo de tributar los indios*, 116–18.

27. *Annals of Juan Bautista* in *Los Anales de Juan Bautista*, ed. Luis Reyes García (Mexico City: CIESAS, 2001), 184–85.

28. The proceedings of the case have been published in *Códice Osuna accompañado de 158 páginas inéditas encontradas in el Archivo General de la Nación*, ed. Luis Chávez Orozco (Mexico City: Instituto Indigenista Interamericano, 1947), 13–16 [hereafter *Codex Osuna*].

29. *Annals of Juan Bautista*, 196–97, and *Codex Chimalpahin* 2:119. Castañeda de Paz, "Historia de una casa real," 6, argues that we cannot know who this young woman is, as she is described in the *Annals* only as "the daughter of the late don Diego"; she lists two different noble don Diegos to make the point. However, it is highly likely that only one man would be termed "the late don Diego" with no further explanation considered necessary: this person would have been the recently dead tlatoani. Looking at his genealogy in the *Codex Chimalpahin*, we find a Magdalena who would have been the right age among his household descendants. She was a grandniece, not a daughter, but any young female dependent of the household might have been known in a figurative sense as a "daughter." That Magdalena is not listed as having any children herself, and the young woman in question here did indeed die shortly after her marriage, without issue.

30. *Annals of Juan Bautista*, 198–99. I previously interpreted this passage to mean only that the altepetl had expended great effort to survive. I thank Celso Mendoza for his insightful improvement to my translation; the text is referencing the tradition of blood sacrifice.

31. Lockhart, *The Nahuas*, 118.

32. This segment of the *Annals of Juan Bautista* is transcribed and translated into English in CamillaTownsend, *Annals of Native America: How the Nahuas of Colonial Mexico Kept Their History Alive* (New York: Oxford University Press, 2016), chap. 2.

33. The tradition of public weeping as a way of making a memorable statement is found in many places. See for instance the document published by James Lockhart as an appendix to *The Nahuas After the Conquest*: "Grant of a house site, San Miguel Tocuillen, Tetzcoco region, 1583." Miguel Leon Portilla reprinted the document with the apt title, "And Ana Wept," in *In the Languages of Kings: An Anthology of Mesoamerican Literature,* ed. Miguel Leon Portilla and Earl Shorris (New York: Norton, 2001), 366–67.

34. *Annals of Juan Bautista,* 214–15.

35. *Annals of Juan Bautista,* 218–19.

36. *Annals of Juan Bautista,* 220–23.

37. *Annals of Juan Bautista,* 220–21. For the full text of the song, see Camilla Townsend, "'What in the World Have You Done to Me, My Lover?': Sex, Servitude and Politics among the Pre-conquest Nahuas," *Americas* 62 (2006): 349–89.

38. *Cartas de Valderrama,* 160–61.

39. María Justina Sarabia Viejo, *Don Luis de Velasco, Virrey de Nueva España* (Seville: Escuela de Estudios Hispano-Americanos, 1978), 470–71.

40. *Annals of Juan Bautista,* 238–39.

41. *Annals of Juan Bautista,* 222–23.

42. *Annals of Juan Bautista,* 230–31, 278–81.

43. *Codex Osuna,* 32–38.

44. On the ancient spiritual associations with Tepeyac, see Rodrigo Martínez Baracs, "De Tepeaquilla a Tepeaca, 1528–1555," *Andes* 17 (2006). On the Franciscan provincial's 1556 mention of Marcos's new painting at Tepeyac, and the subsequent decision by the archbishop to launch an investigation into possible idolatry, see Edmundo O'Gorman, *Destierro de Sombras: Luz en el orígen de la imagen y culta de Nuestra Señora de Guadalupe* (Mexico City: Universidad Nacional Autónoma de México, 1986). Readers can find the 1556 testimony relating to Marcos in Ernesto de la Torre Villar and Ramiro Navarra de Anda, eds., *Testimonios Históricos Guadalupanos* (Mexico City: Fondo de Cultura Económica, 1982), 63. On the question of whether the Marcos who did the painting is the same as the Marcos found in the *Annals of Juan Bautista*, see Townsend, *Annals of Native America,* chap. 2. The *Annalsof Juan Bautista* lists all the painters who worked for the Franciscans in the mid-1560s, and only one is named "Marcos." That figure is perceived as a leader among the painters and takes a leading role in the text, so it is logical to think that he is probably the one known for the extraordinary painting of a few years earlier.

45. There is no sixteenth-century evidence for the existence of Juan Diego. See Stafford Poole, *The Guadalupan Controversies in Mexico* (Stanford, CA: Stanford University Press, 2006).

46. *Annals of Juan Bautista*, 254–55, 258–59.

47. *Annals of Juan Bautista*, 238–39.

48. *Annals of Juan Bautista*, 288–89.

49. *Annals of Juan Bautista*, 262–63.

50. *Annals of Juan Bautista*, 258–59.

51. *Annals of Juan Bautista*, 250–51.

52. *Annals of Juan Bautista*, 248–49.

53. For a full study of this remarkable figure, see Camilla Townsend, "Mutual Appraisals: The Shifting Paradigms of the English, Spanish and Powhatans in Tsenacomoco, 1560–1622," in *Early Modern Virginia: Reconsidering the Old Dominion*, ed. Douglas Bradburn and John C. Coombs (Charlottesville: University of Virginia Press, 2011), 57–89.

54. The Provincial's letter is preserved in the Archivo General de Indias, RG Mexico, vol. 280, Feb. 1563; the text can be found in Camilla Townsend, ed., *American Indian History: A Documentary Reader* (London: Wiley-Blackwell, 2009), 31–33.

55. We learn of the argument in the letter (in Townsend, *American Indian History*); the friar occasionally recounts Paquiquineo's responses, but we cannot directly hear his voice.

56. The best treatment of this expedition orchestrated by Jesuits is Charlotte Gradie, "Spanish Jesuits in Virginia: The Mission That Failed," *Virginia Magazine of History and Biography* 96 (1988): 131–56.

57. *Cartas de Valderrama*, 187.

58. *Annals of Juan Bautista*, 148–49.

59. See Ethelia Ruiz Medrano, "Fighting Destiny: Nahua Nobles and Friars in the Sixteenth-Century Revolt of the Encomenderos against the King," in *Negotiation within Domination: New Spain's Indian Pueblos Confront the Spanish State*, ed. Ethelia Ruiz Medrano and Susan Kellogg (Boulder: University Press of Colorado, 2010).

60. *Annals of Juan Bautista*, 318–19.

61. *Codex Osuna*, 77–78.

62. These phenomena are evident in the *Annals of Juan Bautista* and are discussed in Townsend, *Annals of Native America*, chap. 2.

63. Chimalpahin commented explicitly on what historians can see: that the royal family per se did not continue to rule. However, there are complexities surrounding Chimalpahin's declaration as to the ending of the royal line, in the sense that some who governed later in the century were related to the royal family through the network of intermarriage among the nobility of the central valley. See Castañeda de Paz, "Historia de una casa real." Those governing figures were nevertheless from other altepetls in their primary identity.

64. This is the text known as the *Annals of Juan Bautista*. For more on the rotation of perspective as found in the *Annals*, see Camilla Townsend, "Glimpsing Native American Historiography: The Cellular Principle in Sixteenth-Century Nahuatl Annals," *Ethnohistory* 56 (2009): 625–50.

Chapter 8

1. The events (and the details) of this paragraph all come from the work of the indigenous historian now known as Chimalpahin. Don Domingo de San Antón Muñón Chimalpahin Cuauhtlehuanitzin, *Annals of His Time*, ed. and trans. James Lockhart, Susan Schroeder, and Doris Namala (Stanford, CA: Stanford University Press, 2006), 224–25. For a more complete study of his life than is found in this chapter, see Camilla Townsend, *Annals of Native America* (New York: Oxford University Press, 2016), chap. 4. On what his writings reveal about indigenous political concepts, see Susan Schroeder, *Chimalpahin and the Kingdoms of Chalco* (Tucson: University of Arizona Press, 1991).

2. Chimalpahin does not say, "I was there." But I assume he was present because he states: "We Indians [*timacehualtin*] helped." Elsewhere in the book he sometimes uses the phrase *timacehualtin* to talk about Indians in general ("We Indians must pay a tax," for example) but he does *not* do so when he is talking about a specific group of Indians of which he was not a part. In such cases he says *in macehualtin* ("the Indians"). So I believe it is safe to assume that he was present; the details he mentions would also indicate as much, for only an eyewitness would have had access to them. On my decision to translate *macehualtin* as "Indians" rather than "commoners" see Camilla Townsend, "Don Juan Buenaventura Zapata y Mendoza and the Notion of a Nahua Identity," in *The Conquest All Over Again*, ed. Susan Schroeder (Brighton: Sussex Academic Press, 2010). There, I discuss only the choices Zapata occasionally made in this regard, but I have since found that "macehualtin" serves to express the idea of "indigenous people" in numerous Nahuatl texts.

3. The full story with citations is in chap. 3. Quecholcohuatzin was later named "don Jerónimo," the "don" indicating that he was of a noble family, just as we would expect. Chimalpahin tells us that he was from Amaquemecan's sub-altepetl of Iztlacozauhcan, while his own grandparents were from the sub-altepetl of Tzacualtitlan Tenanco. He also tells us that the noble families of the various Amaquemecan sub-altepetls all intermarried with each other, so the families were at least distantly related.

4. He quoted the section on the different continents that can be found in Enrico Martínez, *El Reportorio de los tiempos* (Mexico City, 1606). His reading of Martínez will be discussed later in this chapter.

5. David Eltis and David Richardson, *Voyages: The Trans-Atlantic Slave Trade Database*, http://www.slavevoyages.org. For commentary on how blind to this reality we have long been, see Henry Louis Gates, *Black in Latin America* (New York: New York University Press, 2011), 59–60.

6. See Frederick Bowser, "Africans in Spanish American Colonial Society," in *The Cambridge History of Latin America,* ed. Leslie Bethell, vol. 2 (New York: Cambridge University Press, 1984); Colin Palmer, *Slaves of the White God: Blacks*

in Mexico, 1570–1650 (Cambridge, MA: Harvard University Press, 1976); Herman Bennett, *Africans in Colonial Mexico: Absolutism, Christianity, and Afro-Creole Consciousness, 1570–1640* (Bloomington: Indiana University Press, 2003). The most recent contribution is Pablo Sierra Silva, *Urban Slavery in Colonial Mexico: Puebla de los Angeles, 1531–1706* (New York: Cambridge University Press, 2018).

7. "Census de la población del Virreinato de Nueva España en el siglo XVI [1570]," *Boletín del Centro de Estudios americanistas de Sevilla de Indias* (February/March 1919): 44–62. Eight thousand was the number of men; there were more Spanish women than African women.

8. Report from Pedro de Vega regarding the population of Mexico City, Puebla and other cities, 1595, cited in María Elena Díaz, "The Black Blood of New Spain: Limpieza de Sangre, Racial Violence, and Gendered Power in Early Colonial Mexico," *William and Mary Quarterly* 61, no. 3 (2003): 503. These population figures are debatable, as there was no such thing as a census that meets our modern standards. Some historians have estimated the black population to be much higher, but most have not.

9. Chimalpahin, *Annals of His Time*, 26–27. Numerous annals mention the horrendous epidemic that began in 1576. The most graphic is the *Annals of Tecamachalco*. Sahagún expressed the fear harbored by the friars that literally all the indigenous would die.

10. The 1570 "census de la población" (see n. 7) reported about 60,000 indigenes. Confirming this, in the 1560s, specific tributary counts for the city's barrios placed the count at about 22,000 tribute-paying heads of household. Normally in this period, the multiplier to include family members would be higher than three, but in a situation in which indigenous children were dying of disease at extremely high rates, it is probably about right. In the early 1600s, tributaries were counted at roughly 8,000 (see Charles Gibson, *The Aztecs Under Spanish Rule* [Stanford, CA: Stanford University Press, 1964], 142, 379, and 462.) Using the same multiplier, we get a number in the area of 24,000 indigenous people in the early 1600s. Even if we reject the hypothetical multiplier, the count of the number of tributaries tells us the population had dropped by almost two-thirds.

11. Nicole Von Germeten, *Black Blood Brothers: Confraternities and Social Mobility for Afro-Mexicans* (Gainesville: University Press of Florida, 2006).

12. Bennett in *Africans in Colonial Mexico* focuses on the ways in which people of African descent in Mexico City were able to empower themselves, often by making the most of fissures that existed between state authorities and the church.

13. On relations between Africans and Indians in the nearby town of Cholula, see Norma Angelica Castillo Palma and Susan Kellogg, "Conflict and Cohabitation between Afro-Mexicans and Nahuas in Central Mexico," in *Beyond Black and Red: African-Native Relations in Colonial Latin America*, ed. Matthew Restall (Albuquerque: University of New Mexico Press, 2005); see also Matthew Restall, *The Black Middle: Africans, Mayas, and Spaniards in Colonial Yucatan* (Stanford,

CA: Stanford University Press, 2009). Networking and interactions with other groups is a major element of Sierra Silva, *Urban Slavery*.

14. Díaz, "The Black Blood of New Spain," includes a fine analysis of the records of the investigation. For more on "coronation" ceremonies in the New World influenced by actual African political traditions, see Walter Rucker, *Gold Coast Diasporas: Identity, Culture, and Power* (Bloomington: University of Indiana Press, 2015).

15. Díaz, "Black Blood of New Spain." Antonio Carrión, *Historia de la ciudad de Puebla de los Angeles* (Puebla: José Cajica, 1970 [1897]), 2:20–24. For a classic work on maroon communities, see Richard Price, *Maroon Societies: Rebel Slave Communities in the Americas* (Baltimore: Johns Hopkins University Press, 1979).

16. Díaz, "Black Blood of New Spain," 507–8. See also Von Germeten, *Black Blood Brothers*, 77–78.

17. Chimalpahin describes the abscess and the failed attempt to drain it. The people blamed inept Spanish doctors, see Chimalpahin, *Annals of His Time*, 200–201.

18. The anonymous report submitted by one of the members of the Audiencia appears in full in Luis Querol y Roso, "Negros y mulatos de Nueva España," *Anales de la Universidad de Valencia* 12, no. 9 (1931–32): 141–53. It includes a mention of one report by a black woman that a black man had tried to use witchcraft against her. This type of accusation was common and would normally have been referred to the office of the Inquisition. See Laura Lewis, *Power, Witchcraft and Caste in Colonial Mexico* (Durham, NC: Duke University Press, 2003).

19. Chimalpahin, *Annals of His Time*, 212–13. Chimalpahin refers to "Nuestra Señora of Huitzillan" and Huitzillan was the preconquest name for a place near to which in his own era the Hospital Nuestra Señora de la Misericordia stood—the same place that later allowed the executed black people to be buried in its graveyard. Spanish sources made a direct connection to Nuestra Señora de la Misericordia, whose confraternity members had been involved with the protest of the enslaved woman's death. See Von Germeten, *Black Blood* Brothers, 77. On Huitzillan, see Barbara Mundy, *The Death of Tenochtitlan, The Life of Mexico City* (Austin: University of Texas Press, 2015).

20. Chimalpahin, *Annals of His Time*, 214–15.

21. *Annals of His Time*, 216–17.

22. *Annals of His Time*, 218–19.

23. *Annals of His Time*, 218–19.

24. Vicente Riva Palacio claimed that he had read about this somewhere. His account shows the influence of Chimalpahin. See Vicente Riva Palacio, *El Libro Rojo, 1520–1867* (Mexico City: Díaz de León, 1870).

25. Luis Querol y Roso, "Negros y mulatos de Nueva España." The city authorities in writing to Puebla's cabildo mentioned the element of witchcraft. See Díaz, "Black Blood of New Spain."

26. Chimalpahin, *Annals of His Time*, 218–23. Díaz in "Black Blood of New Spain" does an excellent job of analyzing the discourse in the context of emerging European

notions of racial purity. However, it is not at all clear how much of the street gossip among the indigenous as reported by Chimalpahin originally came from Spaniards. Certainly much of what the indigenous said makes more sense in the precolonial context than in any other.

27. Modern historians working with the Spanish sources have understandably been more than willing to believe that the enraged black population really did plot to bring the Spaniards down. However, Chimalpahin was closer to the black population—he seems to have socialized with Afro-Mexicans—and so I am inclined to accept his presentation of events rather than theirs. Certainly to whatever extent the Spanish sources were based on statements made by Portuguese slave traders who claimed to speak fluent Angolan, we can discount them. In addition, Sierra Silva in *Urban Slavery* points out that the people accused, the leadership of the black cofradías (brotherhoods), as embedded as they were in the city's power structure, with access to high elites, were not likely to attach their hopes to violent upheaval.

28. Chimalpahin, *Annals of His Time*, 224–25.

29. *Annals of His Time*, 222–23.

30. *Annals of His Time*, 224–25.

31. This fact, like most of what we know about Chimalpahin, comes from his own writings. See Chimalpahin, *Las Ocho Relaciones*, ed. Rafael Tena (Mexico City: Consejo Nacional para la Cultura y las Artes, 1998), 1:249.

32. This can be deduced from their ages at their deaths in 1606; Chimalpahin, *Annals of His Time*, 90–91. On his family tree and its significance, see Schroeder, *Chimalpahin and the Kingdoms of Chalco.*.

33. See n. 3, this chapter, as well as n.1, chap. 3.

34. Nearly all of Chimalpahin's writings take the form of the xiuhpohualli. It does not seem to be imposed in any sense whatsoever, but undoubtedly reflects the format in which he was first introduced to the material.

35. Chimalpahin, *Annals of His Time*, 166–67.

36. Chimalpahin's *Annals of His Time* is written in the third person. It records elements from the earlier history of Mexico City, but only begins to convey the sense of having been written by someone who actually witnessed the events in around 1590, when Chimalpahin was eleven. He also later wrote that he had lived there "desde muy niño" ("from young childhood"), which he would not have said if he were older than twelve upon his arrival.

37. Chimalpahin, *Annals of His Time*, 38–39.

38. For the history of the church, see Rodrigo Martínez Baracs, "El Diario de Chimalpahin," *Estudios de cultura náhuatl* 38 (2007), 288–89. In Europe, monks of an order of San Antonio Abad ran hospitals, but in this case, it was simply the name chosen for a church.

39. Chimalpahin, *Annals of His Time*, 60–61.

40. Arthur J. O. Anderson and Charles Dibble, eds., *Florentine Codex: General History of the Things of New Spain* (Salt Lake City: University of Utah Press and School of

American Research, 1950–1982), 6:35–36. I thank Louise Burkhart for the improvement of the translation.

41. Don Juan Buenaventura Zapata y Mendoza, *Historia cronológica de la Noble Ciudad de Tlaxcala*, ed. Luis Reyes García and Andrea Martínez Baracs (Tlaxcala: Universidad Autónoma de Tlaxcala, 1995), 180–83. These events are also mentioned in the *Annals of Tlaxcala*. For a full study, see Travis Jeffres, "'In Case I Die Where I Am Selected to Be Sent': Coercion and the Tlaxcalan Resettlement of 1591," *Ethnohistory* 66 (2019): 95–116.

42. Chimalpahin, *Annals of His Time*, 36–37.

43. *Annals of His Time*, 62–63.

44. *Annals of His Time*, 64–65.

45. *Annals of His Time*, 70–71. On the word "macehualtin" see n.2, this chapter.

46. For more on this, see Tatiana Seijas, *Asian Slaves in Colonial Mexico* (New York: Cambridge University Press, 2014). On the Hospice San Jacinto, founded 1601, see Seijas, 125–26.

47. Saint Augustine, *Confessions*, ed. R. S. Pine-Coffin (New York: Penguin, 1961), 34. For a study of Chimalpahin's references to Adam and Eve and the use he made of Saint Augustine in his own work, see Townsend, *Annals of Native America*, chap. 4.

48. Scholars can trace the kinds of possessions people liked to collect through studies of wills. See James Lockhart, *The Nahuas After the Conquest* (Stanford, CA: Stanford University Press, 1992).

49. Art historians have studied the creative works of art that emerged in Mexico after artisans were exposed to Asian silks and porcelains. Donna Pierce and Ronald Otuska, eds., *Asia and Spanish America: Transpacific Artistic and Cultural Heritage, 1500–1850* (Denver: Denver Art Museum, 2009). See also Carmen Yuste López, *El comercio de la Nueva España con Filipinas, 1590–1795* (Mexico City: Instituto Nacional de Antropología e Historia, 1984).

50. Chimalpahin knew quite a bit about her under this name. See *Annals of His Time*, 298–301.

51. *Annals of His Time*, 66–67.

52. The most complete treatment of Pedro Dionisio is found in María Castañeda de la Paz, "Historia de una casa real: origen y ocaso del linaje gobernante en México-Tenochtitlan," *Nuevo Mundo Mundos Nuevos* (2011): 8–10.

53. Huanitzin was back from Honduras and living with his wife by 1526. If we assume that they began to have children immediately, then the eldest, a girl, was born about 1527, and the oldest boy, don Cristóbal, about 1528. This makes sense, as he was elected gobernador in the mid-1550s, and that probably could not have happened if he were younger than in his late twenties at that time. Five more children were then born over the course of the 1530s, before their father's death in 1541. Tezozomoc was the second to last. See Arthur J. O. Anderson and Susan Schroeder, eds., *Codex Chimalpahin* (Norman: University of Oklahoma Press, 1997), 1:173.

54. Chimalpahin, *Annals of His Time*, 66–67.

55. Chimalpahin, *Annals of His Time*, 58–59. He literally says don Antonio "couldn't hear things" but the implication was that he couldn't understand things (which is how Lockhart et al. read it as well). Chimalpahin later mentions Valeriano's death in 1605. For more on this most interesting figure, see Castañeda de la Paz, "Historia de una casa real," and Davíd Tavárez, "Nahua Intellectuals, Franciscan Scholars, and the *Devotio Moderna* in Colonial Mexico," *Americas* 70, no. 2 (2013): 203–10. On Isabel's marriage to Valeriano, see *Codex Chimalpahin* 1:173.

56. Chimalpahin, *Annals of His Time*, 90–91.

57. *Annals of His Time*, 100–101.

58. For the full story of this remarkable decades-long project, see Vera Candiani, *Dreaming of Dry Land: Environmental Transformation in Colonial Mexico City* (Stanford, CA: Stanford University Press, 2014). Candiani does a fine job of demonstrating why it was rational and cost-effective for the city's leaders to continue to depend on a conscripted indigenous labor force.

59. Chimalpahin, *Annals of His Time*, 110–11. Chimalpahin uses one verb (*mococoya*), which is used to refer to both illness and injury.

60. We know that he read them because he quotes both of them directly.

61. Louise Burkhart includes a catalog of Nahuatl doctrinal sources as an appendix to *The Slippery Earth: Nahua-Christian Moral Dialogue in the Sixteenth Century* (Tucson: University of Arizona Press, 1989).

62. It was the work of fray Juan Bautista Viseo that largely constituted this burst of productivity (see n.63 for an example. There is an impressive literature on these friars, and more recently, on the Christian Nahuas who worked with them. An interested reader should begin with the opening chapters of Burkhart's *Slippery Earth*. An excellent recent piece is Tavárez, "Nahua Intellectuals." His footnotes provide a thorough guide to the various contributions.

63. Preface to Juan Bautista Viseo, *Sermonario en lengua Mexicana* (Mexico City: Casa de Diego López Dávalos, 1606). A copy of this work, like many of the early Mexican imprints, is housed in the New York Public Library.

64. For a textual study demonstrating how scholars deduce that he began his magnum opus (now called *Las Ocho Relaciones*) in this year, see Townsend, *Annals of Native America*, chap. 4.

65. "Eighth Relation" in *Las Ocho Relaciones*, 2:305–9. For a complete chart of all the sources mentioned by Chimalpahin, including one elderly woman, see Schroeder, *Chimalpahin*, 18–19.

66. *Las Ocho Relaciones*, 2:317. I have a small but very important disagreement with Rafael Tena regarding the translation and have thus amended it. He interprets the meaning to be that the group made a copy of some old written accounts, whereas I am certain that the text means that they brought people together and made presentations of old oral accounts (*quicenquixtique y huehuetlahtolli*), which were then transcribed. This is important, for it means that Chimalpahin was reading a transcription of a rich verbal performance.

67. *Las Ocho Relaciones*, 2:309.

68. Chimalpahin included lengthy statements by Tezozomoc in his writings, one of them dated 1609. Indeed, it is only through Chimalpahin that Tezozomoc's statements survive at all. It is theoretically possible that the two never actually met and that the writings were simply delivered to Chimalpahin at Tezozomoc's orders. On a realistic level, however, such a thing is inconceivable. A matter of such consequence to them both would have been handled in person, especially in an age when *all* important transactions were handled in person.

69. More often than referring to having written something, Tezozomoc mentioned vouching for the authenticity of the statements. Thus it is very possible that he was reading pictographic statements or reciting aloud to Chimalpahin (or to someone else) in some cases.

70. "Eighth Relation" in *Las Ocho Relaciones*, 2:273.

71. Tezozomoc in *Codex Chimalpahin* 1:60–61.

72. "Eighth Relation," in *Las Ocho Relaciones*, 2:295.

73. *Las Ocho Relaciones*, 2:360–61.

74. David Tavárez, "Reclaiming the Conquest," in *Chimalpahin's Conquest,* ed. Susan Schroeder, Anne J. Cruz, Cristián Roa-de-la-Carrera, and David Tavárez (Stanford,CA: Stanford University Press, 2010), 29–30.

75. "First Relation" in *Las Ocho Relaciones*, 1:29.

76. "Second Relation" in *Las Ocho Relaciones* 1:65; and "Fourth Relation" in *Las Ocho Relaciones* 1:307.

77. Chimalpahin, *Annals of His Time*, 194–95. The story is extensive and is treated (in pieces) through 201.

78. *Annals of His Time*, 196–97. He writes, "*Macama ytalhuillo.*"

79. *Annals of His Time*, 222–23.

80. See Revelation 20:13. I would like to thank Robert Taber for this insightful contribution. I would not have recognized the biblical allusion, but it is most definitely there.

81. See Martin Nesvig, "The 'Indian Question' and the Case of Tlatelolco," in *Local Religion in Colonial Mexico,* ed. Martin Nesvig (Albuquerque: University of New Mexico Press, 2006).

82. The script does not seem to have survived, but the performance was summarized by an audience member. Antonio de Ciudad Real, *Tratado curioso y docto de las grandezas de la Nueva España* (Mexico City: Universidad Nacional Autónoma de México, 1976 [1584]).

83. "Seventh Relation" in *Las Ocho Relaciones*, 2:230–31.

84. See Gregorio Martin del Guijo, *Diario.* 2 vols. (Mexico City: Editorial Porrúa, 1952).

85. For an analysis of these riots, see Alejandro Cañeque, *The King's Living Image: The Culture and Politics of Vice-regal Power in Colonial Mexico* (New York: Routledge, 2004).

86. *Annals of Tlaxcala* in Camilla Townsend, ed., *Here in This Year: Seventeenth-Century Nahuatl Annals of the Tlaxcala-Puebla Valley* (Stanford, CA: Stanford University Press, 2010), 176–77.

87. James Lockhart, Susan Schroeder, and Doris Namala, introduction to *Annals of His Time*, 12. The editors believe it is highly unlikely that Chimalpahin wrote more for several reasons: (1) by 1615, he was already slowing down; (2) the work ends in the middle of the page, not the way it would end if it were merely that a final set of pages were lost, as he *never* wasted paper; and (3) Sigüenza y Góngora, who received his papers, wrote a note that he had specifically looked for the ending but could find nothing more of this nature anywhere among the documents.

88. Fernando de Alva Ixtlilxochitl, *Obras Históricas* ed. Edmundo O'Gorman (Mexico City: Universidad Nacional Autónoma de México, 1975–77), 1:523. O'Gorman, having found this preface in different places in different copies of Ixtlilxochitl's work, places it before the earlier "Sumaria relación de la historia general." However, Amber Brian found it at the start of Ixtlilxochitl's final work, "The Historia Chichimeca" in his autograph manuscripts. See Brian, "Don Fernando de Alva Ixtlilxochitl's Narratives of the Conquest of Mexico," in *The Conquest All Over Again*, ed. Susan Schroeder (Brighton: Sussex Academic Press, 2010); and Brian, "The Original Alva Ixtlilxochitl Manuscripts at Cambridge University," *Colonial Latin American Review* 23, no. 1 (2014): 84–101.

89. Amber Brian, *Alva Ixtlilxochitl's Native Archive and the Circulation of Knowledge in Colonial Mexico* (Nashville, TN: Vanderbilt University Press, 2016). For a detailed summary of Ixtlilxochitl's life based on historical documents, see Camilla Townsend, "The Evolution of Ixtlilxochitl's Scholarly Life," *Colonial Latin American Review* 23, no. 1 (2014): 1–17. The latter is the first article in a special issue devoted to Ixtlilxochitl.

90. Townsend, *Annals of Native America*, 154–55.

91. David Brading, *The First America: The Spanish Monarchy, Creole Patriots, and the Liberal States, 1492–1867* (Cambridge: Cambridge University Press, 1991). For a fascinating study of the way in which indigenous elites—including but not limited to Chimalpahin and Ixtlilxochitl—were involved in the production of the creole fantasies about indigenous peoples, see Peter Villella, *Indigenous Elites and Creole Identity in Colonial Mexico, 1500–1800* (Cambridge: Cambridge University Press, 2016). For the ways in which eighteenth-century elites became fixated on finding medical cures from among the ancient lore of the Indians, see Lance Thurner, "Lizards and the Idea of Mexico," *Nursing Clio*, April 12, 2018. https://nursingclio.org/2018/04/12/lizards-and-the-idea-of-mexico.

Epilogue

1. On the survival of the xiuhpohualli for a longer period in Tlaxcala, see Camilla Townsend, "Don Juan Buenaventura Zapata y Mendoza and the Notion of a Nahua Identity," in *The Conquest All Over Again* ed. Susan Schroeder (Brighton: Sussex

Academic Press, 2010). On the Nahuas' later colonial production of what are called primordial titles or *títulos*, see the work of Stephanie Wood, including "Don Diego García de Mendoza Moctezuma: A Techialoyan Mastermind?" *Estudios de cultura náhuatl* 19 (1989): 245–68, and *Transcending Conquest: Nahua Views of Spanish Colonial Mexico* (Norman: University of Oklahoma Press, 2003); as well as the work of Robert Haskett, including *Visions of Paradise: Primordial Titles and Mesoamerican History in Cuernavaca* (Norman: University of Oklahoma Press, 2005).

2. An excellent guide to the socioeconomic patterns of the colonial period is the classic work by James Lockhart and Stuart Schwartz, *Early Latin America* (New York: Cambridge University Press, 1983).

3. Each of these subjects pertains to a large and growing literature. For entrées into the literature, I recommend the following recent works: Pablo Sierra Silva, *Urban Slavery in Colonial Mexico: Puebla de los Angeles, 1531–1706* (New York: Cambridge University Press, 2018) and Jessica Nelson Criales, "'Women of Our Nation': Gender and Christian Indian Communities in the United States and Mexico, 1724–1850," *Early American Studies* 17, no. 4 (2019)..

4. There is extensive literature on both Sor Juana and the history of the Virgin of Guadalupe. To begin, see Camilla Townsend, "Sor Juana's Nahuatl," *Le Verger* 8 [Paris] (2015): 1–12; and Stafford Poole, *The Guadalupan Controversies in Mexico* (Stanford, CA: Stanford University Press, 2006).

5. A clearly written overview of the period is E. Bradford Burns, *The Poverty of Progress: Latin America in the Nineteenth Century* (Berkeley: University of California Press, 1980).

6. For a full study of the modern movement among Nahuatl speakers, see Kelly McDonough, *The Learned Ones: Nahua Intellectuals in Postconquest Mexico* (Tucson: University of Arizona Press, 2014). The Nahuatl-Nahuatl dictionary is that of John Sullivan, Eduardo de la Cruz Cruz, Abelardo de la Cruz de la Cruz et al., *Tlahtolxitlauhcayotl* (Chicontepec, Veracruz: IDIEZ, 2016). Nahuatl scholars and writers Victoriano de la Cruz Cruz and Refugio Nava presented papers at the 2012 Northeastern Group of Nahuatl Studies Conference at Yale University, making reference to the metaphorical concept of a Sixth Sun. Other writers around the world have been deeply influenced by work in Nahuatl, such as Duncan Tonatiuh, who publishes children's stories in English based on Nahua themes and motifs.

Appendix

1. Most archaeologists excavate and analyze magnificent sites. In Mexico's Nahua territory, the greatest among these is the Aztec Templo Mayor in today's Mexico City, excavated 1978–1982. The lead archaeologist was Eduardo Matos Moctezuma. His publications in Spanish are voluminous. For an English introduction, see *Life and Death in the Templo Mayor* (Boulder: University Press of Colorado, 1995). Other archaeologists dedicate their time to the study of ordinary people's lives in less

grand locales; their work is also profoundly illuminating. See Michael E. Smith, *The Aztecs* (London: Blackwell, 1996).

2. I find the most helpful English edition of what remains to us of Columbus's logbook (a copy prepared by Bartolomé de las Casas) is Oliver Dunn, ed., *The Diario of Christopher Columbus's First Voyage to America* (Norman: University of Oklahoma Press, 1989). The only surviving text dating from the years of the conquest of Mexico is a set of letters to the king written by Hernando Cortés himself. See Hernán Cortés, *Letters from Mexico*, ed. Anthony Pagden (New Haven, CT: Yale University Press, 1986). In later years, other participants also wrote of their experiences, the most famous being Bernal Díaz de Castillo. An excellent English edition is Bernal Díaz, *The Conquest of New Spain*, ed. J. M. Cohen (New York: Penguin Books, 1963). Not long after the conquest, proselytizing friars began to record their thoughts, among them such figures as the Dominican Fray Diego Duran, *The History of the Indies of New Spain*, ed. Doris Heyden (Norman: University of Oklahoma Press, 1994 [1964]).

3. See Michael Coe, *Breaking the Maya Code* (New York: Thames & Hudson, 1992). It was a scholar namedDavid Stuart, who had regularly gone to Mexico as a child with his anthropologist parents, who spoke enough of the language to first recognize this.

4. This is part of a relatively lengthy life history carved at Piedras Negras, Guatemala. See Linda Schele's translation in Coe, *Breaking the Maya Code*, 266–67.

5. The leading scholar of the pictorial histories is Elizabeth Hill Boone. See her foundational *Stories in Red and Black: Pictorial Histories of the Aztecs and Mixtecs* (Austin: University of Texas Press, 2000) and *Cycles of Time and Meaning in the Mexican Books of Fate* (Austin: University of Texas Press, 2007). Today numerous young art historians follow in her footsteps, among them Lori Boornazian Diel, *The Tira de Tepechpan: Negotiating Place Under Aztec and Spanish Rule* (Austin: University of Texas Press, 2008)and *The Codex Mexicanus: A Guide to Life in Late Sixteenth-Century New Spain* (Austin: University of Texas Press, 2018).

6. These chapter subtitles come from the well-studied and much-loved *Florentine Codex*.

7. Classic works include (for the Maya) Linda Schele and David Freidel, *A Forest of Kings: The Untold Story of the Ancient Maya* (New York: William Morrow, 1990) and (for the Aztecs) Alfredo López Austin, *Hombre-Dios: Religión y política en el mundo náhuatl* (Mexico City: Universidad Nacional Autónoma de México, 1973), translated by Russ Davidson with Guilhem Olivier as *The Myth of Quetzalcoatl: Religion, Rulership, and History in the Nahua World* (Boulder: University Press of Colorado, 2015); Inga Clendinnen, *Aztecs: An Interpretation* (New York: Cambridge University Press, 1991); Davíd Carrasco, *City of Sacrifice: The Aztec Empire and the Role of Violence in Civilization* (Boston: Beacon Press, 1999). Frances Berdan has combined her deep knowledge of archaeology and of the Spanish-influenced sources to write the best compendium available, *Aztec Archaeology and Ethnohistory* (New York: Cambridge University Press, 2014).

8. In Mexico, Angel María Garibay had long studied the Nahuatl language, and his student, Miguel León-Portilla, published select source extractions as *Visión de los Vencidos* (Mexico City: Universidad Nacional Autónoma de México, 1959), later translated into English by Lysander Kemp as *The Broken Spears: The Aztec Account of the Conquest of Mexico* (Boston: Beacon Press, 1962) and into many other languages as well. Meanwhile, a leading American historian, Charles Gibson, had grown increasingly convinced of the importance of Nahuatl sources, as he indicated in *The Aztecs Under Spanish Rule* (Stanford, CA: Stanford University Press, 1964); at the same time Charles Dibble and Arthur Anderson pursued their great work, the English translation of the *Florentine Codex*, working directly from the Nahuatl rather than the Spanish glosses. See the entry in the annotated bibliography at the end of the appendix.

9. Louise Burkhart established a field with her book, *The Slippery Earth: Nahua-Christian Moral Dialogue in Sixteenth-Century Mexico* (Tucson: University of Arizona Press, 1989). For a fine recent contribution by one of her students, see Ben Leeming, "Micropoetics: The Poetry of Hypertrophic Words in Early Colonial Nahuatl," *Colonial Latin American Review* 24 (2015): 168–89.

10. James Lockhart likewise established a field with his great work, *The Nahuas After the Conquest* (Stanford, CA: Stanford University Press, 1992). The contributions of his students appear throughout this book. One of them took over Lockhart's position at UCLA and carried his methodology farther afield, to a study of the Mixtecs. See Kevin Terraciano, *The Mixtecs of Colonial Oaxaca: Ñudzahui History, Sixteenth through Eighteenth Centuries* (Stanford, CA: Stanford University Press, 2001).

11. Probably the single most important realization was that of the French linguist Michel Launey, "The Features of Omnipredicativity in Classical Nahuatl," *STUF: Journal of Linguistic Typology and Universals* [Berlin] 57 (2002): 1–13.

12. Those who did productive work with annals include Federico Navarrete Linares, who has compared annalistic accounts of the Nahua origin myths; the late Luis Reyes García, who worked with annals from the Puebla-Tlaxcala valley; Susan Schroeder, who worked with Chimalpahin's texts; and Rafael Tena, whose translations of several sets of annals have been inordinately valuable.

13. Walter Mignolo argued that as the remaining texts offered merely snippets of frozen text and failed to do justice to the once lively, vibrant oral tradition, it was a form of imperialism to study them. Miguel León-Portilla fought back. See his "Have We Really Translated the Mesoamerican 'Ancient Word'?" in *On the Translation of Native American Literatures*, ed. Brian Swann (Washington, DC: Smithsonian Institution Press, 1992). For Mignolo's full argument, including certain aspects of singular merit, see his *Darker Side of the Renaissance: Literacy, Territoriality, and Colonization* (Ann Arbor: University of Michigan Press, 1995).

14. David Lowenthal, *The Past is a Foreign Country* (New York: Cambridge University Press, 1985).

15. A thoughtful study by a psychologist of the fine line that historians and history teachers must walk, and the inherent difficulties of their task in teaching others to do the same, is Sam Wineburg, *Historical Thinking and Other Unnatural Acts: Charting the Future of Teaching the Past* (Philadelphia: Temple University Press, 2001).

16. A case in point: A recent article by Greg Anderson, "Retrieving the Lost Worlds of the Past: The Case for an Ontological Turn," *American Historical Review* 120 (2015): 787–810, effectively questions the use of such terms as "democracy" and "tyranny," which are ubiquitous in our studies of the ancient classical world. The author demonstrates how differently the people of the time thought about their polity and their dedication to their gods. I found the piece extraordinarily compelling, yet it was clear to me that had the author been making a case for the depth of difference between ourselves and an ancient American people, I would have condemned him as irresponsible. In short, the cultural prism through which we unintentionally look nearly always requires unique critical commentary in order to be rendered visible in each particular situation.

17. For a product of this moment in the debate, see Joyce Marcus, *Mesoamerican Writing Systems: Propaganda, Myth, and History in Four Ancient Civilizations* (Princeton, NJ: Princeton University Press, 1992).

18. James Lockhart was of this school of thought, as am I. A recent volume focusing on the question of what we can and cannot learn from the sources available to us in regard to one particular community is Jongsoo Lee and Galen Brokaw, eds., *Texcoco: Prehispanic and Colonial Perspectives* (Boulder: University Press of Colorado, 2014).

19. For instance, scholars have loved the notion of *yolia*, which they have understood as being closely akin to the European notion of the soul. However, careful scholarship has now proven that the word *yolia* as it is presently understood was a production of the Spanish era. See Justyna Olko and Julia Madajczak, "An Animating Principle in Confrontation with Christianity? De(Re)Constructing the Nahua 'Soul,'" *Ancient Mesoamérica* 30 (2019): 1–14.

20. These include the *Annals of Tlatelolco*, the *Annals of Cuauhtitlan*, the beginning of the *Codex Aubin*, the annals written by Tezozomoc and Chimalpahin, the *Bancroft Dialogues*, and the early segment of the work of don Juan Zapata. I also draw judiciously from don Fernando de Alva Ixtlilxochitl. He wrote in Spanish and seemed to feel increasingly free to develop his own thoughts, but his earliest work is clearly a reflection of older sources he had in hand. Likewise, the *Florentine Codex* is a mix of extraordinary detail coming to us in the words of people who came of age before the conquest, combined with statements that were very obviously made in response to leading questions posed by Spaniards with the intent to please the hearer. Readers will see that in some ways I trust the *Codex* to be a truly indigenous source—whenever it is not conveying a message desirable or even relevant to Europeans—and in other ways I do not. For more on this subject, see the relevant entries in the annotated bibliography found in the appendix.

Bibliography

Adorno, Rolena. *Colonial Latin American Literature: A Very Short Introduction*. New York: Oxford University Press, 2011.

Adorno, Rolena, ed. *From Oral to Written Expression: Native Andean Chronicles of the Early Colonial Period*. Syracuse, NY: Maxwell School of Citizenship and Public Affairs, 1982.

Alchon, Suzanne. *A Pest in the Land: New World Epidemics in Global Perspective*. Albuquerque: University of New Mexico Press, 2003.

Altman, Ida. *The War for Mexico's West: Indians and Spaniards in New Galicia, 1524–1550*. Albuquerque: University of New Mexico Press, 2010.

Alva, Jorge Klor de. "La historicidad de los coloquios de Sahagún." *Estudios de cultura náhuatl* 15 (1982): 147–84.

Anderson, Greg. "Retrieving the Lost Worlds of the Past: The Case for an Ontological Turn." *American Historical Review* 120 (2015): 787–810.

Andrews, Richard. *Introduction to Classical Nahuatl*. Norman: University of Oklahoma Press, 2003 [1975].

Ardren, Traci, ed. *Ancient Maya Women*. Lanham, MD: Rowman & Littlefield, 2002.

Arroyo, Salvador. "The Discovery of the Caja de Agua of Tlatelolco: Mural Painting from the Dawn of New Spain." *Colonial Latin American Review* 22 (2013): 19–38.

Augustine, Saint. *Confessions*. Edited by R. S. Pine-Coffin. New York: Penguin Books, 1961.

Barlow, Robert. "Anales de Tula, Hidalgo, 1361–1521." *Tlalocan* 3 (1949): 2–13.

Bennett, Herman. *Africans in Colonial Mexico: Absolutism, Christianity, and Afro-Creole Consciousness, 1570–1640*. Bloomington: Indiana University Press, 2003.

Benton, Bradley. *The Lords of Tetzcoco: The Transformation of Indigenous Rule in Post-conquest Central Mexico*. New York: Cambridge University Press, 2017.

Berdan, Frances. *Aztec Archaeology and Ethnohistory*. New York: Cambridge University Press, 2014.

Berdan, Frances. "Economic Alternatives under Imperial Rule: The Eastern Aztec Empire." In *Economies and Polities of the Aztec Realm*, edited by Mary G. Hodge and Michael E. Smith. Albany: State University of New York Press, 1994.

Bierhorst, John, ed. *Ballads of the Lords of New Spain*. Austin: University of Texas Press, 2009.

Bierhorst, John, ed. *Cantares Mexicanos*. Stanford, CA: Stanford University Press, 1985.

Bierhorst, John, ed. *History and Mythology of the Aztecs: The Codex Chimalpopoca*. Tucson: University of Arizona Press, 1992.

Bleichmar, Daniela. "History in Pictures: Translating the Codex Mendoza." *Art History* 38 (2015): 682–701.

Bleichmar, Daniela. "Painting the Aztec Past in Early Colonial Mexico: Translation and Knowledge Production in the Codex Mendoza." *Renaissance Quarterly* 72, no. 4 (Fall 2019).

Blitz, John. "Adoption of the Bow in Prehistoric North America." *North American Archaeologist* 9 (1988): 123–45.

Boone, Elizabeth Hill. *Cycles of Time and Meaning in the Mexican Books of Fate*. Austin: University of Texas Pres, 2007.

Boone, Elizabeth Hill. *Stories in Red and Black: Pictorial Histories of the Aztecs and Mixtecs*. Austin: University of Texas Press, 2000.

Boone, Elizabeth Hill, and Gary Urton, eds. *Their Way of Writing: Scripts, Signs and Pictographies in Pre-Columbian America*. Washington, DC: Dumbarton Oaks, 2011.

Boone, Elizabeth, Louise Burkhart, and David Tavárez, eds. *Painted Words: Nahuatl Catholicism, Politics, and Memory in the Atzacualco Pictorial Catechism*. Washington, DC: Dumbarton Oaks, 2017.

Borucki, Alex, David Eltis, and David Wheat. "Atlantic History and the Slave Trade to Spanish America." *American Historical Review* 120 (2015): 433–61.

Bowser, Frederick. "Africans in Spanish American Colonial Society." In *The Cambridge History of Latin America*, vol. 2, edited by Leslie Bethell. New York: Cambridge University Press, 1984.

Brading, David. *The First America: The Spanish Monarchy, Creole Patriots, and the Liberal State, 1492–1867*. New York: Cambridge University Press, 1991.

Braswell, Geoffrey. *The Maya and Teotihuacan: Reinterpreting Early Classic Interaction*. Austin: University of Texas Press, 2003.

Brewster, Paul G. "The Foundation Sacrifice Motif in Legend, Folksong, Game and Dance." *Zeitschrift für Ethnologie* 96 (1971): 71–89.

Brian, Amber. *Alva Ixtlilxochitl's Native Archive and the Circulation of Knowledge in Colonial Mexico*. Nashville, TN: Vanderbilt University Press, 2016.

Brian, Amber. "Don Fernando de Alva Ixtlilxochitl's Narratives of the Conquest of Mexico." In *The Conquest All Over Again*, edited by Susan Schroeder. Brighton, England: Sussex Academic Press, 2010.

Brian, Amber. "The Original Alva Ixtlilxochitl Manuscripts at Cambridge University." *Colonial Latin American Review* 23 (2014): 84–101.

Brian, Amber, Bradley Benton, and Pablo García Loaza, eds. *The Native Conquistador: Alva Ixtlilxochitl's Account of the Conquest of New Spain*. College Park: Pennsylvania State University Press, 2015.

Brokaw, Galen, and Jongsoo Lee, eds. *Fernando de Alva Ixtlilxochitl and His Legacy.* Tucson: University of Arizona Press, 2016.

Brooks, Francis. "Moteuczoma Xocoyotl, Hernán Cortés, and Bernal Díaz del Castillo: The Construction of an Arrest." *Hispanic American Historical Review* 75 (1995): 149–83.

Bruhns, Karen Olsen, and Karen Stothert. *Women in Ancient America.* Norman: University of Oklahoma Press, 1999.

Brumfiel, Elizabeth. "Weaving and Cooking: Women's Production in Aztec Mexico." In *Engendering Archaeology: Women and Prehistory*, edited by J. M. Gero and M. W. Conkey. New York: Cambridge University Press, 1991.

Burkhart, Louise. *Before Guadalupe: The Virgin Mary in Early Colonial Nahuatl Literature.* Albany, NY: Institute for Mesoamerican Studies, 2001.

Burkhart, Louise. "Mexica Women on the Home Front: Housework and Religion in Aztec Mexico." In *Indian Women of Early Mexico,* edited by Susan Shroeder, Stephanie Wood, and Robert Haskett. Norman: University of Oklahoma Press, 1997.

Burkhart, Louise. *The Slippery Earth: Nahua-Christian Moral Dialogue in Sixteenth-Century Mexico.* Tucson: University of Arizona Press, 1989.

Burns, E. Bradford. *The Poverty of Progress: Latin America in the Nineteenth Century.* Los Angeles: University of California Press, 1980.

Candiani, Vera. *Dreaming of Dry Land: Environmental Transformation in Colonial Mexico City.* Stanford, CA: Stanford University Press, 2014.

Cañeque, Alejandro. *The King's Living Image: The Culture and Politics of Vice-regal Power in Colonial Mexico.* New York: Routledge, 2004.

Carillo Castro, Alejandro. *The Dragon and the Unicorn.* Mexico City, 2014 [1996].

Carmack, Robert, ed. *The Legacy of Mesoamerica: History and Culture of a Native American Civilization* Albany, NY: Institute for Mesoamerican Studies, 1996.

Carochi, Horacio, S.J. *Grammar of the Mexican Language.* Edited by James Lockhart. Stanford, CA: Stanford University Press, 2001 [1645].

Carrasco, David. *City of Sacrifice: The Aztec Empire and the Role of Violence in Civilization.* Boston: Beacon Press, 1999.

Carrasco, David, and Scott Sessions, eds. *Cave, City, and Eagle's Nest: An Interpretive Journey through the Mapa de Cuauhtinchan No. 2.* Albuquerque: University of New Mexico Press, 2007.

Carrasco, David, Lindsay Jones, and Scott Sessions, eds. *Mesoamerica's Classic Heritage: From Teotihuacan to the Aztecs.* Boulder: University of Colorado Press, 2000.

Carrasco, Pedro. "Royal Marriages in Ancient Mexico." In *Explorations in Ethnohistory: The Indians of Central Mexico in the Sixteenth Century*, edited by H. R. Harvey and H. Premm. Albuquerque: University of New Mexico Press, 1984.

Carrasco, Pedro. *The Tenochca Empire of Ancient Mexico: The Triple Alliance of Tenochtitlan, Tetzcoco, and Tlacopan.* Norman: University of Oklahoma Press, 1999.

Carrión, Antonio. *Historia de la Ciudad de Puebla de los Angeles.* Puebla, Mexico: José Cajica, 1970 [1897].

Castañeda de Paz, María. "Historia de una casa real: Origen y ocaso del linaje gobernante en México-Tenochtitlan." *Nuevo Mundo, Mundos Nuevos* (2011): 1–20.

Castillo Palma, Norma Angelica, and Susan Kellogg. "Conflict and Cohabitation between Afro-Mexicans and Nahuas in Central Mexico." In *Beyond Black and Red: African-Native Relations in Colonial Latin America*, edited by Matthew Restall. Albuquerque: University of New Mexico Press, 2005.

Celestino Solis, Eustaquio, and Luis Reyes García, eds. *Anales de Tecamachalco, 1398–1590*. Mexico City: Centro de Investigaciones y Estudios Superiores en Antropología Social, 1992.

Chang Rodríguez, Raquel. *La apropriación del signo: tres cronistas indígenas del Perú*. Tempe: Arizona State University Press, 1988.

Chapman, Anne. "Port of Trade Enclaves in Aztec and Maya Civilizations." In *Trade and Market in the Early Empires*, edited by Karl Polyani, Conrad Arensberg, and Harry Pearson. Glencoe, IL: Free Press, 1957.

Chávez Baldera, Ximena. "Sacrifice at the Templo Mayor of Tenochtitlan and Its Role in Regard to Warfare." In *Embattled Bodies, Embattled Places: War in Pre-Columbian Mesoamerica and the Andes*, edited by Andrew Scherer and John Verano. Washington, DC: Dumbarton Oaks, 2014.

Chávez Orozco, Luis, ed. *Códice Osuna accompañado de 158 páginas inéditas encontradas en el Archivo General de la Nación*. Mexico City: Instituto Indigenista Interamericano, 1947.

Chimalpahin Quauhtlehuanitzin, don Domingo de San Antón. *Annals of His Time*. Edited by James Lockhart, Susan Schroeder and Doris Namala. Stanford, CA: Stanford University Press, 2006.

Chimalpahin Quauhtlehuanitzin, don Domingo de San Antón. *Chimalpahin's Conquest*. Edited by Susan Schroeder, Anna J. Cruz, Cristián Roa-de-la-Carrera, and David Tavárez. Stanford, CA: Stanford University Press, 2010.

Chimalpahin Quauhtlehuanitzin, don Domingo de San Antón. *Codex Chimalpahin*. Edited by Arthur J. O. Anderson and Susan Schroeder. 2 vols. Norman: University of Oklahoma Press, 1997.

Chimalpahin Quauhtlehuanitzin, don Domingo de San Antón. *Las Ocho relaciones y el Memorial de Colhuacan*. Edited by Rafael Tena. 2 vols. Mexico City: Conaculta, 1998.

Chipman, Donald. "Isabel Moctezuma." In *Struggle and Survival in Colonial Latin America*, edited by David Sweet and Gary Nash. Los Angeles: University of California Press, 1981.

Chipman, Donald. *Moctezuma's Children: Aztec Royalty under Spanish Rule*. Austin: University of Texas Press, 2005.

Ciudad Real, Antonio de. *Tratado curioso y docto de la grandeza de la Nueva España*. Mexico City: Universidad Nacional Autónoma de México, 1976 [1584].

Clendinnen, Inga. *Aztecs: An Interpretation*. New York: Cambridge University Press, 1991.

Clendinnen, Inga. "'Fierce and Unnatural Cruelty': Cortés and the Conquest of Mexico," *Representations* 33 (1991): 65–100.

Cline, S. L., ed. *The Book of Tributes: Early Sixteenth-Century Nahuatl Censuses from Morelos.* Los Angeles: UCLA Latin American Center Publications, 1993.

Coe, Michael. *Breaking the Maya Code.* New York: Thames & Hudson, 1992.

Colmenares, David. "How the Aztecs Got a Pantheon: The Creation of Ancient Religion in New Spain." PhD diss., Department of Spanish, Columbia University, 2019.

Colston, Stephen. "'No Longer Will There Be a Mexico': Omens, Prophecies and the Conquest of the Aztec Empire." *American Indian Quarterly* 5 (1985): 239–58.

Cope, R. Douglas. *The Limits of Racial Domination: Plebeian Society in Colonial Mexico City, 1660–1720.* Madison: University of Wisconsin Press, 1994.

Cortés, Hernán. *Letters from Mexico.* Edited by Anthony Pagden. New Haven, CT: Yale University Press, 1986.

Crapo, Richley, and Bonnie Glass-Coffin, eds. *Anónimo Mexicano.* Logan: Utah State University Press, 2005.

Criales, Jessica Nelson. "'Women of Our Nation': Gender and Christian Indian Communities in the United States and Mexico, 1725-1850." *Early American Studies* 17, no. 4 (fall 2019).

Cuevas, Mariano, ed. *Cartas y otros documentos de Hernán Cortés.* Seville: F. Díaz, 1915.

Curcio-Nagy, Linda. *The Great Festivals of Colonial Mexico City.* Albuquerque: University of New Mexico Press, 2004.

Daniels, Peter, and William Bright, eds. *The World's Writing Systems.* New York: Oxford University Press, 1996.

De la Torre Villar, Ernesto, and Ramiro Navarra de Anda, eds. *Testimonios Históricos Guadalupanos.* Mexico City: Fondo de Cultura Económica, 1982.

Diamond, Jared. *Guns, Germs, and Steel.* New York: Norton, 1997.

Díaz, Bernal. *The Conquest of New Spain.* Edited by J. M. Cohen. New York: Penguin Books, 1963.

Díaz, Bernal. *Historia verdadera de la conquista de la Nueva España.* Mexico City: Porrúa, 1960.

Díaz, María Elena. "The Black Blood of New Spain: Limpieza de Sangre, Racial Violence, and Gendered Power in Early Colonial Mexico." *William & Mary Quarterly* 61 (2003): 479–520.

Díaz Balsera, Viviana. *The Pyramid under the Cross: Franciscan Discourses of Evangelization and the Nahua Christian Subject in Sixteenth-Century Mexico.* Tucson: University of Arizona Press, 2005.

Dibble, Charles, ed. *Historia de la Nación Mexicana.* Madrid: Porrúa, 1963.

Diehl, Richard. *The Olmecs: America's First Civilization.* New York: Thames & Hudson, 2004.

Diel, Lori Boornazian. *The Codex Mexicanus: A Guide to Life in Late Sixteenth-Century New Spain.* Austin: University of Texas Press, 2018.

Diel, Lori Boornazian. *The Tira de Tepechpan: Negotiating Place Under Aztec and Spanish Rule*. Austin: University of Texas Press, 2008.

Don, Patricia Lopes. *Bonfires of Culture: Franciscans, Indigenous Leaders, and Inquisition in Early Mexico, 1524–1540*. Norman: University of Oklahoma Press, 2010.

Dunn, Oliver, ed. *The Diario of Christopher Columbus's First Voyage to America*. Norman: University of Oklahoma Press, 1989.

Durán, fray Diego. *The History of the Indies of New Spain*. Edited by Doris Heyden. Norman: University of Oklahoma Press, 1994 [1964].

Durston, Alan, and Bruce Mannheim, eds. *Indigenous Languages, Politics, and Authority in Latin America: Historical and Ethnographic Perspectives*. Notre Dame, IN: University of Notre Dame Press, 2018.

Edmonson, Munro. *The Book of the Year: Middle American Calendrical Systems*. Salt Lake City: University of Utah Press, 1988.

Elliott, John. "Introductory Essay" to Hernando Cortés, *Letters from Mexico*, edited by Anthony Pagden. New Haven, CT: Yale University Press, 1986.

Eltis, David, and Allen Tullos. *Voyages: The Trans-Atlantic Slave Trade Database*. http://www.slavevoyages.org.

Escalante Gonzalbo, Pablo. "El Patrocinio del arte indocristiano en el siglo XVI. La iniciativa de las autoridades indígenas en Tlaxcala y Cuauhtinchan." In *Patrocinio, colección y circulación de las artes*, edited by Gustavo Curiel. Mexico City: UNAM, 1997.

Evans, Susan Toby. *Ancient Mexico and Central America*. New York: Thames & Hudson, 2013 [2004].

Farris, Nancy. *Tongues of Fire: Language and Evangelization in Colonial Mexico*. New York: Oxford University Press, 2018.

Fenn, Elizabeth. *Pox Americana: The Great Smallpox Epidemic of 1775–82*. New York: Hill & Wang, 2001.

Fernández Armesto, Felipe. "Aztec Auguries and Memories of the Conquest of Mexico." *Renaissance Studies* 6 (1992): 287–305.

Foster, Michael, and Shirley Gorenstein, eds. *Greater Mesoamerica: The Archaeology of West and Northwest Mexico*. Salt Lake City: University of Utah Press, 2000.

Fuentes, Patricia, ed. *The Conquistadors: First Person Accounts of the Conquest of Mexico*. Norman: University of Oklahoma Press, 1993.

García Castro, René. *Indios, territorio y poder en la provincia Matlatzinca: La negociación del espacio politico de los pueblos otomianos, siglos XV-XVII*. Toluca: Colejio Mexiquense, 1999.

García Icazbalceta, Joaquín, ed. *Nueva colección de documentos para la historia de México*. Liechtenstein: Kraus Reprints, 1971 [1886].

García Loaeza, Pablo. "Deeds to be Praised for All Time: Alva Ixtlilxochitl's *Historia de la nación chichimeca* and Geoffrey of Monmouth's *History of the Kings of Britain*." *Colonial Latin American Review* 23 (2014): 53–69.

Gates, Henry Lewis. *Black in Latin America*. New York: New York University Press, 2011.

Gero, J. M., and M. W. Conkey, eds. *Engendering Archaeology: Women and Prehistory*. New York: Cambridge University Press, 1991.

Gibson, Charles. *The Aztecs Under Spanish Rule*. Stanford, CA: Stanford University Press, 1964.

Gibson, Charles. *Tlaxcala in the Sixteenth Century*. New Haven, CT: Yale University Press, 1952.

Gillespie, Susan. *Aztec Kings: The Construction of Rulership in Mexica History*. Tucson: University of Arizona Press, 1989.

Gómara, Francisco López de. *Cortés: The Life of the Conqueror by His Secretary*. Edited by Leslie Byrd Simpson. Los Angeles: University of California Press, 1965.

Gómez García, Lidia. *Los anales nahuas de la ciudad de Puebla de los Angeles, siglos XVI y XVII*. Puebla, Mexico: Ayuntamiento de Puebla, 2018.

Gómez García, Lidia, Celia Salazar Exaire, and María Elena Stefanón, eds. *Anales del Barrio de San Juan del Rio*. Puebla, Mexico: Benemérita Universidad Autónoma de Puebla, 2000.

Gonzalbo Aizpuru, Pilar. *Historia de la educación en la época colonial: El mundo indígena*. Mexico City: El Colegio de México, 1990.

Gradie, Charlotte. "Spanish Jesuits in Virginia: The Mission that Failed." *Virginia Magazine of History and Biography* 96 (1988): 131–56.

Graulich, Michel. *Moctezuma: Apogeo y Caída del Imperio Azteca*. Mexico City: Ediciones Era, 2014 [1994].

Gruzinski, Serge. *Conquest of Mexico: The Incorporation of Indian Societies into the Western World, 16th–18th Centuries*. London: Blackwell, 1995.

Guijo, Gregorio Martín del. *Diario*. 2 vols. Mexico City: Porrúa, 1952.

Haskett, Robert. *Indigenous Rulers: An Ethnohistory of Town Government in Colonial Cuernavaca*. Albuquerque: University of New Mexico Press, 1991.

Haskett, Robert. *Visions of Paradise: Primordial Titles and Mesoamerican History in Cuernavaca*. Norman: University of Oklahoma Press, 2005.

Hassig, Ross. "The Maid of the Myth: La Malinche and the History of Mexico." *Indiana Journal of Hispanic Literatures* 12 (1998): 101–33.

Hassig, Ross. *Polygamy and the Rise and Demise of the Aztec Empire*. Albuquerque: University of New Mexico Press, 2016.

Hassig, Ross. *Time, History and Belief in Aztec and Colonial Mexico*. Austin: University of Texas Press, 2001.

Heitman, Carrie, and Stephen Plog. *Chaco Revisited: New Research on the Prehistory of Chaco Canyon, New Mexico*. Tucson: University of Arizona Press, 2015.

Hernández Sánchez-Barba, Mario, ed. *Hernando Cortés: cartas y documentos*. Mexico City: Porrúa, 1963.

Herren, Ricardo. *Doña Marina, la Malinche*. Mexico City: Planeta, 1992.

Himmerich y Valencia, Robert. *The Encomenderos of New Spain.* Austin: University of Texas Press, 1991.

Hodge, Mary G., and Michael E. Smith, eds. *Economies and Polities of the Aztec Realm.* Albany: State University of New York Press, 1994.

Horn, Rebecca. *Postconquest Coyoacan: Nahua-Spanish Relations in Central Mexico, 1519–1650.* Stanford, CA: Stanford University Press, 1997.

Houston, Stephen, John Baines, and Jerrold Cooper. "Last Writing: Script Obsolescence in Egypt, Mesopotamia and Mesoamerica." *Comparative Studies in Society and History* 45 (2003): 430–79.

Hutton, Ronald. *Blood and Mistletoe: The History of the Druids in Britain.* New Haven, CT: Yale University Press, 2009.

Ixtlilxochitl, Fernando de Alva. *Obras Completas.* 2 vols. Edited by Edmundo O'Gorman. Mexico City: Universidad Nacional Autónoma de México, 1975–77.

Jeffres, Travis. " 'In Case I Die Where I Am Selected To Be Sent': Coercion and the Tlaxcalan Resettlement of 1591." *Ethnohistory* 66 (2019): 95–116.

Justeson, John, and Terrence Kaufman. "A Decipherment of Epi-Olmec Hieroglyphic Writing." *Science* 259 (1993): 1703–11.

Kalyuta, Anastasia. "El arte de acomodarse a dos mundos: la vida de don Pedro de Moctezuma Tlacahuepantli segun los documentos del Archivo General de la Nación (México) y el Archivo General de Indias (Sevilla)." *Revista Española de Antropología Americana* 41 (2010): 471–500.

Kartunnen, Frances. *An Analytical Dictionary of Nahuatl.* Norman: University of Oklahoma Press, 1992 [1983].

Kartunnen, Frances. "Rethinking Malinche." In *Indian Women of Early Mexico,* edited by Susan Schroeder, Stephanie Wood, and Robert Haskett. Norman: University of Oklahoma Press, 1997.

Kartunnen, Frances, and James Lockhart, eds. *The Art of Nahuatl Speech: The Bancroft Dialogues.* Los Angeles: UCLA Latin American Center Publications, 1987.

Kauffmann, Leisa. *The Legacy of Rulership in Fernando de Alva Ixtlilxochitl's Historia de la nación chichimeca.* Albuquerque: University of New Mexico Press, 2019.

Kaufman, Terrence. "Native Languages of Mesoamerica." In *Atlas of the World's Languages.* New York: Routledge, 1994.

Keen, Benjamin. *The Aztec Image in Western Thought.* New Brunswick, NJ: Rutgers University Press, 1971.

Kellogg, Susan. "The Women's Room: Some Aspects of Gender Relations in Tenochtitlan in the Late Pre-Hispanic Period." *Ethnohistory* 42 (1995): 563–76.

Kicza, John, and Rebecca Horn. *Resilient Cultures: America's Native Peoples Confront European Colonization, 1500–1800.* Boston: Pearson, 2013.

Kirchoff, Paul, Lina Odena Güemes, and Luis Reyes García, eds. *Historia Tolteca Chichimeca.* Mexico City: Instituto Nacional de Antropología e Historia, 1976.

Kranz, Travis. "The Tlaxcalan Conquest Pictorials." PhD diss., UCLA, Department of Art History, 2001.

Lanyon, Anna. Malinche's *Conquest*. St Leonards, Australia: Allen & Unwin, 1999.

Lanyon, Anna. *The New World of Martín Cortés*. New York: DaCapo, 2003.

Launey, Michel. "The Features of Omnipredicativity in Classical Nahuatl." *STUF: Journal of Linguistic Typology and Universals* [Berlin] 57 (2002): 1–13.

Launey, Michel. *An Introduction to Classical Nahuatl*. New York: Cambridge University Press, 2011 [1979].

Lee, Jongsoo. *The Allure of Nezahualcoyotl: Pre-Hispanic History, Religion, and Nahua Poetics*. Albuquerque: University of New Mexico Press, 2008.

Lee, Jongsoo. "The Aztec Triple Alliance: A Colonial Transformation of the Prehispanic Political and Tributary System." In *Texcoco: Prehispanic and Colonial Perspectives*, edited by Jongsoo Lee and Galen Brokaw. Boulder: University of Colorado Press, 2014.

Lee, Jongsoo, and Galen Brokaw, eds. *Texcoco: Prehispanic and Colonial Perspectives*. Boulder: University of Colorado Press, 2014.

Leeming, Ben. "Micropoetics: The Poetry of Hypertrophic Words in Early Colonial Nahuatl." *Colonial Latin American Review* 24 (2025): 168–89.

Lehmann, Walter, and Gerdt Kutscher, eds. *Geschichte der Aztekan: Codex Aubin und verwandte Documente*. Berlin: Gebr. Mann, 1981.

Leibsohn, Dana. *Script and Glyph: Pre-Hispanic History, Colonial Bookmaking, and the Historia Tolteca Chichimeca*. Washington, DC: Dumbarton Oaks, 2009.

Lekson, Stephen, ed. *The Archaeology of Chaco Canyon: An Eleventh-Century Pueblo Regional Center*. Santa Fe, NM: School of American Research, 2006.

León-Portilla, Miguel. *Bernardino de Sahagún: First Anthropologist*. Norman: University of Oklahoma Press, 2002.

León-Portilla, Miguel. *The Broken Spears*. Boston: Beacon Press, 1962 [1959].

León-Portilla, Miguel, ed. *Cantares Mexicanos*. 3 vols. Mexico City: Universidad Nacional Autónoma de México, 2011.

León-Portilla, Miguel, ed. *Coloquios y doctrina cristiana*. Mexico City: Universidad Nacional Autónoma de México, 1986.

León-Portilla, Miguel. *Fifteen Poets of the Aztec World*. Norman: University of Oklahoma Press, 1992.

León-Portilla, Miguel. "Have We Really Translated the Mesoamerican Ancient Word"? In *On the Translation of Native American Literatures*, edited by Brian Swann. Washington, DC: Smithsonian Institution Press, 1992.

León-Portilla, Miguel, and Earl Shorris, eds. *In the Language of Kings: An Anthology of Mesoamerican Literature*. New York: Norton, 2001.

Lewis, Laura. *Power, Witchcraft and Caste in Colonial Mexico*. Durham, NC: Duke University Press, 2003.

Lockhart, James. *The Nahuas After the Conquest*. Stanford, CA: Stanford University Press, 1992.

Lockhart, James. *Nahuas and Spaniards: Postconquest Central Mexican History and Philology*. Stanford, CA: Stanford University Press, 1991.

Lockhart, James. *Nahuatl as Written*. Stanford, CA: Stanford University Press, 2001.

Lockhart, James. "Some Nahua Concepts in Postconquest Guise." *History of European Ideas* 6 (1985): 465–82.

Lockhart, James, ed. *We People Here: Nahuatl Accounts of the Conquest of Mexico*. Los Angeles: University of California Press, 1993.

Lockhart, James, and Stuart Schwartz. *Early Latin America*. New York: Cambridge University Press, 1983.

López Austin, Alfredo. *The Myth of Quetzalcoatl: Religion, Rulership, and History in the Nahua World*. Translated by Russ Davidson with Guilhem Olivier from the Spanish *Hombre-Dios: Religión y política en el mundo náhuatl*. Boulder: University Press of Colorado, 2015 [1973].

López Austin, Alfredo. "The Research Method of Fray Bernardino de Sahagún." In *Sixteenth-Century Mexico: The Work of Sahagún*, edited by Munro Edmonson. Albuquerque: University of New Mexico Press, 1974.

López Luján, Leonardo. *The Offerings of the Templo Mayor of Tenochtitlan*. Boulder: University Press of Colorado, 1994.

López de Meneses, Amada. "Tecuichpotzin, hija de Moctezuma." In *Estudios cortesanos: recopilados con motive del IV centenario de la muerte de Hernán Cortés*. Madrid: Consejo Superior de Investigaciones Científicas, 1948.

López Rayón, Ignacio, ed. *Proceso de residencia instruido contra Pedro de Alvarado y Nuño de Guzman*. Mexico City: Valdes y Redondas, 1847.

Lowenthal, David. *The Past Is a Foreign Country*. New York: Cambridge University Press, 1995.

Madajczak, Julia. "Nahuatl Kinship Terminology as Reflected in Colonial Written Sources from Central Mexico: A System of Classification." PhD diss., University of Warsaw, Poland, 2014.

Malanga, Tara. "'Earth Is No One's Home': Nahuatl Perceptions of Illness, Death, and Dying in the Early Colonial Period, 1520–1650." PhD diss., Rutgers University, Department of History, 2019.

Marcus, Joyce. *Mesoamerican Writing Systems: Propaganda, Myth, and History in Four Ancient Civilizations*. Princeton, NJ: Princeton University Press, 1992.

Martínez, Enrico. *El Reportorio de los tiempos e historia natural de Nueva España*. Mexico City: Novum, 1991 [1606].

Martínez, José Luis, ed. *Documentos Cortesianos*. Mexico City: Fondo de la Cultura Económica, 1990.

Martínez Baracs, Andrea. *Un Gobierno de indios: Tlaxcala, 1519–1750*. Mexico City: Centro de Investigaciones y Estudios Superiores en Antropología Social, 2008.

Martínez Baracs, Rodrigo. *Convivencia y utopia: El gobierno indio y español de la "ciudad de Mechuacan," 1521–1580*. Mexico City: Científica, 2017 [2005].

Martínez Baracs, Rodrigo. "De Tepeaquilla a Tepeaca, 1528–1555." *Andes* 17 (2006).

Martínez Baracs, Rodrigo. "El Diario de Chimalpahin." *Estudios de cultura náhuatl* 38 (2007).

Martínez Martínez, María del Carmen. *Martín Cortés: pasos recuperados (1532–1562)*. León, Spain: Universidad de León, 2018.

Matos Moctezuma, Eduardo. *Life and Death in the Templo Mayor*. Boulder: University Press of Colorado, 1995.

McDonough, Kelly. *The Learned Ones: Nahua Intellectuals in Postconquest Mexico*. Tucson: University of Arizona Press, 2014.

Medina Lima, Constantino, ed. *Libro de los guardianes y gobernadores de Cuauhtinchan*. Mexico City: Centro de Investigaciones y Estudios Superiores en Antropología Social, 1995.

Megged, Amos. *Social Memory in Ancient and Colonial Mesoamerica*. New York: Cambridge University Press, 2010.

Mendoza, Celso. "Scribal Culture, Indigenous Modes and Nahuatl-Language Sources, 16th through 18th Centuries." In *Oxford Research Encyclopedia of Latin American History*, edited by William Beezley. New York: Oxford University Press, forthcoming 2020.

Mengin, Ernst, ed. *Unos annales de la nación Mexicana*. Copenhagen: Einar Munksgaard, 1945.

Metzer, David. *First Peoples in a New World: Colonizing Ice Age America*. Los Angeles: University of California Press, 2009.

Mignolo, Walter. *The Darker Side of the Renaissance: Literacy, Territoriality and Colonization*. Ann Arbor: University of Michigan Press, 1995.

Miller, Mary, and Karl Taube. *An Illustrated Dictionary of the Gods and Symbols of Ancient Mexico and the Maya*. London: Thames & Hudson, 1993.

Mills, Kenneth, William B. Taylor, and Sandra Lauderdale Graham, eds., *Colonial Latin America: A Documentary History*. Wilmington, DE: Scholarly Resources, 2002.

Molina, fray Alonso. *Vocabulario en Lengua Castellana y Mexicana y Mexicana y Castellana*. Mexico City: Porrúa, 1992.

Monmouth, Geoffrey of. *History of the Kings of Britain*. Edited by Lewis Thorpe. London: Folio Society, 1969.

Motolinía, fray Toribio de Benavente. *Historia de los Indios de la Nueva España*. Madrid: Alianza, 1988 [1555].

Mundy, Barbara. *The Death of Tenochtitlan, the Life of Mexico City*. Austin: University of Texas Press, 2015.

Nava Nava, Refugio. *Malintzin Itlahtol*. Warsaw, Poland: Faculty of Liberal Arts, 2013.

Navarrete Linares, Federico, ed. *Historia de la venida de los mexicanos y otros pueblos*. Mexico City: Instituto Nacional de Antropología e Historia, 1991.

Navarrete Linares, Federico. *Los orígenes de los pueblos indígenas del valle de México: Los altepetl y sus historias*. Mexico City: Universidad Autónoma de México, 2015.

Nelson, Ben. "Mesoamerican Objects and Symbols in Chaco Canyon Contexts." In *The Archaeology of Chaco Canyon: An Eleventh-Century Pueblo Regional Center*, edited by Stephen Lekson. Santa Fe, NM: School of American Research, 2006.

Nesvig, Martin. "The 'Indian Question' and the Case of Tlatelolco." In *Local Religion in Colonial Mexico,* edited by Martin Nesvig. Albuquerque: University of New Mexico Press, 2006.

Nesvig, Martin. *Promiscuous Power: An Unorthodox History of New Spain.* Austin: University of Texas Press, 2018.

Nesvig, Martin. "Spanish Men, Indigenous Language, and Informal Interpreters in Postcontact Mexico." *Ethnohistory* 19 (2012): 739–64.

Offner, Jerome. "Ixtlilxochitl's Ethnographic Encounter: Understanding the Codex Xolotl and Its Dependent Alphabetic Texts." In *Fernando de Alva Ixtlilxochitl and His Legacy*, edited by Galen Brokaw and Jongsoo Lee. Tucson: University of Arizona Press, 2016.

Offner, Jerome. *Law and Politics in Aztec Texcoco.* New York: Cambridge University Press, 1983.

O'Gorman, Edmundo. *Destierro de Sombras: Luz en el orígen de la imagen y culta de Nuestra Señora de Guadalupe.* Mexico City: Universidad Nacional Autónoma de México, 1986.

Olivier, Guilhem. *Mockeries and Metamorphoses of an Aztec God: Tezcatlipoca, "Lord of the Smoking Mirror."* Boulder: University Press of Colorado, 2003.

Olko, Justyna. *Insignia of Rank in the Nahua World: From the Fifteenth to the Seventeenth Century.* Boulder: University Press of Colorado, 2014.

Olko, Justyna, and Agnieska Brylak. "Defending Local Autonomy and Facing Cultural Trauma: A Nahua Order Against Idolatry, Tlaxcala 1543." *Hispanic American Historical Review* 94 (2018): 573–604.

Olko, Justyna, and Julia Madajczak. "An Animating Principle in Confrontation with Christianity? De(Re)constructing the Nahua 'Soul.'" *Ancient Mesoamerica* 30 (2019): 1–14.

Orozco y Berra, Manuel, ed. *Noticia histórica de la conjuración del Marqués del Valle, 1565–1568.* Mexico City: R. Rafael, 1853.

Otte, Enrique. "Nueve Cartas de Diego de Ordás." *Historia Mexicana* 14, no. 1 (1964): 102–30 and 14, no. 2 (1964): 321–38.

Oudijk, Michel, and Laura Matthew, eds. *Indian Conquistadors: Indigenous Allies in the Conquest of Mesoamerica.* Norman: University of Oklahoma Press, 2007.

Oudijk, Michel, and Matthew Restall. "Mesoamerican Conquistadors in the Sixteenth Century." In *Indian Conquistadors: Indigenous Allies in the Conquest of Mesoamerica*, edited by Michel Oudijk and Laura Matthew. Norman: University of Oklahoma Press, 2007.

Pacheco, Joaquín, ed. *Colección de documentos inéditos relativos al descubrimiento, conquista y colonización de las posesiones españolas en América y Oceania.* 42 vols. Madrid: Manuel Bernaldos de Quirós, 1864–84.

Palmer, Colin. *Slaves of the White God: Blacks in Mexico, 1570–1650.* Cambridge, MA: Harvard University Press, 1976.

Paso y Troncoso, Francisco del, ed. *Historia de las Cosas de Nueva España: Códices matritenses.* 3 vols. Madrid: Hauser y Menet, 1906–7.

Pasztory, Esther. *Teotihuacan: An Experiment in Living*. Norman: University of Oklahoma Press, 1997.

Pennock, Caroline Dodds. *Bonds of Blood: Gender, Lifestyle and Sacrifice in Aztec Culture*. London: Palgrave Macmillan, 2008.

Pérez Rocha, Emma, and Rafael Tena, eds. *La nobleza indígena del centro de México después de la conquista*. Mexico City: Instituto Nacional de Antropología e Historia, 2000.

Pierce, Donna, and Ronald Otuska, eds. *Asia and Spanish America: Transpacific Artistic and Cultural Heritage, 1500–1850*. Denver, CO: Denver Art Museum, 2009.

Pillsbury, Joanne, Patricia Sarro, James Doyle, and Juliet Wiersema. *Design for Eternity: Architectural Models from the Ancient Americas*. New York: Metropolitan Museum of Art, 2015.

Pillsbury, Joanne, Timothy Potts, and Kim Richter, eds. *Golden Kingdoms: Luxury Arts in the Ancient Americas*. Los Angeles: Getty Publications, 2017.

Pizzigoni, Caterina. *The Life Within: Local Indigenous Society in Mexico's Toluca Valley*. Stanford, CA: Stanford University Press, 2012.

Pizzigoni, Caterina. *Testaments of Toluca*. Los Angeles: UCLA Latin American Center Publications. Stanford, CA: Stanford University Press, 2007.

Pizzigoni, Caterina, and Camilla Townsend, eds. *Indian Life After the Conquest: The De la Cruz Family Papers of Colonial Mexico*. Unpublished manuscript.

Pollack, John H. "Native American Words, Early American Texts." PhD diss., Department of English, University of Pennsylvania, 2014.

Polyani, Karl, Conrad Arensberg, and Harry Pearson, eds., *Trade and Market in the Early Empires*. Glencoe, IL: Free Press, 1957.

Pomar, Juan. "Relación de Tetzcoco." In *Relaciones de Nueva España*, edited by Germán Vázquez. Madrid: *Historia* 16, 1991.

Poole, Stafford. *The Guadalupan Controversies in Mexico*. Stanford, CA: Stanford University Press, 2006.

Prem, Hanns. *The Ancient Americas: A Brief History and Guide to Research*. Salt Lake City: University of Utah Press, 1997 [1989].

Price, Richard. *Alabi's World*. Baltimore, MD: Johns Hopkins University Press, 1991.

Price, Richard. *Maroon Societies: Rebel Slave Communities in the Americas*. Baltimore, MD: Johns Hopkins University Press, 1979.

Querol y Roso, Luis. "Negros y mulatos de Nueva España." *Anales de la Universidad de Valencia* 12 (1931–32): 141–53.

Quiñones Keber, Eloise, ed. *Codex Telleriano-Remensis*. Austin: University of Texas Press, 1995.

Restall, Matthew. *The Black Middle: Africans, Mayas, and Spaniards in Colonial Yucatan*. Stanford, CA: Stanford University Press, 2009.

Restall, Matthew. *Seven Myths of the Spanish Conquest*. New York: Oxford University Press, 2003.

Restall, Matthew. *When Montezuma Met Cortés: The True Story of the Meeting that Changed History*. New York: HarperCollins, 2018.

Restall, Matthew, and Amanda Solari. *2012 and the End of the World: The Western Roots of the Maya Apocalypse*. Lanham, MD: Rowman & Littlefield, 2011.

Reyes García, Luis, ed. *¿Como te confundes? ¿Acaso no somos conquistados? Los anales de Juan Bautista*. Mexico City: Centro de Investigaciones y Estudios Superiores en Antropología Social, 2001.

Reyes García, Luis. *Cuauhtinchan del Siglo XII a XVI*. Wiesbaden, Germany: Franz Steiner, 1977.

Reyes García, Luis, ed. *Documentos sobre tierras y señorios en Cuauhtinchan*. Mexico City: Instituto Nacional de Antropología e Historia, 1978.

Riedler, Renée. "Materials and Technique of the Feather Shield Preserved in Vienna." In *Images Take Flight: Feather Art in Mexico and Europe, 1400-1700*, edited by Alessandra Russo, Gerhard Wolf and Diana Fane. Florence, Italy: Kunsthistorisches Institut in Florenz, 2015.

Robertson, Donald. *Mexican Manuscript Painting of the Early Colonial Period: The Metropolitan Schools*. New Haven, CT: Yale University Press, 1959.

Ricard, Robert. *The Spiritual Conquest of Mexico*. Los Angeles: University of California Press, 1966 [1933].

Riva Palacio, Vicente. *El Libro Rojo, 1520–1567*. Mexico City: Díaz de León, 1870.

Ross, Kurt. *Codex Mendoza: Aztec Manuscript*. Fribourg: Miller Graphics, 1978.

Rucker, Walter. *Gold Coast Diasporas: Identity, Culture, and Power*. Bloomington: University of Indiana Press, 2015.

Ruiz Medrano, Ethelia. "Fighting Destiny: Nahua Nobles and Friars in the Sixteenth-Century Revolt of the Encomenderos against the King." In *Negotiation within Domination: New Spain's Indian Pueblos Confront the Spanish State*, edited by Ethelia Ruiz Medrano and Susan Kellogg. Boulder: University Press of Colorado, 2010.

Ruiz Medrano, Ethelia. *Mexico's Indigenous Communities: Their Lands and Histories, 1500–2010*. Boulder: University Press of Colorado, 2010.

Ruiz Medrano, Ethelia, and Susan Kellogg, eds. *Negotiation within Domination: New Spain's Indian Pueblos Confront the Spanish State*. Boulder: University Press of Colorado, 2010.

Russo, Alessandra, Gerhard Wolf and Diana Fane, eds. *Images Take Flight: Feather Art in Mexico and Europe, 1400–1700*. Florence, Italy: Kunsthistorisches Institut in Florenz, 2015.

Sahagún, Fray Bernardino de, ed. *The Florentine Codex: General History of the Things of New Spain*. Edited by Arthur J. O. Anderson and Charles Dibble. Santa Fe and Salt Lake City: School of American Research and University of Utah, 1950–1982.

Salomon, Frank, and Jorge Urioste, eds. *The Huarochirí Manuscript: A Testament of Ancient and Colonial Andean Religion*. Austin: University of Texas Press, 1991.

Sampeck, Kathryn. "Pipil Writing: An Archaeology of Prototypes and a Political Economy of Literacy." *Ethnohistory* 62 (2015): 469–94.

Sanders, William, Jeffrey Parsons, and Robert Santley. *The Basin of Mexico: Ecological Processes in the Evolution of a Civilization*. New York: Academic Press, 1979.

Sarabia Viejo, María Justina. *Don Luis de Velasco, Virrey de Nueva España*. Seville: Escuela de Estudios Hispano-Americanos, 1978.

Schele, Linda, and David Freidel. *A Forest of Kings: The Untold Story of the Ancient Maya*. New York: William Morrow, 1990.

Scherer, Andrew, and John Verano, eds. *Embattled Bodies, Embattled Places: War in Pre-Columbian Mesoamerica and the Andes*. Washington, DC: Dumbarton Oaks, 2014.

Schmandt-Besserat, Denise. *How Writing Came About*. Austin: University of Texas Press, 1996.

Schmandt-Besserat, Denise. *When Writing Met Art: From Symbol to Story*. Austin: University of Texas Press, 2007.

Scholes, France, and Ralph Roys. *The Maya Chontal Indians of Acalan-Tixchel: A Contribution to the History and Ethnography of the Yucatan Peninsula*. Norman: University of Oklahoma Press, 1968 [1948]

Scholes, France, and Eleanor Adams, eds. *Cartas de Valderrama*. Mexico City: Porrúa, 1961.

Scholes, France, and Eleanor Adams, eds. *Sobre el modo de tributar los indios de Nueva España a Su Majestad, 1561–64*. Mexico City: Porrúa, 1958.

Schroeder, Susan. *Chimalpahin and the Kingdoms of Chalco*. Tucson: University of Arizona Press, 1991.

Schroeder, Susan. "The First American Valentine: Nahua Courtship and Other Aspects of Family Structuring in Mesoamerica." *Journal of Family History* 23 (1998): 341–54.

Schroeder, Susan. *Tlacaelel Remembered: Mastermind of the Aztec Empire*. Norman: University of Oklahoma Press, 2016.

Schroeder, Susan. "The Truth about the Crónica Mexicayotl." *Colonial Latin American Review* 20 (2011): 233–47.

Schroeder, Susan, Stephanie Wood, and Robert Haskett, eds. *Indian Women of Early Mexico*. Norman: University of Oklahoma Press, 1997.

Schwaller, John. "Broken Spears or Broken Bones? The Evolution of the Most Famous Line in Nahuatl." *Americas* 16 (2009): 241–52.

Seijas, Tatiana. *Asian Slaves in Colonial Mexico*. New York: Cambridge University Press, 2014.

Sierra Silva, Pablo. *Urban Slavery in Colonial Mexico: Puebla de los Angeles, 1531–1706*. New York: Cambridge University Press, 2018.

Sigal, Pete. "The Cuiloni, the Patlache and the Abominable Sin: Homosexualities in Early Colonial Nahua Society." *Hispanic American Historical Review* 85 (2005): 555–94.

Sigal, Pete. "Queer Nahuatl: Sahagún's Faggots and Sodomites, Lesbians and Hermaphrodites." *Ethnohistory* 54 (2007): 9–34.

Siméon, Rémi. *Dictionnaire de la Langue Nahuatl*. Paris: Imprimerie Nationale, 1885.

Simpson, Leslie Byrd. *Many Mexicos*. Berkeley: University of California Press, 1963 [1941].

Skopyk, Bradley. "Undercurrents of Conquest: The Shifting Terrain of Agriculture in Colonial Tlaxcala." PhD diss., York University, Department of History, 2010.

Smith, Michael. *The Aztecs*. London: Blackwell, 1996.

Smith, Michael. *At Home with the Aztecs: An Archaeologist Uncovers Their Daily Life*. New York: Routledge, 2016.

Sousa, Lisa. *The Woman Who Turned into a Jaguar, and Other Narratives of Native Women in Archives of Colonial Mexico*. Stanford, CA: Stanford University Press, 2017.

Spence, Michael. "From Tzintzuntzan to Paquime: Peers or Peripheries in Greater Mesoamerica?" In *Greater Mesoamerica: The Archaeology of West and Northwest Mexico*, edited by Michael Foster and Shirley Gorenstein. Salt Lake City: University of Utah Press, 2000

Suárez de la Peralta, Juan. *Tratado del descubrimiento de las Indias y su conquista*. Edited by Giorgio Perissinotto. Madrid: Alianza, 1990.

Sullivan, John, Eduardo de la Cruz Cruz, Abelardo de la Cruz de la Cruz, Delfina de la Cruz de la Cruz, Victoriano de la Cruz Cruz, Sabina Cruz de la Cruz, Ofelia Cruz Morales, Catalina Cruz de la Cruz, Manuel de la Cruz Cruz. *Tlahtolxitlauhcayotl*. Chicontepec, Veracruz: IDIEZ, 2016.

Sullivan, Thelma, ed. *The Primeros Memoriales*. Norman: University of Oklahoma Press, 1997.

Szoblik, Katarzyna. *Entre los papeles de ocelote entono mi canto, yo Quetzalpetlatzin: El lugar de la mujer dentro de la oralidad nahua*. Mexico City: Centro de Estudios de Antropología de la Mujer, 2016.

Tavárez, David. *The Invisible War: Indigenous Devotions, Discipline, and Dissent in Colonial Mexico*. Stanford, CA: Stanford University Press, 2011.

Tavárez, David. "Nahua Intellectuals, Franciscan Scholars, and the *Devotio Moderno* in Colonial Mexico." *Americas* 70 (2013): 203–10.

Tedlock, Dennis. *2000 Years of Mayan Literature*. Los Angeles: University of California Press, 2010.

Tena, Rafael, ed. *Anales de Cuauhtitlan*. Mexico City: Cien de México, 2011.

Tena, Rafael, ed. *Anales de Tlatelolco*. Mexico City: Conaculta, 2004.

Tena, Rafael. *La religión Mexica*. Mexico City: Instituto Nacional de Antropología e Historia, 1993.

Tena, Rafael, ed. *Tres crónicas mexicanas: Textos recopilados por Domingo Chimalpahin*. Mexico City: Conaculta, 2012.

Terraciano, Kevin. *The Mixtecs of Colonial Oaxaca: Ñudzahui History, Sixteenth through Eighteenth Centuries*. Stanford, CA: Stanford University Press, 2011.

Terraciano, Kevin. "Three Texts in One: Book XII of the Florentine Codex." *Ethnohistory* 57 (2010): 51–72.

Thomas, Hugh. *Conquest: Montezuma, Cortés and the Fall of Old Mexico*. New York: Simon & Schuster, 1993.

Thurner, Lance. "Lizards and the Idea of Mexico." *Nursing Clio*, April 12, 2018. https://nursingclio.org.

Todorov, Tzvetan. *The Conquest of America: The Question of the Other*. New York: Harper, 1984.

Tomlinson, Gary. *The Singing of the New World: Indigenous Voice in the Era of European Contact*. New York: Cambridge University Press, 2007.

Tortorici, Zeb. "'Heran Todos Putos': Sodomitical Subcultures and Disordered Desire in Early Colonial Mexico." *Ethnohistory* 54 (2007): 35–67.

Tortorici, Zeb. *Sins Against Nature: Sex and Archives in Colonial New Spain*. Durham, NC: Duke University Press, 2018.

Townsend, Camilla, ed. *American Indian History: A Documentary Reader*. London: Wiley-Blackwell, 2009.

Townsend, Camilla. *Annals of Native America: How the Nahuas of Colonial Mexico Kept Their History Alive*. New York: Oxford University Press, 2016.

Townsend, Camilla. "Burying the White Gods: New Perspectives on the Conquest of Mexico." *American Historical Review* 108 (2003): 659–87.

Townsend, Camilla. "Don Juan Buenaventura Zapata y Mendoza and the Notion of a Nahua Identity." In *The Conquest All Over Again,* edited by Susan Schroeder. Brighton: Sussex Academic Press, 2010.

Townsend, Camilla. "The Evolution of Alva Ixtlilxochitl's Scholarly Life." *Colonial Latin American Review* 23 (2014): 1–17.

Townsend, Camilla. "Glimpsing Native American Historiography: The Cellular Principle in Sixteenth-Century Nahuatl Annals." *Ethnohistory* 56 (2009): 625–50.

Townsend, Camilla, ed. *Here in This Year: Seventeenth-Century Nahuatl Annals of the Tlaxcala-Puebla Valley*. Stanford, CA: Stanford University Press, 2010.

Townsend, Camilla. *Malintzin's Choices: An Indian Woman in the Conquest of Mexico*. Albuquerque: University of New Mexico Press, 2006.

Townsend, Camilla. "Mutual Appraisals: The Shifting Paradigms of the English, Spanish and Powhatans in Tsenacomoco, 1560–1622." In *Early Modern Virginia: Reconsidering the Old Dominion,* edited by Douglas Bradburn and John C. Coombs. Charlottesville: University of Virginia Press, 2011.

Townsend, Camilla. *Pocahontas and the Powhatan Dilemma*. New York: Hill & Wang, 2004.

Townsend, Camilla. "Polygyny and the Divided Altepetl: The Tetzcocan Key to Pre-conquest Nahuatl Politics." In *Texcoco: Prehispanic and Colonial Perspectives,* edited by Jongsoo Lee and Galen Brokaw. Boulder: University Press of Colorado, 2014.

Townsend, Camilla. "Slavery in Pre-Columbian America." In *The Cambridge World History of Slavery,* vol. 2, edited by Craig Perry, David Eltis et al. New York: Cambridge University Press, forthcoming 2020.

Townsend, Camilla. "Sor Juana's Nahuatl." *Le Verger* 8 (2015): 1–12.

Townsend, Camilla. "'What in the World Have You Done to Me, My Lover?': Sex. Servitude, and Politics among the Pre-Conquest Nahuas as Seen in the *Cantares Mexicanos*." *Americas* 62 (2006): 349–89.

Townsend, Richard. *State and Cosmos in the Art of Tenochtitlan*. Washington, D.C.: Dumbarton Oaks, 1979.

Ulloa, Modesto. *La hacienda real de Castilla en el reinado de Felipe II*. Madrid: Seminario Cisneros, 1986.

Urton, Gary. *Inka History in Knots: Reading Khipus as Primary Sources*. Austin: University of Texas Press, 2017.

Vail, Gabrielle, and Andrea Stone. "Representations of Women in Postclassic and Colonial Maya Literature and Art." In *Ancient Maya Women,* edited by Traci Ardren. Lanham, MD: Rowman & Littlefield, 2002.

Valton, Emilio, ed. *El Primer Libro de alfabetización en América*. Mexico City: Robedo, 1949 [1569].

Van Deusen, Nancy. *Global Indios: The Indigenous Struggle for Justice in Sixteenth-Century Spain*. Durham, NC: Duke University Press, 2015.

Velázquez, Primo Feliciano, ed. *Códice Chimalpopoca: Anales de Cuauhtitlan y Leyenda de los soles*. Mexico City: Imprenta Universitaria, 1945.

Veyne, Paul. *Did the Greeks Believe in Their Myths? An Essay on the Constitutive Imagination*. Chicago: University of Chicago Press, 1988.

Villella Peter. *Indigenous Elites and Creole Identity in Colonial Mexico, 1500–1800*. New York: Cambridge University Press, 2016.

Viseo, fray Juan Bautista. *Sermonario en lengua Mexicana*. Mexico City: Casa de Diego López Dávalos, 1606.

Von Germeten, Nicole. *Black Blood Brothers: Confraternities and Social Mobility for Afro-Mexicans*. Gainesville: University Press of Florida, 2006.

Wade, Lizzie. "Feeding the Gods: Hundreds of Skulls Testify to the Monumental Scale of Human Sacrifice in the Aztec Capital." *Science* 360 (2018): 1288–92.

Wake, Eleanor. *Framing the Sacred: The Indian Churches of Colonial Mexico*. Norman: University of Oklahoma Press, 2010.

Watson, Kelly. *Insatiable Appetites: Imperial Encounters with Cannibals in the North Atlantic World*. New York: New York University Press, 2015.

West, Robert, and John Augelli. *Middle America: Its Land and Peoples*. New Jersey: Prentice-Hall, 1989 [1966].

Whittaker, Gordon. "The Principles of Nahuatl Writing." *Göttinger Beiträge zur Sprachwissenschaft* 16 (2009): 47–81.

Wineburg, Sam. *Historical Thinking and Other Unnatural Acts: Charting the Future of Teaching the Past*. Philadelphia: Temple University Press, 2001.

Wood, Stephanie. "Don Diego García de Mendoza Moctezuma: A Techialoyan Mastermind?" *Estudios de Cultura Náhuatl* 19 (1989): 245–68.

Wood, Stephanie. "Nahuatl Terms Relating to Conquest." Paper presented at the Conference of the American Historical Association, New York City, January 2015.

Wood, Stephanie. "Nahua Women Writing and Speaking." Paper presented at the Northeastern Nahuatl Studies Group, Yale University, May 2016.

Wood, Stephanie. *Transcending Conquest: Nahua View of Spanish Colonial Mexico.* Norman: University of Oklahoma Press, 2003.

Yannakakis, Yanna. "How Did They Talk to One Another? Language Use and Communication in Multilingual New Spain." *Ethnohistory* 59 (2012): 667–75.

Yuste López, Carmen. *El comercio de la Nueva España con Filipinas, 1590–1795.* Mexico City: Instituto Nacional de Antropología e Historia, 1984.

Zapata y Mendoza, don Juan Buenaventura. *Historia cronológica de la noble ciudad de Tlaxcala.* Edited by Luis Reyes García and Andrea Martínez Baracs. Tlaxcala: Universidad Autónoma de Tlaxcala, 1995.

Index

Note on index: For the benefit of digital users, indexed terms that span two pages (e.g., 52–53) may, on occasion, appear on only one of those pages